Practical Measurement
in
Physical Education and Sport

Practical Measurement
in
Physical Education and Sport

Harold M. Barrow, P.E.D.
Professor Emeritus of Physical Education
Wake Forest University
Winston-Salem, North Carolina

Rosemary McGee, Ph.D.
Professor of Physical Education
The University of North Carolina at Greensboro
Greensboro, North Carolina

Kathleen A. Tritschler, Ed.D.
Assistant Professor of Sport Studies
Guilford College
Greensboro, North Carolina

Karen Uhlendorf, Ed.D. Photographer

FOURTH EDITION

Lea & Febiger   Philadelphia • London • 1989

Lea & Febiger
600 Washington Square
Philadelphia, PA. 19106-4198
U.S.A.
(215)922-1330

Lea & Febiger (UK) Ltd.
145a Croydon Road
Beckenham, Kent BR3 3RB
U.K.

First Edition, 1964
 Reprinted May, 1966, February, 1968, and March, 1970

Second Edition, 1971
 Reprinted March, 1973, May, 1976, June, 1978

Third Edition, 1979

Fourth Edition, 1989

Library of Congress Cataloging in Publication Data
Barrow, Harold Marion, 1909-
 Practical measurement in physical education and sport / Harold M.
Barrow, Rosemary McGee, Kathleen A. Tritschler; Karen Uhlendorf,
photographer.—4th ed.
  p. cm.
 Rev. ed. of: A practical approach to measurement in physical
education. 3rd ed. 1979.
 Includes bibliographies and index.
 ISBN 0-8121-1216-4
 1. Physical fitness—Testing. I. McGee, Rosemary, 1926-
II. Tritschler, Kathleen A., 1948-   III. Barrow, Harold Marion, 1909-
Practical approach to measurement in physical education. IV. Title.
GV436.B3   1989
613.7--dc19   88-34035
                                                              CIP

PRINTED IN THE UNITED STATES OF AMERICA

Print number: 6 5 4 3 2 1

05/03/90

Preface

The field of physical education has undergone major changes since the first edition of this text was released in 1964. As an academic discipline, physical education has become increasingly more sophisticated and diversified; research has defined and expanded the bodies of knowledge in over a dozen subdisciplines. Consistent with this broader focus, academic units of "physical education" in institutions of higher education have been renamed "physical education and sport," "physical education and exercise science," "sport studies," etc. The physical education and sport-related professions are also more diversified than they were a quarter of a century ago. Today's "physical educator" may, of course, still be found teaching and coaching in our schools. He or she may, however, just as likely be found serving the public in a community recreation program, a private health club, or a corporate fitness program. He or she may be employed in a position with a title of "facility director," "promotions manager," "sports medicine director," "aerobics instructor," "athletic trainer," or the like.

Measurement skills and knowledge are a necessary part of the professional preparation of all modern-day physical education and sport practitioners. The objective of this text is to aid the pre-service and in-service physical education and sport professional in the development of requisite measurement skills and knowledge.

This edition retains the distinguishing and popular characteristics of previous editions. It is highly practical in its approach and content, measurement instruments and interpretation tables are complete and ready for use, and there is a conscientious focus on measurement in all three educational domains. Also retained is a glossary to encourage accurate use of measurement and evaluation terminology.

Readers will find, however, that this newest edition differs from earlier editions in several ways. Most notably, the text has been reorganized, and well over half of the content has been newly written specifically for this edition. With this new content, the authors have tried to reflect some of the major changes in the field of physical education and sport. Included in this edition are many new, highly practical measurement instruments that have been developed consistent with sophisticated measurement theory. While previous editions focused on measuring participants in school physical education, intramural, and athletic programs, this edition provides instruction and tests, scales, and inventories for the measurement of active persons between the ages of 4.5 and 85+ years of age! Readers will also notice that much of the text language is less formal. Personal pronouns and parenthetical comments make the text more readable (and enjoyable!) for the beginning student of measurement.

Content Features

The text is organized into two major sections. Part I, which comprises the first five chapters, presents the "how to do" foundational information necessary for effective and efficient measurement and evaluation. The chapters are ordered logically, as a potential user would need the knowledge. Part II, Chapters 6 through 10, provides the specifics needed for measurement and evaluation of fitness, sport skills, cognitive learnings, affective learnings, and programs in physical education and sport.

Chapter 1 is an overview of measurement and evaluation in physical education and sport settings. The student is introduced to the basic language of measurement and evaluation, and is provided with a historical perspective of measurement in physical education and sport. Testimonials from real-life physical education and sport professionals help the student appreciate the many ways that measurement can be used.

Chapter 2 begins with suggestions for locating a specific measurement instrument in the area of physical education and sport. The learner is then instructed in evaluating available tests, scales, and inventories. Validity and reliability are discussed for both norm-referenced and criterion-referenced tests. Additionally, test bias is presented as an important psychometric consideration.

The third chapter focuses on administrating measurement instruments. Checklists are included for administering various kinds of performance tests, rating scales, knowledge tests, and affective scales. The checklists specify the administrator's activities prior to, just before and during, and just after administering the test and later. The checklists address considerations from the standpoint of the test/scale taker as well as the test/scale itself.

Chapter 4, completely rewritten for this edition, presents descriptive statistical and graphic techniques necessary for basic analysis and interpretation of measurement scores. Many sample calculations and practice problems are given; the examples are realistic and meaningful. Also included is a longer problem set, with answers provided at the end of the chapter. Emphasis throughout the chapter is on understanding the appropriate use and interpretation of statistics. Students are encouraged to use a hand calculator or a computer, so they won't get bogged down unnecessarily in formulas and calculations.

The final chapter in Part I addresses the issue of grading, one of the most common uses of measurement in school physical education programs. The content reflects an updating of current thought and practice related to grading. Sample grading schemes are given as well as a chart for evaluating a grading system. Although students who are not majoring in school physical education might wish to skip this chapter, the authors have found that most students find the content interesting because they have been the subjects (or victims!) of grading for a dozen or more years.

Part II begins with recommendations and instruments for the measurement of physical fitness. Chapter 6 content reflects the latest thinking about health-related and skill-related fitness. All but one of the fitness tests presented are new to this edition. Fitness tests are included for children, adolescents, adults, and the elderly. Appropriate norm-tables or criterion standards are provided for all tests.

Chapter 7 presents sports skills tests in 15 different activities. Included are 27 different skills tests, 12 of which are new additions to this edition. The Rhythmic Aerobics Rating Scale and the Allen Volleyball Diagnostic Instrument are especially noteworthy.

Chapter 8 addresses procedures for developing and evaluating both norm-referenced and criterion-referenced knowledge tests. Item writing and item analysis are emphasized.

Chapter 9, on affective measurement in physical education and sport, provides a comprehensive treatment of social measures, attitude measures, and self-concept measures. Sixteen different inventories are presented, eight of which are new to this edition. Scales appropriate for in-school and out-of-school use are included, as are scales that focus on physical education, physical activity, physical estimation, and athletic participation.

The final chapter of the text, Chapter 10, focuses on program evaluation. Included are measures for the evaluation of youth sport programs, college athletics, intramurals, and physical education programs at the elementary, secondary, and college levels.

Acknowledgements

Special indebtedness is acknowledged to a number of people, especially to our colleagues at Wake Forest University, the University of North Carolina at Greensboro, and Guilford College. Appreciation is extended to Ms. Gaylor Callahan in the Reference Department of Jackson Library at the University of North Carolina at Greensboro for extensive help with interlibrary loans, and to Dr. Betty Place-Beary, reference librarian at Guilford College, for further assistance. A special thanks is extended to Dr. Karen Koehler who expedited the background research for new materials.

Recognition and appreciation is given to Dr. Andrea Farrow for updating and revising Chapter 7 on sport skills tests and for critiquing the chapter on grading. We are also indebted to Dr. Janet M. Fisher for sharing her professional expertise in the area of motor development. Finally, a special acknowledgement is extended to Dr. Karen Uhlendorf for contributing the photographs that introduce each chapter.

Winston-Salem, NC   Harold M. Barrow
Greensboro, NC   Rosemary McGee
Greensboro, NC   Kathleen A. Tritschler

Contents

Part I. Foundations of Measurement

Chapter 1. Introduction to Measurement

Chapter 2. Selection of a Measurement Instrument

Chapter 3.   Administration of Measurement Instruments

Chapter 4.   Analysis of Measurement Scores

Chapter 5.   Grading in Physical Education

Part II.   Tests, Scales, Inventories

Chapter 6.   Measurement of Fitness for Health and Skill

Chapter 7.   Tests of Specific Sports Skills

Chapter 8. Knowledge Testing

Chapter 9.   Affective Measures

Chapter 10.   Measurement for Program Evaluation

PART I

Foundations of Measurement

1

Introduction to Measurement

History reveals that as humans became more civilized they also became more scientific, and subsequently sought more exact ways to measure. In the United States the history of measurement in physical education and sport has paralleled the growth and development of research and the rise of the field to a more respected position in the educational spectrum. For many decades knowledge and skills in the area of measurement have been considered important for graduate study in the field of physical education and sport. But today measurement skills and knowledge are also deemed a necessary part of the professional preparation of physical education teachers, athletic coaches, sports medicine specialists, and sport management professionals. Employers assume that candidates for positions of leadership in the field of physical education and sport understand the potential value of accurate measurement, are familiar with a variety of measurement tools, know how to administer tests and inventories, and can evaluate the results of such measurements. The objective of this text is to aid you in developing these requisite measurement skills and knowledge.

The first chapter provides an overview of the study of measurement. This overview is organized into three main sections. The first section introduces you to the basic language of measurement. The second section provides a brief history of measurement in physical education and sport. The final section attempts to answer the newspaper reporter's traditional questions of who?, what?, why?, when?, and how? as we begin to explore the role of measurement in the environments of modern-day physical education and sport.

THE LANGUAGE OF MEASUREMENT

There are several key terms that often cause confusion among students beginning their study of measurement. Already in the two paragraphs that you have just read, you came across the words "tests," "inventories," "measurement," and "evaluation." We suspect that you have some idea of what is meant by each of these terms, but you may need some clarification to understand exactly how these terms are used in this area of study.

Test, Measurement, Evaluation

For every student the word "test" surely conjures up a vivid picture of writing answers to questions presented on a page of paper. ("Test" may even stimulate a grumbling in your stomach!) However, in the study of measurement in physical education and sport, "test" is applied in a broader sense. *Test refers to any specific instrument, procedure, or technique used by a test administrator to elicit a response from the test taker.* Tests always specify a particular protocol, but vary greatly in their form. In physical education and sport contexts, some tests are paper-and-pencil instruments that require a written response directly from the student, athlete, or client. Many of our tests, however, employ physical devices such as stopwatches, tape measures, skinfold calipers, or even treadmills. Some tests restructure the normal sport environment with cones, ropes, and targets with associated point values. Many of our tests yield objective estimates of the characteristic of interest; others, known as *rating scales* yield subjective estimates. Most physical education and sport tests and rating scales attempt to assess a characteristic of an individual student, athlete, coach, or administrator, but some tests and rating scales are designed to assess characteristics of groups, teams, and programs.

"Test" generally is used to describe instruments, procedures, and techniques that result in responses that can be evaluated in terms of their correctness. Instruments, procedures, and techniques that assess affective qualities of one's interests, attitudes, beliefs, or personal values can be included within the general definition of "test." They are however, more commonly referred to as *inventories* to emphasize that they do not have clearly defined right and wrong answers. In this text, *measure* is used to connote tests, rating scales, and inventories. When speaking collectively about different tests, scales, and inventories, *"measurement instruments"* and *"assessment tools"* are used synonomously.

The term *battery* is used to refer to a group of several tests, scales, or inventories intended to be administered in succession to the same subject or subjects. The group of measures is usually designed to accomplish a closely related set of measurement objectives.

Measurement refers to the process of administering a test or inventory. The usual result of measurement is quantitative data that are characteristically expressed in numerical form. These data are referred to as *scores*. Qualitative assessments usually result in assignment of words or phrases such as "excellent" or "is characteristic of the student."

Evaluation refers to the process of interpreting the results of measurement. Test scores and qualitative assessments are evaluated by making comparisons with preconceived criteria in order to make judgments about people or appropriate courses of action. In other words, evaluation is the process of making qualitative judgments based upon measurement evidence. But then, these judgments are usually subjected to careful examination that often require another round of measurement and re-evaluation.

Norm-Referenced and Criterion-Referenced Tests

There are two broad classifications of measurement instruments that are referred to as *norm-referenced* and *criterion-referenced*. These are also important terms for the beginner in measurement.

Norm-referenced tests are designed by the test developer to measure individual differences so one person's score on such a test can be compared to the scores of other similar persons who have taken the same test. These scores are known as *norms*. From tables of norms, one's score is interpreted in terms of how it compares to the scores of other similar persons' scores. The standardized tests that you have taken through your years of schooling were norm-referenced tests. Perhaps you re-member being told that you scored, for example, at the 85th percentile; this meant that you scored equal to or better than 85% of the other similar students. The majority of physical education and sport tests that have been developed to date are norm-referenced.

In recent years, however, more and more *criterion-referenced tests* have been developed. In this type of testing *test scores are compared, not to each other, but to a standard that is referenced to a criterion behavior.* The criterion behavior is a sat-isfactory level of performance, so performers whose scores meet or exceed the standard are claimed to be *masters* and those whose scores fall below the standard are *nonmasters*. There are no limits to the number of persons who may achieve mastery on the test. In fact, a teacher may be proud indeed if all of his/her students meet or exceed the standard on a criterion-referenced test in which the standard is keyed to a meaningful criterion behavior! American Red Cross cer-tification tests and refereeing certification tests are examples of criterion-refer-enced tests.

Laboratory and Field Tests

There are many highly sophisticated and precise tests, e.g., treadmill tests and reaction time tests, that can only be given in exercise physiology or motor learning laboratories. *Laboratory tests typically require specialized equipment and spe-cialized training on the part of the test administrator.* Another distinguishing feature of laboratory tests is that they are usually administered to only one person at a time. These features make laboratory tests impractical for use by most physical education and sport practitioners.

The alternative to laboratory tests is *field tests. Field tests require no prohibitively expensive equipment and little, if any, specialized training.* Additionally, they are time-effective, in that they can often be administered to a group of individuals simultaneously. Field tests must, of course, be accurate measures of the char-acteristic under investigation, but often these measures are less precise than laboratory tests of the same characteristic. Depending upon the intended use of the measurement, however, this lack of precision is often deemed acceptable or even preferable due to the gained advantages in practicality. This text is devoted to the presentations and discussion of field tests appropriate for use by the physical education and sport practitioner in settings such as schools, camps, YMCAs, YWCAs, private clubs, and gymnasiums.

BRIEF HISTORY OF MEASUREMENT IN PHYSICAL EDUCATION AND SPORT

Testing and measurement in physical education and sport in America is only a little over a century old. Its history can be divided roughly into periods ex-tending from about 1860 to the present (Table 1–1). These periods can be loosely categorized by the prevailing interests of the times. It should be realized, how-ever, that there are no clear-cut lines of demarcation separating them. These periods merely indicate the times when the specific measurement types came into prominence. The first three periods clearly reflected an emphasis on the physical capacity of humans, while the latter periods indicate emphases on

Table 1–1. *Major Periods in the History of Measurement in Physical Education and Sport in the United States*

Predominant Testing Focus of Period	Approximate Years of Emphasis
Anthropometic Measurements	1860–1890
Strength Testing	1880–1910
Cardiovascular Testing	1900–1925
Athletic Ability Testing	1900–1930
Social Measurements	1920–present
Sports Skills Testing	1920–present
Program Evaluation	1930–present
Knowledge Testing	1940–present
Physical Fitness Testing	1940–present

efficiency and performance abilities, and on the "wholeness" of the physical performers.

Anthropometric Measurements

The oldest form of measurement, known as *anthropometry*, is the measurement of human body parts. Anthropometry was of interest in ancient India and later in Egypt where study was undertaken to find one part or component of the body that could be used as a common measure for all body parts. Egyptians, for example, believed that the length of the middle finger could be used as a common measure; the knee should be 5 finger lengths from the ground and one's arm reach should be 8 finger lengths. (Are you proportioned like this? Try it and see!)

The early Greeks also practiced anthropometry in their studies of body proportions. Hippocrates, the "father of modern medicine," believed that body symmetry and proportion were related to health. Greek artists studied body symmetry and proportion for aesthetic reasons. The Greek athlete alone rivaled the gods as subjects for sculpturing!

Interest in anthropometry is also responsible for the beginning of the testing and measurement movement in physical education in the United States. In 1861 Edward Hitchcock, a medical doctor, was hired at Amherst as the director of student health. He initiated yearly measurements of all students. His detailed records included such factors as height, weight, age, reach, girth, vital capacity, and selected strength measures. The ultimate purpose of Hitchcock's measurement was to define the ideal physical proportions of man.

To the work of Hitchcock was added the significant efforts of Dudley Allen Sargent. Sargent was hired in 1878 to oversee the health of students at Harvard University. During his tenure there, Sargent devised more than 40 different measurements of anthropometric types and used them to prescribe a program of exercise for each student. His system was subsequently adapted for use in both public schools and colleges and in YMCAs across the nation. Sargent actively promoted testing and measurement by publishing the first manual on measurement and by writing numerous articles for professional journals.

Anthropometric measurement is still practiced today. There are, however, few physical educators who identify themselves as specialists in this area of measurement. The anthropometric researchers of today usually focus their attention on elite athletes and dancers. These researchers have added body fat measures to the traditional measures of height, weight, and girth.

Strength Measurement

Around 1880, interest in anthropometry began to wane as interest in strength testing waxed. Although Hitchcock had included some strength testing in his program at Amherst, the real pioneer in this area was Sargent. Sargent, along with an anthropologist named William T. Brigham, experimented with the newly invented dynamometer, and devised a strength test battery comprised of measures of the legs, back, hand grip, and arms. His strength test battery also included a measure of lung vital capacity, made possible by the invention of the spirometer. (This lung function measure may seem odd to you, but it remained at least vestigially a part of strength testing for several decades.)

Strength testing has never truly gone out of vogue in the measurement area, although it never again received the attention that it did in the period of 1880 to 1910. In the 1920s interest in strength testing was revived to some extent and several new tests were developed. The best known of these was one by Frederick Rand Rogers.[31] His scheme of testing differed from others in the manner of test construction. His test was devised in a scientific manner and was shown to have high relationship with general athletic ability. Roger's ingenious use of the Strength Index and the Physical Fitness Index made his test one of the true classics in the field.

Strength testing today occurs both in the exercise physiology laboratory and in the gymnasium and weight training room. In the laboratory, this testing employs dynamometers, cable tensiometers, and various electronic machinery such as the Cybex. Field tests of strength require the performer to lift maximal loads of free weights or plates on Universal or Nautilus machinery.

Cardiovascular Measurement

At the turn of the century, measurement interests again began to shift. The new interests were concerned with the efficiency of heart and vessel function. Just as strength testing had taken on new meaning with the invention of the dynamometer, cardiovascular testing changed as a result of Mosso's invention of the ergograph in 1884. Physiologists studied the effects of fatigue and the relationship of muscular work to the circulatory system, while physical educators sought methods of testing the cardiovascular efficiency of the body. The first test of cardiac function, the Blood Ptosis Test, was published by C.W. Crampton in 1905.[18] Crampton's seminal test was based upon changes in heart rate and blood pressure as one assumes a standing position from a starting supine position. E.C. Schneider designed a similar but a more sophisticated test that was used during World War I to assess the fitness of military aviators.[32] This test included a measure of one's ability to recover to normal after a measured exercise bout. In 1931, W.W. Tuttle presented his Pulse-Ratio Test that specified a block stepping protocol to standardize exercise bouts.[33] Tuttle's test influenced L. Brouha and his co-workers in their 1943 development of the Harvard Step Test.[13] This test subsequently inspired the development of less strenuous field tests of cardiovascular function such as the Tecumseh Step Test and the Queen's College Step Test.[25,30]

The Balke Treadmill Test was developed in 1952.[6] This development led the way to increased sophistication in the laboratory measurement of cardiovascular function related to exercise stress. Despite strong validity and reliability evidence, sophisticated laboratory tests that require specialized training and expensive equipment are clearly not feasible for the practitioner. The need for a valid and reliable field test of cardiovascular fitness was, perhaps, best met through the efforts of Dr. Kenneth Cooper. In 1968 he published *Aerobics* in which he proposed a practical field test of cardiovascular fitness that he had originally developed for the United States Air Force.[14] His test required a simple-to-administer, 12-minute walk/run during which performers tried to cover as much distance on a measured track as possible. It seemed too good to be true, but Cooper's 12-Minute Walk/Run Test was validated against treadmill performances in the laboratory. Since that time, numerous other walk/run field tests have been developed. Cooper himself even developed alternate versions of his test, including a 1.5-Mile Run Test, a 3-Mile Walk Test, a 12-Minute Swim Test, and a 12-Minute Cycle Test.[15]

Athletic Ability Testing

Interest in athletic ability testing was largely a result of the "new physical education" movement inspired by the philosophies of Wood, Gulick, and Hetherington. As sports and games became an important part of the school physical education curriculum, concomitant interest in the measurement of athletic ability developed. However, this movement was not restricted to the public schools. Even before the turn of the century the YMCA and the Turners had developed pentathlon tests of athletic achievement. The Athletic Badge Tests were developed in 1913 by the American Playground Association with standards for both boys and girls. Test items were heavily weighted with track and field events along with a few items like the rope climb and vault. Colleges began to follow the lead of these other organizations because even leaders in the strength testing movement such as Sargent had begun to realize that strength per se was not as important as the way strength was used for effective performance.

The 1920s were particularly significant for the field of measurement. Before this period much of the work done in measurement was unscientific and based on empiricism. Standards were arbitrarily established by the test maker in most instances and were not clearly identified. No provision was made for increments in scoring tables as performance reached the more difficult levels of attainment, nor were there ways to equate scores on different tests. During this era, however, new statistical techniques became available and more scientifically constructed tests were developed. Validity and reliability of tests were improved and better means of developing scoring tables were used.

Pioneer work in the field of scientific test construction was done by C.H. McCloy of the University of Iowa. He developed achievement scales for boys in track and field, gymnastics, games, and swimming. Some new luminaries appeared on the scene with tests in the areas of motor ability and performance. David K. Brace of Texas developed a motor ability test that was later revised by McCloy and became known as the Iowa Revision of the Brace Test.[12,29] This revised test was termed a motor educability test, claiming to measure one's potential to learn new motor skills. Frederick Cozens devised a test of general athletic ability for college men.[17] All of these test were developed in accordance with the newest scientific approaches in research and statistics. These early tests served as models for modern test construction.

In the late 1920s and early 1930s, the concept of measuring general qualities was explored further and several well-constructed tests were developed in general motor ability, motor capacity, and motor educability. McCloy again revised a test developed by Brace, and published the General Motor Capacity Test.[28] This test presumably was a test of innate performance; it yielded a Motor Quotient that is the motor analogue of the Intelligence Quotient. In the same era, Humiston developed a motor ability test for women.[24]

The popularity of the notions of general motor ability, motor capacity, and motor educability continued into the late 1950s. A widely used motor ability test for college men and junior and senior high school boys was designed by Barrow in 1953.[7] Subsequent motor learning research evidence began to suggest the high task specificity of motor skills.[20,21] As a result, the use of generalized motor measurements is today questioned by many measurement experts.

Sports Skills Testing

As already mentioned, the initial use of sports skills tests was the Athletic Badge Test in 1913. However, great interest in this testing area did not develop until the 1920s. Brace presented one of the earliest skills tests for basketball.[11] Skills tests to measure achievement in specific sports were devised by statistically determining a few simple test items that could effectively measure the total activity of that sport. During the decades of the 1920s, 1930s, and 1940s, tests were devised for nearly every sport, and norms were established for appropriate age and gender groups. However, sports skills test construction continues today because these early tests were designed to reflect the rules and techniques of their day. As you know, many sports have undergone major rule and technique changes, so many older tests are no longer appropriate. Furthermore, the norms of decades ago often no longer match the performance skills of modern sport participants.

Today's sports skills tests are being developed against even more stringent standards and by using even more sophisticated measurement techniques. AAHPERD-sponsored committees have gotten together experts from across the nation to develop quality sports skills tests.[23] These new tests are characterized by conscientious presentation of validity and reliability evidence and by updated performance norms.

Social Values Measurement

During the 1920s attention was first directed toward some of the intangibles that had been attributed to well-directed physical education programs. Since character, personality, and other social values had been considered outcomes of the new sports and games program and were stated as objectives, it seemed logical that status and improvement in them should be measured in some way. McCloy again made a major contribution to testing by developing one of the first character inventories.[27] B.E. Blanchard devised a Behavior Rating Scale for the measurement of character and personality in physical education classes.[8]

In more recent years, affective measurement has focused on the interests and motivations of performers and on the self-concept and body image of participants in physical activity programs. As researchers in the subdiscipline of sport psychology identified psychological constructs that they wished to study, they typically had to figure out ways to measure these abstract phenomena. Sport psychology researchers have been responsible for the development of many new affective measurement instruments.

Program Evaluation

As school programs in physical education grew in number and quality, there was a corresponding need to evaluate them to answer the calls for accountability of tax dollars. In the 1930s the subjective elements that go into program evaluation began to be quantified. The first such quantitative device to receive wide recognition was devised by LaPorte and his committee.[26] Since that time program evaluation instruments have been developed for nearly all school and non-school physical education and sport programs. These include program evaluation instruments for all levels of school physical education, intramurals, athletics, and youth sport. One recent aspect of this area of measurement is a focus on the processes of effective teaching and coaching. Instruments have been developed that require observation of these physical activity leaders as they perform their leadership roles.[20]

Knowledge Testing

Knowledge testing has probably always been a part of school physical education programs; however, most attempts to measure knowledge have been done through the use of teacher-made tests. Although these tests serve an important function, they have not been scientifically constructed and devised. Standardized tests are certainly a rarity in physical education and sport, though a few notable exceptions exist. The first knowledge test reported in the literature was a test of knowledge related to basketball, developed by J.C. Bliss.[9]

In 1969 AAHPER published *Knowledge and Understanding in Physical Education*, presenting the body of knowledge for elementary and secondary schools.[5] The Educational Testing Service of Princeton, New Jersey, developed standardized tests from this publication. These tests became known as the Cooperative Physical Education Tests.[16] Unfortunately these tests never gained much popularity. AAHPERD now boasts a series entitled *Basic Stuff* that identifies the essential body of knowledge in six subdiscipline areas of physical education and sport.[2] As yet, no standardized tests have been developed from these materials.

Physical Fitness Testing

In a sense, a form of fitness testing has always been done. Individuals have been assessed for their ability to meet the requirements of their environment. This was true in World War II, which followed in the wake of two decades of scientific test-making in physical education. Great stress was placed on fitness, and this emphasis brought about a rush to develop fitness tests. These tests were geared to the needs of the war era. They could be mass administered and easily scored and interpreted. All branches of the armed forces devised fitness tests with appropriate norms for both genders. A number of such tests were also developed for school and college groups. Among the latter were Cureton's 14-Item Motor Fitness Test at Illinois and Bookwalter's Indiana Motor Fitness Index.[10,19]

After World War II, President Eisenhower became an advocate for the development of the physical fitness of school-aged American children. His advocacy was largely in response to the shocking results of the Kraus-Weber Test, which suggested that most American children were less than minimally fit, and significantly less fit than European children. AAHPER got into the act in 1958 with publication of the *Youth Fitness Test* for school-aged children.[4] This test has undergone revisions through the years, but in general it has always attempted to measure physical characteristics related to effective athletic performance.

In the 1970s a major philosophical influence drastically changed the focus of fitness testing. It changed from the assessment of qualities of athletic performance to that of health-related performance. In 1980, AAHPERD developed the *Health-Related Physical Fitness Test.*[1] This test included only components believed to be related to health and functional capacity. In 1988, AAHPERD revised this test and titled it *Physical Best.*[3] The emphasis on health-related physical fitness remained the same; however, it cut new ground by setting criterion standards below which one's health or functional capacity would likely be negatively affected.

WHO USES MEASUREMENT?

Measurement is a universal practice, something that all persons engage in either informally or formally. Professionals in the field of physical education and sport are no exception. Instructors, administrators, coaches, sport performers, and researchers use measurement for a variety of purposes and in a variety of settings. They perform measurement in both school and non-school settings such as YMCAs, YWCAs, private health clubs, employee fitness centers, and summer camps. Below are testimonials from real-life physical education and sport professionals who readily acknowledge the use of measurement in their jobs.

"I use testing in my physical education classes to chart student progress through sport skill units. For example, at the beginning of a basketball unit, I record scores for my students in a 30-second speed shooting test, on a dribble test, and on a wall pass test. I have them repeat these same tests at the end of the unit. Students really seem to enjoy the objective evidence of their improvement!"
—High School Physical Education Teacher

"The YMCA has developed a physical fitness test battery that we administer to our members to help them set realistic exercise goals."
—Director of YMCA Branch

"We are currently working on an instrument that will be used to evaluate the effectiveness of our coaching staff."
—College Athletic Director

"My staff uses a 40-yard dash, a mile-run test, vertical jump, and strength tests to help us make initial cuts from the team. The tests also serve as a great motivator—so the returning players come back ready to go each fall!"
—High School Football Coach

"In my research I have used a variety of physiological tests to measure things like maximum oxygen consumption and respiratory function, and I've also used perceived exertion scales to determine levels of work in stress tests."
—Exercise Physiologist

"Our most extensive use of testing involves range of motion tests as our athletes rehabilitate an injury, but we also have used strength testing to help identify athletes who might be likely to incur an injury during the season."
—Athletic Trainer

"I have developed a gymnastics potential test which we give free of charge to anybody who thinks that he or she might be interested in learning gymnastics. We have a lot of parents bring very young children in to be tested. Each one hopes that they have a Nadia or a Kurt!"
—Owner of a Private Gymnastics Academy

"People at our school use testing for the IEPs–the Individualized Education Programs. The tests are basically designed to show parents the progress that the child has shown with respect to the guidelines of the IEP."
—Adapted Physical Education Teacher

"I use soccer skill tests in dribbling and kicking to group the children for further instruction. I also think the tests add a game-like fun quality to their practices."
—Youth Sport Soccer Coach

"Upon rising in the morning I check my body temperature and resting heart rate. If either of these is abnormal, it may indicate a state of being or becoming over-trained. Also, I perform skinfold tests to determine my body fat percentage. I monitor this in the weeks before an upcoming contest in order to lose body fat, and not muscle, at an optimal rate."
—Professional Bodybuilder

"I was required to take a written knowledge test in order to be certified as an aerobics instructor. My students are tested informally everyday. I ask them to monitor their workout intensities by periodic checking of exercise heart rates."
—Private Aerobics Instructor

WHAT SORTS OF THINGS ARE MEASURED?

When an individual is the object of measurement in a physical education or sport setting, the purpose is usually to assess learning or achievement of the individual in one of the three educational domains. Tests in the *psychomotor* domain measure motor skill, motor development, and physical fitness. Psychomotor tests are generally of two kinds—those that test the *product* of a motor performance (like the speed, accuracy, or consistency of a tennis serve) and those that test the *process* that is employed in the performance (e.g., determining the pattern that is used in performing the tennis serve). *Cognitive* tests measure acquired knowledge relating to techniques, rules, and strategies of sports, and concepts relating to the development and maintenance of physical fitness and the prevention of injuries. Tests in the *affective* domain assess interests, attitudes, feelings, and values in relationship to purposeful physical activity. Some of these tests also assess psychological constructs such as aggressiveness, exercise addiction, and pre-competitive anxiety.

Individuals can also be the object of measurement when job effectiveness is assessed. Paper-and-pencil instruments have been developed to measure the effectiveness of physical education teachers, coaches, and athletic administrators.

Groups are sometimes the object of measurement in physical education and sport. A group that we find most interesting is, of course, the athletic team. Qualities of the team, such as team cohesiveness, are assessed with the ultimate purpose of determining ways to optimize team performance.

Measurement is also applied to athletic, instructional, and recreational programs as part of an overall evaluation process. A program may be evaluated in one of two ways. First, it may be evaluated when measurement techniques are applied directly to components of the program; second, it may be evaluated indirectly by measuring the status and progress of the products of the program, i.e., the participants or graduates.

WHY MEASURE?

Since measurement is a universal practice engaged in by humans in many aspects of their lives, there are many possible answers to the question, "Why measure?". In general, however, most intentional human behavior consists of a process that involves establishing of some value or criterion, the exercising of a judgment, and a follow-up involving a choice. Most of the time this process is informal. For instance, in all sports, evaluations occur whenever a player or a coach must make a choice—when a golfer selects a 5-iron rather than a 6-iron, when a basketball player shoots rather than passes to a teammate, when a football coach decides to go for the fourth down yardage rather than punting! Physical education and sport professionals face a myriad of choices as they go about performing their jobs. Most of the time the evaluations of their choices will be informal. Informal evaluations can sometimes, however, be inaccurate and even biased because of their highly subjective nature. Formal measurement is a prerequisite to evaluations that are more likely to be honest and accurate. So perhaps a general answer to the question of "Why measure?" is "to formalize the evaluation process." It must be realized, though, that tests are merely the tools of measurement. The test itself never makes decisions; the test user does!

There are, however, more specific answers to the question of "Why measure?" that are worth discussing. These answers are based upon the ways in which test results are used by physical education and sport professionals.

Classification

Classification implies a grouping of individuals for instruction or activity. At times, performers of similar skill or fitness levels are grouped to enhance instruction, practice, or competition. This is done with the belief that such a grouping better meets the needs of the participants than would a grouping in which participants have a heterogenous mix of skill and/or fitness levels. There are times, however, when a heterogeneous grouping is desired, for example, to form teams of near-equal abilities or to enhance interpersonal relationships.

Classification is accomplished by using, either alone or in combination, basic ability tests, fitness tests, sport skill tests, social scales, and attitude scales. Unfortunately, classification is one application of test scores that is not used to its fullest by physical education instructors and coaches because of the perceived inconvenience of testing. Many times, a quickly administered observational screening test is all that is required to make sound grouping judgments. The instructional or competitive benefits derived from better groupings are usually worth the time and effort.

Motivation

The use of test results for motivational purposes is somewhat nebulous, but nevertheless significant. Students and players often can be motivated to perform at their maximum because of their inherent competitive spirit, because they are anxious to make the best possible showing, and because the activity itself is important to them. This is true for performers of all ages. They should, however, be encouraged to perform well, as they compete against themselves and not always against other members of the group. Self-improvement and self-realization are the keys to effective motivation through the use of testing.

Psychomotor Learning

Motor learning specialists have determined that performance feedback is essential for learning to occur. Through the use of lines, ropes, cones, and targets, sport skill tests often provide greater performance feedback than is available in the natural sport environment. Therefore, sport skill tests can be used by instructors and coaches to create an effective and interesting practice situation for learners. The scores, per se, do not even have to be tallied or recorded.

This is also true for fitness tests. Most fitness tests require a maximum effort on the part of the test taker. As such, the tests themselves can be used by fitness leaders to provide a good workout for the participants.

Affective and Cognitive Learning

There are other uses of tests that are especially appropriate for physical education teachers. Tests can be used to stimulate class discussions about issues related to personal health, sportsmanship, or attitudes toward competition. Similarly, tests can be used by a teacher to illustrate bodily functions and stimulate cognitive understanding of exercise physiology.

Guidance

Guidance concerns are so interwoven throughout the whole realm of test scores and their uses that it is difficult to delineate them. A series of test scores can provide a cumulative record to provide a complete picture of the physical, social, and academic status of an individual. The more complete the information, the better the counseling can be for that individual.

Of particular value to instructional counseling in physical education and sport are diagnostic tests, prognostic tests, and proficiency tests. *Diagnostic tests are designed to identify weaknesses.* On the basis of diagnostic test results, fitness instructors, PE teachers, and coaches can prescribe exercises, learning activities, or skill drills that are needed to remediate the identified weakness. *Prognostic tests are designed for determining levels of potential skill development.* Such tests are concerned with capacity and ultimate skill attainment. As predictors of skillful players, they could be especially valuable to coaches. Unfortunately, there are only a few good prognostic tests available at the present time. This area of test development needs much work. *Proficiency tests* are beginning to receive considerable attention. *They are being used to determine placement at appropriate skill levels and to justify exemption from required coursework.* For example, on the basis of his or her score on a tennis proficiency test a student could be placed in an intermediate tennis class or be excused from a required beginning tennis course.

Proficiency tests are criterion-referenced, based on the concept of mastery learning.

Grading

Test scores are used more often for grading purposes than for any other reason. In one way this appears sound because it assures at least some objectivity in the assignment of grades. In another way it may be questionable if this is the sole application of test scores. Grades probably should not be based exclusively on test scores, nor should test scores be relegated to this one narrow purpose.

Grades can reflect attainment, improvement, and a standard of achievement. They are educational indices to help students understand levels of competency. Grades are relative, however, because they must be interpreted in relation to the tests used, the group tested, and the standards that the teacher believes to be appropriate for a particular group. Chapter 5 of this text is devoted entirely to the topic of grading.

Research

The research uses of the test results in physical education and sport are many and varied. Practitioners and theoreticians in all of our subdisciplines conduct research. The variables under investigation are often operationally defined in terms of scores generated by a particular measurement instrument. Thus, test results generally provide the data that are analyzed in order to answer the problem under investigation. Researchers realize that the quality of their research hinges on the quality of the data they collect. They are, therefore, concerned that the measurement tools are good and that they are administered accurately.

Vocational Suitability

Physical performance tests are increasingly being used by employers to determine applicant's suitability for particular jobs. Military, fire, and police personnel are now commonly subjected to such testing, though performance testing also occurs in the private business sector.

Knowledge tests are also used to ensure qualified practitioners and professionals in some areas of physical education and sport. Certification tests are now regularly being used by the aerobics industry. And, the American College of Sports Medicine has developed certification tests for many areas of sports medicine.

WHEN IS MEASUREMENT DONE?

You can surely guess that the answer to this question is, "Anytime." Testing can be done daily, monthly, yearly, or over even longer time periods. Testing should be done when it can contribute positively to instructional, recreational, or athletic objectives. It should *not* be done when it detracts from more important learning or performance goals. In general it is believed that testing should take no more than 10% of the allotted time for a program. This is, however, only a rough guideline.

An important distinction is made between *summative* and *formative* evaluations. These terms have to do with the timing of testing. *Summative evaluations are the result of testing that is conducted at the end* (or "summation," get it?) *of an identified class or program.* This is the commonly used pattern of test administration when tests are used for grading purposes or for evaluating programs of instruction. *Formative evaluations rely on testing at a variety of times during the ongoing program, i.e., while skills, knowledges, and/or attitudes are still developing* (or "forming," get it?). Both measurement and learning specialists strongly endorse the use of formative evaluations. And, believe it or not, students actually appreciate tests that give them important feedback about their performance in a class while there is still time for them to work on any problems before the unit ends.

HOW IS MEASUREMENT DONE?

Measurement data derive from a variety of testing techniques. Some of these techniques yield data that are numerical, i.e., quantitative in nature and can be tabulated and statistically summarized. Other techniques yield data that are generally in the form of written words and phrases, i.e., qualitative. No one technique will be best for use in all situations. A person knowledgeable and skilled in measurement will have the ability to discern which of the many available techniques will best meet the needs of a particular measurement and evaluation situation. Following are brief descriptions of several types of data collection tools that the measurement specialist in physical education and sport has at his or her disposal.

Physical Performance Tests

These include sport skill tests and physical fitness tests similar to those provided for you in Chapters 6 and 7 of this text. In general, *these types of tests have a structured protocol under which the test taker is required to perform a physical task within strictly specified conditions.* The resulting product of the performance (e.g., tennis serve, vertical jump, or softball pitch) is measured (e.g., speed timed, distance scored, and target values scored). This measurement is then compared to the preconceived definition of a "good" performance upon which the test was designed in order to evaluate the quality of the physical performance.

Rating Scales, Checklists, and Inventories

These differ from physical performance tests in that the process, rather than the product, of a physical performance or behavior is measured. The assessment typically requires the test administrator to make either yes-no judgments regarding the presence or absence of a specified behavior, or to rate on a numerical scale the degree to which a behavior is demonstrated. In some cases the data resulting from use of rating scales, checklists, and inventories are compared with preconceived definitions of correctness or desirability, but more commonly these measurement techniques are used to determine the status quo in the development or maturing of behaviors.

Written Tests and Self-Report Scales

These measurement techniques require a written response on the part of the examinee. After a dozen or so years of schooling we are sure that you are intimately familiar with written tests and realize that the many different types of written tests vary greatly in the response requirements for the examinee. Objective tests typically require the examinee to indicate the true or best choice from among two or more alternatives. Subjective tests require the respondent to provide a word, phrase, or entire essay in response to a particular query. Written tests are used to measure one's achieved knowledge or aptitude for cognitive learning, so responses are evaluated in terms of their correctness.

Self-report scales differ from written tests in that they are used to measure attitudes, beliefs, feelings, and opinions of the respondent. Although preconceived desirable responses are generally identified, such affective responses cannot be evaluated strictly in terms of correctness. In fact, great care must be taken by the administrator of a self-report scale to communicate the importance of an honest response on the part of the examinees. Examinees must be thoroughly convinced that no harm will come to them should their responses be deemed undesirable. If this is not achieved, the self-report scale becomes useless as a measurement instrument.

Sociometric Inventories

Sociometric inventories allow for measurement of the amount and nature of organization within a social group in order to identify patterns of relationships among the group members. The sociometric inventory starts by asking group members to indicate their feelings about each other. Its results simply and graphically show who would like to be grouped with whom for a particular activity. It can be carried a step further to permit the group members not only to choose those with whom they want to be grouped, but also to reject those with whom they do not want to be grouped. In the final analysis, sociometric instruments indicate which individuals are accepted and which are not. These findings can provide the basis for classification of group members into cooperative and productive units, location of group leaders and social "outcasts" or "loners," and identification of gangs or cliques that might resist integration into the total group.

Sociometry, the process of using and interpreting sociometric inventories, might be used for a variety of social groups in physical education and sport settings. Examples of such groups include athletic teams, athletic coaching staffs, physical education classes, physical education department faculty members, preprofessional clubs or professional organizations, and employee fitness workout groups.

Questionnaires and Interviews

These measurement tools can obtain information directly from individuals regarding the present status of their behaviors, beliefs, attitudes, or interests. Questions are asked directly of the respondent. In the case of the questionnaire the questions and answers are in a written form; the interview might be rightfully termed an "oral questionnaire," for the questions and answers are exchanged orally either in a personal face-to-face interview or over the telephone.

These measurement techniques have been used extensively in physical education and sport research, for they can be designed to answer nearly any research question. They are also a favorite measurement technique of administrators. However, there is a major concern associated with their use, for questionnaires and interviews are seldom subjected to testing to determine whether or not the questions actually yield consistent and honest answers that can be interpreted in an unbiased fashion. (This type of testing is described in Chapter 2.) It is recommended that if an alternate method for obtaining the same measurement data exists that has been subjected to such quality testing, that one refrain from use of homemade questionnaires and interviews. Or, if an acceptable measurement alternative does not exist, enroll in a course in which you learn the intricacies of questionnaire and interview design and analysis before you blindly attempt to use these valuable measurement techniques.

Anecdotal Records

The anecdotal record is a means of recording the actual behavior of a student, athlete, or client. Perhaps its techniques apply best in the area of affective learnings, although its use is certainly not limited strictly to this area. *The anecdotal record may be defined as a written objective record of an incident in the life of a student/ athlete/client as observed by a teacher/coach/leader.* Anecdotal information becomes much more meaningful when a number of observations are made because it is always dangerous to draw a conclusion from too few samples. When a number of observations are made, patterns of conduct emerge and behavior trends become quite evident, thus giving greater insight into the problems and social adjustments of the person being observed. The anecdotal record should never be a time-consuming task for the report is a short, concise description of significant incidents. This technique in physical education and athletic settings should probably not be applied to an entire class or team, but should be used in special cases in order to better understand certain students with special problems.

Autobiographies

Teachers and coaches use various means to understand their charges. If educators are to make the fullest use of their opportunities for guidance, they should understand more about each individual's needs, problems, and ambitions. A technique designed to obtain some of this information is the autobiography. It is similar to the anecdote except that it is written by the student/ athlete instead of the teacher/coach. *An autobiography is a self-written story about some phase of the writer's own life and experience.* If stories are done well, they give a good picture of attitudes, feelings, and actions concerning the indicated phase or topic addressed. For instance, the teacher may want to learn something about Jerry's past experience in fitness activities and his attitude toward fitness. Jerry's autobiography will reveal much insight into what he has done to become fit and the importance he attaches to fitness.

SUMMARY

We hope you now feel oriented to the area of measurement. You have learned some of the basic language that is used in measurement, gained a historical perspective, and explored the who?, what?, why?, when?, and how? of measurement in modern-day physical education and sport.

We would like to conclude this chapter by challenging you to interview someone you know, who currently is working in the area of physical education or sport, about the use of testing in his or her job. Ask specifically how he or she uses tests. Which tests are used? When are they given? Why are they given? You might even ask if you could observe the next time a test is given. If the professional you talk with does not use tests often, then ask what the limitations are that restrict their use. Perhaps after a few weeks of study in the area of measurement, you might share some ideas with him or her that might make test use more feasible in that setting.

REFERENCES

1. American Alliance for Health, Physical Education, Recreation, and Dance: Health-Related Physical Fitness Test Manual. Reston, VA, AAHPERD, 1980.
2. American Alliance for Health, Physical Education, Recreation, and Dance: Basic Stuff Series 1. Reston, VA, AAHPERD, 1987.
3. American Alliance for Health, Physical Education, Recreation, and Dance: Physical Best: The American Alliance Physical Fitness Education & Assessment Program. Reston, VA, AAHPERD, 1988.
4. American Association of Health, Physical Education, and Recreation: Youth Fitness Test Manual. Washington, D.C., AAHPER, 1958.
5. American Association of Health, Physical Education, and Recreation: Knowledge and Understanding in Physical Education. Washington, D.C., AAHPER, 1969.
6. Balke, B.: Correlation of static and physical endurance. I. A test of physical performance based on the cardiovascular and respiratory response to gradually increased work. Air University, USAF School of Aviation Medicine, Project No. 21-32-004, Report No. 1, April, 1952.
7. Barrow, H.M.: Motor Ability Tests for College Men. Minneapolis, Burgess, 1957.
8. Blanchard, B.E.: A behavior frequency rating scale for measurement of character and personality in physical education. Research Quarterly, 7:56, May, 1936.
9. Bliss, J.C.: Basketball. Philadelphia, Lea & Febiger, 1929.
10. Bookwalter, K.W.: Test manual for Indiana University motor fitness indices for high school and college age men. Research Quarterly, 14:356–365, December, 1943.
11. Brace, D.K.: Testing basketball technique. American Physical Education Review, 29:159–165, April, 1924.
12. Brace, D.K.: Measuring Motor Ability. New York, A. S. Barnes, 1927.
13. Brouha, L.: The step test: A simple method of measuring physical fitness for muscular work in young men. Research Quarterly, 14:31–36, March, 1943.
14. Cooper, K.H.: Aerobics. New York, Bantam, 1968.
15. Cooper, K.H.: The Aerobics Program for Total Well-Being. New York, Bantam, 1982.
16. Cooperative Tests and Services. AAHPER Cooperative Physical Education Tests. Princeton, NJ, Educational Testing Service, 1970.
17. Cozens, F.W.: The Measurement of General Athletic Ability for College Men. Eugene, OR, University of Oregon Press, 1929.
18. Crampton, C.W.: A test of condition. Medical News, 88:529, September, 1905.
19. Cureton, T.K.: Physical Fitness Appraisal and Guidance. St. Louis, C.V. Mosby, 1947.
20. Darst, P.W., Mancini, V.H., and Zakrajsek, D.B.: Systemic Observation for Physical Education. West Point, NY, Leisure Press, 1983.
21. Henry, F.M.: Specificity versus generality in learning motor skills. Proceedings of the College Physical Education Association, 61:127, 1958.
22. Henry, F.M.: Increased response for complicated movements and a memory drum theory of motor reaction. Research Quarterly, 31:448–458, 1960.
23. Hopkins, D.R., Schick, J., and Plack, J.J.: Skills Test Manual—Basketball for Boys and Girls. Reston, VA, AAHPERD, 1984.
24. Humiston, D.: A measurement of motor ability in college women. Research Quarterly, 8:181–185, May, 1937.
25. Katch, F.I., and McArdle, W.D.: Nutrition, Weight Control, and Exercise. 3rd Ed. Philadelphia, Lea & Febiger, 1988, pp. 222–224.
26. LaPorte, W.R.: The Physical Education Curriculum. Los Angeles, College Book Store, 1955.
27. McCloy, C.H.: Character building through physical education. Research Quarterly, 2:41–61, October, 1931.
28. McCloy, C.H.: The measurement of general motor capacity and general motor ability. Research Quarterly, 5:46–61, March, 1934.
29. McCloy, C.H.: An analytical study of the stunt type test as a measure of motor educability. Research Quarterly, 28:46–55, October, 1957.

30. Montoye, H.J.: Physical Activity and Health: An Epidemiologic Study of an Entire Community. Englewood Cliffs, NJ, Prentice-Hall, 1975.

31. Rogers, F.R.: Physical capacity tests in the administration of physical education. New York, Teachers College, Columbia University, Contribution to Education No. 173, 1925.

32. Schneider, E.C.: A cardiovascular rating as a measure of physical fatigue and efficiency. JAMA, 74:1507, May, 1920.

33. Tuttle, W.W.: The use of the pulse-ratio test for rating physical efficiency. Research Quarterly, 2:5–8, May, 1931.

2

Selection of a Measurement Instrument

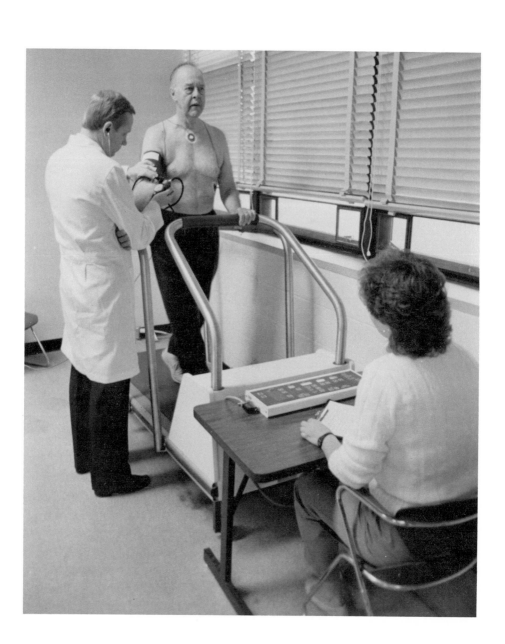

2

Selection of a Measurement Instrument

In the first chapter you learned that there are many different types of measurement instruments and many reasons for testing. The purpose of this chapter is to help you find and select a good measurement instrument to match your measurement goals. Since there is limited time available in physical education and sport programs for formal testing, it is obvious that the available time must be used well. Finding a measurement instrument to use is not especially difficult, for there are many readily available sources, and there are reference guides to help you locate particular types of tests. What *is* sometimes difficult, however, is evaluating the instruments you locate. You may wonder how you will be able to decide which of the existing instruments is the best one for you to use. The processes of locating and evaluating measurement instruments are explained in this chapter.

SOURCES OF MEASUREMENT INSTRUMENTS

New tests, scales, and inventories to assess qualities of interest to physical education and sport professionals are being developed literally every day. However, this is no easy or quick task. Quality test construction requires knowledge of measurement theory; thus persons who have not had at least one course in measurement probably should refrain from attempts to develop measurement instruments. Test construction is also a time-consuming endeavor. For most professionals, construction of one's own measurement instrument is not a viable alternative. Most of us will turn to instruments that have been developed and validated, i.e., determined to be sound, by others. Thus the first task addressed in this chapter is how to locate measurement instruments.

Measurement Textbooks

Before you read any further you should take several minutes to explore the wide variety of tests, scales, and inventories provided for you in the second half of this textbook. Perhaps the most obvious source of measurement instruments for physical education and sport purposes is the physical education and sport measurement textbook. Besides the one that you are now reading, there are many other such texts.[2-7,9,13,16] These texts typically present a selection of existing measurement instruments in an abbreviated form, but give appropriate references to find or purchase the complete instrument. Often the texts' authors will also provide a helpful, informative critique of the measurement instruments.

There are also some physical education and sport tests published in book form. These books can usually be found in university libraries, but may also be purchased for personal use directly from the publisher. The two biggest publishers of physical education and sport measurement instruments are the American Alliance of Health, Physical Education, Recreation, and Dance (AAHPERD) and Human Kinetics Publishers.

Journals, Dissertations, and Theses

The instruments described in measurement texts often can be located in their original form in professional journals, dissertations, and theses. So it is also possible to search these original sources directly rather than relying on the secondary measurement text source. A reference guide entitled *Completed Research in Physical Education* is most helpful in locating specific tests, scales, and inventories that originally were produced as dissertations or theses. Although numerous periodical guides may be used to locate tests that have been published in professional journals, an especially valuable reference source for the physical education and sport professional is *The Physical Education Index*.

Buros' Guides

A comprehensive approach for locating commercially published measurement instruments is to utilize the *Mental Measurement Yearbooks*, published by the Buros Institute of Mental Measurements. Volumes of these yearbooks are housed in the reference section of most university libraries. They are an invaluable source of test information for persons in all areas of education and psychology. Each volume contains information on new and substantially revised tests, scales, and inventories that have been published since the last volume of the yearbook. A typical entry includes: test, title, author, publisher, price, a brief description of the test, a description of the persons for whom the test was developed, administration time requirements, and reliability and validity data (concepts to be discussed later in this chapter). The entry may also include test references and a critical evaluation by a knowledgeable reviewer who notes any particular concerns about the test development, administration, interpretation, or scoring. See Figure 2–1 for a sample entry from *The Ninth Mental Measurements Yearbook*.[10]

Supplementing the *Mental Measurement Yearbooks* is Buros' *Tests in Print*. This reference aid is a bibliography of all tests that have appeared in preceding volumes of the yearbooks. This guide will also be found in the reference section of university libraries.

CRITERIA FOR EVALUATION

Before buying a new car, most people will determine the qualities of each car and then evaluate the qualities based upon how they intend to use the car. An expensive car that has superior road handling, sleek lines, and plush interior is right for some persons, but others need a less expensive car with good gasoline mileage and a roomy interior for the family. So it is with measurement tools. Each instrument must be evaluated in terms of its intended use. Some tests need to be very accurate and precise because they will be used to make a critical decision, e.g., whether or not a certain person is admitted into a prestigious program such as the NASA astronaut program. Other tests need to be quick,

AAHPERD Health Related Physical Fitness Test. Ages 6–17; 1980; 4 tests: Distance Run, Skinfolds, Sit-Ups, Sit-and Reach Test; manual (77 pages); personal fitness record (4 pages); cumulative fitness record (4 pages); class composite record (1 page); superior fitness award certificate (1 page); 1983 price data: $.15 per cumulative fitness record; $.15 per personal fitness record; $.10 per class composite record; $.25 per superior fitness award certificate; $3.95 per manual; $4.25 per specimen set; administration time not reported; American Alliance for Health, Physical Education, Recreation and Dance.

TEST REFERENCES

1. Ford, H.T., Jr., Puckett, J.R., Drummond, J.P., Sawyer, K., Gantt, K., and Fussell, C. Effects of three combinations of polymetric and weight training programs on selected physical fitness test items. PERCEPTUAL AND MOTOR SKILLS, 1983, 56, 919–922.

2. Pissanos, B.W., Moore, J.B. and Reeve, T.G. Age, sex, and body composition as predictors of children's performance on basic motor abilities and health-related fitness items. PERCEPTUAL AND MOTOR SKILLS, 1983, 56, 71–77.

Fig. 2–1. Sample entry from *The Ninth Mental Measurements Yearbook.* (From Mitchell, J.V. (Ed.): The Ninth Mental Measurements Yearbook. Volume I. Lincoln, NE, University of Nebraska Press, 1985, p. 1. Used by permission of the publisher.)

easy to administer, and can be less accurate because they will be used for a less critical decision. An example of this would be a decision about how to group students for instruction in a physical education class, because a person who is initially put into the wrong group can easily be switched when the error is discovered.

Two broad categories of qualities must be taken into consideration when evaluating a test, scale, or inventory for possible use. These are *administrative feasibility* and *psychometric qualities.*

Administrative Feasibility

The user of a test needs to carefully examine the test, scale, or inventory before selecting it for use. In fact, it is recommended that the user actually take the test. The test user also needs to pay close attention to what the test author has specified regarding the persons for whom the test was developed, the stated purpose of the test, and recommended administration procedures. Each of these topics is explored further in the following sections.

Test Population. For whom was the instrument developed? Many measurement instruments have been developed for high school and college-age students; far fewer instruments exist for young children, adults, the elderly, and special handicapped populations. Some tests have been developed for both males and females; others are designed only for one gender. A test originally developed for one population would, in some cases, clearly be inappropriate for use with a different population. Other times, the difference is less critical. For example, sport skill tests developed for college age performers often can be used with high school students.

Test Purpose. What is the stated purpose of the test? What exactly is it supposed to measure? The answers to these questions are critical to the test selection process. For example, is a "physical fitness" test designed to measure health-related or athletic performance-related aspects of fitness? Is the test designed to diagnose specific areas of weakness or simply to classify levels of fitness? Is a basketball knowledge test intended to assess more than one's knowledge of rules? The test user must be sure that he or she understands the purpose of the test. A measurement instrument cannot measure something it is not intended to measure. Using a test inappropriately would be like trying to use a hammer to saw a board. It simply will not do the job.

Group Size for Administration. How is the measurement instrument to be administered? May the test be given to a group, or must it be administered individually? What special training is needed to give or interpret the test?

Administration Time. How much time is needed to administer the test, and when is the test to be given? Is the test to be given before or after initial instruction has occurred? Is the test to be given on one day or two or more?

Administration Environment. What are the conditions or environment within which the test is to be given? Is the test to be given in a classroom, the gymnasium, or an outside field? Are special markings or special pieces of equipment required?

Administrative Costs. Is there a fee for use of the test? What is it? What is the cost of any special equipment that is needed?

These feasibility qualities are evaluated by comparing the match between the actual test and your intended use of the test. The closer the match the better. You will not always find the perfect measurement instrument—one that matches your intended use exactly. While some of the test restrictions can be "lived with," others will make the use of a particular test totally prohibitive. There are, however, no clear-cut rules by which to evaluate the administrative feasibility of a measurement instrument. The test user is the best person to decide what is or is not feasible in his or her particular circumstances. Additional points on administrative feasibility are discussed in Chapter 3.

Psychometric Qualities

"Psychometry" refers to the academic specialization of testing and measurement. Psychometric qualities are those of test *validity, reliability, objectivity,* and *freedom from group bias.* These fancy sounding terms are *values that result from tests of a measurement instrument usually conducted by the author of the measurement instrument being evaluated.* It is the responsibility of the test author to do such testing and to communicate the results to potential users of the test. Returning to the car analogy, this testing is similar to the testing for gasoline mileage, braking ability, and impact resistance that a car manufacturer does before offering a car for sale. Knowledge of the results of these performance tests helps the automobile consumer decide the worth of this product. Knowing something about the psychometric qualities of a measurement instrument helps the user decide its worth. Before deciding upon a particular test, the user must be convinced that the test measures what it is supposed to measure (*validity*), measures with consistency (*reliability*), yields accurate scores (*objectivity*), and is fair to members of all groups for whom the test is intended (*freedom from group bias*).

The qualities of validity, reliability, objectivity, and freedom from group bias are important for literally *all* types of tests. There is a difference, however, in how validity and reliability are defined and evaluated for norm-referenced and criterion-referenced measurement instruments. (Do you remember from Chapter 1 that norm-referenced tests compare the performances of individuals while criterion-referenced tests compare performances to a cut-off score that represents the level of mastery?) Because most published tests in physical education and sport are of the norm-referenced variety, the psychometric qualities of this type of measurement instrument are discussed first.

Validity of Norm-Referenced Tests. Validity is the single most important consideration in test evaluation. Generally, it refers to *the degree to which a test, scale, or inventory measures what it is supposed to measure.* More specifically, the concept of validity refers to the "appropriateness, meaningfulness, and usefulness of the specific inferences made from test scores."[1] The process of test validation involves the accumulation of different types of evidence to support different types of inferences made from the test scores.

It is important to realize that no test, scale, or inventory can be judged to be 100% valid, nor valid for all circumstances. Validity always refers to the degree to which accumulated evidence supports specific inferences made from test scores, so it can only be evaluated in terms of a particular purpose and for a particular group. A test designed to measure the health-related fitness of college students is not likely to be valid if administered to young children in an attempt to measure their motor coordination.

Since tests are developed for a variety of purposes and since validity is evaluated only in terms of purpose, it is not surprising that several types of validity evidence can be gathered. Generally we refer to the three categories of norm-referenced validity evidence as *content validity, criterion-related validity*, and *construct validity.* These are discussed in the sections that follow. As you read, do not forget that each of these types of validity evidence is used to demonstrate that the measurement instrument is, in fact, measuring what it is supposed to measure.

Content Validity. Content-related validity evidence demonstrates the *"degree to which the sample of items, tasks, or questions on a test are representative of some defined universe or domain of content."*[1] Perhaps this is most easily explained by *non*-examples. What would you think about a final examination that included questions about content that had not been taught in the course? (It would be pretty awful, huh?) What would you think of a basketball skill test battery that did not include a shooting test? Chances are that you would not think either of these tests was very good. In fact, you would be questioning the *content validity* of the tests.

Content validity is most important in the initial phases of test development. Expert judgment is often essential to define exactly what is to be measured by the content of the test, scale, or inventory. Positive examples may help you to understand this concept even better.

> *Example #1.* For a written test of intermediate tennis knowledge, the test author demonstrated content validity by providing a "blueprint" that specifies the test items that address knowledge of rules, history, skill and technique, strategy, and equipment and facilities. (See "Intermediate Tennis Test" by Reynolds in Chapter 8.)
>
> *Example #2.* Content validity was established for a basketball skill test battery by a committee of measurement experts who identified the four essential skills of basketball as shooting, passing, dribbling, and defensive movement. This was deduced from a survey of professional, college, high school, and elementary school basketball coaches. The coaches were asked to identify essential basketball skills and to suggest performance tests to measure those skills. (See the "AAHPERD Basketball Test for Boys and Girls" in Chapter 7.)

Criterion Validity. *"Criterion-related evidence demonstrates that test scores are systematically related to one or more outcome criteria."*[1] This is perhaps the easiest of the categories of validity to understand. Criterion-related evidence will be either *predictive* or *concurrent*.

Predictive evidence demonstrates the degree to which a test can predict how well an individual will do in a future situation. An example that every college student is familiar with is the use of the SAT (Scholastic Aptitude Test) and ACT (American College Testing). The scores from these tests, taken during one's junior or senior year in high school, are used to predict future success in college. The validation of these tests involved statistically correlating test scores with the criterion of freshman year grade point averages for thousands of students. (The statistical technique of correlation is explained in Chapter 4. If you are not familiar with this concept, you might want to turn to the appropriate section of that chapter now to read about correlation.) Validity was claimed because, in general, students who scored high on the SAT or ACT also received high grades in college, while those with low test scores tended to receive low grades. Of course, no test will have perfect predictive validity. (How did the SAT do in predicting your freshman grade point average? Did you, or one of your friends, do much better than the SAT had predicted?)

Concurrent evidence demonstrates the degree to which scores of the test being validated are related to some other valid criterion standard available at the same time. When validating measurement instruments in physical education and sport, alternate criteria that are considered valid include such things as the expert judgments of coaches, tournament results or competition scores, laboratory measurements, and scores from similar already-validated tests that are intended to measure the same thing as the new test (but may not do it as well, quickly, easily, or cheaply).

As is true of predictive validity evidence, concurrent validity evidence is evaluated statistically, by calculation of a correlation coefficient. The correlation coefficient represents the strength of the linear relationship between the test scores and the scores representing the criterion. The higher the correlation coefficient, i.e., the closer it is to the maximal value of 1.00, the stronger the validity evidence is believed to be. Usually a coefficient of .70 is interpreted as demonstrating strong validity evidence. However, the acceptability of the validity coefficient really depends on the appropriateness of the criterion, as well as on the purpose and the intended use of the test.

The following examples of how concurrent evidence was used to demonstrate criterion validity for actual measurement instruments may prove helpful to you.

> *Example #1.* The author of a field hockey ball control skill test demonstrated concurrent validity by correlating test scores with a criterion measure of expert rankings of players based upon subjective evaluations of their stickwork skills. The value of this correlation was .63. (See "Chapman Ball Test" in Chapter 7.)
>
> *Example #2.* The validity of using the sum of skinfold measurements to estimate percentage of body fat was demonstrated by correlating skinfold sums with body fatness as measured in the laboratory by underwater weighing techniques. The concurrent validity coefficients were .85 for adult females and .89 for adult males. (See College Norms for the "AAHPERD Health-Related Physical Fitness Test" in Chapter 6.)

Construct Validity. The evidence collected to demonstrate construct validity can be either logical or statistical in form, but both forms *focus on the test score* *as a measure of the characteristic of interest.* If a test score has real meaning then a person who is believed to possess a lot of the characteristic of interest should receive a high score on the test, while a person with little or none of the characteristic should receive a low score. Test scores are demonstrated to be valid to the extent that the scores agree with the expectations. Hopefully, the following examples will help to illustrate this idea.

> *Example #1.* One would expect low-handicap golfers to score better than high-handicap golfers on a valid test of golf skill. (Right?) Construct validity was claimed by the author of a golf skill test battery when the mean score for golfers with handicaps between 0 and 12 was significantly better than the mean score for golfers with handicaps between 13 and 18; and, the average handicap golfers' mean score was significantly better than that of golfers with handicaps of 19 or greater (See "Rowlands Golf Skills Test Battery" in Chapter 7.)
>
> *Example #2.* Children's scores on an inventory designed to assess children's attitudes toward physical activity were found to be positively related to active involvement in physical activity. In other words, children who expressed positive attitudes on the test tended to be physically active, while children who had negative attitudes tended to be less active. Construct validity was claimed on the basis of this evidence. (See "Children's Attitude Toward Physical Activity" in Chapter 9.)

Validity of Criterion-Referenced Tests. The concept of validity explained for norm-referenced tests remains basically the same when applying this concept to criterion-referenced tests. There are, however, different techniques that must be used to validate this type of measurement instruments.[11,12] Validity can be demonstrated either through the use of logical or statistical evidence. The logical approach is termed *domain-referenced validity*; the statistical approach is *decision validity.*

Domain-Referenced Validity. Every criterion-referenced test has a performance measure that is referenced to a criterion behavior that can be used to distinguish masters from nonmasters. Validation of this type of test involves *showing that the items sampled by the test adequately represent the criterion behavior.* In this case, "domain" is used to represent the criterion behavior.

Consider the task of validating an officiating rules examination for volleyball officials. The first step in the validation process would be to identify, in detail, the complete *domain* of volleyball rules. The next step might be to classify the rules into categories such as ball handling violations, serving violations, rules about positions and interchange, and substitution rules. Finally a procedure would be developed to systematically sample from the domain in such a way that the entire domain was adequately represented by the sample of items.

Domain-referenced validity may sound very similar to the description of content validity. It should, for there are many similarities! The main difference, however, lies in the careful definition of the domain that represents the criterion behavior for domain-referenced validity.

Decision Validity. Decision validity evidence demonstrates that the measurement instrument can accurately classify individuals as masters or nonmasters. One method by which this is done is through identification of *contrasting groups,* i.e., groups of individuals who are known to be either masters or nonmasters of the characteristic assessed by the criterion-referenced test that is under investigation. These persons are then given the test, and classified as masters or nonmasters based upon their scores on the test in relation to the specified cut-off score.

Validity is demonstrated when most of the known masters are accurately classified as masters by the test, and known nonmasters are accurately classified as nonmasters by the test.

This type of validity can be estimated by a *contingency coefficient, C,* that represents the proportion of the total test group who are accurately classified by the test.[13] A value that approaches 1.00 indicates near-perfect classification, while a coefficient value of .50 indicates that the test classification was no better than chance. Krippendorff suggests that values of .80 or higher are desirable.[8] The *C* value is easily calculated from a contingency table by summing the number of accurate master-master classifications plus the number of nonmaster-nonmaster classifications, then dividing by the total group size to find the proportion.

The following is an example of how a variation of the contrasting groups method was used to demonstrate decision validity in the development of an actual sport skill test. Usually contrasting groups are groups such as professionals vs. amateurs. In this example the criterion groups were students who had received at least eight classes of archery instruction (instructed group) vs. those who had received fewer than eight classes of instruction (uninstructed). Although the test authors used a correlation statistic (a phi coefficient) to estimate the accuracy of classification, Table 2–1 demonstrates how the *C* value could have been calculated from the contingency table of their classifications.

> *Example.* The test authors tested instructed students and uninstructed students on their newly-developed "Criterion-Referenced Test for Archery." After determining the cut-off score that maximized correct classifications, the authors reported that 42 of the 47 instructed group students were accurately classified as masters and 26 of the 31 uninstructed students were accurately classified as nonmasters.[14]

A Few More Words about Validity. Remember that validity is the single most important psychometric quality of a measurement instrument. We hope you now understand that each of the validity procedures is merely a different way by which test authors can demonstrate that their measurement instrument really measures what it is supposed to be measuring. In the next section we turn to a discussion of reliability, the second most important psychometric quality. It is not sufficient that a test measures what it is supposed to measure, it must do so consistently (*reliability*). Reliability and validity are, however, related. *A valid test is always reliable, but a reliable test is not necessarily valid.* (Can you reason why this is so?)

Reliability of Norm-Referenced Tests. Are you a reliable person? Reliability as a measurement concept means essentially the same thing as it does in everyday English. A reliable person is dependable and consistent; a reliable test is also dependable and consistent. *Reliability denotes the degree to which a meas-*

Table 2–1. Example of Calculation of Contingency Coefficient from Contingency Table

	Criterion Groups	
	Instructed (n = 47)	Uninstructed (n = 31)
Masters	42	5
Nonmasters	5	26

$$C = \frac{(42 + 26)}{(47 + 31)} = \frac{68}{78} = .87$$

urement instrument consistently measures whatever it measures. This is why a test can be reliable without being valid. The test might measure something besides what it is supposed to measure, but as long as it does so consistently it is considered reliable. (I have a bathroom scale that is reliable. It consistently measures 10 pounds less than my true body weight.) A reliable measurement instrument gives us confidence that an individual's score would be essentially the same if the test, scale, or inventory were readministered. It also gives us confidence that there would be consistency in the magnitude of score differences between any two examinees.

A reliable test is not affected to any large degree by random errors that might improve an individual's score on one day but hurt it on another day. Examples of such random errors are boredom and fatigue, inconsistent test administration, distracting noise, uncomfortable temperatures, lack of warm-up, and cheating. High reliability of tests, scales, and inventories can be achieved only if sources of error are reduced or eliminated.

As was true of validity, reliability can be demonstrated by several different types of evidence. A reliability coefficient is, however, always calculated from the evidence. The theoretical range of reliability coefficients is from a low of .00 to a high of 1.00. No test, however, is ever perfectly reliable, for there are always some measurement errors that cannot be eliminated even under the best of testing conditions. Reliability is usually easier to achieve than validity, so reliability coefficients are usually expected to be higher than corresponding validity coefficients.

Since reliability can be determined in several different ways, "reliability coefficient" is really a generic term. Each reliability coefficient estimates a different type of consistency. For norm-referenced tests we will discuss *test-retest, internal consistency,* and *parallel forms* reliability. This will be followed by a discussion of reliability of criterion-referenced tests.

Test-Retest Reliability. *Test-retest reliability coefficients estimate stability, or consistency over time.* In this process of test evaluation, the *same* individuals are administered a test *twice* within a relatively short period. The relationship between the two sets of scores is then determined by one of two statistical methods. One method is to correlate the two sets of scores by the *Pearson product-moment correlation,* the same correlation statistic that was used for estimating concurrent and predictive validity. The resulting correlation coefficient is reported as the test-retest reliability coefficient, symbolized by $r_{xx'}$. The second method for estimating test-retest reliability is to use *analysis of variance* to calculate an *intraclass correlation coefficient.* This reliability estimate is symbolized by $R_{xx'}$. (Analysis of variance, an inferential statistical technique, is not described in this text. Baumgartner and Jackson provide an example of the calculation of the intraclass correlation coefficient in Chapter 3 of their measurement text.)[2]

You may be wondering which of these two reliability coefficient methods is better. The intraclass correlation coefficient is preferred because it is a more appropriate statistic for the situation that exists when testing for reliability. The product-moment correlation is actually designed to establish the relationship between two different variables, such as SAT scores and freshman year grade point averages. It is not really appropriate for use in univariate situations as we have when correlating repeated measures on the same variable. You will, however, find the $r_{xx'}$ reliability coefficient reported in older tests for it was used exclusively until the late 1970s.

Test-retest reliability is the most commonly reported type of reliability for measurement instruments in physical education and sport for it is especially suited for tests that require motoric responses. One of the important decisions that must be made when attempting to demonstrate test-retest reliability is the length of the time interval between the test administrations. If too little time passes, scores are likely to be affected by fatigue. If too much time passes, scores may vary due to learning or real physical changes. So ideally, both the size of the test-retest coefficient and the length of the test-retest time interval should be reported. An example of how test-retest reliability was estimated for an actual test follows.

> *Example.* In development of a basketball test battery, males and females between the ages of 10 and college-age were tested and a few days later were re-tested on the four basketball tests that comprise the battery. Test-retest reliability was reported for each of the tests by means of the intraclass correlation coefficient. For the "Control Dribble Test," Rxx' ranged from .93 to .97 for females, and .88 to .95 for males. (See "AAHPERD Basketball Test for Boys and Girls" in Chapter 7.)

Internal Consistency Reliability. *Internal consistency reliability implies consistency within a test, scale, or inventory across a single administration.* In other words, it tells us that persons taking the test perform similarly throughout all parts of the test or from trial to trial. A common type of internal consistency reliability is termed *split-half reliability*. The total test is dividing into two comparable halves with an equal number of questions or number of trials per half. Each examinee's score is determined for each half, then the two half-scores are correlated. Split-half reliability is claimed to the extent that there is consistency between performances on the two halves of the test.

The split-half reliability coefficient must be interpreted with care, however, because longer tests tend to be more reliable than shorter tests. The correlation coefficient for the two halves of a test underestimates the reliability of the full test. The split-half reliability coefficient is therefore adjusted by the *Spearman Brown prophecy formula* to reflect the reliability of the total test. This formula is:

$$r \text{ of total test} = \frac{2 \ (r \text{ of halves})}{1 + (r \text{ of halves})} \qquad \text{Formula 2–1}$$

For example, suppose a 10-trial pitching accuracy test were divided into two halves, with the odd-numbered trials comprising one half and the even-numbered trials comprising the other half. If the split-half reliability coefficient is calculated to be .60, then the Spearman Brown formula estimates the reliability of the 10-trial test to be .75. (Check this by plugging .60 into the above formula!)

An intraclass correlation coefficient may also be calculated to estimate internal consistency reliability. Again, it is actually preferred over estimates that use the Pearson product-moment correlation. Not only is the analysis of variance a more appropriate statistic for this univariate situation, but additionally it is not necessary to reduce the trials to two sets to calculate the intraclass correlation coefficient. This is a distinct advantage for use with motor skill or fitness tests that have several trials. Reducing the trials to two groups masks the effect of any systematic increase or decrease across the trials. The analysis of variance approach is sensitive to differences across the trials and would result in a lower internal consistency reliability estimate.

Since the advent of computers to handle the long, involved arithmetic, internal consistency reliability is also being determined by other approaches. These approaches employ one of the Kuder-Richardson formulas, *KR-20* or *KR-21*, or Cronbach's formula for *coefficient alpha*. These approaches to demonstrating the internal consistency of a test are similar to that of the split-half method. Essentially, they provide a reliability coefficient that represents the average of all possible split-halves.

Parallel Forms Reliability. Parallel forms of a test are designed to be identical in every way but the actual items included on the test. They have the same number of items, the same level of difficulty, the same directions for administration, scoring, and interpretation, and they test the same variable. *Parallel forms reliability, also know as equivalent forms and/or alternate forms reliability, implies consistency from one form to another.* Parallel forms are seldom generated for any measurement instrument except a written test, scale, or inventory. They are used most often in research studies where one form is used for pretesting and the other form is used for posttesting. Whenever parallel forms are available, it is important to know that an examinee's score will be minimally affected by the form of the test that is taken. The *coefficient of equivalence*, r_{ab}, is the reliability estimate that results from the correlation of the sets of scores for individuals who have been administered both forms of the test during the validation process. R_{ab}, the corresponding intraclass correlation coefficient, is determined via the analysis of variance approach.

Interpreting Reliability Coefficients. Though we seldom accept a reliability coefficient lower than .70, the different types of reliability estimates cannot be interpreted identically. Remember that they represent different types of consistency which may be simpler or harder to achieve for different types of tests and for different groups of individuals. For example, tests that require maximal effort expenditures such as strength tests often report reliabilities of .85 or greater, while tests with high accuracy demands such as a pitching test often report reliabilities less than .85. Additionally, motor skill tests for beginners are often higher in reliability than tests designed for intermediates. And, as already mentioned, longer tests tend to be more reliable than shorter tests.

Standard Error of Measurement. To interpret a reliability estimate, it is sometimes helpful to determine the measurement error in each test score. This is accomplished by estimating the *standard error of measurement* from the test standard deviation (a measure of variability discussed in Chapter 4) and reliability coefficient as given in Formula 2–2.

$$SE_m = s \sqrt{1 - \text{(reliability coefficient)}} \qquad \text{Formula 2–2}$$

For example, suppose that the standard deviation for a set of vertical jump scores is 2 inches and the reliability coefficient of the test is .91. In this case the standard error of measurement is estimated to be .6 inch.

$$SE_m = 2 \sqrt{1 - .91} = .6 \text{ inch}$$

What does this mean? The standard error of measurement can be used to tell how precise any particular individual's score is. Assume that a particular athlete jumped 15 inches. If he were to retake this vertical jump test 100 times, we would expect his score to fall between 14.4 and 15.6 inches 68 times out of the 100 jumps. In other words, *the obtained score $\pm$ 1 SE_m creates a 68% confidence interval for any individual's test score.* The smaller the standard error of measurement, the more faith we have in the precision of the obtained test scores. High reliability coefficients generally mean low measurement errors. Low reliability coefficients indicate large measurement errors and yield test scores that are imprecise.

Reliability for Criterion-Referenced Tests. *Criterion-referenced reliability is defined as consistency of classification.* Reliability is judged by the consistency with which examinees are classified as masters or nonmasters by the test. Usually this is determined by administering the same mastery test to the same individuals on two different occasions. The test results are then tallied on a contingency table as depicted in Table 2–2. In this example, 80 examinees took a mastery test twice. Thirty-four were judged to be masters on both test administrations, 30 were judged as nonmasters on both occasions, 9 were judged masters on Day 1 but nonmasters on Day 2, and 7 nonmasters on Day 1 were judged as masters on Day 2. The reliability is estimated by calculation of the *proportion of agreement*, symbolized by *P*. The calculation of *P* is identical to that of the *C*-value explained earlier in this chapter. The number of consistent classifications is divided by the total number of examinees. In this example, *P* is .80. This reliability coefficient is interpreted similarly to *C*, the contingency coefficient that was calculated to estimate decision validity. The interpretable range of *P* are values between .50 and 1.00, because values less than .50 would indicate classification poorer than that of chance.

Objectivity. *Objectivity* is also a consistency measure. *It implies consistency in the scoring of a measurement instrument,* rather than consistency in performance. An estimate of the consistency in scoring is especially critical when scoring involves subjectivity, such as in scoring gymnastics performances or using a rating scale of most any kind. *Interjudge objectivity refers to the consistency of scoring for independent judges; intrajudge objectivity refers to the consistency of scoring for individual scorers.* The objectivity estimates are obtained through use of correlation and are interpreted the same as reliability coefficients.

Freedom from Bias. Test bias is related to validity, but deserves a special note because of its potential to impact on society. *Test bias becomes a concern whenever a test is administered to a group of individuals who have experiential backgrounds that are noticeably different from those of the group for whom the test was developed and on*

Table 2–2. Example of Calculation of Proportion of Agreement from Contingency Table

| | | Day 2 | |
		Masters	Nonmasters
Day 1	Masters	34	9
	Nonmasters	7	30

$$P = \frac{34 + 30}{80} = .80$$

whom the test was standardized.[15] Among the factors that can affect differences in experiential backgrounds are ethnic heritage, socioeconomic status, and gender. Unfairness can result when the use of test scores requires large inferential leaps, such as when scores on standardized tests are used to determine admission to desired educational programs or jobs.

Bias can be identified both at the level of a single item and for a complete test. One of the clues that an item might be biased is a particular item that is disproportionately hard (or easy) for the special group. At the level of the complete test, one can look for differences in mean scores, group differences in reliability, and group differences in prediction of some criterion variable. Freedom from bias is a worthy goal in the development and validation of measurement instruments that are intended to be used for testing of a broad spectrum of individuals.

In physical education and sport settings, the major potential source of test bias is gender. Especially when selecting a psychomotor test one should try to determine whether the test is gender appropriate. Often the test developer will account for gender differences by providing different norm tables for the interpretation of the scores for males and females. They may also specify differences in the test administration to account for gender differences. For example, females may use shorter distances or lighter weights in psychomotor tests that have a significant strength or power element. The test user should specifically look for how gender differences have been accounted for in sports skills and fitness tests.

SELECTING FROM THE ALTERNATIVES

After identifying as many instruments as you can that could serve your purpose, it is time to conduct a comparative evaluation. In most cases, the following step-by-step evaluation process will help you to select the best instrument from among the alternatives.

Step 1. Perhaps in the long run, it is best to first eliminate all of the instruments that clearly are administratively infeasible for one reason or another. Does the instrument require too much time? Does it require expensive equipment that cannot be purchased at this time?

Step 2. The next step is to carefully consider the factor of validity. Is one instrument more appropriate for testing the population that you are interested in? If content validity is a major concern, do the items included in one of these tests better match the content that you wish to test? Or, simply, does one instrument have a higher validity coefficient than any of the others?

Step 3. The next factor that should be considered is reliability. All else being equal, one would naturally select the most reliable measurement instrument. Seldom, however, is the decision this simple! The most reliable test might be considerably longer than a test that has a slightly lower reliability coefficient. Remember also that reliability coefficients that have been determined by different methods (that is, test-retest, split halves, etc.) cannot be interpreted as being equivalent.

Step 4. Return to the factor of administrative feasibility to reconsider any other information that you have about an instrument. Re-think the requirements for administration, scoring, and interpretation. Also consider the factors of objectivity and freedom from bias.

At this point, you most likely have selected an instrument for use. Congratulations if you have! But what if you have not? If you have narrowed the choices to a couple of possibilities you might proceed by trying out the two tests on a small sample of persons drawn from, or similar to, the intended population.

If, however, you cannot locate any acceptable instruments, then clearly the logical solution is to develop your own instrument. But remember the earlier caution that test construction is time-consuming and requires special knowledge. Perhaps at this point you might try to locate an expert in your locale who can assist you in the development of a measurement instrument. Do not be shy to ask for help, for not only must you design the new instrument, but you should also collect the necessary validation data. Anyone who understands measurement will appreciate your situation and, hopefully, will come to your aid.

SUMMARY

In this chapter you learned how to locate and evaluate measurement instruments. Specifically, you learned that the evaluation process includes attention to both *administrative feasibility* and to the *psychometric qualities* of the instrument. After eliminating from consideration those instruments that are not administratively feasible, you will select for use an instrument that measures what it is supposed to measure (*validity*), measures with consistency (*reliability*), yields accurate scores (*objectivity*), and is fair to members of all groups for whom the test is intended (*freedom from group bias*).

REFERENCES

1. American Educational Research Association, American Psychological Association, & National Council on Measurement in Education: Standards for Educational and Psychological Testing. Washington, DC., American Psychological Association, 1985, pp. 9–11.
2. Baumgartner, T.A., & Jackson, A.S.: Measurement for Evaluation in Physical Education and Exercise Science. 3rd Ed. Dubuque, Wm. C. Brown, 1987.
3. Bosco, J.S., and Gustafson, W.F.: Measurement and Evaluation in Physical Education, Fitness, and Sports. Englewood Cliffs, NJ, Prentice-Hall, 1983.
4. Clarke, H.H., and Clarke, D.H.: Application of Measurement to Physical Education. 6th Ed. Englewood Cliffs, NJ, Prentice-Hall, 1987.
5. Collins, D.R., and Hodges, P.B.: A Comprehensive Guide to Sports Skills Tests and Measurement. Springfield, Charles C Thomas, 1978.
6. Johnson, B.L., and Nelson, J.K.: Practical Measurements for Evaluation in Physical Education. 4th Ed. Edina, MN, Burgess, 1986.
7. Kirkendall, D.R., Gruber, J.J., and Johnson, R.E.: Measurement and Evaluation for Physical Educators. 2nd Ed. Champaign, IL, Human Kinetics, 1987.
8. Krippendorff, K.: Content Analysis: An Introduction to Its Methodology. Beverly Hills, CA, Sage, 1980.
9. Miller, D.K.: Measurement by the Physical Educator: Why and How. Indianapolis, Benchmark Press, 1988.
10. Mitchell, J.V. (ed.): The Ninth Mental Measurements Yearbook. Volume I. Lincoln, NE, University of Nebraska Press, 1985, p. 1.
11. Popham, W.J.: Modern Educational Measurement. Englewood Cliffs, NJ, Prentice-Hall, 1981.
12. Safrit, M.J.: Evaluation in Physical Education. 2nd Ed. Englewood Cliffs, NJ, Prentice-Hall, 1981.
13. Safrit, M.J.: Introduction to Measurement in Physical Education and Exercise Science. St. Louis: Times Mirror/Mosby, 1986.
14. Shifflett, B., and Schuman, B.J.: A criterion-referenced test for archery. Research Quarterly for Exercise and Sport, 53:330–335, 1982.
15. Thorndike, R.L.: Applied Psychometrics. Boston, Houghton Mifflin, 1982.
16. Verducci, F.M.: Measurement Concepts in Physical Education. St. Louis, Mosby, 1980.

3

Administration of Measurement Instruments

3

Administration of Measurement Instruments

The proper selection of tests is of little value unless testing programs are conducted in an efficient manner. Carefully administered tests provide maximum accuracy for valid and reliable results and insure that time has been used well. Efficiency of testing in all three learning domains is the result of careful step-by-step planning and preparation. There must be understanding of the techniques to be used and competence in the actual administrative procedures along with proper utilization of space and time, effective use of personnel, and an adequate follow-up process.

It is essential that the teacher/coach has an appreciation for the effective utilization of time. The actual time allotted to the physical education class or the athletic practice is shortened because of time invested in changes of clothing, showering, and administrative procedures. Unless special precautions are taken to conserve the remaining portion of class or practice time, testing might consume more than its proportional share of the total time allotment and result in excessive loss of instruction/practice. Time should not be saved, however, at the expense of accurate scores.

The program of measurement should be organized as an integral part of the total program and with definite purposes in mind. When it is organized in this manner, the time devoted to testing is not wasted. Testing becomes a part of the instructional setting and thereby a learning activity in itself. Although there is no steadfast rule in the matter of time allotment, it is generally accepted that performance and knowledge testing should take no more than 10% of instructional time. If tests are used as instructional devices, however, and if they serve a number of purposes, the time commitment is justified.[3]

Test results are only as valid as the data that have been collected through testing techniques. Tests carelessly administered, or tests administered to students/players who are not motivated, provide results that may have little value. Students/players have not really been tested until they have given maximum effort, nor are their scores accurate unless the test has been properly administered.[6]

Since tests vary according to objectives, purposes, and type, no standard rules may be established to cover all administrative procedures. Some general suggestions can be made, however, for purposes of simplicity. Administrative suggestions are made for specific tests in the chapters where these tests are presented.

ADMINISTERING PERFORMANCE TESTS

Checklists are presented to help the test administrator be more efficient. Additionally, some general statements about marking test areas, order of administering items, organization of groups, score cards, and scoring may prove helpful.

Markings

The test administrator should modify test directions and *markings* only when it is assured that the proposed change or changes will not affect the scores or use of the scores. The field or floor should be laid out properly and marked for rapid scoring in such events as throws, jumps, and kicks for distance. A football field that has been marked into 5-yard zones provides an excellent layout for estimating throwing and kicking distances to the nearest yard. Perhaps the simplest way to set up a standing broad jump station is to use a line already on the floor as the takeoff line and secure a tape measure to the floor at right angles to this line. Scoring can be done by observing across the tape measure the distance of the best jump.

Order of Administering Test Items

If test instructions call for a specific arrangement, that pattern should be followed explicitly. If not, the test administrator can establish an *order* with certain principles in mind: (1) the stations and all traffic patterns should be arranged to accommodate the flow of traffic by performers, (2) the stations should be arranged to offset fatigue and should be placed from the least strenuous to the most strenuous, or they should be spaced so that alternate sets of muscles are tested, (3) the stations should be clearly identified by name or number so that rotational procedures will be clear, and (4) safety should be considered in the placement of events that might be dangerous if they are permitted to overlap.

Organization of Groups[2]

There are three main ways to *organize a group* for testing. The most effective use of time is made when a large number is tested at one time. Many tests can be administered on a *mass* basis. For example, one examiner can explain, demonstrate, and administer all tests to all students at the same time. This is a great time-saver. However, this system can be used only when it is feasible for the performers to score themselves. A variation of this method pairs the students with partners. While one partner is tested, the other partner serves as scorer and recorder after which the partners exchange roles. This method saves time and may be used whenever the test items are adaptable to its use, e.g., Sit-Ups.

Another organizational scheme is to divide the group into *squads;* each squad works independently. This method works best when each station operates on a comparable time basis so that all the squads may rotate simultaneously. If squads are already organized for instruction and practice, it is efficient to have each squad tested on a particular test item by the squad leader or by a trained assistant. Either squad cards or individual cards may be used to record scores, in this case. Squad organization should not be used, however, if the subsequent order of tests handicaps certain squads.

When groups are large in number and the order of events is not important, or when some stations require more time than others, the best method of organization and rotation is on a *station-to-station* basis. Here the performers rotate from one station to another as individuals and do not remain with any particular group or squad. They are scored by trained assistants at each station and carry an individual score card with them. This approach is sometimes not feasible when younger children are tested.

On some occasions it may be effective to combine two or more of these methods of organization. For example, the squads can rotate from one test to another on a station-to-station basis. On other occasions, the mass technique of testing may be used for one or two items and then a shift can be made to the squad or station-to-station method for the other items. No single plan of organization will fit all situations.

Score Cards[2]

There are several kinds of *score cards* and various methods for reading scores. Various score cards may be seen in Chapter 7. The particular testing situation dictates the kind of card to use. The *class roll sheet* has names of all group members in alphabetical order with spaces for their scores and other pertinent data. This type of score card can be used more readily when one examiner administers and scores all test items, or when the station-to-station method is used and each station has class roll sheets. In any event, this method expedites the conversion of raw scores to scale scores and presents an overview of class performance. The *squad card* is used sometimes when the squads rotate from station to station and the squad leaders carry the squad cards with them. It is a smaller version of the class roll sheet and has the same characteristics. It is more flexible, however, and permits the squads to score themselves under the direction of squad leaders or a trained tester.

Perhaps the best method, certainly the most flexible, for recording scores is the *individual score card*. All performers carry a card with them and assume responsibility for its care. This card usually is designed for specific tests and generally provides space for such information as the performer's name, class, date, age, weight, height, raw scores, and converted scores. If the scores can be summed, as is the case with all standard scores, there should be a place for a composite score. In most cases, a 5″ × 8″ card is adequate. This individual card is generally used when the performers score for each other or when they rotate from station to station independently and are scored by a trained assistant. Since performers must assume responsibility for their cards and also share in the rotational procedures, they share to a greater extent in the testing process and at the same time learn self-direction. In addition, they can see their scores, and they have a better idea of their achievement status.

Methods of Scoring

Naturally, there is some relationship between the organization of the group, the type of score card used and the *method of scoring*. *Scoring by instructor/coach* is perhaps the most time-consuming and should be used only when the utmost in accuracy is essential. The instructor/coach may do the scoring when one squad is being tested while the other squads are participating in alternate activities, or when the nature of the test is such that only a highly specialized person can administer it. Posture and nutrition tests fall into this category.

Scoring by partners is the method generally used when the tests are administered on a mass basis. The class or team is divided into partners and, while an examiner administers the tests and supervises them, scores are judged and recorded by the partner who is not taking the test at the time. Partners may also do the scoring within the squad. When the partner method of scoring is employed, it is essential that the director of testing emphasize the correct scoring techniques to be followed.

When tests are administered on a squad basis, generally they are administered and *scored by a squad leader.* The preparation of the squad leaders should be done at training sessions prior to the testing period. This system is especially effective when a student leadership program is in operation and when student leaders are already trained in test administration techniques.

When tests are administered on a station-to-station basis, *scoring by trained examiners* is usually the practice. They have been instructed in methods of judging and scoring at training sessions prior to the actual testing. These trained individuals may be students, faculty members, professional students from teacher-training programs, paraprofessionals, or interested, nonschool personnel, such as parents.[8]

Checklist

The administrative suggestions[1-3,5,7,8] presented in the checklist for administering performance tests are given in 3 categories: (1) prior to testing, (2) just before and during testing, and (3) just after testing and later. The checklist also addresses concerns about the performer who will be taking the tests and about the test itself. Several checklists are included to facilitate administrative procedures, each following the pattern set by the first one. They can be refined with use. The checklists for administering performance tests and rating scales are related to the psychomotor assessment of performers while they are actually "doing" the activity. The checklist for administering knowledge tests is to expedite assessment in the cognitive, "knowing," domain, and the checklist for administering affective scales is used with "feeling" assessments. The first checklist is the most complete and should be referred to even when administering other types of assessments.

Checklist of Procedures for Administering Performance Tests*

Time	Procedures Related to the Performer	Procedures Related to the Test

Prior to Administering the Test	Decide on reason(s) for administering test(s)
	Review tests for validity and reliability
	Select most suitable test(s) for purpose(s)
	  Grouping
	  Diagnosis
	  Grading
	  Process, formative measure
	  Product, summative measure
	Review for efficiency of administration
	  Facilities
	  Time
	  Personnel
	  Equipment
	  Money
	Orient students/players
	  Purposes of taking test
	  How results will be used
	  Any special directions
	Explain and demonstrate test items as they should be performed
	Get students/players familiar with test(s)[7]
	Provide practice time
	Diagram location of test stations and indicate traffic flow of performers
	Consider safety factors such as spotters, warm-up, hazards, discipline
	Motivate students/players for optimum performance
	Tell performers if scores will be posted
	Plan activity for early finishers and uninvolved performers
	Plan adjustments for mainstreamed performers
	Decide on make-up and re-take policies
	Get parental permission, if indicated
	Get administrative permission, if necessary
	Check for medical restrictions
		Schedule space
		Take test(s) as administrator to gain understanding of it
		Decide on class organization
		  Mass
		  Squad
		  Individual
		  Combination
		Decide if scoring by instructor, partner, squad leader, trained tester, or some combination
		Make a check-off list of all equipment and materials needed including quantity
		Order any equipment needed that is not already in inventory
		Estimate time needed for each item
		Practice giving test(s)
		Plan and complete floor/field markings
		  Prepare 2 or 3 stations for items which take more time
		  Be alert to traffic flow from station to station
		    Fatigue–administer aerobic items last, allow rest between stations, if necessary
		    Safety–avoid crossing areas where performance is underway
		    Specifications in test directions
		Secure personnel to help administer test
		Train assistants (judges, scorers, recorders, etc.)
		  Conduct workshops
		  Have assistants take test(s)
		  Clarify test directions
		  Explain organizational plan for performers
		  Go over plan for setting up stations
		  Point out safety precautions
		  Explain and practice use of specialized equipment
		  Explain and practice scoring procedures
		  Determine procedures for incorrect performance or for mistakes during trials
		  Explain procedures following completion of test(s)
		  Inform helpers of time and place to report
		Prepare score cards and duplicate

*Checklist of Procedures for Administering Performance Tests** **Continued**

Time	Procedures Related to the Performer	Procedures Related to the Test
Prior to Administering the Test *Continued*		Make card consistent with organizational plan for taking and scoring test(s) (mass, squad, individual)
		Consider using individual score cards as the most preferable
		Provide space to record all trials
		Provide norms on reverse of card for ease and promptness of interpretation. Drawing a profile is possible if test has multiple items.
		Indicate norms or criterion score
		Use columns instead of rows for accuracy in adding scores of trials
		Include space for comments by performer, assistant, and/or teacher/coach
		Write-out standardized directions in the second person
		Write-out scoring procedures for assistants and performers
		Arrange stations and label
		Post diagram of traffic flow and order of taking tests
		At arrival
		During testing
		At completion
		Have spare equipment in reserve
		Provide space for warm-up
		Review procedures in case of injury

*Checklist of Procedures for Administering Performance Tests** **Continued**

Time	Procedures Related to the Performer	Procedures Related to the Test
Just Before and During Administration	Tell the performers again what each test is and why is it being given Explain testing and scoring procedures Demonstrate the test items, if appropriate. Skills tests should be demonstrated but motor ability items are not usually Remind performers of safety points Respond to questions Provide warm-ups specific to the test items Administer practice trials Motivate performers to perform well and give maximum effort Encourage performers to help one another with administration Administer test(s) in a positive and efficient manner Maintain discipline to enhance performance and safety Provide for performers who finish early Anticipate and reduce potentially embarrassing situations Circulate to supervise whole process so traffic flow, safety, emergency, and other concerns can be monitored. The test administrator should not be tied down at any one responsibility	Check facility for lighting, cleanliness, safety Place equipment and supplies Check for proper placement and safety of all equipment Check that all assistants are present and prepared Make mental notes of testing situation Student/player reactions Smoothness of administrative procedures Changes to be made in the future
Just After the Test and Later	Interpret results as promptly as possible As a group Individually, if indicated Compare results with criterion-referenced standards or norm-related standards Protect privacy of individual scores Do not embarrass any performer Share results with parents, if appropriate Discuss the testing process with the performers Thank performers for their cooperation and motivated participation	Collect score cards Analyze test results. Use computer, if appropriate Apply results to the purpose(s) for administering the test(s) Note changes to be made in procedures the next time administered Return all equipment to proper storage Remove markings (tape or painted lines) from testing area Thank assistants for their help Evaluate results in relation to purpose(s) of giving test(s) Study results to identify ways to improve instruction File copy of results

*Adapted from Logsdon, B.J.: Physical Education for Children, Philadelphia, Lea & Febiger, 1984. McGee, R.: Evaluation of processes and products, p. 415.[5]

ADMINISTERING RATING SCALES[2,4]

A rating scale organizes the process of observation by making and recording judgments about degrees of the quality, trait, or factor being examined. Physical education and athletic objectives have many desirable outcomes that are intangible and do not lend themselves easily to objective techniques of measurement. Rating scales are helpful under at least three conditions: (1) when no objective measurement technique is available for measuring a quality, (2) when the existing devices for measurement are not administratively feasible or practical, or (3) when it appears expedient to supplement objective measurement with subjective ratings.

The function of the rating scale is a subjective estimate, but if it is properly constructed and used, it will help to narrow the gap between subjective and objective assessment. Rating scales are excellent means of quantifying the many hard-to-measure variables in physical education and sport. They make observation more accurate and serve to focus the attention of the instructor/coach and the performer on the important aspects of the movement.

Some activities can be evaluated only subjectively, such as diving and gymnastics. Most activities, however, result in a score depicted in time or game points. The score is the product measure, the end result of the movement. Some instructors/coaches and performers consider ratings inappropriate for such activities, thinking that form is not important as long as the results are successful. For people who are just learning skill patterns, however, instruction and asessment in recommended, well accepted movement patterns has merit.

Rating scales are usually used to evaluate performance while it is in process. A form rating of a golf swing, a floor exercise routine, a side stroke, a tennis serve, and a basketball rebound are examples. Form rating scales are most appropriately used at beginning levels of learning when the basic patterns of form are being established. At higher levels of skill, individuals tend to customize the movement to fit their unique body build and timing. Deviations from commonly accepted classic skill patterns are obvious in Olympic level performers and are not considered nearly so serious at that level as they would be if present at lower skill levels. Imagine someone telling Dick Fosbury that his high jump "flop" was poor form!

When an activity as a whole is being evaluated, the use of ratings should be considered because the whole movement is generally more important than the sum of its parts. For this reason, ratings are far more effective in the testing of some skill and game situations than are more objective skill tests. The ultimate outcomes identified in behavioral objectives describe criteria for the "whole" situation. Occasionally, the highest scorers on some skill tests are not the best players in game situations. A skill test is but a part of a whole. This "whole"' combines many facets into one totality including skill, knowledge, fitness, attitude, and perhaps others. These facets are all used in game situations to give a performance quality. Game performance or quality cannot be measured by any single test battery, but only by some type of subjective measurement. All coaches use ratings either consciously or subconsciously in selecting squads, choosing starting lineups, and evaluating opponents.

Rating scales are useful assessment tools in the affective area as well as the psychomotor and are evident when measuring attitudes, leadership, competitiveness, motivation, and behavior. Usually used, however, as measures of performance while in process, they are also suitable for program evaluations.

The checklist for Administering Rating Scales should be used in conjunction with the Checklist of Procedures for Administering Performance Tests. Only the additional points specific to Rating Scales will be added here. Samples of rating scales are shown in Chapter 7.

Checklist of Procedures for Administering Rating Scales

Time	Procedures Related to the Performer	Procedures Related to the Test

Prior to Administering a Rating Scale	Discuss rating scale with performers
	Analyze each part of the skill to be observed
	Discuss the meaning of scoring terms. Try to identify scoring categories which either use terms specific to the activity or are defined in relation to the activity
	Practice using the rating scale with performers
		Analyze activities and qualities to be assessed
		Develop rating scale or find a suitable one
		Be attentive to
		  Purpose
		  Traits, qualities
		  Activities determined and defined
		  Sub-division of traits if using scale as a diagnostic tool, i.e., parts of batting
		  Categories of scoring
		  Provision for final index score
		  Type of rating scale
		    Comparison scales
		    Graphic scales
		    Descriptive scales
		    Numerical scales
		    Combination scales
		Duplicate rating scale and share with performers
		Practice using rating scale and discuss results among raters so all have the same anchor point

Just Prior to and During Use of a Rating Scale	Review rating scale
	Answer questions if clarification is needed
	Encourage the best performance possible
		Have several instructors, coaches, performers rate so a combined score is possible. If using 5 raters, throw out high and low scores
		Be alert to rater errors[4]
		  Halo effect–letting other information influence rating
		  Error of logic–rating similarly on factors which seem to be, but are not, related
		  Error of contrast–rating in relation to self, as rater
		  Error of central tendency–avoiding very high and low ratings and rating toward the middle of the scale

Checklist of Procedures for Administering Rating Scales **Continued**

Time	Procedures Related to the Performer	Procedures Related to the Test
Just Prior to and During Use of a Rating Scale *Continued*		Proximity error–rating similarly the factors assessed close together in time or space
		Error of leniency–rating consistency too high or compensating for that possibility by rating consistently too low
		Error of bias
		Sex
		Appearance
		Rater inflation
		Observe performer long enough to have confidence in rating
		Observe actual performance. Do not rate from memory.
		Use videotape procedures, if possible. Provides feedback for performer and for rater
		Rate everyone in group on one skill before progressing to next skill. Do not rate one performer on several items and then rate next performer
		Be in a good position to observe performance
Just After Using a Rating Scale and Later	Interpret rating to performer	Have raters and performers evaluate rating scale and make suggestions for revisions
	Get comments from performers	Revise rating scale
	Have follow-up conferences	Decide how results can be used to enhance teaching
		Make summary notations about process of using rating scale to have for reference when using the scale again

ADMINISTERING KNOWLEDGE TESTS

The instructor/coach who has cognitive objectives for his/her program will want to assess knowledge of the activity. Administrative procedures should be as carefully planned as when administering motor performance measures. Assurance that test scores in the "knowing" domain are valid is equally essential. Assuming that the knowledge test itself is well constructed, the test administration will influence the test results. Points for the teacher/coach to consider when administering a knowledge test are noted in the checklist that follows. Other topics related to administering tests, which might be helpful in the cognitive area as well, are included on the checklists for psychomotor tests, rating scales, and affective scales.

Checklist of Procedures for Administering Knowledge Tests

Time	Procedures Related to the Student/Player	Procedures Related to the Test
Prior to Administering a Knowledge Test	Discuss the date for taking the test Describe the content Review for the test Share sample test items with students/players Tell students/players how test scores will be used	Prepare and duplicate the test Prepare and duplicate the answer sheet Try to use a standardized answer sheet if giving an objective test Arrange for a classroom in which to administer the test so students/players will not have to sit on the ground/floor/bleachers Identify students/players who will need help taking test and arrange for the help or for another time to administer the test to them
Just Prior to and While Taking the Knowledge Test	Explain scoring so students/players will know whether or not to guess at answers about which they are not quite sure Explain use of answer sheet Answer procedural questions Teach and encourage students to cover their answer sheets as they work Put relevant words on blackboard to help with spelling if giving a subjective test	Check number of copies of test and answer sheets Have extra pencils available Check lighting, seating, and temperature in room Be available to clarify questions Supervise
Just After and Following Administration of Knowledge Test	Return answer sheets and test papers to students/players to go over and discuss. Learning is still taking place Explain grading system Discuss comments about confusing items Get reactions about the test and its use	Grade promptly Use computer to process an item analysis if available Discard bad test items Re-score and re-assign grades Use the results for the intended purpose Note items needing revision Revise items Use results to make changes in teaching Keep a record of results

ADMINISTERING AFFECTIVE SCALES

Assessments in the affective domain are taken to help students/players understand how their "feeling" selves interact with their "doing" and "knowing" selves. Usually, measures in the affective domain are more sensitive so special precautions need to be taken when administering these scales and using the results. The discussion of affective measures in Chapter 5 on Grading states that assessments in this domain generally are not included in achievement grades. Not all assessments need to be a part of a grade to be justified. Many assessments are made of students/players that never become a part of a final grade. This does not detract, however, from the value of students/players knowing their status on such measures as attitude, self-concept, body-image, competitiveness, and sportsmanship. There are some scales, however, in which it would not be appropriate to report scores of individual measures, such as measures of social distance. The checklist for administering affective measures identifies some unique aspects of using these assessment tools. They are referred to as scales, or inventories, instead of tests because they are not graded in the traditional sense.

Checklist of Procedures for Administering Affective Scales

Time	*Procedures Related to the Student/Player*	*Procedures Related to the Affective Scale*
Prior to Administering the Scale	Describe the scale to be used why it is being given how the results will be used Encourage honesty Describe procedures to insure privacy Self-scoring Anonymity Obtain signed human subjects consent forms if scale is of a sensitive nature or if individual results are to be used	Alert the school administration of your plans to administer an affective scale and the nature of it Study scales and select most appropriate one(s) for the purpose(s) Duplicate, if not copyrighted, or order commercially Prepare for interpretative discussion with students/players
Just Before and While Taking and Affective Scale	Encourage carefulness Provide adequate time Guarantee privacy of scores to encourage honesty Reiterate that scores will not be used as part of a grade, if, indeed, that is true	Give directions carefully Usually, do not have students/players put names on answer sheets. Either have them score the scales themselves or use the individual answer sheets to arrive at a group score. i.e., What is the sportsmanship index of our school? What is the attitude of our students toward coeducational classes? What is the cohesiveness index of our team? Be available to handle procedural matters
Just After Taking an Affective Scale and Later	If appropriate, have students/players score their own scales, if individual scores are desired, describing the procedure step by step Discuss the experience of taking the scale and reacting to the findings Reassure the students/players of the confidentiality of the information if individual scoring had to be done by the instructor/coach Do not break your promise about confidentiality of information Encourage individual conferences. Make referrals to qualified school personnel, if indicated, but only with approval of student/player	Interpret the scoring of the scale, generally Encourage individual conferences for follow-up Evaluate process of using an affective tool Make notes for future use and revisions

SUMMARY

Effective evaluation always includes measurement, followed by analysis and use of results. Test data have many uses. In the final analysis, to be of most value they must be applied to improve either the product or the process. A significant phase of evaluation is what happens after results are used. Regardless of whether measurement is applied directly to product or process, a follow-up is indicated. The follow-up is usually revealed through a redirection of aims and objectives, a replanning of the process with a prescription of change in some process factors, and a general raising of standards in all areas of process. All of this requires further evaluation. Thus, the follow-up implies that evaluation is a continuous, ongoing process.

A yearly plan, whether for the instructional, intramural, or athletic program in a school or non-school setting, should identify any psychomotor, cognitive, and affective measures that will be used. Such a yearly plan puts the administrative procedures for assessment tools in context. The instructor/coach/administrator wants to plan carefully to obtain accurate scores in an efficient manner. This is the challenge because important decisions will be made about students/players/employees on the basis of the assessment information.

REFERENCES

1. Barrow, H.M.: The ABC's of testing. Journal of Health, Physical Education, Recreation, 33:35–37, May-June, 1962.
2. Barrow, H.M., and R. McGee: A Practical Approach to Measurement in Physical Education. 3rd Ed. Philadelphia, Lea & Febiger, Chapter 4, Administration of Tests, pp. 53–65, and Chapter 17, Rating Scales in Physical Education, pp. 535–548, 1979.
3. Baumgartner, T.A., and A.S. Jackson: Measurement for Evaluation in Physical Education. 3rd Ed. Dubuque, Iowa, Wm. C. Brown Company, 1987.
4. Irwin, D.M., and M.M. Bushnell: Observational Strategies for Child Study. New York, Holt, Rinehart and Winston, 1980.
5. Logsdon, B.J., et al.: Physical Education for Children: A Focus on the Teaching Process. 2nd Ed. Philadelphia, Lea & Febiger, 1984.
6. Nelson, J.K., and J.J. Dorociak: Reducing administration time while improving reliability and validity of fitness tests. Journal of Physical Education, Recreation, and Dance, 53:63–65, January, 1982.
7. Plowman, S.A., D.N. Hastad, and J.R. Marett: A workshop model that works—Implementation strategies for health related fitness testing. Journal of Physical Education, Recreation, and Dance, 54:46–47, February, 1983.
8. Wall, J.: Organizational hints on test administration. Canadian Association for Health, Physical Education and Recreation Journal, 31–32, September-October, 1982.

4

Analysis of Measurement Scores

After measurement scores have been collected, they must be analyzed to give them meaning. Every measurement textbook has one of these—a chapter on statistics. Now tell the truth, are you holding your breath, anticipating something akin to having your teeth drilled without novocaine? Well, believe it or not, this will not be too unpleasant even for those of you with a severe case of mathematics anxiety. The statistics needed to analyze measurement scores require little more mathematics sophistication than knowledge of addition, subtraction, multiplication, and division. Occasionally you will need to determine square roots, but please feel free to use a calculator to obtain those values. In fact, please use your calculator or a computer any time you wish, for it is not productive for you to get bogged down in statistical formulas and calculations. The real importance of this chapter for the physical education and sport practitioner lies in the selection of appropriate statistics for a given situation, the interpretation of statistical values, and the subsequent decisions that are made based upon available evidence.

FAMILIARIZING YOURSELF WITH THE SCORES

Units of Measurement

It is important to note the units in which your scores are recorded and to make sure that you clearly understand the behavior that was measured by these scores. For example, do the scores represent time to complete a particular task measured in minutes and seconds, the distance that an object was projected in feet and inches, or perhaps a judge's estimation of the skillfulness of a performance based on a 10-point scale? It is also important to remind yourself whether a high score or a low score represents the better performance.

Before analyses can be performed, many measurement scores may also need to be converted to a common unit of measurement to facilitate the mathematical manipulation of values. For example, a set of scores for the standing long jump recorded in feet and inches should probably be converted to inches for subsequent analyses.

Types of Scores

Measurement scores can be classified in many different ways. How scores are classified influences the calculations that can be done on them and the interpretations of the calculations.

Continuous Vs. Discrete. One important classification system categorizes scores as being either continuous or discrete. *A continuous score has a potentially infinite number of values because the precision of measurement is limited only by the precision of the measurement instrument.* Between any two recorded values of a continuous score exist countless other values that could be expressed as fractions of these numbers. For example, using a hand-held stopwatch one would probably measure a 50-yard sprint to the nearest tenth of a second; using an electronic timer the same score would likely be recorded in thousandths of a second. *A discrete score is limited to a specific number of values and is seldom expressed as a fraction.* The score for a round of golf, the number of successful free-throws in 20 attempts, and the score on an end of arrows are all examples of discrete scores.

When averaging continuous scores, it is appropriate and logical to use fractions or decimals to report average values. However, using fractions or decimals to report discrete scores is often artificial and sometimes even nonsensical. (Have you heard that American families now have an average of 1.9 children? Have you heard that my basketball team had an average of 12.4 free throw attempts per game last season? I wonder how many times we sank that .4 free-throw!) Extra care must be taken when interpreting fractional discrete values.

Level of Measurement. Another way to classify scores is to categorize them according to their level of measurement—as *ratio, interval, ordinal,* or *nominal* scores. These different levels of scores result from the qualities that are measured and the ways in which measurements occur. It is important to know the level of measurement represented by your data because different statistical operations are valid only with certain levels of measurement. Ratio and interval data are more precise than ordinal and nominal data and allow greater latitude in choice of statistic than do ordinal and nominal data.

Ratio. Ratio scores have both a common interval of measurement between each possible value and a true zero point at which "0" means no amount of the quality being measured. Ratio scores permit comparisons of the ratio of one score value to another, e.g., determining that a shot put of 40' is twice as far, and therefore twice as good, as a 20' shot put. Distances, times, weights, and points scored are common examples of ratio scores used in physical education and sport settings.

Interval. Interval scores also have a common interval of measurement between score values, but have no true zero point. If a "0" is recorded for an interval score, it is not meant to imply that absolutely no amount of the quality being measured exists. For example, a "0" on a sportsmanship test generally would not mean that the test taker is absolutely devoid of sportsmanship. Because there is not a true zero to use as a reference point, it would be inappropriate to conclude that someone who scores 40 on a sportsmanship test is twice as good a sport as someone who scores 20 on the same test.

Ordinal. Ordinal scores do not have a constant interval between possible score values, but there is a hierarchical order to the scores that allows one to characterize one test taker as having performed better than another. Finishes in a cross country race, team standings in a league, and ranked-order preferences for members of an all-star team are all examples of ordinal scores. Because of the lack of constant intervals between score values, ordinal scores should never be summed and arithmetically averaged.

Nominal. Nominal scores simply use numbers to represent membership to different categories. They cannot be ordered in terms of goodness or badness, nor can the score values be summed and arithmetically averaged. For example, a researcher who uses a "1" to code gender for female athletes and a "2" for male athletes should not attempt to find the average gender of the research subjects by adding the 1s and 2s and dividing by the total number of subjects. (How silly it would be to try to interpret an average gender of 1.7!) Nominal scores are seldom used in physical education and sport measurement.

If you would like to check your understanding of these two ways of classifying scores, then refer to Table 4–1. For each of the measurements listed, first identify whether it is discrete or continuous, then identify the level of measurement as ratio, interval, ordinal, or nominal. Correct answers are given at the bottom of the table.

NONSTATISTICAL DATA INSPECTION

The number of scores you need to analyze usually determines which of several nonstatistical and/or statistical data inspection techniques are used. In general, the larger the number of scores the more helpful it will be to precede statistical analyses with use of one or more of the nonstatistical data inspection techniques presented here.

Frequency Tables

Listed in Table 4–2 are vertical jump scores for a group of junior high school girls attending a summer volleyball camp. The scores are rounded to the nearest inch of fingertip reach at the height of the jump. As they are listed, the scores are hard to interpret. The camp director is unable to tell the girls with much precision about the average performance of the group or about the performance of individual girls.

Simple Frequency Tables. Contrast the random lists of scores in Table 4–2 with the simple frequency table presented in Table 4–3. In Table 4–3, the column labeled "Score" lists all obtained score values in descending order, with the best score always listed first. The "f" column indicates the frequency of occurrence of each particular score value (consistent with the result of the hand tally). The column labeled "cum f" lists the cumulative frequency, starting at the bottom

Table 4–1. *Practice in Classifying Types of Measurement Scores*

Instructions: Classify each of the following as either discrete or continuous, then reclassify each as ratio, interval, ordinal, or nominal.

1. Standing broad jump score (to nearest half-inch)
2. Place of team finish in a tournament
3. Temperature at game time (in degrees farenheit)
4. Number of football jersey

Answers: 1. continuous, ratio	2. discrete, ordinal
3. continuous, interval	4. discrete, nominal

Table 4–2. *Vertical Jump Scores (in inches) for 50 Junior High Girls*

88	86	88	90	90	91	87	89	91	89
87	87	85	85	88	91	95	89	87	87
86	87	85	89	91	86	88	87	83	90
90	86	86	88	89	89	86	94	88	92
92	90	89	90	89	91	90	88	89	88

Table 4–3. *Simple Frequency Table for Vertical Jump Scores (in inches) for 50 Junior High Girls*

Score	Tally	f	cum f	%	cum %
95	/	1	50	2	100
94	/	1	49	2	98
92	/ /	2	48	4	96
91	/ / / / /	5	46	10	92
90	/ / / / / / /	7	41	14	82
89	/ / / / / / / / /	9	34	18	68
88	/ / / / / / / /	8	25	16	50
87	/ / / / / / /	7	17	14	34
86	/ / / / / /	6	10	12	20
85	/ / /	3	4	6	8
83	/	1	1	2	2

of the frequency table and accumulating frequencies up to the total number of scores at the highest obtained score value. The "%" and "cum %" columns give the same information as the "f" and "cum f" columns expressed in terms of percentage of the total number of scores.

From this table it is easy to see that the scores ranged from a high of 95 inches to a low of 83 inches, a difference of 12 inches. It is also easy to see that the majority of scores fell between the values of 86 and 91 inches, with the single most common score being 89 inches. From the "cum %" column one can easily determine that one-half (50%) of the girls jumped a height of no more than 88 inches, the height of the standard volleyball net for females. What decisions do you think that the camp director could now make regarding setting and spiking practices?

Grouped Frequency Tables. A variation of the simple frequency table is the grouped frequency table. This table serves the same purposes as the simple frequency table, but differs in definition of the score values, i.e., the "Score" column values. Instead of identifying the frequencies for individual score values, frequencies are reported for specified score intervals. This becomes useful when there are so many different score values with low incidences of occurrence that the simple frequency table becomes cumbersome and difficult to interpret.

A grouped frequency table is constructed by forming 10 to 20 score intervals that will include all obtained score values. Fifteen score intervals with an odd-numbered interval size is usually considered ideal. The score intervals are determined by dividing the difference between the largest and smallest scores by 15, and rounding the result to the nearest whole number. This number defines the score interval that should probably be used. The next step is to define the top interval to contain the best score. If the interval size is odd, the midpoint of this top interval should be a multiple of the interval size. If the interval size is even, the smallest score of this top interval should be a multiple of the interval size.

Using the guidelines given in the above paragraph, try to construct a grouped

Table 4–4. *Number of Bent-leg Curl-ups in One Minute by High School Boys*

47	60	72	37	26	48	74	51	52	39
30	76	60	57	57	49	50	44	38	64
67	55	50	58	81	66	57	61	69	29
16	64	47	5	36	61	51	53	38	55
56	34	44	52	50	48	59	45	46	41

Table 4–5   Grouped Frequency Table for Number of Bent-leg Curl-ups in One Minute by High School Boys

Score Interval	Tally	f	cum f	%	cum %
78–82	/	1	50	2	100
73–77	/ /	2	49	4	98
68–72	/ /	2	47	4	94
63–67	/ / / /	4	45	8	90
58–62	/ / / / / /	6	41	12	82
53–57	/ / / / / / /	7	35	14	70
48–52	/ / / / / / / / /	9	28	18	56
43–47	/ / / / / /	6	19	12	38
38–42	/ / / /	4	13	8	26
33–37	/ / /	3	9	6	18
28–32	/ /	2	6	4	12
23–27	/	1	4	2	8
18–22	/	1	3	2	6
13–17	/	1	2	2	4
8–12		0	1	0	2
3–7	/	1	1	2	2

frequency table for the scores given in Table 4–4. After you finish, compare your grouped frequency table to the one in Table 4–5. Do we agree? Did you also decide to use an interval size of 5? Do you see that the top interval of 78 to 82 includes the best score of 81? Do you also see that the top interval is defined such that the midpoint of the interval (i.e., 80) is a multiple of 5, the interval size? Good for you!

In the grouped frequency table, notice that the "f" column identifies the number of scores that fell within each defined score interval. When an interval is defined such as 28–32, all scores of 28, 29, 30, 31, and 32 are combined to yield the frequency. When measuring curl-ups, a discrete variable, only completed curl-ups are counted, so whole numbers are the only possible values. There should be no real confusion regarding the interval within which to record any particular score. When measuring continuous variables, however, it is important to realize that a score that is rounded to 28 actually represents scores from 27.5 to 28.4999999. Remember that one traditionally rounds up fractions of 0.5 or greater, and rounds down fractions less than 0.5. Do you see that the score interval of 28–32 actually represents scores that range from 27.5 to 32.4999999? However, since it is somewhat inconvenient to write a long number like 32.4999999, we usually abbreviate and say that the top of the score interval is 32.5. These values are called the *real limits* of the score interval of 28–32. The 27.5 is called the *lower real limit*, and the 32.5 is called the *upper real limit*.

Frequency Polygons and Histograms

It has been said that a picture may be worth a thousand words, thus a graphical representation is sometimes used to communicate the scores of a group of students, athletes, or clients. The most popular types of graphs for this purpose are the frequency polygon and the histogram.

Frequency Polygons. Frequency polygons are line graphs in which measurement scores or score intervals are charted on the horizontal axis and the associated frequencies are given on the vertical axis. Individual scores are then plotted at the intersection of the appropriate points on the two axes. If score intervals

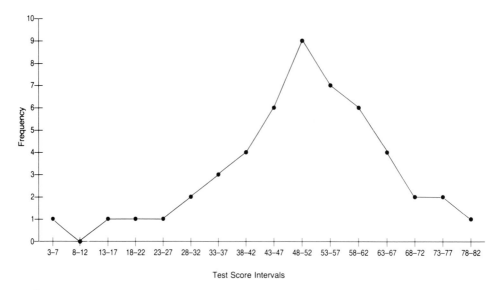

Fig. 4–1. Frequency polygon of number of curl-ups in one minute.

greater than 1 are used to form the frequency polygon, then the points used to plot the score should be midpoints of the intervals given on the horizontal axis.

Histograms. Histograms are bar graphs that either chart scores or score intervals on the horizontal axis and frequencies on the vertical axis, or vice versa. The width of each bar usually represents the width of the score interval.

Figures 4–1 and 4–2 both depict the curl-up scores given in Table 4–4. Figure 4–1 displays this information as a frequency polygon, and Figure 4–2 is in histogram form. Notice that both graphs use the test score intervals that were calculated for the construction of the grouped frequency table in Table 4–5. Also

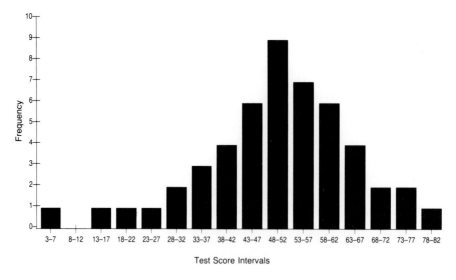

Fig. 4–2. Histogram of number of curl-ups in one minute.

notice that the score intervals are ordered from low to high as one reads from left to right across the horizontal axis. The choice of whether to use a frequency polygon, a histogram, or a frequency table to display measurement scores is largely a matter of personal preference.

STATISTICAL DATA ANALYSIS

Statistical data analysis involves the calculation of values, or indices that summarize various characteristics of the measurement data. Two broad categories of statistics are used in measurement analyses to serve very different purposes. *Descriptive statistics* are used to meaningfully summarize many scores via calculation of a single index. Descriptive statistics are an integral part of every quantitative measurement analysis. *Inferential statistics* are not employed in every measurement analysis. They are used only when measurement personnel are interested in making inferences from a sample to a population, i.e., from the group of persons who were actually measured to persons who were not measured, but who are believed to be similar to those who were.

Sound confusing? Perhaps a quick example will help. If a coach takes a set of pre-season measurements on her team members, it is likely that she is interested simply in summarizing and thus describing the measurements of the current group of players. She is not immediately concerned with any athletes other than those who are currently playing on her team. As such, the coach would calculate appropriate *descriptive statistics.* Another coach has been using a new training technique for some of his players. He is curious whether the improvements that he has measured are probably due to "flukes" in measurement, or whether they represent real improvements that would likely occur for most players should he employ the new training technique with the entire team. This coach would calculate one or more *inferential statistics* to answer his question. Do you see that the second coach is interested in making "inferences" from the group of players who were actually measured to similar players who were not measured?

The calculation and interpretation of descriptive statistics is fairly straightforward, and the limitations for their appropriate use are easily grasped by undergraduate students. Thus, the following text will be limited to discussion of descriptive statistics. For explanations and examples of how inferential statistics are used with measurement data in physical education and sport settings, you may refer to texts by Bosco and Gustafson, Johnson and Nelson, or Verducci.[3,5,10]

All descriptive statistics describe different qualities of a set of measurement data. *Measures of central tendency are used to describe the average or common score of a group of scores. Measures of variability describe the extent of similarity or difference in a set of scores. Measures of relative position determine how a particular individual's score compares to the scores of others in a data set.* The fourth category of descriptive statistics that will be discussed are *measures of relationship.* These statistics indicate the *nature of the relationship between two sets of measurement data.*

Measures of Central Tendency

All measures of central tendency attempt to represent an entire set of data values with a single value. How does one do this? Ever since grade school you have been computing and using the arithmetic *mean* to report the "average" or typical score. In sport settings you are familiar with the use of batting averages, earned run averages, and the like to represent typical performances of sport skills during athletic competitions. Although the mean is the most frequently used measure of central tendency, it is not the only statistic that can be used to represent a typical score. The *median* and the *mode* are two other commonly used measures of central tendency. Each of these indices is most appropriate for a different level of measurement. The mode is appropriate for nominal data, the median for ordinal data, and the mean for interval and ratio data.

Mode. The mode, symbolized by *Mo*, is defined as *the most commonly occurring value.* A formula is not even required to determine this value! One simply inspects a frequency table, graph, or even the raw scores themselves and notes which score occurs most frequently. The mode for 8, 6, 6, 6, 5, 3, 3 is the value 6. The mode for the data given in Table 4–3 is 89 inches.

The mode can give one a quick but rough sense of the typical score. It is, however, believed to be an unstable measure of central tendency because it can be affected to a large extent by the value of one or two scores. Another problem with the use of the mode is that a data set can have two or more modes. Therefore, the mode is of limited value, and is seldom used for ordinal, interval, and ratio data. It is, however, the only appropriate measure of central tendency for nominal level data. For example, the mode would be used to describe the typical pattern of voting for all-star players in a tournament.

Median. Just as a median on the highway divides the road into two halves, the statistical median divides the data set into two equal halves. The median, or *Mdn*, is *a single value that is greater than half the scores and smaller than half the scores.* The median of a set of measurement scores is found by ordering all of the data values from best to worst, then determining the middle point of this distribution, i.e., the value of the 50th percentile.

Although researchers often need to find the exact value of the median, physical education teachers, coaches, exercise specialists, and other practitioners usually find the approximate value of the median by following these simple guidelines. If the number of scores is odd, then the median is the value of the score that is in the middle position of the distribution. The median of 15, 12, 11, 9, 7, 5, 4 is 9, the value of the fourth of seven scores. If the number of scores is even, the median is the arithmetic average of the values of the two middle scores of the distribution. The median of 15, 12, 11, 9, 7, 5, 4, 2 is 8, the arithmetic average of 9 and 7.

The median is more stable than the mode, for it considers only the position and not the exact value of each and every score. However, what it gains in stability, it loses in precision. The median is the ideal measure of central tendency for ordinal data. It is also the most appropriate measure of central tendency for interval and ratio data sets that have extreme scores. (This condition will be discussed further after the next section of text.) The median may not be used for nominal data because nominal data cannot be ordered in terms of goodness to badness. (Did you figure that out before we told you?)

Mean. The mean, symbolized by either $\overline{X}$ or *M*, is *the arithmetic average of the scores in a distribution.* It is calculated by summing the values of all the scores, then dividing by the number of scores that were summed. This is expressed by the formula:

$$\overline{X} = \frac{\Sigma X}{N}$$

Formula 4–1

Table 4–6. *Relationship Between Central Tendency Statistics and Levels of Measurement*

	Interval/Ratio	Ordinal	Nominal
Mode	Ok to use	Ok to use	is BEST
Median	Ok to use (BEST if extreme scores)	is BEST	is WRONG
Mean	is BEST if no extreme scores	is WRONG	is WRONG

where the symbol Σ tells one to sum, X refers to each of the score values, and N is the number of scores.

Since the mean takes into account each and every score value, it is considered a more precise and stable index than either the mode or the median. It is the most appropriate measure of central tendency for both interval and ratio data. It should never be used for describing the central tendency of ordinal or nominal data.

Using the Median with Interval/Ratio Data. If there are extremely high or extremely low scores in the distribution, the mean will yield an artificially high or low index of typical performance because the mean will be inflated or deflated by the extreme values. In these cases, the median becomes the preferred measure of central tendency.

Let us share with you an example that will vividly illustrate this point. Imagine a high school basketball team that reports that the average height of its starting line-up is 6'0". They got this figure by calculating the mean of the five players' heights. Suppose they have four starters who are 5'9" and one "long, tall drink of water" who measures in at 7' even. In this case, the height of the 7-footer tends to artificially inflate the mean value. The mean is "artificial" in the sense that it does not do a very good job of representing the typical height of the starting team, because only one player was actually taller than 6'. The median value of 5'9" would actually give a better idea of the *typical* height of these five young men. Because not all cases will be so obvious, be sure to check for extreme high or low values before selecting the mean as the measure of central tendency for interval and ratio data.

Table 4–6 summarizes the recommendations for use of the mean, median, and mode with nominal, ordinal, and interval/ratio data.

Would you like to try your hand at determining the mode, median, and mean for the small set of scores? Refer to Table 4–7 and calculate all three of the measures of central tendency for the scores that are given. Check your answers

Table 4–7. *Practice in Calculating Measures of Central Tendency*

Instructions: The following scores represent bench press scores (in lbs.) for healthy, active males over the age of 65. Calculate the mode, median, and mean.

420
140
130
120
100
100
100
90

Answers: Mo = 100 lbs., *Mdn* = 110 lbs., $\overline{X}$ = 150 lbs.

with those given at the bottom of the table. Since these numbers represent bench press scores, which of the three measures of central tendency do you think would be most appropriate? The data are ratio in nature, so you might think that the mean would be best. Did you, however, notice the one extreme score of 420 lbs.? Because of this score, the median would probably do a better job of representing the typical bench press performance of the older gentlemen. (Oh, by the way, the man who pressed 420 was a successful competitive weightlifter most of his life.)

Measures of Variability

Measures of central tendency describe the typical score for a group, but alone they do not sufficiently describe a set of scores. *Both a measure of central tendency and a measure of variability are needed to adequately describe a set of measurement scores.*

Consider the following example comparing the heights of the starters on two basketball teams:

> *Team A*   5'4"   5'5"   6'0"   6'7"   6'8"
> *Team B*   5'10"   5'11"   6'0"   6'1"   6'2"

The mean height of both teams is 6'0" and the median height of both is 6'0", yet the teams are very different in terms of their players' heights. Team A is blessed with two very tall players, a 6-footer, and two very short players. Team B players all hover close to the 6-foot mark. Measures of variability *describe the characteristic of spread in the scores.* The three most commonly used measures of variability are the *range,* the *semi-interquartile range,* and the *standard deviation.*

Range. The range, or *Rng,* is simply *the numerical difference between the highest and the lowest scores.* (In some measurement texts you may find the range defined as the highest score minus the lowest score plus 1. This minor change in the definition merely takes into account the real limits of the score values. For practical purposes you may use either definition of the range.) If the range is small, like that for Team B, one knows that the scores are grouped close together and the measurements are relatively homogeneous in nature. If the range is large, it indicates more heterogeneity in the scores.

For ratio, interval, and ordinal scores the range can give a very quick, rough estimate of the spread of the scores. However, it is unstable because it only takes into account the two extreme scores. Frequent or extreme gaps in the score distribution can easily distort this measure of variability.

Semi-Interquartile Range. The semi-interquartile range, symbolized by Q, is used to determine *the spread of the middle 50% of the scores taken from the median.* The formula for calculating the semi-interquartile range is:

$$Q = \frac{Q_3 - Q_1}{2}$$

Formula 4–2

The values Q_3 and Q_1 refer, respectively, to the 75th and the 25th percentiles. In most cases, physical education and sport practitioners may approximate the values of the 75th and 25th percentiles in a manner similar to finding the median, or the 50th percentile. One simply needs to find those points that define the upper and lower one-fourth of the distribution. Once the locations of these points are found, the values of Q_3 and Q_1 will either be the value of the score

Table 4–8.   Sample Calculation of the Semi-Interquartile Range

X		
10		
9		
8		$Q = \dfrac{Q_3 - Q_1}{2}$
8	$Q_3 = 8$	
8		
7		
7		$= \dfrac{8 - 5.5}{2}$
7	$Mdn = 7$	
7		
7		
6		$= 1.25$
6	$Q_1 = 5.5$	
5		
3		
3		
1		

that represents that point or the average of the two scores on either side of the defined point. By then subtracting the Q_1 from Q_3 and dividing by 2, we get this measure of variability. See Table 4–8 for an example of this calculation.

A small Q value indicates a small spread in scores, whereas a large Q indicates a large spread in scores. In interpreting the semi-interquartile range, this value can be added to and subtracted from the median. It should be realized that the median plus Q will approximate the value of Q_3, but will not equal it exactly. The same is true of the median minus the Q value and Q_1.

The interquartile range is a more stable measure of variability than the range because it does not take into account the more extreme scores that fall in the upper 25% and lower 25% of the distribution. *It is appropriately used whenever the median is reported as the measure of central tendency.*

Standard Deviation. *The standard deviation is the appropriate measure of variability whenever the mean is selected as the measure of central tendency.* It is the most stable of all variability measures because its calculation takes into account every score in the distribution.

The standard deviation, symbolized by s or SD, is theoretically a measure that indicates the spread of the middle 68% of the scores taken from the mean. However, it is commonly defined as *the average deviation of the scores about the mean.* If you read the above words carefully, you might have a guess of what we need to do to find this value. First one must calculate the *deviation* scores by subtracting the mean from each and every score. To then find an *average* deviation, you'd probably guess that we need to add the deviations and then divide by the number of scores. Close, but not quite right, because the sum of the deviation scores would always equal zero. Instead, we need to square each deviation score before summing them, then divide by the number of score values, and finally take the square root (or "unsquare") the obtained value. The formula is:

$$s = \sqrt{\frac{\Sigma (X - \overline{X})^2}{N}}$$

Formula 4–3

where X refers to each individual score, $\overline{X}$ is the mean for the distribution, and N is the total number of scores in the distribution.

Formula 4–3 can become cumbersome when dealing with anything but whole numbers, so an alternative formula exists that you may find easier:

$$s = \sqrt{\frac{\Sigma X^2}{N} - \overline{X}^2} \qquad \text{Formula 4–4}$$

The sample calculation in Table 4–9 makes use of both formulas. As is demonstrated, these formulas are computationally equivalent.

Regardless of the formula used to calculate the value of the standard deviation, the interpretation is the same. A small standard deviation indicates that scores are close together, while a large standard deviation indicates that the scores are widely spread.

Why don't you take a few minutes and try to calculate the range, semi-interquartile range, and standard deviation for the data in Table 4–7? Do you agree that the range is 330 lbs., the semi-interquartile range is 17.5 lbs., and the standard deviation is 103.3 lbs.? Since the median was the preferred measure of central tendency, the semi-interquartile range is the preferred measure of variability.

Relationship of Mean and Standard Deviation. If you know both the mean and standard deviation of a set of scores, you can get a pretty good idea of what the distribution would look like graphically, especially if the distribution is *normal*, or "bell-shaped." (You may be familiar with such a distribution in relationship to grading. Teachers who grade "on the normal curve" give the majority of students Cs, and only a small percentage of students receive As and Fs and slightly larger percentage of students get Bs and Ds.) If a set of scores is normally distributed, then a curious relationship exists between the mean and standard deviation. Virtually all the scores, i.e., over 99% of them, will be within three

Table 4–9. Sample Calculation of Standard Deviation Employing Formulas 4–3 and 4–4

$\overline{X}$	$(X - \overline{X})$	$(X - \overline{X})^2$	
2	-1	1	$s = \sqrt{\dfrac{\Sigma(X - \overline{X})^2}{N}}$
1	-2	4	
4	1	1	$= \sqrt{\dfrac{10}{5}}$
3	0	0	
5	2	4	
$\Sigma = 15$		$\Sigma = 10$	
$\overline{X} = 3$			$= 1.4$

X	X^2	
2	4	$s = \sqrt{\dfrac{\Sigma X^2}{N} - \overline{X}^2}$
1	1	
4	16	$= \sqrt{\dfrac{55}{5} - 9}$
3	9	
5	25	
$\Sigma = 15$	$\Sigma = 55$	
$\overline{X} = 3$		$= 1.4$
$\overline{X}^2 = 9$		

standard deviations above and below the mean. Furthermore, about 95% of all the scores will be within two standard deviations above and below the mean. And, about 68% of the scores will fall within one standard deviation of either side of the mean. These relationships are depicted graphically in Figure 4–3.

As an example, suppose that you have analyzed a set of scores and found the mean to be 63 and the standard deviation to be 8. In this case, the mean plus 3 standard deviations (63 + 8 + 8 + 8) is equal to 87. The mean minus 3 standard deviations (63 − 8 − 8 − 8) is equal to 39. To the extent that the distribution is normal, we can expect virtually all of the scores to be between 39 and 87. Approximately 95% of the scores will be between 47 and 79, and 68% of the scores will be spread between the score values of 55 and 71. It is important to realize that each distribution will have its own mean and its own standard deviation that are calculated based on the particular scores in that distribution.

It is also important to realize that many distributions will not be normally distributed, especially when working with samples or small populations. However, many of the variables of interest in physical education and sport settings will be normally distributed in their underlying populations even if the sample does not appear to be. Understanding the theoretical relationship between the mean and the standard deviation for normal distributions can help one to interpret the standard deviation of any distribution.

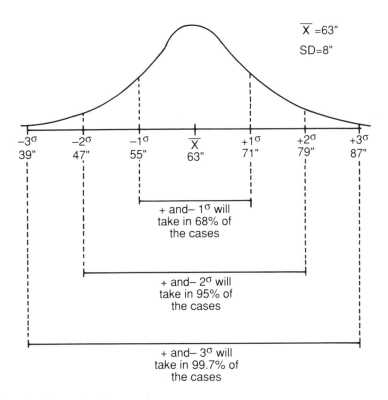

Fig. 4–3.   Area under the normal curve.

Measures of Relative Position

Measures of relative position are used to describe how any one score compares to the rest of the scores in a distribution. A major advantage of such measures is that they standardize the interpretation of scores by converting raw scores to a common scale. This also makes it possible to compare the performance of an individual on two or more different types of measure. For example, imagine the following scores for Angela in a track and field unit: Shot put = 38 feet, 50-yard dash = 8.2 seconds, and running long jump = 14 feet. Which was Angela's best event? How did she do compared to her classmates? The raw scores themselves are not sufficient to answer either of these questions. They could easily be answered if the raw scores were reported as measures of relative position. The two most frequently used measures of relative position are *percentile ranks* and *standard scores*.

Percentile Ranks. A percentile rank, symbolized by *PR*, tells *the percentage of scores in the distribution that are equal to or poorer than a given score*. If a score of 32 equals the percentile rank of 85, then 85% of the scores in the distribution are 32 or poorer. If a score of 68 equals the percentile rank of 95, then 95% of the scores are equal to or poorer than 68. Percentile ranks are easily determined from careful inspection of the *"cum %"* column of the frequency table. The following formula may, however, be used to calculate a percentile rank for either simple or grouped frequency tables:

$$PR \text{ for } X = \frac{\dfrac{cum\ f\ in\ int.}{below} + \dfrac{X - lrl}{int.\ size}(f)}{N}(100) \qquad \text{Formula 4-5}$$

where X is the score of interest, *cum f in int. below* refers to the cumulative frequency in the interval below the interval within which the score of interest falls, *lrl* is the lower real limit of the interval within which the score of interest falls and *f* is the frequency of the interval within which the score of interest falls. An example is probably needed. Let us calculate the percentile rank for a score of 60, using the grouped frequency given in Table 4-5.

$$PR \text{ of } 60 = \frac{35 + \dfrac{60 - 57.5}{5}(6)}{50}(100)$$

$$= \frac{35 + \dfrac{2.5}{5}(6)}{50}(100)$$

$$= 76\%$$

Percentile ranks are especially appropriate for ordinal data because the only requirement of the scores is that they can be ordered from good to poor. Percentile ranks are, though, perfectly appropriate to use for interval and ratio data.

Percentile Norms. Percentile ranks are frequently used in interpreting the performance of individual students on published tests such as the AAHPERD Basketball Skill Test for Boys and Girls. But these percentile ranks have been calculated based upon the performances of hundreds of youngsters across the nation, thus they are usually referred to as *national norms*. For most sport skill and fitness tests separate norms are presented according to age and gender. But before any table of published norms is used, it must be determined that the norms will provide an appropriate comparison. Specifically, it must be determined that the sample on which the norms are based is similar to local performers who will be taking the test. Norms based on a dissimilar group and norms that are over a decade old are suspect, and should not be used.

The physical education and sport professional may choose to develop *local norms*. The procedure for developing local norms ideally requires a minimum of 100 scores. After a frequency distribution is constructed, the cumulative frequency values are rounded to whole numbers.

Standard Scores. Norms may also be reported as standard scores. There are many different types of standard scores, but all *transform raw scores into a new derived score that describes how far, in standard deviation units, the raw score is from some reference point such as the mean of the distribution.* These measures of relative position are only appropriate for use with interval and ratio data. Two of the most common standard scores are the *z-score* and the *T-score*.

z-Score. A raw score is transformed to a z-score simply by subtracting the mean from the raw score, then dividing by the standard deviation. The formula is:

$$z = \frac{X - \overline{X}}{s} \qquad \text{Formula 4–6}$$

where X is the value of the individual raw score, $\overline{X}$ is the group mean, and s is the group standard deviation. A raw score exactly equal to the group mean will be transformed to a z-score of 0. A raw score that happens to be exactly one standard deviation above the mean will yield a z-score of $+1.00$. A raw score that is exactly two standard deviations below the mean will equal a z-score of -2.00. Remember the relationship between the mean and standard deviation for normal distributions? Since z-scores are expressed in standard deviation units, virtually all raw scores will derive z-scores between -3.00 and $+3.00$.

Do you also remember Angela and her track and field performances in the shot put, the 50-yard dash, and the running jump? Do you remember that we wanted to know her best event, and how she did in each event in comparison to her classmates? Well, suppose, based upon the class mean and standard deviation for each event, that we calculate Angela's z-scores for these events as $+2.46$, -0.12, and $+1.08$. Since the performances are now expressed in standard units of measurement, we can easily determine that her best event was the shot put. We can also determine that she was one of the top performers on the shot put, that she performed a little below the class mean in the dash, and that she performed equal to or better than about 84% of her classmates on the running long jump. (Do you see where the 84% comes from? The area of the normal curve below the mean includes 50% of the distribution of scores, and the area between the mean and $+1$ standard deviation includes another 34%.) Table 4–10 can be used to calculate the exact percentage of cases associated with any particular z-score. For positive z-scores, one must remember to add 50% to

Table 4–10.*   *Percentage Parts of the Total Area under the Normal Probability Curve Corresponding to Distances on the Base Line between the Mean and Successive Points from the Mean in Units of Standard Deviation†*

Units	.00	.01	.02	.03	.04	.05	.06	.07	.08	.09
0.0	00.00	00.40	00.80	01.20	01.60	01.99	02.39	02.79	03.19	03.59
0.1	03.98	04.38	04.78	05.17	05.57	05.96	06.36	06.75	07.14	07.53
0.2	07.93	08.32	08.71	09.10	09.48	09.87	10.26	10.64	11.03	11.41
0.3	11.79	12.17	12.55	12.93	13.31	13.68	14.06	14.43	14.80	15.17
0.4	15.54	15.91	16.28	16.64	17.00	17.36	17.72	18.08	18.44	18.79
0.5	19.15	19.50	19.85	20.19	20.54	20.88	21.23	21.57	21.90	22.24
0.6	22.57	22.91	23.24	23.57	23.89	24.22	24.54	24.86	25.17	25.49
0.7	25.80	26.11	26.42	26.73	27.04	27.34	27.64	27.94	28.23	28.52
0.8	28.81	29.10	29.39	29.67	29.95	30.23	30.51	30.78	31.06	31.33
0.9	31.59	31.86	32.12	32.38	32.64	32.90	33.15	33.40	33.65	33.89
1.0	34.13	34.38	34.61	34.85	35.08	35.31	35.54	35.77	35.99	36.21
1.1	36.43	36.65	36.86	37.08	37.29	37.49	37.70	37.90	38.10	38.30
1.2	38.49	38.69	38.88	39.07	39.25	39.44	39.62	39.80	39.97	40.15
1.3	40.32	40.49	40.66	40.82	40.99	41.15	41.31	41.47	41.62	41.77
1.4	41.92	42.07	42.22	42.36	42.51	42.65	42.79	42.92	43.06	43.19
1.5	43.32	43.45	43.57	43.70	43.83	43.94	44.06	44.18	44.29	44.41
1.6	44.52	44.63	44.74	44.84	44.95	45.05	45.15	45.25	45.35	45.45
1.7	45.54	45.64	45.73	45.82	45.91	45.99	46.08	46.16	46.25	46.33
1.8	46.41	46.49	46.56	46.64	46.71	46.78	46.86	46.93	46.99	47.06
1.9	47.13	47.19	47.26	47.32	47.38	47.44	47.50	47.56	47.61	47.67
2.0	47.72	47.78	47.83	47.88	47.93	47.98	48.03	48.08	48.12	48.17
2.1	48.21	48.26	48.30	48.34	48.38	48.42	48.46	48.50	48.54	48.57
2.2	48.61	48.64	48.68	48.71	48.75	48.78	48.81	48.84	48.87	48.90
2.3	48.93	48.96	48.98	49.01	49.04	49.06	49.09	49.11	49.13	49.16
2.4	49.18	49.20	49.22	49.25	49.27	49.29	49.31	49.32	49.34	49.36
2.5	49.38	49.40	49.41	49.43	49.45	49.46	49.48	49.49	49.51	49.52
2.6	49.53	49.55	49.56	49.57	49.59	49.60	49.61	49.62	49.63	49.64
2.7	49.65	49.66	49.67	49.68	49.69	49.70	49.71	49.72	49.73	49.74
2.8	49.74	49.75	49.76	49.77	49.77	49.78	49.79	49.79	49.80	49.81
2.9	49.81	49.82	49.82	49.83	49.84	49.84	49.85	49.85	49.86	49.86
3.0	49.865									
3.1	49.903									
3.2	49.93129									
3.3	49.95166									
3.4	49.96631									
3.5	49.97674									
3.6	49.98409									
3.7	49.98922									
3.8	49.99277									
3.9	49.99519									

*Adapted from *Biometrika Tables for Statisticians.* Edited by E.S. Pearson and H.O. Hartley. Vol. 1, 1954.

†From Mathews, D.K.: *Measurement in Physical Education.* 4th Ed. Philadelphia, W.B. Saunders Co., 1973. Reprinted by permission of the publishers and the author.

the tabled value. For negative z-scores, the percentage of cases is calculated by subtracting the tabled percentage for any given z-score from 50%.

T-score. A T-score is a z-score expressed in a form that does not necessitate negative values nor decimals. A z-score is transformed into a T-score by multiplying the z-score by 10 and adding 50:

$$T = 10(z) + 50 \qquad \text{Formula 4–7}$$

Let us try a couple. A z-score of $+1.00$ is equivalent to a T-score of 60, because $10(+1.00) + 50$ equals 60. A z-score of -1.50 becomes a T-score of 35, because

$10(-1.50) + 50$ equals 35. A z-score of 0, the mean score, is equivalent to 50. When raw scores are transformed to T-scores the new distribution has a mean of 50 and a standard deviation of 10. Virtually all raw scores will derive T-score values between 20 and 80. Figure 4–4 depicts the relationship among raw score standard deviations, z-scores, and T-scores.

Measures of Relationship

The final category of descriptive statistics that will be discussed is the category of measures of relationship. These statistics *describe whether and to what degree a relationship exists between two sets of measurement scores.* The degree of relationship is expressed as a correlation coefficient. A correlation coefficient close to +1.00 or to −1.00 will be obtained if the two sets of scores are highly related. A coefficient close to .00 will be obtained when the scores are not related in any systematic way. See the graphical depiction of these relationships in Figure 4–5.

Many different measures of relationship are appropriate for different levels of measurement, and to describe different patterns of quantitative relationships. Described here are the *Spearman rank order correlation* and the *Pearson product moment correlation.* Both of these measures of relationship describe the strength and the direction of linear relationships between two measurement variables. The Spearman statistic was developed for use when one or both of the variables to be correlated is expressed in ranks, representing ordinal data. The Pearson correlation is for use only with interval and ratio level data.

Two cautionary notes are needed prior to discussing the calculation of these measures of relationship. First, the data that you are working with must be paired. That is, *the two sets of scores must have come from measurement of the same persons, or teams, or objects, etc.* The relationship that will be described is that of the measurement on variable X for Subject 1 with that of variable Y for Subject 1, variable X for Subject 2 with variable Y for Subject 2, etc. If this is not true, there is no logical way to "pair" the data. The second caution is that the data should be bivariate. In other words, the X and Y variables should represent measures of two different characteristics, not two measures of the same variable.

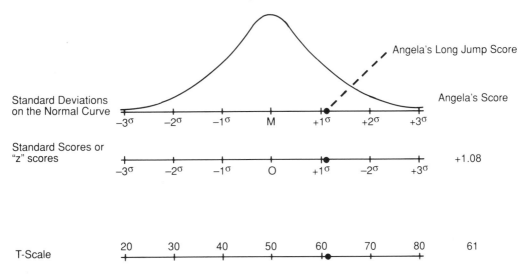

Fig. 4–4.   A comparison of various scales.

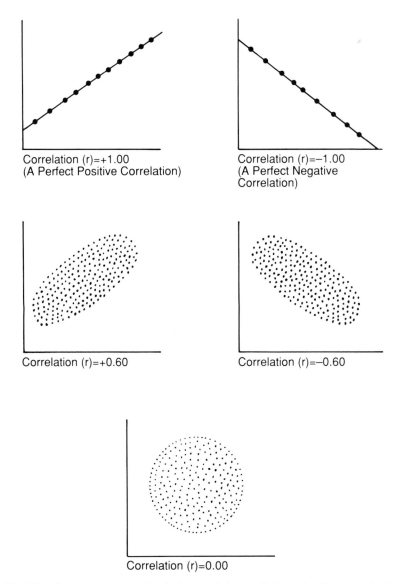

Fig. 4–5. Scattergrams associated with correlation coefficients of various magnitudes. (From Jaeger, R.M.: Statistics: A Spectator Sport. Beverly Hills, CA, Sage, 1983, p. 73. Reprinted by permission of Sage Publications, Inc.)

Spearman Rank Order Correlation. The first step in calculating the Spearman correlation is to report both variables in terms of ranks. If one variable is expressed in ranks and the other variable is reported as an interval or ratio variable, the interval/ratio variable must be transformed to ranks before calculating the Spearman correlation. When ranking scores, the best score is given the rank of 1. If more than one person receives the same score, the tied ranks are averaged. For example, if two performers share the third highest score, they are each assigned the average of ranks 3 and 4, or 3.5.

The next step is to determine the quantitative difference between the rank on variable X and the rank on variable Y for each subject. For example, if one subject has a rank of 6 on variable X and a rank of 2 on variable Y, then the difference between the ranks is a value of 4. Each of these rank difference values is then squared, and the squared values are summed for all subjects.

The next, and final, step is to simply plug the appropriate values into the formula to calculate the Spearman *rho* value:

$$rho = 1 - \frac{6 \Sigma (DR)^2}{N (N^2 - 1)} \qquad \text{Formula 4–8}$$

where DR is the difference between the ranks, N refers to the number of subjects or pairs of data, and 6 is a constant.

See Table 4–11 for a sample calculation of Spearman *rho*. In this example the X variable represents team standing in a small college football league. The Y variable is average game attendance, rounded to the nearest 50. Note that the X variable is already in rank form, but Y scores need to be converted to ranks.

The Spearman *rho* correlation coefficient will vary between -1.00 and $+1.00$. A plus sign indicates a positive relationship between the two variables. In other words, high ranks on one variable tend to be associated with high ranks on the other variable, and low ranks are associated with low ranks. A minus sign preceding the value of rho indicates a negative or an inverse relationship in which high ranks on one variable are associated with low ranks on the other variable. The numerical value of the correlation coefficient tells the strength of the relationship between the two variables. The guidelines in Table 4–12 will give you a general idea about how to interpret the magnitude of *rho*. These are, however, rough estimates that will vary according the nature of the actual variables that are measured.

Pearson Product Moment Correlation. The Pearson correlation, symbolized by r, is the most appropriate measure of relationship when the scores to be

Table 4–11.   Sample Calculation of Spearman Rank Order Correlation

Team	League Standing X	Average Attendance Y	Y in Ranks	DR	(DR)²
A	1	850	2	−1	1
B	2	1000	1	1	1
C	3	600	3.5	−.5	.25
D	4	600	3.5	.5	.25
E	5	500	5	0	1
F	6	200	8	−2	4
G	7	250	7	0	0
H	8	400	6	2	4
				$\Sigma =$	11.5

$$rho = 1 - \frac{6 \Sigma (DR)^2}{N (N^2 - 1)}$$
$$= 1 - \frac{6 (11.5)}{8 (64 - 1)}$$
$$= 1 - \frac{69}{504}$$
$$= 1 - .12$$
$$= + .88$$

Table 4–12.   *Guidelines for Interpretation of the Magnitude of Spearman rho and Pearson r*

Correlation Coefficient	Strength of Relationship
± .90 or greater	very strong
± .70 to .89	strong
± .50 to .69	moderate
± .30 to .49	weak
less than ± .30	little if any correlation

correlated are both interval or ratio level measures. The Pearson correlation will give a more precise estimate of relationship than will the Spearman because the actual values of every score are taken into account in the calculation of the Pearson r. The Spearman procedures should only be used on interval and ratio data when a quick, rough estimate of the measure of relationship is needed.

The purpose of the Pearson correlation is identical to that of the Spearman. The only real difference is that interval or ratio scores are used rather than ranks. The Pearson r correlation coefficient will also range from -1.00 to $+1.00$. *It is interpreted identically to that of the Spearman rho.*

The major problem with the Pearson correlation procedure is that the formula is long and highly susceptible to errors. A hand calculator is a must if working with large data sets, but use of a computer is really the best idea. The Pearson r is calculated by:

$$r = \frac{N \, \Sigma(XY) - (\Sigma X)(\Sigma Y)}{\sqrt{[\, N \, \Sigma(X^2) - (\Sigma X)^2\,][\, N \, \Sigma(Y^2) - (\Sigma Y)^2\,]}} \qquad \text{Formula 4–9}$$

where X represents the scores on one variable, Y represents the scores on the second variable, XY is the cross-product of the paired X and Y scores, and N is the number of subjects. See Table 4–13 for a sample calculation of the Pearson r correlation coefficient. In this example the X scores are the number of golf putts sunk in 10 trials at a distance of 5 feet. The Y scores are the number of putts sunk in the same number of tries from twice the distance. The resulting

Table 4–13.   *Sample Calculation of Pearson Product Moment Correlation*

Golfer	Putts at 5 Feet X	Putts at 10 Feet Y	X^2	Y^2	XY
A	9	7	81	49	63
B	7	7	49	49	49
C	7	4	49	16	28
D	6	5	36	25	30
E	5	2	25	4	10
	$\Sigma = 34$	$\Sigma = 25$	$\Sigma = 240$	$\Sigma = 143$	$\Sigma = 180$

$$r = \frac{N \, \Sigma(XY) - (\Sigma X)(\Sigma Y)}{\sqrt{[N \, \Sigma(X^2) - (\Sigma X)^2][N \, \Sigma(Y^2) - (\Sigma Y)^2]}}$$

$$= \frac{5\,(180) - (34)(25)}{\sqrt{[5\,(240) - (34)^2][5\,(143) - (25)^2]}}$$

$$= \frac{900 - 850}{\sqrt{[1200 - 1156][715 - 625]}}$$

$$= \frac{50}{\sqrt{3960}}$$

$$= +.79$$

r value indicates the strength and direction of the relationship between putting performances at these two distances. (Before you look at Table 4–13, what is your guess? Will the r value be positive? How strong will the relationship be?)

USE OF COMPUTERS

The nonstatistical and statistical data analysis techniques presented in this chapter can be extremely time-consuming with large numbers of scores. Computer programs to do the tedious work are available both for mainframe computers and microcomputers. Many of these programs will construct both frequency tables and graphs for you and calculate descriptive statistics.

Available for use on mainframe computers at many universities, agencies, and industries are the FREQUENCIES and CONDESCRIPTIVE programs in the SPSS-X package, and the FREQ, MEANS, and SUMMARY programs in the SAS package.[9,8] Another popular statistics package is MINITAB.[7] This is an excellent statistics package for beginners because it is interactive (i.e., giving answers on the terminal screen as one works) and is very accepting of variations in command language.

There are many software programs availabe for use with microcomputers that can aid in the analysis of measurement scores in physical education and sport. One of the better microcomputer packages available is *Statistics with Finesse*.[2] Its programs run on either the Apple II or the IBM-PC.

In addition to statistics programs, programs are available to meet a wide variety of measurement needs. For example, there are programs to interpret fitness test battery scores, programs to calculate percentage of body fat from skinfold measures, programs to analyze game statistics, and programs to store and calculate grades. The Research Consortium of AAHPERD has published a directory of available computer software.[1]

SUMMARY

In this chapter you have learned several different techniques that can be used to analyze measurement scores. You learned how to develop frequency tables and graphs to summarize a data set. You also learned statistical techniques to describe the central tendency and variability of a data set. Additional techniques were learned to describe how an individual examinee performs in relation to a group, and to describe the linear relationship between two paired data sets. These techniques can be performed by hand or by use of appropriate computer programs.

May we now challenge you to test your new knowledge of measurement score analysis by working the problems presented in Table 4–14? You may, of course, do these problems by hand or by use of a computer. Or perhaps best of all, would be to do the problems both by hand and by computer, so you can compare the answers and the procedures. Do not be distressed if there are small differences between the hand calculations and the computer results; some computer programs use slightly different formulas for some of the statistical procedures. You will find our answers to the problems at the end of this chapter. Good luck!

Table 4–14. **Practice in Analyzing Measurement Scores**

Student	Vertical Jump (inches) (X)	Standing Long Jump (inches) (Y)
A	9	65
B	10	72
C	7	62
D	6	55
E	4	44
F	7	62
G	7	56
H	9	70
I	4	54

1. (a) Calculate the *mean, median,* and *mode* for the vertical jump for the nine elementary school students.
   (b) Which of the measures of central tendency is preferred for these data? Explain.
2. (a) Calculate the *range, semi-interquartile range,* and *standard deviation* for the vertical jump scores.
   (b) Which of the variability measures is preferred? Explain.
3. (a) Calculate the *percentile rank, z-score,* and *T-score* for Student D on the vertical jump.
   (b) Describe how Student D performed on the vertical jump in comparison to the other children.
4. (a) Construct a *scattergram* showing the relationship between the vertical jump and the standing long jump scores.
   (b) From the pattern of data points on the scattergram, describe the relationship between the two jumps.
5. (a) Calculate the *Pearson's product moment correlation* between the vertical jump scores and the scores on the standing long jump.
   (b) Interpret the Pearson's r value.
6. (a) Convert both sets of scores to ranks, then calculate *Spearman's rank order correlation.*
   (b) Which of the two correlation measures is preferred for these data? Explain.

REFERENCES

1. Baumgartner, T.A., and Cicciarella, C.: Directory of Computer Software with Application to Physical Education. 2nd Ed. Reston, VA, AAHPERD, 1987.
2. Bolding, J.: Statistics with Finesse. Fayetteville, AR, J. Bolding, 1985.
3. Bosco, J.S., and Gustafson, W.F.: Measurement and Evaluation in Physical Education, Fitness, and Sports. Englewood Cliffs, NJ, Prentice-Hall, 1983.
4. Jaeger, R.M.: Statistics: A Spectator Sport. Beverly Hills, CA, Sage, 1983.
5. Johnson, B.L., and Nelson, J.K.: Practical Measurements for Evaluation in Physical Education. 4th Ed. Edina, MN, Burgess, 1986.
6. Mathews, D.K.: Measurement in Physical Education. 4th Ed. Philadelphia, W.B. Saunders, 1973.
7. Ryan, T.A., Joiner, B.L., and Ryan, B.F.: MINITAB Student Handbook. Boston, Duxbury Press, 1976.
8. SAS Institute: SAS User's Guide: Basics 1982 Edition. Cary, NC, SAS Institute, 1982.
9. SPSS Inc.: SPSS-X User's Guide. New York, McGraw-Hill, 1983.
10. Verducci, F.M.: Measurement Concepts in Physical Education. St. Louis, C.V. Mosby, 1980.

Answers to Problems to Table 4–14

1. (a) $\overline{X} = 7$, $Mdn = 7$, and $Mo = 7$.
   (b) Since these are ratio level data and the data have no extreme scores and are normally distributed (as evidenced by the common mean, median, and mode), the mean is preferred.

2. (a) $Rng = 6.0$, $Q = 1.5$, and $s = 2.0$ (Note that the range is an inclusive range, and the Q value is calculated using the approximation method.)
   (b) Since the mean is the preferred measure of central tendency, the standard deviation is the preferred measure of variability.

3. (a) PR of 33, z-score $= -.50$, and T-score $= 45$.
   (b) The PR tells us that Student D performed equal to or better than 33% of the other children; the z and T values tell that his vertical jump was one-half standard deviation below the class mean.

4. (a) Scattergram of vertical jump and standing long jump scores:

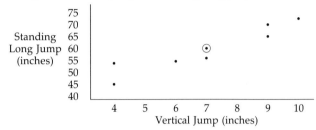

   (b) In general, students who received high scores on the vertical jump also tended to receive high scores on the standing long jump; students who scored lower on the vertical jump also scored lower on the standing long jump. The scattergram suggests a strong positive correlation between the two sets of scores.

5. (a) $r = +.92$ ($\Sigma X = 63$, $\Sigma Y = 540$, $\Sigma X^2 = 477$, $\Sigma Y^2 = 33010$, and $\Sigma(XY) = 3917$.)
   (b) The r value suggests that there is a very strong positive correlation between vertical jump and standing long jump scores.

6. (a) $rho = +.98$.
   (b) The Pearson product moment is preferred because the data are ratio in nature. There is loss of precision in reducing the actual values to ranks, so the r value is actually more precise than the rho value.

5

Grading in Physical Education

Grading probably causes the most consternation of any aspect of education. Doubtless, grades are a chore to teachers and an enigma to students. Several reasons emerge to account for frustrations with grading. There is vagueness in defining levels of excellence, there are varying grading scales, not all measures easily convert to a 100-point scale, there is indecision about where to make cut-offs, there is difficulty with grading small classes fairly, and there is confusion about what to include in the grade and how to weigh each factor.

Two recent additions to the long list of grading frustrations are grade inflation and the diversity of factors included in grades. The interpretation of grades is so varied that grades are becoming meaningless. An A is not always a symbol of excellence; it may be the result of no more than above average work. A C has represented average work traditionally, but a B is now the most frequently occurring grade. Grade inflation has eroded the commonly held interpretations. Until recently, if a student received B in a beginning tennis class, one could expect that student to play a better than average game for a beginner and to know something about the rules, strategy, and techniques of the game. Currently, that same B could mean that the student tried hard, improved greatly, and/or attended regularly. That grade would not necessarily reflect the level of performance the student attained. The humanistic atmosphere in education is to be applauded, but the realities of accountability and credibility must still be faced.

SPECIAL GRADING CONCERNS

Some measurement practices have the potential to make grading more effective and efficient. To address these concerns, *criterion-referenced* grading, *sex-fair* grading, *ability grouping, multiple grades, improvement scores,* and *computer-assisted grading* are topics discussed in this chapter.

Traditionally grades have been norm-referenced. Students were compared with others of their peer group and made to feel that they were competing for achievement. Currently, *criterion-referenced* grading is becoming more prevalent. This is the result of criterion-referenced learning, also known either as task-referenced or mastery learning, i.e., the practice of holding students, teachers, and school systems accountable by setting specific standards of achievement. The tasks are set by the teacher, sometimes in conjunction with students, and

77

reflect the learning requirements for a course, unit, or lesson. The students are then assessed in relation to their achievement in accomplishing the tasks set.

The implication may seem to be that criterion-referenced assessment has become the only acceptable way to measure student achievement. This is not intended. There will be times when a norm-referenced assessment will be meaningful and helpful to the student, just as there will be times when self-referenced assessment will be appropriate. What is intended, however, is that criterion-referenced assessment be given more consideration. In the past, norm-referenced evaluation has been almost the sole basis of assigning grades and has, consequently, contributed to grading problems such as how to arrive at grades for small groups. Criterion-referenced assessment demands a more precise statement of objectives and also makes clear the learning expectations. This type of assessment is prevalent in school systems or states with system-wide or state-wide competency based curricula. Competency levels are determined with norm-referenced information, and subsequent testing for students' achievement uses a criterion-referenced orientation.

Often mastery learning can be assessed periodically within a unit reflecting formative evaluation. Even at these times, the teacher must use some norm-based frame of reference to establish the levels of mastery that would be reasonable for students to achieve at various stages in the unit. The summative measure could be either criterion-referenced or norm-referenced, depending on how the grade is to be used and on the levels of achievement that have been set. It seems reasonable to expect that a criterion-referenced measure used for summative purposes would be somewhat congruent with the norm expectations of the group. This may not be true, however, in school systems using competency based curricula that are trying to upgrade the level of student performance by expecting more of teachers and students.

Since the advent of Title IX legislation requiring coeducational enrollment in physical education classes, there has been concern about *sex-fair* grading. For performance evaluation where size, strength, and/or speed are involved, separate standards are usually needed for each sex. Knowledge, participation, and effort, aspects often included in a grade, would not and should not require separate standards. Deutsch addressed this topic: "The dilemma which must be addressed is if the same standard is used for both boys and girls, the result may be [that] lower grades occur for one sex. On the other hand, if one uses a double standard, this may serve to perpetuate sex differences. It would seem that, if a grade is based solely upon innate factors which favor one sex (i.e., flexibility for women; upper limb strength for men), different standards should be used. If a grading plan encompasses a balance in skill factors and includes a process and product orientation, a single standard is in order thereby facilitating the equity orientation."[3]

McGonagle and Stevens[18] have suggested an approach to sex-fair grading, which they submitted to the Illinois State Board of Education. The plan places more emphasis on the quality of the movement than on the results of the movement, especially for results of movements in which there is a distinct strength advantage. "Skills are scored on a range of 0 to 3 and the total score is incorporated into the department grading system for a unit grade."[18] In this way, students can be evaluated on their skill performance using the same criteria without regard to sex. An example from volleyball illustrates the system they recommend using at Evanston Township High School in Illinois.

Sex-Fair Grading for Volleyball Skill

Each area of evaluation is scored from 0 to 3 points.

	Possible	Example
Serve		
Successful serves (3 tries)	3	2
Toss	3	2
Strike	3	3
Follow-through	3	2
Bump		
Successful bumps (3 tries)	3	2
Legs	3	3
Arms	3	2
Hands	3	2
Overhead Set		
Successful sets (3 tries)	3	3
Legs	3	3
Arms	3	2
Hands	3	2
Total Skill Test Points	36	28
Points to Grade Conversion		
30–36	A	
24–29	B (from example, 28 points = B)	
17–23	C	
14–16	D	
13 and less	NC (no credit)	
Example as applied to Evanston Township High School Grading System		
Participation	40%	A
Effort	30%	A
Skill	20%	B
Written test *only 10%*	10%	B
Unit Grade		A–

Notice that some of the skill assessment is objective, but most is subjective. The teacher can select the aspects of the activity to be evaluated and the methods of assessing them. The example above further shows the role of the skill assessment in the overall physical education grades as used in the Evanston system. These weightings could be adjusted to fit the grading philosophy of the teacher/school system. The example shows one way to accommodate sex-fair grading in the skill area. There need be no separate sex standards for participation, effort, and written test grades.

Ability grouping is advocated within classes if enrollments are not homogeneous. If ninth to twelfth graders with diverse skill levels are enrolled in the same class, subgroupings will help with instruction as well as with grading. Groupings require a little administrative time at the beginning of a unit. The potential to enhance the learning environment and fairness in grading, however, seems to justify the time. Ability grouping is one of the primary ways of meeting Title IX legislative requirements and assigning sex-fair grades.

When handicaps place a restriction on the degree of proficiency a mainstreamed student can attain in fitness or sports skills, some adjustment should be made. The special student should receive a fair and encouraging grade within the limits of the handicap.

Often confronted with large classes of many different skill levels that meet two to five times a week, the physical educator has resorted to including participation, effort, and improvement as components of the grade. This is inconsistent with other subject fields and tends to distort the meaning of a grade in physical education. For this reason, there is worth in considering a physical education grading plan that shows *multiple grades*. One grade would represent achievement in the motor performance and knowledge related to the unit of instruction; this is the "real" grade comparable to grades received in other subjects. Participation, effort, and improvement grades could be reported separately for physical education just as they could be for other subject areas. Adding or averaging these grades makes the overall physical education grade unintelligible and less informative than the use of multiple grades. The grading example presented later in the chapter shows a plan using multiple grades.

Lashuk,[14] writing in the *Journal of the Canadian Association for Health, Physical Education, and Recreation,* presented a different approach to multiple grades. He argued that traditional techniques of classroom grading are seldom applicable to physical education classes because other subject areas report grades related solely to cognitive objectives. Since physical education has objectives in several domains, it should report grades of achievement in each of the areas that comprise its mandate. Lashuk advocated a grading system and report card unique to physical education. In this multiple grading plan, the uniqueness of physical education could be accommodated.

It is difficult to evaluate *improvement* because the increment of gain varies in value. It becomes increasingly more difficult to improve as one becomes more skilled. For example, it is easier for a golfer to cut a golf score 10 strokes from 120 to 110 than to reduce the score from 80 to 70. The change score, the difference between pre- and post-measures, traditionally has been treated as if it were a valid component in the grading formula. Recent work by East[4] addresses and adjusts for the inequity of scores along an improvement continuum. His computer program is available for those who wish to make the improvement score a meaningful part of the overall physical education grade. The improvement grade also provides another opportunity for a 2- to 3-track multiple grading system. If such information is deemed important to report, improvement can be assessed and reported separately from the grade that reflects actual achievement.

Computer-assisted grading software[4,12,16,20,21] is available to make grading procedures more efficient for teachers. In addition, once established, the printed results provide more information for students and parents. Computer programs such as GRADES, ELECTRONIC GRADES, REPORT CARD, GRADEPOINT, HELPER, and NIBBLE GRADE BOOK are listed in the references and are well worth the attention of the physical educator. These programs have the capability to average, weigh, convert to standard or norm scales, give mean, standard deviation, scale, and convert scores to letter grades. If a grade book program is unavailable, grade reports can be created using a spread sheet program.

PURPOSES

Physical education is a part of total education. To achieve this portion of education, objectives have been established to serve as guides and to indicate direction. It has been suggested that grades be used to indicate the student's achievement in terms of the stated objectives. These grades have several purposes and are useful for the following groups.

Students. Grades are useful to students. Grades may indicate standing within the group with respect to established objectives. They may represent standing in relation to the mastery level of content that has been predetermined. They may motivate the student to greater efforts. In addition, the students' attitudes toward physical education and their feelings about themselves may be influenced.

There is, however, a major danger inherent in grades. Since the grades themselves are frequently more tangible than the goals they represent, they sometimes become ends for the student rather than means. Grades are often the primary object that the student seeks. The student should, however, be more interested in the degree of progress toward the objectives as well as the outcomes they represent. This condition is more likely to occur when the grades are fair representations of the achievement of objectives.

Parents. Grades enable parents to follow the progress and achievement of their children. Parents can be informed about the overall objectives of physical education and of the objectives for specific units and then can be furnished the facts about their child's progress in reaching the objectives. Grades probably provide one of the more important links between the parent and the school. Expanded report cards and student/teacher/parent conferences can be beneficial.

Teachers. Grades serve manifold purposes for the teacher. First, they encourage the teacher to make a competent evaluation of each student, thus providing a more comprehensive understanding of the individual. Second, they furnish information to assist in the teacher's role of helping students to learn. In addition, the teacher is provided with data that can be used to evaluate the effectiveness of the program and the quality of the teaching. Grades indirectly reflect a teacher's philosophy of education, professional attitudes, and goals.

Administrators. Grades have become absolutely necessary for the school administrator. Both educational accountability and administrative decisions frequently stem from interpretations of the performance records of students. Grades are used as a basis for graduation and promotion, for academic honors, for college entrance, and for guidance. Physical education grades should be considered in conjunction with other academic grades whenever academic decisions are made about students. If they represent pupil progress and achievement, they should become a part of the permanent records of the school.

MEASURABLE FACTORS

There is no standard method of grading. All good systems, however, have certain characteristics and are based on definite well-established criteria. The system of grading reflects the basic beliefs and philosophy of the grader. The kind of grades (or whether there are grades at all in physical education) depends on the instructor's philosophy and on the policies of a particular school system.

If a program is to accomplish the recognized, well-rounded objectives of physical education, the grade must be a composite of a number of factors. Procedures for evaluating each factor must be determined. Certainly, a large proportion of a student's grade should be based on the results of objective tests that measure the skills acquired, the fitness developed, and the knowledges learned.

Psychomotor Factors. Probably the most commonly used factors for grading purposes in physical education are skill in the activity, game performance, and fitness. These factors should be weighted as logic dictates and usually according to the time allotted to each. In the skills area, the grade for each sport might be determined with several measures: a skill test, performance on a team, tournament standing in individual sports, and a subjective analysis of the student's ability to play the sport. When skill tests are not feasible, the student's ability in the various skills of the sport can be measured by rating devices.

Cognitive Factors. A portion of the grade should be related to the cognitive domain based on understandings, applications, and analysis of the activity. Usually included are questions related to rules, performance, strategy, techniques, history, and information concerning physiology, fitness, and conditioning. Knowledge tests for fitness, sports, and other activities are generally of the objective type. Standardized tests may be employed, but usually the well-constructed, homemade test is better for local use.

Affective Factors. In the affective area, the student should be evaluated, but probably not "graded" in the sense of an official recording. If it is a matter of record, the affective grade should be separate from the grade representative of achievement in motor and cognitive objectives. Such a multiple grade system is practiced in many schools. This practice isolates the affective assessment. The affective grade submitted by the teacher should be free of personal bias and have no bearing on cognitive and motor assessments. The affective assessment might include evaluation of such factors as attitude, appreciation, sportsmanship, cooperation, helpfulness, and leadership. A liberal definition of the affective domain would even include social qualities. There is some thought, however, that the social area should be identified by a domain of its own.

Affective/social qualities are assessed best on the basis of observation and ratings by both the teacher and students themselves. Self-appraisal records must be used judiciously, however, since some students tend to rate themselves too severely and some too leniently. Numerous checklists and rating scales are available. Several are included in Chapter 9. These devices are valuable for measuring such subjective factors as responsibility, behavior, and self-concept.

Questionable Factors. Items such as showers, absences, uniforms, and punctuality have been used in grading. These *administrative concerns* seem out of place and are questioned as suitable factors in grading. They should be considered by departmental policies and not as part of grading procedures. Grades that represent showers and uniforms are held by many to be inconsistent with modern philosophies of physical education and should be eliminated. These factors are important and should be emphasized, but they should not become factors in grades. When included, they are viewed as a weapon to enforce desired student behavior. Grades based on these items would be entirely misleading to both parents and administrators.

The practice of grading partly on *participation* is not uncommon. Those who would lower a grade because of excessive excuses from participation argue that the student who does not participate cannot hope to achieve the objectives of the course. More logically, a participation grade might be justified as a supplement to imperfect and incomplete skill assessments. Nevertheless, those who are opposed to grading directly on participation contend that absences from class are reflected in the achievement of the student anyway, and thus participation is an inconsequential factor. It is probably true that the final status of any student in well-organized programs of physical education will be somewhat lower as a result of reduced participation.

Effort is another factor mentioned frequently in any discussion of the grading process. Effort is used as a factor of grading because it serves to motivate students. It is similar to improvement in that it is difficult to evaluate. In the early stages of learning, it is easy to identify the effort being put forth by the learner. Many times, in order to accomplish a little, the learner must expend a great amount of effort. As the student becomes more proficient, however, accomplishment is possible with less effort. The record breaker in a mile run usually comes in with knees high and in full stride, whereas the last-place runner invariably is plodding along struggling to keep moving toward the finish line. It is virtually impossible to attach a value to levels of effort. It does make sense, however, to grade on level of achievement that can be evaluated and that definitely is related to effort.

CRITERIA FOR GRADES

Relation to Objectives. It is appropriate to reemphasize that grades must be determined in relation to the objectives that have been stated. It is necessary to determine what each student should be able to achieve in each unit of instruction. The grade should then indicate the student's degree of proficiency in the established objectives of the program. The final grade usually reflects a combination of the psychomotor and cognitive achievement of the student in relation to the unit objectives.

Validity. Validity, in respect to grading, simply means that grades truthfully measure the qualities or factors intended. Grades should honestly represent the achievements for which they are purportedly a symbol. The validity of most grading systems is lessened somewhat by the fact that the physical educator must measure the immeasurable or the difficult to measure if he/she is to be consistent with the idea that grades must be related to objectives. Frequently, the intangibles are more valuable than the measurable qualities in the quest for good living. For example, such qualities as team spirit and a willingness to sacrifice oneself for the good of the group are important in team games and sports, but it is difficult to assign a degree of attainment to them. Validity can never be as high as desired. When the intangibles are objectified something is inevitably lost in the process, in the same manner that something is lost when a circle is squared or when a poem is translated.

The validity of the grading system is enhanced if there is congruency of values, objectives, procedures, and evaluation.[10] For example, if a program emphasizes the motor development of the student, the values, objectives, procedures, and evaluation should be consistent with that emphasis. The orientation toward humanistic education has put a renewed emphasis on self-concept and self-direction, on helpful, caring interpersonal relationships, and on aesthetic sense. This emphasis may be stressed more than the psychomotor and intellectual growth of the student. If this is the case, certain values, objectives, and procedures accrue, and the evaluation procedures must be congruent with that curricular philosophy. The same is true of curricula that emphasize the fitness objective of physical activity; evaluative procedures must be consistent with that thrust.

Reliability. The system must report consistently whatever it does report. The reliability of the grading system may be determined by asking the question, "Will the system be apt to obtain the same grades for students if their performances were reassessed?" An affirmative answer means that the system has reliability.

Objectivity. Objectivity in grading means the degree to which different instructors will arrive at the same grade for the same student when they have access to the same information. This implies, of course, that objective tests should be used when they are available in order to eliminate bias and subjective opinion. All important objectives of physical education, however, cannot be measured in quantitative terms. When no objective tests are available to measure a particular factor, subjective methods must be used, but these methods should be objectified as much as possible. Even when objective tests are used, the subjective is not entirely eliminated in grading since levels of achievement are arbitrarily set by the instructor.

When grades are given subjectively by the instructor, care must be taken that they are not based on vague factors or carelessly awarded. The subjective can be made more reliable only when it is objectified, and this is best done through the prudent use of rating scales and checklists.

Understandability. Grades must be understandable to the student and to parents and should be easily interpreted by the teacher. Students must know the basis on which the grades are given, and they must understand how the system operates. The student should have a feeling for what the grade will be before it is assigned. Time should be devoted to the explanation of grades. Interpretation is best accomplished through the results of objective tests in relation to levels on a scale or in relation to preset criterion standards. Such tests and accompanying interpretation leave little doubt about what a grade actually means.

Weightings. Since all factors in grading are not of equal importance, it is common procedure to weigh the measurable elements according to their relative importance. The final answer in weighing the various factors must be determined logically by the teacher. In some cases, it is appropriate for the students to be involved in this process.

There is no agreement about how the three domains of psychomotor, cognitive, and affective should be weighted. For reasons of logic, the psychomotor achievement is generally weighted heaviest, the cognitive assessment is weighted next heaviest, and the affective usually receives the lightest weight in the grade if it receives any at all. Not only does the teacher have to weigh the three domains of learning according to their relative importance, but he/she also needs to weigh the factors within each domain according to their emphasis. Several skill measures may have been used that need to be weighted according to their contributions to the overall physical performance assessment for the student. It is impossible for a grade to reflect everything in the unit, but it should represent an adequate sampling of all the experiences presented. Properly weighted factors should result in a meaningful achievement grade for each student.

Discrimination. Grades need to discriminate between levels of attainment whether they are norm-referenced or criterion-referenced. Norm-referenced grades reflect a continuum of performance levels in relation to how other students performed. They are reported by letters, numbers, or descriptive statements indicative of a broad range of student performance.

Criterion-referenced grades, on the other hand, must also discriminate, but they do it in terms of those who pass or fail at an established level of attainment. A cutting point could be set at a high mastery level equivalent to an A or B normative grade. On the other hand, it could be set at D to indicate the line between a pass or fail situation. The criterion-referenced grade must be somewhat influenced by the logical application of the cutting point decided by the teacher and partially determined by what the teacher knows students can be reasonably expected to attain. The discrimination is based, however, on whether the student does or does not meet the criterion standard, regardless of how the student's performance compares with other students.

Administrative Economy. The grading system must operate within the framework of time, cost, and personnel efficiency. The most important consideration concerns time. A teacher's first duty is to teach. An undue amount of time should not be spent in implementing a complicated grading system. A grading system should work as a tool to improve instruction, not to hinder it. The objectives to be used as a basis for grading must be kept to a minumum. Too many factors complicate the process and make grades uninterpretable. Several computer software programs are listed in the references in the hope that teachers will become proficient in this time-saving technology.

METHODS OF GRADING

A method of grading that is based on sound philosophy and well-established criteria is appropriate. One of the essential requirements of any grading system is that the instructor is able to justify the grade that has been awarded. Although it is necessary to adhere to certain criteria and principles in grading, there is no standardized method or technique; this is probably appropriate. Many difficulties must be overcome in designing a grading system, but when a system is set up on some rational basis in the light of the local program and philosophy, many of these difficulties resolve themselves.

Current dissatisfactions with traditional grading systems have brought to surface many alternative plans. Several have merit and, even if not adequate alone, they can be used in combination with other systems or for special purposes. Two points seem evident: The student is becoming an active participant in the grading process and is no longer simply the grade recipient; and, second, the grading system can be flexible to adapt to ability groups, age levels, and units and consequently might change from time to time and from unit to unit. Malehorn[17] discussed "Ten Better Measures than Giving Grades" stating that traditional grading can no longer be defended. As one of the advocates against traditional grading, he stated, "Marks are misleading and incomplete at best; and at worst they are inhibiting and traumatizing."

There are numerous methods of grading, but in general they all end up similar to one of these three types: (1) the more conventional letter or numerical grade such as A, B, C, D, and F or 82, 96, and 75; (2) the dichotomous pass-or-fail,

Satisfactory/Unsatisfactory method; and (3) the written or oral descriptive type. Regardless of the format, however, the systems place varying amounts of emphasis on the role of the student in the process. The teacher's role has always been assumed. Increased student involvement in grade determination, a current trend, seems a worthy goal.[15]

Letter Grades, Number Grades. Letter grades expressed as A, B, C, D, and F and number grades expressed as 5, 4, 3, 2, and 1 or 97, 86, 72, 65, and 45 are essentially the same. Although the number grades have not been used as extensively as the letter grades, the letter grades frequently must be converted to numbers when grade points are computed.

Letters and numbers represent gradations in the quality of work performed by students. Table 5–1 shows further translations of the gradations into words and numbers. The exact symbol system to be used is often a total school policy.

Numerical grades based on a scale of 100 are computed as percentages. The percentage score is obtained by dividing the attained score by the highest possible score and multiplying by 100. For example, if Jerry scores 33 on a test where 40 is the highest possible score, the score of 34 is divided by 40 and multiplied by 100 and equals 85%. This is the system used for most knowledge testing.

One problem concerning letter grades is arriving at an average for the single final mark. The student's several letter grades are converted into numerical scores, sometimes weighted, and summed for a numerical total. This total may be averaged by dividing by the number of grade weightings. A system of converting letter grades into numerical values is shown in Table 5–2. This conversion table is used in the examples that follow later in the chapter.

The convenience of this conversion system is the multiple of 3 that represents all of the solid grades. Some would question a weighting of even 1 for an F. It is difficult to imagine, however, that a student would not absorb some learning if only present in a class. This point, however, is not as important as the 12, 9, 6, and 3 weightings for A, B, C, and D grades, respectively.

Self-Evaluation. Self-evaluations are usually used in conjunction with other methods of assessing grades. They can be made on each assignment or test as well as on the unit as a whole. Self-assessments are viewed as important means by which students assume more responsibility for their own learning. LaPoint[13] indicated several disadvantages and advantages of self-grading. Among disadvantages, he listed that "administrators need to be kept more closely informed of the class activities, some students may lack the honesty needed for self-grading, and students may become less accurate as the process continues throughout the year." Among the advantages, LaPoint listed an increased personal responsibility and an increased awareness of results on the part of the student.

The research findings are mixed. Some have found students prone to evaluating themselves higher than justified, especially when first adopting this system.[11] Others have reported self-ratings worthy of consideration when guidelines are established and when individual conferences are conducted to discuss the self-assigned grades.[7]

Students need to be taught how to use self-evaluation wisely. This type of involvement in evaluation seems especially appropriate when the students have set their own goals as well as the means to achieve them. Once these criteria

Table 5–1. Alternative Grade Symbols

Grade	Grade	Grade	Grade	Grade	Grade (T-Score)	Grade (T-Score)	Grade (Percentage)	Grade (Percentage)	Grade (Percentile)
5	4	1	A	E-Excellent Superior	70–80	65 & above	95–100	90–100	80–100
4	3	2	B	G-Good Above Average	60–69	55–64	88–94	80–89	60–79
3	2	3	C	A–Average Satisfactory	40–59	45–54	80–87	70–79	40–59
2	1	4	D	I–Inferior Below Average	30–39	35–44	70–79	60–69	20–39
1	0	5	F	F–Failure Unsatisfactory	20–29	34 & below	Below 70	Below 60	0–19

Table 5–2.   Numerical Conversion Table for Letter Grades

A = 12	B− = 8	D+ = 4
A− = 11	C+ = 7	D = 3
B+ = 10	C = 6	D− = 2
B = 9	C− = 5	F = 1

are established in writing and/or in conference, students evaluate their progress toward their set goals. Self-evaluation is not effective if sprung on the students on a one-shot basis. The responsibility for self-evaluation needs to be a regular part of the instructional setting throughout the year. Students soon become accustomed to the procedures and achieve some objectivity and consistency in assessing the worth of their own work.

Contract Grading. This system can be applied to the entire class or to each student. The class contract establishes the type, quantity, and quality of work to be accomplished to achieve various grades. These decisions can be made by the teacher, but are usually more effective if jointly planned by the students and the teacher. Individual contracts are designed by each student and include setting the goals, methods for realizing them, and the grading procedures. Since each contract is different, each grading system is tailor-made to fit the contract. It is essential that the methods of evaluation are agreed upon jointly by the teacher and each student and specifically stated in the written contract.[1]

Peer Evaluations. Subjective ratings by classmates of skill performance, contributions to the team, sportsmanship, helpfulness, and such factors involve students in the evaluation process. Guidelines need to be established covering such topics as impartiality, analysis of skills to be observed, and the use of rating scales. Probably several students should be involved in the ratings for each student. Both the raters and the students being rated can learn from these experiences. Ratings identify important concepts and inform the student of his/her status in each. The ratings can lead to discussions between the raters and the rated and between the teacher, the raters, and the rated. Some evidence suggests that peer ratings can have a high degree of consistency and can show good agreement with instructor ratings.[2]

With adequate training, high school and college students are capable of making peer evaluations. In the lower grades, peer evaluations are valuable to give students experience and understanding but probably should not be included as part of the final grade. The process does, however, at whatever educational level, involve the students in the instructional strategy.

Pass-Fail.[1,22] The criteria for a passing grade are established at the beginning of the course and should be decided jointly by the students and teacher. Students pass who meet the criteria; students fail who do not. Often, however, failing students are allowed to continue working until a passing standard can be achieved. Some educators prefer this plan because it increases the motivation to learn and decreases the motivation to earn grades. This plan, however, "eliminates competition for grades but fails to distinguish excellent students from average or poor."[22] The pass-fail plan of grading is similar to mastery learning. A standard is set and, if achieved, mastery is claimed. In this case, passing is analogous to mastery. Often, however, mastery is set at a higher standard than just passing. If the pass-fail system is used, it probably should be supplemented by individual conferences to discuss achievement toward various objectives of physical education.

Pass/no pass or credit/no record[1] is a variation of the pass-fail plan. This system credits the student only if work is of at least passing quality. If it is not passing work, no official record is made that the student was ever exposed to the instruction. This is similar to the pass-fail option, except there is no record of failure. Students are free to elect challenging and exploratory courses with no fear of tarnishing their academic records. Students are informed of their status by the usual appraisal methods.

Descriptive Statements. Statements are frequently more meaningful to parents and students than the more traditional letter or number grades. Phrases or words generally used are "excellent," "fair," "unsatisfactory," "improving," "needs to," "applying," "seems unable," and "showing progress toward." These words or phrases may be in the form of a checklist or rating scale, and evaluation may be made in an objective or a subjective manner. This method can become more elaborate and take the form of a short anecdotal record in which an analysis is written of the student's status and achievement. There is no doubt of the value of this scheme, but for the instructor with a large number of students, such reports are prohibitive because of time. In addition, it is relatively easy to describe the good performer and the poor performer, but it becomes increasingly more difficult to describe the many who are in the large middle-average group. In these many instances, the descriptive method can become a perfunctory and meaningless device.

Descriptive statements, narrative comments, and written evaluations are all terms for a prose account of the results of evaluative procedures. These are done "periodically to sum up a student's strengths and weaknesses."[22] They are criticized as being too subjective and too time-consuming. They are beneficial, however, if carefully constructed because they are unique to each student. Pools of statements are available on computers. Teachers select the appropriate phrases and the computer composes the statement.

Rating Scales. Gebhardt[8] suggested a modification of the descriptive statement which is organized into a rating scale and enumerates the crucial components of the unit. The student is evaluated on 10 to 15 components related to the stated objectives. This replaces the single, symbolic grade with a profile. Gebhardt claimed that this system gives more information than the simplistic A through F system and is more convenient to use than comments of teachers. It has some special merit for physical education because it can accommodate the myriad factors that are included in the physical education grade. The rating scale can include effort, improvement, and cooperation in addition to achievement in skills and understandings without having to transform them into a single grade.

Individual Conferences. Conferences may follow testing sessions in skill and understandings and can be used for analytical remarks. The testing results are not used for determining grades translated into A, B, C, D, and F or perhaps even pass-fail, but are used to help each student understand personal achievements. Individual conferences can be used in conjunction with descriptive statements serving the purpose of "report cards." It is true, however, that students are still likely to want to know their grades.

One variation is the inclusion of parents in the conference.[6] This practice is no longer considered appropriate only when a disciplinary action is indicated, but is viewed as a more thorough involvement of students, teachers, and family in the education process. Individual and parent conferences are used often for special cases with unique problems and to help to clarify school policies. They should be used routinely so that students do not view them as indicated only when something is wrong. Parental involvement in conferences is difficult because of working schedules, but such meetings are considered worthwhile in spite of the extra effort needed to conduct them.

SAMPLE SYSTEMS OF GRADING

A grading system should be adopted which can meet most of the criteria discussed earlier in the chapter. At the same time, it must be flexible enough to meet the needs of the local situation. It is best for the individual teachers and schools to develop grading systems that fit their procedures and reflect their own philosophy and curriculum. It is essential, however, that all teachers in a physical education department adopt a grading plan that is implemented consistently among teachers. Otherwise, students will compare the different plans and think they are being treated unfairly.

Converting Raw Scores. Before it is possible to arrive at a final grade, it is necessary to convert raw scores to scale scores or grades. Table 5–3 will help illustrate this procedure by depicting the scores for 22 students who took a badminton wall test of skill using the forehand. Several alternatives are presented which need to be considered in light of a teacher's grading philosophy. Since grading is arbitrary, the alternative can be selected that is most congruent with the grading philosophy of the teacher and/or school. The alternatives presented are related to the alternative grading symbols presented earlier in Table 5–1.

Table 5–3 shows that the beginning badminton students scored from 22 to 40 on a timed wall test. An important concept is that no maximum score related to the examples in Table 5–3. Plan 1 uses natural breaks in the distribution to assist with the designation of letter grades. This is a helpful procedure when assigning grades for small groups. It is not as possible with large groups because likely there will be no natural breaks and the distribution will look normal. For Plans 2 and 3, T-scores were used, which had been computed for this skill test using 496 beginning badminton players who had been previously tested. The grade conversion from T-score to letter grade for Plan 2 is more strict than that for Plan 3 and follows the cut-off levels for the first T-score equivalencies on Table 5–1. For example, a player who scored 32 on the skill test would receive a T-score of 56; that is equivalent to a C using the first T-score cut-offs in Table 5–1. On the other hand, if a more generous conversion scale is desired, the second T-scale equivalency on Table 5–1 could be used. In this case, this same student who scored a 32 would still have a T-score of 56 but would be assigned a grade of B. The different T-score conversions to grades shown in Table 5–1 illustrate only two options the teacher has to implement a philosophical position on grading; one is fairly strict and the other one more generous. Many other variations are possible.

Then T-scores were computed for just the 22 students in this beginning badminton class. Because of the small number, the distribution of scores is not

Table 5–3. *Alternative Ways of Converting Badminton Wall Test Scores*

Raw Scores	No. of Students	Natural Breaks Plan 1	T-Scores Computed on Previous Classes N = 496	#1 Plan 2	#2 Plan 3	T-Scores Computed on This Class N = 22	#1 Plan 4	#2 Plan 5	% of Best Score	Plan 6
40	1	A	88	A	A	70	A	A	100	A
39			84			68			98	
38	1	A–	80	A	A–	66	B	A–	95	A
37	1	A–	76	A	A–	64	B	A–	93	A
36	1	A–	72	A	A–	62	B	A–	90	A
35			68			60			88	
34	1	B+	64	B	B+	58	C	B+	85	B
33	1	B	60	B	B	56	C	B	83	B
32	4	B	56	C	B	54	C	B	80	B
31	2	B	52	C	B	52	C	B	78	C
30			48			50			75	
29	2	C+	44	C	C+	48	D	C+	73	C
28	1	C	40	C	C	46	D	C	70	C
27	1	C	36	D	C	44	D	C	68	D
26	1	C	32	D	C	42	D	C	65	D
25	1	D	28	F	D	40	F	D	63	D
24	1	D	24	F	D	38	F	D	60	D
23	1	D	20	F	D	36	F	D	58	F
22	2	D	16	F	D	34	F	D	55	F
	22									

normal so the T-scale reflects that. The natural breaks and the strict or liberal orientation of the teacher are reflected in the grades assigned in Plans 4 and 5.

Another alternative to converting raw scores to grades is to use a percentage procedure such as shown in Plan 6. In this case, the highest score made on the skill test by these 22 students, 40, is assumed to be the maximum score, and all other scores are converted to a percentage of this score. Then the numerical percentage is converted to a letter grade using the 10-point scale shown in the second to last column of Table 5–1.

Table 5–4 shows the scores made by the same 22 students on a knowledge test covering the content of the badminton unit. It was possible to make 50 points on the test. In this case, the maximum score possible is known.

Obviously, the test did not discriminate very well and, therefore, probably was not too reliable. Giving the students the benefit of doubt that the test was not a particularly good one, the teacher might use Plan 1 to assign grades. On the other hand, if the student with the highest score knew only 86% of the content on the test, a grade of B might be appropriate, as shown in Plan 2. Natural breaks occur in the distribution, which the teacher should use rather than force grade levels at every 5, 7 or 10 points, for example. In Plan 3, assume that the criterion-referenced level for mastery had been set at 70%. All of the 22 students met this standard and, therefore, passed the knowledge test.

In the previous examples, two sets of scores have been presented along with several alternative ways to assign a letter grade to the performance of each of the 22 students. These examples should help to illustrate the point made earlier that there is no single procedure for assigning grades. Perhaps the arbitrary nature of grading and the importance of the teacher having an established plan and a firm philosophy of grading now seems even more evident!

Letter Grade Example. Table 5–5 shows the assessment of 1 student on a beginning badminton unit. Notice that some factors evaluated are not counted in determining the final single grade. Even so, the student has a report on these factors and is better informed about his/her performance in all facets of the unit objectives. Notice also that the grades in the 5 motor factors are not averaged to get 1 motor grade which would then be weighted 7 times. Each factor has kept its own identity and integrity in the total. In addition, the teacher has avoided 2 additional computational steps that are unnecessary and would distort the total grade. The conversions from letter grades to points are made by referring to Table 5–2. If the student has received an A on all weighted factors,

Table 5–4.   Grades Assigned for a Badminton Knowledge Test

No. of Items Correct	No. of Students	% of 50 pts.	Plan 1	Plan 2	Plan 3
43	4	86	A	B	P
42	1	84	A	B	P
41		82			
40	7	80	B+	C	P
39	5	78	B	C	P
38	4	76	B−	C	P
37		74			
36		72			
35	1	70	C	D	P
	22				

Table 5–5. *Summary of Unit Evaluations*

Student _____   Unit _____   Date _____

Areas	Weighting of Area	Factors	Weighting of Factors		Grade on Factor	Points
Psychomotor	7	Self-Rating of Skill	1	X	B (9)	9
		Peer Rating of Skill	1	X	A– (11)	11
		Teacher Rating of Skill	1	X	B (9)	9
		Tournament Standing	2	X	B (9)	18
		Skill Test, Serve	2	X	A (12)	24
		Improvement	0		A	0
Cognitive	2	Knowledge Test	2	X	B (9)	18
Affective	0	Peer Rating on Helpfulness	0		A	0
		Self-Rating on Helpfulness	0		B	0
		Teacher Rating on Helpfulness	0		B	0
Totals	9		9			89

Comments: Grade:

the total points could have been (9 × 12) 108. All the totals of weighted points for the class could be placed in a frequency distribution so they are organized conveniently for grade decisions: (1) various grade levels, (2) pass-fail cut-off line or other criterion-related levels, (3) qualitative levels expressed in good, fair, excellent, and so forth. The teacher has several ways to convert the 89 points into a final grade:

1. Determine the percentage: 89 ÷ 108 = 82%. Record the numerical grade of 82.
2. Divide the total points by the number of weightings: 89 ÷ 9 = 9.9. Table 5–2 shows 9.9 equals a grade of B+.
3. Compare the 82% with a predetermined standard of accomplishment that would indicate mastery, for example, 80%. Record a "Pass" because the student has exceeded the cut-off point indicating sufficient proficiency in badminton to continue to the intermediate level of instruction.

Descriptive Statement Example. Statements must be based on information, and a summary of performance similar to the one in Table 5–5 is still necessary. It serves, however, only as a basis for the descriptive statement and is not usually transmitted to the parent. An example of what is communicated is given below.

> "Jerry learned the importance of a good serve in badminton. His skill in serving helped him perform well in the tournament play, but he needs to work on his other strokes. His score on the knowledge test covering skills, strategy, and rules of badminton showed good comprehension which he was able to apply in game play. His classmates considered his helpfulness to them in class very valuable."

EVALUATION OF A GRADING SYSTEM

Eble[5] refers to grades as one of the "grubby stuff and dirty work" aspects of teaching. This cannot be refuted. Some unpleasant dimensions of the grading process are tedium, lack of confidence, misinterpretations, and short deadlines. They can be minimized by establishing a grading philosophy, developing an efficient scheme to implement it, involving students in the process, reducing the administrative red tape, and closely tying the evaluation process to the learning process.

A checklist[19] is included to help the preprofessional student evaluate a personal grading system and the teacher in the field to assess the system in use.

Checklist for Evaluating a Grading System

	None	Poor	Fair	Good	Excellent
The grading system:					
1. is based on student performance objectives for the course	___	___	___	___	___
2. samples student performance from all areas of the course	___	___	___	___	___
3. weights the relative contribution of each type of performance on the basis of its relative importance	___	___	___	___	___
4. provides a consistent method for assigning student grades to various levels of student performance	___	___	___	___	___
5. conforms to schoolwide grading policy	___	___	___	___	___
6. is compatible with the grading system used by other teachers teaching related courses	___	___	___	___	___

7. provides an organized, convenient way of recording grades   _____ _____ _____ _____ _____

In determining student grades, the teacher:

8. informs students of the basis and system for determining their grades   _____ _____ _____ _____ _____

9. maintains accurate and complete records of student performance   _____ _____ _____ _____ _____

10. assigns grades that are consistent with the grading system   _____ _____ _____ _____ _____

11. provides students with regular appraisals of their achievement   _____ _____ _____ _____ _____

12. provides useful information about students' achievement to administrators and other teachers within the school   _____ _____ _____ _____ _____

13. provides meaningful information to parents   _____ _____ _____ _____ _____

This form was adapted from the Professional Teacher Education Module Series, Module D–5, Determine Student Grades, developed at The National Center for Research in Vocational Education at The Ohio State University and is used by permission.[19]

REFERENCES

1. Bender, S.A.: The great grading myth. Colorado Journal of Educational Research, *14*:2–15, Summer, 1975.
2. Burke, R.J.: Some preliminary data on the use of self-evaluation and peer ratings in assigning university course grades. Journal of Educational Research, *62*:444–448, July, 1969.
3. Deutsch, H.: Sex fair grading in physical education. The Physical Educator, *41*:137–141, October 1984.
4. East, W.B.: PROGRAM CHANGE, PROGRAM IMPROVE (Computer Programs). Department of Physical Education, East Tennessee State University, Johnson City, TN 37601, 1987.
5. Eble, K.E.: The Craft of Teaching. Washington, Jossey-Bass Publishers, 1977.
6. Ediger, M.: Reporting pupil progress: Alternatives to grading. Educational Leadership, *32*:265–267, January, 1975.
7. Filene, P.G.: Self-grading: An experiment in learning. Journal of Higher Education, *40*:451–458, June, 1969.
8. Gebhardt, R.C.: An alternative to grades. Improving College and University Teaching, *24*:82–83, 86, Spring, 1976.
9. Germundsen, R., and A.D. Glenn: Computer gradebooks: Implications for teachers. The Computing Teacher, 13–15, October, 1984.
10. Hartman, C.L.: Describing behavior: Search for an alternative to grading. Educational Leadership, *32*:274–277, January, 1975.
11. Jackson, C.D.: Students grade themselves. Today's Education, 24–25, October, 1970.
12. Jones, P.M.: Electronic Grades. Computer Software, 327 Central Avenue, Cleveland, MS. 38732.
13. LaPoint, J.D.: Developing student responsibility through self-grading and peer cooperation. Kansas Association for Health, Physical Education, Recreation, and Dance Journal, 9–11, October, 1981.
14. Lashuk, M.: A percentile method of grading physical education. Canadian Journal of Health, Physical Education, and Recreation, 8–11, March–April, 1984.
15. Leary, J.L.: Assessing pupil progress: New methods are emerging. Educational Leadership, *32*:250–252, January, 1975.
16. Lee, N.S.: The Nibble grade book. Nibble Magazine, 14–31, September, 1984.
17. Malehorn, H.: Ten better measures than giving grades. Clearing House, *57*(6):256–257, February, 1984.
18. McGonagle, K., and A. Stevens: A practical approach to sex fair performance evaluation in secondary physical education. Illinios State Board of Education, Springfield, 13, 1981.
19. Ohio State University: The National Center for Research in Vocational Education (James B. Hamilton, Program Director). Determine Student Grades. 2nd Ed. Module D-5—Instructional Evaluation. Professional Teacher Education Module Series. (Report No. ISBN—0-89606-148-5).

Athens, GA: University of Georgia. American Association for Vocational Instructional Materials. (ERIC Document Reproduction Service No. Ed 242 952). 1984.

20. Rogne, P.: Gradepoint. 15530 Zirconium St., N.W., Ramsey, MN 55303.
21. Sensible Software: Report Card. 6619 Perham Dr. W. Bloomfield, MI 48033: 313/339–8877.
22. Time Magazine: Whadjaget? *100*:49, November 27, 1972.

PART II

TESTS, SCALES, INVENTORIES

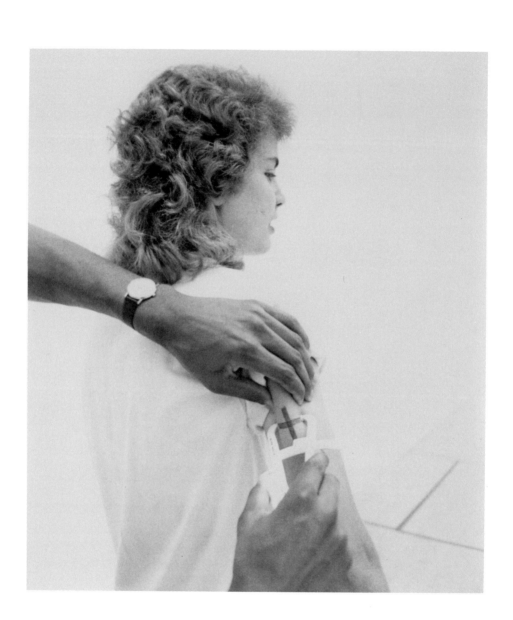

6

Measurement of Fitness for Health and Skill

In this chapter you will learn about the many practical and useful instruments that can be used to measure physical fitness. All of the fitness tests presented in this chapter are *field tests*, designed for use by the physical education and sport practitioner. The tests are easy to administer and interpret and require no sophisticated or expensive equipment. Many of the tests can be administered to more than one person at a time. A wide variety of physical fitness tests will be described in detail, but before presenting the fitness tests, we would like to briefly address a few topics related to the use of physical fitness tests. These topics are: the use of psychomotor taxonomies, the difference between health-related physical fitness and skill-related physical fitness, the difference between fitness testing and medical examinations, and important considerations for the use of fitness tests in schools.

Psychomotor Taxonomies

Classification schemes, commonly referred to as *taxonomies,* have been developed for all three domains of learning. *Cognitive domain taxonomies classify intellectual processes, while affective taxonomies classify interests, attitudes, beliefs, and appreciations.* These taxonomies will be discussed in Chapters 8 and 9, respectively. *Psychomotor taxonomies,* of particular interest for this and the next chapter, *classify motoric abilities and skills.* Understanding of taxonomic relationships is essential to the process of determining objectives, designing appropriate learning experiences, and assessing the extent to which stated objectives are attained. Psychomotor objectives are the primary focus of physical educators who teach in either school or non-school settings. Good physical education teachers are aware of the physical demands of the objectives they set for their students; they attempt to challenge their students with tasks that require motoric responses that span the levels of the taxonomy.

Over the past two decades, a number of different psychomotor taxonomies have been developed.[13,15,19,27] Although all taxonomies are of potential value to the physical education and sport professional, only the Goldberger and Moyer taxonomy will be presented here.[13] This taxonomy has been selected for discussion because it specifically addresses the relationship of physical fitness (Chapter 6) and motor skills (Chapter 7). We feel this is especially important for a psychomotor taxonomy because, "It is the mastery of motor skills and the ability of children [and grown-ups] to incorporate these skills into the games, dances and sports of their culture that provides the stimulus for movement, the stimulus for a series of mechanical, chemical, psychological and social events which in combination contribute to total fitness."[25]

Goldberger and Moyer Taxonomy.[13] The Goldberger and Moyer taxonomy provides a scheme for classifying all human movement—reflexive movements, movements that reflect physical fitness, and movements that demonstrate purposeful motor skills. In developing the taxonomy, the authors modified a three-dimensional movement classification model originally proposed by Mosston.[21] Figure 6–1 depicts both the original Mosston model and the revised taxonomic model. The Goldberger and Moyer model suggests that any human movement can be classified according to three dimensions—its psychomotor attributes that underlie the movement and allow the movement to occur, its anatomical division of body parts developed by the movement, and its psychomotor form. For example, a pull-up test demands the physical attributes of muscular strength and endurance, develops the arms and shoulder girdle region, and is a universal movement form. A football punt demands coordination and power, employs the arms, legs, and trunk, and is a skilled movement form.

Figure 6–2 presents the taxonomy of psychomotor forms in more detail. "Psychomotor forms" refers to different kinds of movements hierarchically ordered according to the developmental sequence that humans experience in learning to move skillfully. Physical educators generally begin their work with elementary school children at the level of universal movement forms. Sublevel 2.11 identifies nonlocomotor forms that allow the creation of a variety of body shapes. Sublevel 2.12 specifies universal locomotor forms such as walking and running. Sublevel 2.13 identifies environment interaction forms in which an obstacle is manipulated. Level 2.2 is the category of conceptual movement forms. These are basic movement forms that have been refined into more generalized movement forms. Examples include the overhand throw, the vertical jump, striking, and static balance forms.

Middle and secondary school physical education teachers teach objectives that primarily draw from levels 3.0 and 4.0. Algorithmic movement forms, levels 3.1, are short-sequenced, self-paced, closed skills such as shooting an arrow or diving. Low organization forms, level 3.2, include both continuous-closed and discrete-open skills such as are needed for most sports skills drills and lead-up activities. Level 3.3 identifies complex movement forms, known as "open skills," that require the performer to adjust to a continually changing environment. Tennis ground and net strokes, basketball dribbling and passing, and softball fielding skills are all examples of movement forms at this level. Highly skilled performers, especially in the sports of gymnastics and figure skating, often work at the 4.1 level of interpretive movement forms in which an existing movement form is used to express feelings. In those same sports one may also see creative movement forms at the 4.2 level. At this level the performer motorically expresses something both new and unique to that performer. Goldberger and Moyer suggested that a classic example of a creative movement form was Dick Fosbury's development of his "flop" in high jumping.

In this chapter you will read about measurement instruments that can be used to assess a variety of the psychomotor attributes that contribute to physical fitness. Of concomitant concern will be the anatomical dimension that identifies

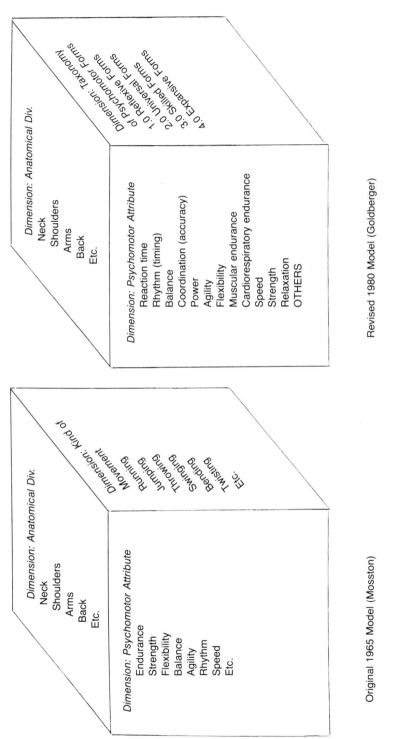

Fig. 6–1.   The three-dimensional model of developmental movement. (From Goldberger, M. and Moyer, S.: A schema for classifying educational objectives in the psychomotor domain. Quest 34(2):137, 1982. Used by permission of Human Kinetics Publishers.)

Level 1.0 Reflexive Movement Forms	**Level 3.0 Skilled Movement Forms**
1.1 Inherited Reflexive Forms	3.1 Algorithmic Movement Forms
1.2 Exploratory Forms	3.2 Low Organization Forms
1.3 Conditioned Reflexive Forms	3.3 Complex Movement Forms
Level 2.0 Universal Movement Forms	**Level 4.0 Expansive Movement Forms**
2.1 Basic Movement Forms	4.1 Interpretive Movement Forms
2.2 Conceptual Movement Forms	4.2 Creative Movement Forms

Fig. 6–2. The taxonomy of psychomotor forms. (From Goldberger, M., and Moyer, S.: A schema for classifying educational objectives in the psychomotor domain. Quest, 34(2):137, 1982. Used by permission of Human Kinetics Publishers.)

the body parts developed by a particular movement form. The movement forms employed are generally those at levels below the 3.2 low organization forms. In Chapter 7 you will read about sports skills tests that measure the qualities of movement forms at or higher than the 3.2 level.

Introduction to Physical Fitness Testing

In a sense, a form of fitness testing has existed since the beginning of formal measurement practices in physical education. Only in the last decade or so, however, have measurement specialists refined their definitions of the components of physical fitness. From the 1940s through the 1970s, physical fitness batteries included a confused array of fitness parameters that drew from the two categories of fitness that we now refer to as health-related physical fitness and skill-related physical fitness (Figure 6–3). It is now generally acknowledged that health-related physical fitness is comprised of cardiorespiratory endurance, muscular endurance, muscular strength, body composition, and flexibility.[8] These qualities have been found to contribute to one's general health by reducing the risk of cardiovascular disease, problems associated with obesity, and chronic back problems.[1] Skill-related physical fitness is defined by those qualities that contribute to successful athletic performance. This category of physical fitness includes the parameters of agility, balance, coordination, speed, power, and reaction time.[8] One of the most important qualities of a good physical fitness test is clear definition of the fitness parameters measured by the test. Few, if any, of the fitness tests developed prior to the 1980s are specific in this way.

Another critical quality of a good fitness test is that the fitness test employ items that are valid measures of each fitness parameter. For example, the run time required for a valid measure of cardiorespiratory endurance is believed to be a minimum of 12 minutes for adults and 9 minutes for children.[17] An item such as the 600-yard walk-run, used in the AAHPER Youth Fitness Test, is now believed to be too short to be a valid measure of cardiorespiratory endurance.[1] Muscular strength, by definition, can be assessed only by requiring the examinee to lift a maximal poundage one time. Thus, a pull-up can be a valid measure of strength only if the examinee's body weight happens to equal the poundage that he/she can lift only one time. The validity of a field test of flexibility can be negatively affected by the examinee's body proportions. The sit-and-reach score of a person with short legs and long trunk and arms will be biased in his or her/favor.

One final caution about the selection and use of fitness tests is needed. *Be sure to administer the physical fitness test exactly as prescribed!* This includes attention

---

HEALTH-RELATED PHYSICAL FITNESS

CARDIORESPIRATORY ENDURANCE (also CIRCULORESPIRATORY ENDURANCE, CARDI-OVASCULAR ENDURANCE, AEROBIC CAPACITY, AEROBIC FITNESS): ability of the circulatory and respiratory systems to efficiently adjust to and recover from exercise. Laboratory assessment = treadmill tests, bicycle ergometer tests. Field assessment = distance runs, distance walks, step tests.

MUSCULAR ENDURANCE: ability of a muscle or group of muscles to continue contracting over an extended time against moderate resistance. Laborabory assessment = dynamometer, tensiometer, Cybex. Field assessment = sit-ups, flexed arm hang, squat thrusts, repeated bench press.

MUSCULAR STRENGTH: ability of a muscle or group of muscles to generate force in a single maximal effort. Laboratory assessment = dynamometer, tensiometer, Cybex. Field assessment = 1RM bench press, 1RM leg press, 1RM squat.

BODY COMPOSITION: determination of the contributions of body fat and lean tissue to total body weight. Laboratory assessment = skinfolds, underwater weighing. Field assessment = skinfolds, height-weight charts.

FLEXIBILITY: range of movement present at body joints. Laboratory assessment = goniometer, flexometer, elgon. Field assessment = sit-and-reach, trunk extensions, splits.

SKILL-RELATED PHYSICAL FITNESS

AGILITY: ability to make successive movements in different directions efficiently and rapidly. Laboratory assessment = film analysis, EMG analysis. Field assessment = shuttle run, line jumps, dodge/agility tests.

BALANCE: ability to maintain equilibrium when one's center of gravity and base of support are altered. Laboratory assessment = film analysis, EMG analysis. Field assessment = stork stand, balance beam walk.

COORDINATION: ability to effectively and efficiently integrate the movements of body parts. Laboratory assessment = film analysis, EMG analysis. Field assessment = ball catch, jump rope, jumping jacks, wand leap.

SPEED: ability to perform rapidly successive movements over a short period of time in a single direction. Laboratory assessment = electronic timing devices. Field assessment = short distance sprints.

POWER: ability of a muscle or group of muscles to generate maximal force in a single explosive effort. Laboratory assessment = EMG analysis, force platform. Field assessment = vertical jump, softball throw for distance.

REACTION TIME/Movement Time (also RESPONSE SPEED): ability to respond rapidly to a stimulus. Laboratory assessment = electronic devices. Field assessment = reaction time stick tests.

Fig. 6–3.   Components of and Assessment of Health-Related and Skill-Related Physical Fitness.

to directions regarding warm-up, practice, the number of trials, specific techniques, equipment, distances, and scoring procedures. Modifications in any of these factors have the potential to affect performance scores, and sometimes to cause injury.

Health-Related Physical Fitness and Medical Examinations

It must be realized that the health-related physical fitness tests that you will read about in this chapter are *not* intended to substitute for a comprehensive medical exam. In fact, medical examinations are required by the American College of Sports Medicine (ACSM) for all but asymptomatic persons under the age of 35 prior to engaging in exercise programs.[4] Medical examinations, especially those that include an exercise stress test, are clearly a more valid and reliable method of assessing one's general health and risk of degenerative and chronic disorders and diseases than any of the practical, easy to administer and interpret field tests of health-related physical fitness described in this chapter.

Recommendations for the Use of Fitness Tests in Schools

Fitness tests have been widely used in schools because it has been assumed that they motivate children to become more fit. Yet, it simply is not known whether this assumption is true. Fox and Biddle discussed the use of fitness testing in schools.[11] Among their recommendations were: (1) that the fitness test be selected with great care because it communicates to the children and their parents what "fitness" is, (2) that teachers recognize that fitness test scores are influenced not only by exercise habits, but also by maturation, genetic ability, skill, level of motivation, and test conditions, and (3) that teachers not concentrate so much on the product of fitness by emphasizing fitness norms and comparisons among children. Rather, fitness testing should be viewed as a means of monitoring progress toward personal fitness goals that can be achieved by participation in realistic exercise programs.

It is also of utmost importance that the test environment be non-threatening. Ideally, it should contribute positively to the child's sense of fitness competence. Confidentiality and sensitivity to the children's needs are also essential. Finally, awards and grades for fitness achievement should not be based solely on the scores of fitness tests. The best rewards for fitness behaviors are those that are derived from the activity itself.

CHILDREN'S HEALTH-RELATED PHYSICAL FITNESS MEASURES

AAHPERD Physical Best Assessment Program*[3]

Purpose. To assess the five health-related fitness components of aerobic endurance, body composition, flexibility, and muscular strength and endurance; each component is referenced to standards associated with minimal risks of degenerative health conditions (e.g., low back disorders, cardiovascular disease, diabetes) that may develop later in life.

Development. Not given in test manual; however, the validity and reliability of all items are described in other sources.

Level and Gender. Girls and boys, ages 5 through 18.

Uses. 1. To compare students to health fitness criterion standards, based on public health research.

2. To motivate students to improve their current fitness status, and to participate in physical activities in their leisure time.

3. To educate students about health-related fitness. The complete Physical Best program is based on an educational model that incorporates cognitive, affective, and psychomotor aspects of learning.

Scoring. Each child's scores on the five test items are compared to the health fitness standards given in Table 6–1 for girls and Table 6–2 for boys.

Comments. The complete Physical Best program includes the fitness assess-

*Reprinted by permission of the American Alliance for Health, Physical Education, Recreation and Dance, 1900 Association Drive, Reston, Virginia 22091.

Table 6–1. Health Fitness Standards for Girls on the AAHPERD Physical Best Test*

			TEST ITEM			
Age	One Mile Walk/Run (minutes)	Sum of Skinfolds (mm)	Body Mass Index	Sit & Reach (cm)	Sit-up	Pull-up
5	14:00	16–36	14–20	25	20	1
6	13:00	16–36	14–20	25	20	1
7	12:00	16–36	14–20	25	24	1
8	11:30	16–36	14–20	25	26	1
9	11:00	16–36	14–20	25	28	1
10	11:00	16–36	14–21	25	30	1
11	11:00	16–36	14–21	25	33	1
12	11:00	16–36	15–22	25	33	1
13	10:30	16–36	15–23	25	33	1
14	10:30	16–36	17–24	25	35	1
15	10:30	16–36	17–24	25	35	1
16	10:30	16–36	17–24	25	35	1
17	10:30	16–36	17–24	25	35	1
18	10:30	16–36	17–24	25	35	1

*Reprinted by permission of the American Alliance for Health, Physical Education, Recreation and Dance, 1900 Association Drive, Reston, Virginia 22091.

ment described here, an educational component kit available for purchase from AAHPERD, and three different awards that may be purchased from AAHPERD. The *Health Fitness Award* recognizes the mastery of the health fitness standards on all items of the Physical Best Assessment Program. The *Fitness Goals Award* is for attainment of individual goals that represent progress in health fitness values, knowledge, and movement/sport/dance abilities. The third type of award, the *Fitness Activity Award*, is given for participation in appropriate physical activity beyond the required physical education program.

Test authors stress the importance of health-related fitness assessment. They specifically do not include nor suggest use of a motor skill assessment. If teachers wish, however, they may test students' motor skills as an aid to goal setting, prescriptive exercise, and physical activity programming.

Table 6–2. Health Fitness Standards for Boys on the AAHPERD Physical Best Test*

			TEST ITEM			
Age	One Mile Walk/Run (minutes)	Sum of Skinfolds (mm)	Body Mass Index	Sit & Reach (cm)	Sit-up	Pull-up
5	13:00	12–25	13–20	25	20	1
6	12:00	12–25	13–20	25	20	1
7	11:00	12–25	13–20	25	24	1
8	10:00	12–25	14–20	25	26	1
9	10:00	12–25	14–20	25	30	1
10	9:30	12–25	14–20	25	34	1
11	9:00	12–25	15–21	25	36	2
12	9:00	12–25	15–22	25	38	2
13	8:00	12–25	16–23	25	40	3
14	7:45	12–25	16–24	25	40	4
15	7:30	12–25	17–24	25	42	5
16	7:30	12–25	18–24	25	44	5
17	7:30	12–25	18–25	25	44	5
18	7:30	12–25	18–26	25	44	5

*Reprinted by permission of the American Alliance for Health, Physical Education, Recreation and Dance, 1900 Association Drive, Reston, Virginia 22091.

Item 1: Aerobic Endurance

Objective. To walk or run one mile at the fastest pace that can be sustained throughout the entire distance.

Facilities and Equipment. A track or other flat, measured area including outside fields or an indoor court. Also needed are a stopwatch, scorecards, and pencils.

Instructions. Students are instructed to run one mile in the fastest possible time. Although walking is permitted, the test administrator should emphasize use of the fastest pace that can be sustained. *Students should be encouraged to practice walking or running the mile prior to the test day. Students should always warm up prior to testing.*

Scoring. The run is scored in minutes and seconds. Elapsed times should be called out to participants (or their partners) as they cross the finish line.

Optional Tests. Any test that requires a duration of at least six minutes is acceptable as an alternative test. For example, a one-half mile walk/run may be used for younger children and a 1.5 mile walk/run may be used for older children.

Item 2: Body Composition

Objective. To measure the degree of body fatness.

Equipment. Skinfold calipers. The caliper selected must exert a constant pressure of 10 grams per square millimeter throughout the range of skinfold thicknesses. Use the best constructed calipers when possible; however, good results are possible with inexpensive plastic calipers.[16]

Instructions. Measure triceps and calf skinfolds. The triceps skinfold is taken on the back of the right arm over the triceps muscle, midway between the elbow and the shoulder. Instruct students to stand erect with arms relaxed and palms facing their legs. The test administrator is to grasp and gently lift a vertical skinfold between the thumb and index finger placed ½-inch (about 1 cm) above the midpoint of the upper arm. The caliper measurement is taken at the midpoint of the upper arm. Repeat the entire procedure three times.

A vertical skinfold measure is taken in the same manner on the inside (medial side) of the right leg. Have the student stand with the right foot on a bench with the knee slightly flexed. The calf measure is taken at the largest part of the calf girth. Grasp and gently lift the skinfold ½-inch above the measurement site; measure at the level of the largest part of the calf. Repeat three times.

Scoring. Record the median (middle value) of the three scores for the triceps and the calf. Sum the two median values to obtain a final score.

Optional Measures. Alternate measures include the sum of the triceps and subscapular skinfolds, the triceps only, or the Body Mass Index.

The subscapular skinfold is taken on the right side of the body, 1 cm below the inferior angle of the scapula, in line with the natural cleavage of the skin. The scapula will protrude when the arm is gently placed behind the back.

The Body Mass Index (BMI) is calculated by dividing body weight (in kilograms) by the square of height (in meters). These values are taken with students clad in lightweight shorts and shirts, and in stocking feet. Weight is the average of two measures, each taken to the nearest 0.5 kilogram. Height is the average of two measures taken to the nearest centimeter.

Comments. Skinfold measures can be taken very reliably after conscientious practice. For further instructions on proper techniques for skinfold measurement, please refer to the excellent article by Jackson and Pollock.[18]

Remember that a body weight measure taken in pounds may be converted to kilograms by dividing by 2.2. Height in inches is converted to meters by dividing by 39.37.

Item 3: Flexibility

Objective. To evaluate flexibility of the lower back and hamstring muscles.

Equipment. Sit and Reach Box, a specially constructed box with a measuring scale with a 23 cm mark in line with the surface for the examinee's feet.

Instructions. Students should warm up by stretching the low back and hamstrings by performing slow, sustained, steady (no bobbing) stretches.

Have students remove shoes and sit at the test apparatus with knees fully extended; heels should be about a shoulder-width apart, and feet should be flat against the box. Arms are extended forward, palms down, with one hand on top of the other. Students then lean forward, extending the fingertips along the ruler as far forward as possible. Four trials are taken; the fourth trial should be held for at least one second.

The trial is invalid and should be readministered if the knees fail to remain fully extended, or if the hands reach unevenly. The test administrator may place one hand lightly on the student's knees to encourage that knees stay extended.

Scoring. The score, measured to the nearest centimeter, is the most distant point reached on the fourth trial by both hands and held for one second.

Comments. Directions for constructing a Sit and Reach Box are given in the Physical Best manual.[3] An inexpensive and convenient alternative is a 12-inch square cardboard box and a yardstick; the yardstick should be placed on the top of the box so the 23 cm mark is in line with the edge of the box where the feet are placed.

Research has found that a head up position is preferred for the sit and reach test.[28]

Item 4: Muscular Strength/Endurance

Objective. To evaluate abdominal muscular strength and endurance by performing repeated sit-ups.

Equipment. Stopwatch and mats.

Instructions. Students should lie on their backs with knees flexed, feet on floor, and heels between 12 and 18 inches from the buttocks. Arms are crossed over chest with hands on opposite shoulders. Feet are held to the mat by a partner. On "ready-go," the student curls to a sitting position, maintaining arm contact with chest. When elbows touch the thighs, the sit-up is completed. The student then uncurls to a position where the midback contacts the mat. Students are to complete as many sit-ups in this manner as possible in one minute. Rest between sit-ups is allowed in either the up or down position.

Scoring. Only correctly performed sit-ups completed in one minute are counted.

Comments. This test may be administered to a large group of students at one time. Partners should be asked to quietly count the number of correct, completed sit-ups.

Item 5: Upper Body Strength/Endurance

Objective. To measure arm and shoulder girdle strength/endurance by performing repeated pull-ups.

Equipment. Metal or wooden bar about 1½ inches in diameter, a doorway gym bar, a piece of pipe, or an inclined ladder.

Instructions. Using an overhand grip (palms outward), students should hang from the bar with legs and arms fully extended. In the hanging position, the feet should not contact the floor. The student raises his/her body with the arms until the chin is positioned over the bar. He/she is to correctly perform as many pull-ups as possible with *no time limit.*

Scoring. Record the number of correctly executed pull-ups that are completed.

Optional Test. None. However, the Vermont modified pull-up may be used to track progress until students can perform at least one pull-up.[23] The modified pull-up is not to be considered an optional test for assessing health fitness status for the Health Fitness Award.

Comments. Research suggests that the thumb over bar position is preferred for the pull-up.[12]

Texas Governor's Fit Youth Today (FYT)[*29]

Purpose. To encourage and promote the attainment and maintenance of a desirable level of fitness among all students. Fit Youth Today is comprised of both a test of functional fitness *and* an enabling curriculum with activities for both the gym and the classroom for the development and maintenance of functional fitness.

Development. The FYT program was developed by public school physical educators and leading medical, fitness, health, and measurement specialists and then reviewed by national medical and fitness experts. During 1986 and 1987, the FYT test was pilot tested throughout the state of Texas on nearly 27,000 children.

A criterion-referenced approach to testing was selected for use because a review of research revealed that children's fitness test scores had fallen over the recent decade. Normative data would have reflected this decline, but norms do not necessarily define what is desirable or acceptable. Particular test items were selected according to their ability to validly and reliably measure fitness in a mass testing situation, and because of what the items might communicate to children about the definition of fitness.

Level and Gender. Both sexes, school grades 4 through 12.

Uses. 1. To provide a means of educating and conditioning students for a lifetime of healthy living.

2. To provide a method of measuring the level of physical fitness in each student.

3. To provide a method of comparing each student's fitness level to a desirable level.

Scoring. Each child's scores on the test items are compared to the criterion standards given for the appropriate gender and grade level.

Comments. The FYT broke new ground by the use of a criterion-referenced

---

*Texas Governor's Commission on Physical Fitness: FYT: Fit Youth Today. Austin, Texas Health and Fitness Foundation, 1988. Used by permission of Donald F. Haydon, Executive Director.

approach to fitness testing; the AAHPERD Physical Best test followed in this mode. In comparing the FYT and the Physical Best tests, there are three major differences. One difference is that the FYT does not have a test of upper body strength and endurance, although the enabling curriculum gives great attention to this area of fitness. The other differences are in the measurement of cardio-respiratory endurance and the measurement of abdominal muscular endurance. The FYT employs more strenuous measures for these areas than does the Physical Best. The Physical Best has a 1-mile run and 1 minute of curl-ups, while the FYT requires a 20-minute jog and 2 minutes of curl-ups. The FYT manual specifies, however, that students should not perform either of these tests until they have been involved in a sound contitioning program for at least 8 weeks.

It is fun to read the FYT manual. It is filled with valuable information and philosophical explanations of the approach to fitness testing, development, and maintenance espoused by the Texas Governor's Commission on Physical Fitness.

Item 1: Steady State Jog

Objective. To measure aerobic fitness.

Purpose. To determine a student's ability to cover a prescribed distance during a 20-minute period.

Rationale. A Steady State Jog was chosen as the measure of cardiorespiratory endurance because 20 minutes was identified as a minimally appropriate duration for the development and maintenance of aerobic fitness. Distance runs generally report reliability coefficients of .70 or greater, and longer tests (of distances up to 3 miles) are more reliable than shorter tests. With maximal oxygen consumption as the criterion, concurrent validity coefficients of .60 to .90 have been reported.

Facilities and Equipment. A measured jogging trail or track is needed for this test. Alternatives include a measured straight-away or other measured distance. The test manual describes how to use a bicycle tire of known circumference to measure a course distance.

Instructions. This test should be given only to students who have completed at least 8 weeks of a sound aerobics conditioning program and who have learned to pace themselves while running.

Students are instructed to jog at a steady rate throughout the 20-minute test. They begin on "Ready, start." Walking should be discouraged; however, it is acceptable if a student can attain the criterion standard by rapid walking or a combination of walking and running. At the end of 20 minutes, the distance covered by each student is recorded to the nearest $\frac{1}{10}$ mile.

Students should engage in cool down activities for 3 to 5 minutes after completion of the test.

The test should not be administered under adverse weather conditions. Avoid days that are hot and humid, are excessively cold, or have high winds.

Scoring. Compare each student's distance to the standard presented in Table 6–3. The student has achieved an acceptable level of cardiorespiratory endurance if his or her score equals or exceeds the standard.

Item 2: Bent-Knee Curl-up

Purpose. To determine abdominal muscular strength and endurance by performing repeated bent-knee curl-ups.

*Table 6–3.   Criterion Referenced Standards for the Fit Youth Today
20-Minute Steady State Jog**

	Distance Covered in 20 Minutes		
Grade Level	*Miles*	*Yards*	*Meters*
	MALES		
4	1.8	3,168	2,896
5	2.0	3,520	3,218
6	2.2	3,872	3,540
7–12	2.4	4,224	3,862
	FEMALES		
4	1.6	2,816	2,574
5	1.8	3,168	2,896
6	2.0	3,520	3,218
7–12	2.2	3,872	3,540

*From Texas Governor's Commission on Physical Fitness: FYT: Fit Youth Today. Austin, Texas Health and Fitness Foundation, 1988. Used by permission of Donald F. Haydon, Executive Director.

Rationale. Clinical orthopedic evidence has shown that lack of abdominal strength is related to the development of low back pain. Furthermore, back problems often improve with abdominal exercise. The task force examined normative data and developed the criterion reference standards by adjusting for age differences. Standards were set that may be more rigorous than needed for maintaining a healthy back, but they can easily be reached by all normal children who are trained and motivated.

Reliability coefficients greater than .77 have been reported for flexed-knee sit-up tests. Content validity is claimed because the muscles used to perform a curl-up are the upper and lower rectus abdominis and the external and internal obliques.

Equipment. Thick mats or other comfortable surfaces on which to recline are required. Also required is a stopwatch or clock with a sweep-second hand.

Instructions. The curl-up procedures are virtually identical to those described for the Physical Best test. However, the time period used in this test is 2 minutes instead of 1 minute.

Students are instructed to establish a pace that will allow them to correctly and continuously execute the criterion standard for their grade within the 2 minutes.

Testing should be conducted only after completion of the training program outlined in the FYT manual.

Scoring. No credit is given for incorrect or incomplete curl-ups, and only one trial is permitted.

Compare each student's score to standards for the appropriate grade level; standards are the same for both genders. Standards are: Grade 4 = 34; Grade 5 = 36; Grade 6 = 38; and Grades 7–12 = 40.

Item 3: Sit and Reach

Purpose. To measure the degree of trunk flexion.

Rationale. Clinical orthopedic evidence has shown that flexibility of the lower back and legs is important for a healthy back. Flexibility contributes to good health because it promotes freedom of movement, reduces muscle soreness, and helps to prevent muscle injury. A touch-your-toes criterion is consistent with minimum standards needed for a healthy back.

Reliability of the sit-and-reach test has been estimated at greater than .84. Construct and content validity are supported from clinical reports, which indicate that people with low back pain often have restricted range of motion in the lower back. Clinical research also shows that stretching exercises for muscle groups in the low back and upper leg regions improve this type of flexibility.

Equipment. A purchased or constructed sit-and-reach measurement apparatus is required. The test manual describes how to construct or improvise this piece of apparatus. It is nearly identical to the sit-and-reach box used for the Physical Best test; the only difference is that the top panel of the box should be marked in half-inches with the 9-inch mark in line with the student's feet. (The Physical Best test uses centimeters, with the 23 cm mark in line with the feet.)

Instructions. The sit-and-reach test is performed similarly to the Physical Best test, but each stretch must be held for at least 3 seconds instead of 1 second. Only four trials should be given on any one test. The farthest point reached is recorded to the nearest ½ inch.

Students should warm-up prior to testing and should have completed the flexibility training protocol prior to testing.

Scoring. Regardless of age, gender, or body size, each child's score is compared to the standard of 9 inches. An acceptable level of flexibility has been achieved if the score equals or exceeds 9 inches.

Comments. The standard set on the Physical Best test is slightly more stringent than that for the FYT; the standard is 2 cm beyond one's toes.

Item 4: Body Composition

Purpose. To identify children who have excess body fat by measuring the skinfold thickness.

Rationale. It has been estimated that 15 to 20% of the annual mortality of Americans can be traced to obesity. A strong relationship has been found to exist between obesity and degenerative diseases such as hypertension, heart disease, stroke, and diabetes. Furthermore, the overwhelming majority of fat children grow to be fat adults.

Skinfolds have been shown to be reliable, over .90, with trained testers; reliability coefficients for novice testers are only slightly lower. Content validity is claimed because much of one's fat content is located subcutaneously. Concurrent validity evidence consists of strong correlations found between total body fatness as measured by underwater weighing and skinfolds. Coefficients typically range from .80 to .90.

Normative data on skinfold thickness are positively skewed. The median of the norm distribution was selected as a conservative and valid benchmark for an acceptable degree of body fatness for health promotion.

Equipment. Needed is a pair of quality skinfold calipers that exerts a constant pressure of 10 grams per square millimeter throughout the range of skinfold thickness and that reads "0" when in a closed position.

Instructions. The triceps and medial calf skinfolds are located and measured in the same manner as the Physical Best test. The FYT manual cautions the tester to place the calipers approximately midway between the crest and the base of the skinfold. One to 2 seconds after the full pressure of the caliper is on the skinfold, read the skinfold thickness to the nearest millimeter. Take three independent measures at each site.

Table 6–4. *Criterion Referenced Standards for the Fit Youth Today*
Body Composition Test*

Grade Level	Sum of Calf and Triceps	Approximate Percent Body Fat
	MALES	
4	23	19
5	26	21
6	29	23
7	29	23
8	29	23
9	27	22
10	25	20
11	23	19
12	23	19
	FEMALES	
4	32	26
5	32	26
6	33	27
7	34	28
8	34	28
9	34	28
10	34	28
11	34	28
12	34	28

*From Texas Governor's Commission on Physical Fitness: FYT: Fit Youth Today. Austin, Texas Health and Fitness Foundation, 1988. Used by permission of Donald F. Haydon, Executive Director.

It is imperative that each student be measured separately, without public comment or display. It is also recommended that the tester interpret measurements individually and privately.

Scoring. The score for each site is the median of the three measures, recorded to the nearest .5 millimeter. The total skinfold score is the sum of the two medians. Compare this score to the appropriate grade and gender standards given in Table 6–4. The student has achieved an acceptable level of body composition if his or her score is equal to or *less than* the standard.

Students with acceptable body fat scores should be encouraged to maintain their weight. However, the instructor should recommend professional consultation if the student is exceptionally thin, for there is the potential of medical or psychological problems.

Comments. The approach taken in the Physical Best test of reporting a range of acceptable skinfold thickness scores is probably preferable to the single score value used by FYT. There is less chance for student misunderstanding of this fitness parameter.

CHILDREN'S SKILL-RELATED PHYSICAL FITNESS MEASURES

AAHPER Youth Fitness Test*[1]

Purpose. To measure status and achievement in the physical fitness objective.

Evaluation. A jury of experts in the form of a committee selected the original items that make up this fitness battery. The Survey Research Center of the University of Michigan selected the schools from which the sample of 8500 boys

*American Association for Health, Physical Education, and Recreation: Youth Fitness Test Manual. Reston, VA, AAHPER, 1976. Used by permission of AAHPERD.

and girls was drawn. The 1958 norms were based on the data from these numbers. The tests were re-normed in 1965 and again in 1975.

Level and Gender. Boys and girls, 9 through 17 years of age.

Time Allotment and Number of Subjects. Two testing periods are necessary for the administration of all items. During the first period the pull-up for boys, the flexed-arm hang for girls, the sit-up, the standing long jump, and the shuttle run can be administered. During the second testing period the 50-yard dash and the 600-yard run-walk can be administered. Optional tests for the 600-yard run are the 1-mile or 9-minute runs for children 10 to 12 years of age, or the 1½ mile or 12-minute runs for children 13 years of age and older. A group of from 30 to 35 can be tested in this way in two 45-minute class periods.

Floor Plan and Space Requirements. A basketball court for the indoor items and a football field with track are the ideal space needs.

Class Organization. The tests can be administered by a combination of mass testing with partners and station-to-station. Half of the group can do sit-ups while the other half score. The same method can be applied to the 600-yard run-walk. The other items can be administered and scored by a trained tester at a station. At the beginning of the period each child is supplied with an individual score card. The events for that day of testing are then all explained and demonstrated before testing gets under way.

General Procedure. 1. All children should be given an appropriate amount of warm-up before testing begins.

2. When a child's medical status is in question, he/she should be excused from the test.

Uses. The test results may be used to indicate present status in fitness. When there is a retest, progress may be noted. From such status and achievement records, many other uses are obvious, such as motivation, grading, guidance, and program appraisal. Comparisons may be made between a child's score and those of others in the group or those of others in the schools throughout the country. Norms have been developed using percentiles based on age.

The child's fitness record may be charted on the profile graph shown in Figure 6–5.

Comments. The AAHPER Youth Fitness Test has been classified here as a skill-related measure, although the items actually reflect a combination of skill-related and health-related measures of physical fitness. Users of the Youth Fitness Test should realize that three of the six items measure skill-related physical fitness. These items are the standing long jump, 50-yard dash, and shuttle run. The other three items—sit ups, pull-ups (boys) or flexed-arm hang (girls), and the optional run tests for the 600-yard run—measure health-related physical fitness. The 600-yard run is not a pure measure of either aspect of fitness; longer distances are needed to adequately measure cardiorespiratory endurance. Part of the popularity of the Youth Fitness Test is attributed to its being a combination of skill-related and health-related physical fitness.

It should be noted that the published norms are now over a decade old. It is unknown whether these norms accurately reflect today's students.

Item 1: Pull-up (For Boys) (Figure 6–4A)

Purpose. To measure arm and shoulder strength.

Facilities and Equipment. A metal or wooden bar approximately 1½ inches in

Fig. 6–4.   (Continued on opposite page)

Fig. 6–4.   Test items for AAHPER youth fitness test. A. Pull-up. B. Flexed-arm hang. C. Sit-up. D. Shuttle run. E. Standing long jump.

diameter is placed at a convenient height. However, for the lower age levels a doorway gym bar can be used. At times it may be necessary to improvise by using such equipment as a basketball goal support or a ladder.

Procedures. The bar is adjusted to such height that the child can hang free of the floor. The boy should grasp the bar with his palms facing away from his body (overhand grasp). He should then raise his body until his chin is over the bar and then lower it again to the starting position with his arms fully extended.

Instructions. You must not lift your knees or assist your pull-up by kicking. You must return to the hang position with the arms fully straight. You will not be permitted to swing or snap your way up.

Scoring. One point is scored each time the child completes a pull-up. Part scores do not count, and only 1 trial is permitted unless it is obvious the child did not have a fair chance on his first trial.

Item 2: Flexed-Arm Hang (For Girls) (Fig. 6–4B)

Purpose. To measure arm and shoulder strength.

Facilities and Equipment. A metal or wooden bar approximately 1½ inches in diameter is placed at the subject's height. A doorway gym bar adjusted at the desired height in a doorway works well. If these items are not available, it is necessary to improvise by using some kind of pole or pipe across bleachers or ladders. A stopwatch is needed.

Procedure. The height of the bar should be adjusted to approximately the standing height of the subject. The child should grasp the bar with an overhand grasp. She then raises her body off the floor with the help of assistants to a position where the chin is above the bar. The elbows should be flexed and the chest should be close to the bar. Two spotters, 1 in front and 1 in back of the subject, are recommended for assistance in getting to the "hang" position. The subject holds the hang position as long as possible. The stopwatch is started as soon as the subject assumes the starting position and is stopped when the chin touches the bar, falls below the bar, or when the subject's head is tilted back to keep the chin above the bar.

Instructions. Grasp the bar with palms facing away from your body. You will be lifted by assistants to a position with your chin just above the bar. Hang in this position as long as possible. It is a violation for your chin to touch the bar or fall below the bar, or for you to tilt your head backward to keep your chin from touching the bar.

Scoring. The score is the elapsed time to the nearest second that the girl maintained the proper hanging position.

PROFILE RECORD

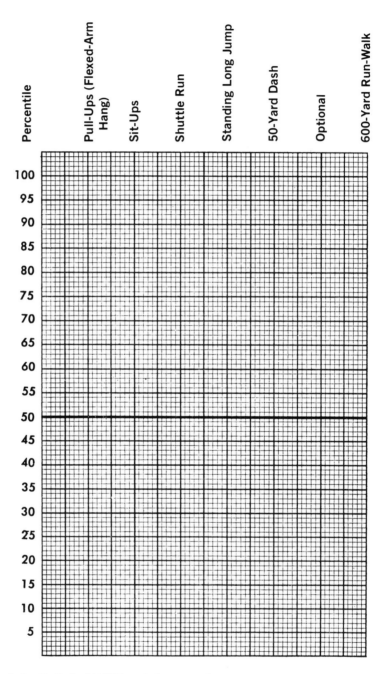

Fig. 6–5. Profile for AAHPER youth fitness test. Plot your personal graph. Use a different color for each trial.

Item 3: Sit-up (Fig. 6–4C)

Purpose. To measure abdominal strength and endurance.

Facilities and Equipment. Mats may be used if they are available; otherwise the floor is satisfactory.

Procedure. The child lies flat on the back with knees bent and feet on the floor with the heels no more than 1 foot from the buttocks. The knee angle should be no less than 90 degrees. The fingers are interlocked and placed behind the neck with the elbows touching the floor. The feet are held securely by a partner. The child then curls up to a sitting position and touches the elbows to the knees. This exercise is repeated as many times as possible in the time requirement.

Instructions. Your fingers must remain interlocked and in contact with the back of your neck at all times. You curl up from the starting position, but you may not push off the floor with an elbow. When you return to the starting position, your elbows must be flat on the floor or mat.

Scoring. One point is scored for each correct sit-up. The score is the maximum number of sit-ups completed in 60 seconds.

Item 4: Shuttle Run (Fig. 6–4D)

Purpose. To measure speed and agility.

Facilities and Equipment. Two lines parallel to each other are placed on the floor 30 feet apart. Since the child must overrun both of these lines, it is necessary to have several feet more of floor space at either end. Two blocks of wood, 2 by 2 by 4 inches, and a stopwatch are needed.

Procedures. The child stands at one of the lines with the 2 blocks at the other line. On the signal to start, he/she runs to the blocks, takes one, and returns to the starting line, and *places* the block behind that line. He/she then returns to the second block, which is carried across the starting line on the way back. Two children can run at the same time if 2 timers are available, or if 1 test administrator has a split-second timer, and of course, if there are 2 sets of blocks. Two trials are permitted. If the children start first at one line and then at the other, it is not necessary to return the blocks after each race. Sneakers should be worn or the children may run barefooted.

Instructions. On the signal to "Go," run as fast as you can to the next line and pick up a block. You should return the block over the second line where you place it on the floor. Do not throw it. Return for the second block, and this time you may run across the starting line as fast as you can without placing the block on the floor.

Scoring. The score is the elapsed time recorded in seconds and tenths of seconds for the better of the 2 trials.

Item 5: Standing Long Jump (Fig. 6–4E)

Purpose. To measure power.

Facilities and Equipment. Tape measure and a mat. Space on the floor or an outdoor jumping pit.

Procedures. The child stands behind a takeoff line with his/her feet several inches apart. Before jumping, the child dips at the knees and swings the arms backward. He/she then jumps forward by simultaneously extending the knees and swinging the arms forward. Three trials are permitted. Measurement is from the closest heel mark to the takeoff line. Indoor administration is best accomplished by placing a tape measure on the floor at right angles to the takeoff line and permitting the child to jump along the line. Measurement can then be made by sighting across the tape to the point of the jump.

Instructions. You must take off from both feet simultaneously, jump as far forward as possible, and land on both feet. Try not to fall backward after the landing. You can jump farther by crouching before the jump and swinging your arms.

Scoring. The score is the distance between the takeoff line and the nearest point where any part of the child's body touches the floor. It is measured in feet and inches to the nearest inch. Only the best trial is recorded.

Item 6: 50-Yard Dash

Purpose. To measure speed.

Facilities and Equipment. An area on a track, football field, or playground with a starting line, a 50-yard course, and a finish line. Two stopwatches or a split-second timer.

Procedures. After a short warm-up period the child takes a position behind the starting line. Best results are obtained when 2 children run at the same time for competition. The starter uses the command, "Are you ready?" and "Go!" The latter is accompanied by a downward sweep of the arm as a signal to the timer. The children run across the finish line. One trial is permitted.

Instructions. You may take any position behind the starting line you wish. On the command, "Go!" you are to run as fast as you can across the finish line. Do not slow up until you are across the finish line. Then you may slow down gradually.

Scoring. The score is the elapsed time to the nearest tenth of a second between the starting and the instant the child crosses the finish line.

Item 7: 600-Yard Run-Walk

Purpose. To measure endurance.

Facilities and Equipment. A track, or an area within a football field, or a square 50 yards on each side of a playground. Stopwatch.

Procedures. Children may run individually or they may run in groups of a dozen or more. When children run in groups, they should be paired into partners. While 1 child runs, the partner listens for the timer to call out the partner's time when he/she crosses the finish line and relays this time to the scorer. Children may interspace running with periods of walking and should be encouraged to pace themselves. When a group is running, the timer can call out times as each child crosses the finish line.

Instructions. Run 3 times around this course (1 time for a football field) and finish at the line, which is clearly marked. You should run as far as you can and then you may have to walk for a short space of time. Try to keep running, however. You must pace yourself by not running too fast at the beginning, but keep going at a speed you think you can maintain.

Scoring. The score is the elapsed time in minutes and seconds.

Optional Tests. 1-Mile or 9-Minute Runs for children 10 to 12 years of age, or the 1½-Mile or 12-Minute Runs for children 13 years of age and older.

*Table 6–5. Pull-Ups and Flexed-Arm Hang**

Pull-Up for Boys
Percentile Scores Based on Age/Test Scores in Number of Pull-Ups

Percentile	Age								Percentile
	9–10	11	12	13	14	15	16	17+	
100th	19	16	18	17	27	20	26	23	100th
85th	5	5	6	7	9	11	11	12	85th
75th	3	4	4	5	7	9	10	10	75th
50th	1	2	2	3	4	6	7	7	50th
25th	0	0	0	1	2	3	4	4	25th

Flexed-Arm Hang for Girls
Percentile Scores Based on Age/Test Scores in Seconds

Percentile	Age								Percentile
	9–10	11	12	13	14	15	16	17+	
100th	78	68	84	68	65	83	69	73	100th
85th	24	24	23	21	26	25	20	22	85th
75th	18	20	18	16	21	18	15	17	75th
50th	9	10	9	8	9	9	7	8	50th
25th	3	3	3	3	3	4	3	3	25th

*From American Alliance for Health, Physical Education, and Recreation: Youth Fitness Test Manual. Reston, VA, AAHPER, 1976. Used by permission of AAHPERD.

Table 6–6. Sit-Up*

Boys (Flexed Leg)
Percentile Scores Based on Age/Test Scores in Number of Sit-ups Performed in 60 Seconds

Percentile	9–10	11	12	13	14	15	16	17+	Percentile
100th	70	60	62	60	73	72	76	66	100th
85th	42	43	45	48	50	50	50	49	85th
75th	38	40	42	45	47	48	47	46	75th
50th	31	34	35	38	41	42	41	41	50th
25th	25	26	30	30	34	37	35	35	25th

Girls (Flexed Leg)
Percentile Scores Based on Age/Test Scores in Number of Sit-ups Performed in 60 Seconds

Percentile	9–10	11	12	13	14	15	16	17+	Percentile
100th	56	60	55	57	52	58	75	66	100th
85th	38	38	38	40	41	40	38	40	85th
75th	34	35	36	36	37	36	35	35	75th
50th	27	29	29	30	30	31	30	30	50th
25th	21	22	24	23	24	25	24	25	25th

*From American Alliance for Health, Physical Education, and Recreation: Youth Fitness Test Manual. Reston, VA, AAHPER, 1976. Used by permission of AAHPERD.

*Table 6–7. Shuttle Run**

Boys

Percentile Scores Based on Age/Test Scores in Seconds and Tenths

Percentile	Age								Percentile
	9–10	11	12	13	14	15	16	17+	
100th	9.2	8.7	6.8	7.0	7.0	7.0	7.3	7.0	100th
85th	10.4	10.1	10.0	9.7	9.3	9.2	9.1	9.0	85th
75th	10.6	10.4	10.2	10.0	9.6	9.4	9.3	9.2	75th
50th	11.2	10.9	10.7	10.4	10.1	9.9	9.9	9.8	50th
25th	12.0	11.5	11.4	11.0	10.7	10.4	10.5	10.4	25th

Girls

Percentile Scores Based on Age/Test Scores in Seconds and Tenths

Percentile	Age								Percentile
	9–10	11	12	13	14	15	16	17+	
100th	8.0	8.4	8.5	7.0	7.8	7.4	7.8	8.2	100th
85th	10.9	10.5	10.5	10.2	10.1	10.2	10.4	10.1	85th
75th	11.1	10.8	10.8	10.5	10.3	10.4	10.6	10.4	75th
50th	11.8	11.5	11.4	11.2	11.0	11.0	11.2	11.1	50th
25th	12.5	12.1	12.0	12.0	12.0	11.8	12.0	12.0	25th

*From American Alliance for Health, Physical Education, and Recreation: Youth Fitness Test Manual. Reston, VA, AAHPER, 1976. Used by permission of AAHPERD.

Table 6–8.   Standing Long Jump*

Boys

Percentile Scores Based on Age/Test Scores in Feet and Inches

Percentile	9–10	11	12	13	14	15	16	17+	Percentile
				Age					
100th	6' 5"	8' 5"	7' 5"	8' 6"	9' 0"	9' 0"	9' 2"	9'10"	100th
85th	5' 8"	5'10"	6' 1"	6' 8"	6'11"	7' 5"	7' 9"	8' 0"	85th
75th	5' 4"	5' 7"	5'11"	6' 3"	6' 8"	7' 2"	7' 6"	7' 9"	75th
50th	4'11"	5' 2"	5' 5"	5' 9"	6' 2"	6' 8"	7' 0"	7' 2"	50th
25th	4' 6"	4' 8"	5' 0"	5' 2"	5' 6"	6' 1"	6' 6"	6' 6"	25th

Girls

Percentile Scores Based on Age/Test Scores in Feet and Inches

Percentile	9–10	11	12	13	14	15	16	17+	Percentile
				Age					
100th	7'11"	7' 0"	7' 0"	8' 0"	7' 5"	8' 0"	7' 7"	7' 6"	100th
85th	5' 5"	5' 7"	5' 9"	6' 0"	6' 3"	6' 1"	6' 0"	6' 3"	85th
75th	5' 2"	5' 4"	5' 6"	5' 9"	5'11"	5'10"	5' 9"	6' 0"	75th
50th	4' 8"	4'11"	5' 0"	5' 3"	5' 4"	5' 5"	5' 3"	5' 5"	50th
25th	4' 1"	4' 4"	4' 6"	4' 9"	4'10"	4'11"	4' 9"	4'11"	25th

*From American Alliance for Health, Physical Education, and Recreation: Youth Fitness Test Manual. Reston, VA, AAHPER, 1976. Used by permission of AAHPERD.

Table 6–9. 50-Yard Dash*

Boys

Percentile Scores Based on Age/Test Scores in Seconds and Tenths

Percentile	Age							
	9–10	11	12	13	14	15	16	17+
100th	7.0	6.3	6.3	5.8	5.9	5.5	5.5	5.4
85th	7.7	7.4	7.1	6.9	6.5	6.3	6.3	6.1
75th	7.8	7.6	7.4	7.0	6.8	6.5	6.5	6.3
50th	8.2	8.0	7.8	7.5	7.2	6.9	6.7	6.6
25th	8.9	8.6	8.3	8.0	7.7	7.3	7.0	7.0

Girls

Percentile Scores Based on Age/Test Scores in Seconds and Tenths

Percentile	Age								Percentile
	9–10	11	12	13	14	15	16	17+	
100th	7.0	6.9	6.0	6.0	6.0	6.0	5.6	6.4	100th
85th	7.8	7.5	7.4	7.2	7.1	7.1	7.3	7.1	85th
75th	8.0	7.9	7.6	7.4	7.3	7.4	7.5	7.4	75th
50th	8.6	8.3	8.1	8.0	7.8	7.8	7.9	7.9	50th
25th	9.1	9.0	8.7	8.5	8.3	8.2	8.3	8.4	25th

*From American Alliance for Health, Physical Education, and Recreation: Youth Fitness Test Manual. Reston, VA, AAHPER, 1976. Used by permission of AAHPERD.

Table 6-10. 600-Yard Run*

Boys

Percentile Scores Based on Age/Test Scores in Minutes and Seconds

Percentile	Age								Percentile
	9–10	11	12	13	14	15	16	17+	
100th	1'52"	1'47"	1'38"	1'26"	1'27"	1'20"	1'21"	1'20"	100th
85th	2'11"	2' 9"	2' 0"	1'54"	1'47"	1'42"	1'40"	1'38"	85th
75th	2'17"	2'15"	2' 6"	1'59"	1'52"	1'46"	1'44"	1'43"	75th
50th	2'33"	2'27"	2'19"	2'10"	2' 3"	1'56"	1'52"	1'52"	50th
25th	2'53"	2'47"	2'37"	2'27"	2'16"	2' 8"	2' 1"	2' 2"	25th

Girls

Percentile Scores Based on Age/Test Scores in Minutes and Seconds

Percentile	Age								Percentile
	9–10	11	12	13	14	15	16	17+	
100th	2' 7"	1'52"	1'40"	1'43"	1'33"	1'41"	1'45"	1'39"	100th
85th	2'30"	2'25"	2'21"	2'16"	2'11"	2'14"	2'19"	2'14"	85th
75th	2'39"	2'35"	2'26"	2'23"	2'19"	2'22"	2'26"	2'24"	75th
50th	2'56"	2'53"	2'47"	2'41"	2'40"	2'37"	2'43"	2'41"	50th
25th	3'15"	3'16"	3'13"	3' 6"	3' 1"	3' 0"	3' 3"	3' 2"	25th

*From American Alliance for Health, Physical Education, and Recreation: Youth Fitness Test Manual. Reston, VA, AAHPER, 1976. Used by permission of AAHPERD.

Table 6–11. **9-Minute/1-Mile Run***

Boys

Percentile Scores Based on Age/Test Scores in Yards/Time

	9-Minute Run—Boys			1-Mile Run—Boys			
Percentile	Age			Age			Percentile
	10	11	12	10	11	12	
	Yards			Time			
100th	2532	2535	2578	5:07	4:44	4:21	100th
85th	2081	2143	2205	7:06	6:43	6:20	85th
75th	1952	2014	2076	7:49	7:26	7:03	75th
50th	1717	1779	1841	9:07	8:44	8:21	50th
25th	1482	1544	1606	10:25	10:02	9:39	25th

Girls

Percentile Scores Based on Age/Test Scores in Yards/Time

	9-Minute Run—Girls			1-Mile Run—Girls			
Percentile	Age			Age			Percentile
	10	11	12	10	11	12	
	Yards			Time			
100th	2157	2180	2203	6:13	5:42	5:08	100th
85th	1801	1824	1847	8:33	8:02	7:28	85th
75th	1702	1725	1748	9:16	8:45	8:11	75th
50th	1514	1537	1560	10:29	9:58	9:24	50th
25th	1326	1349	1372	11:42	11:11	10:37	25th

*From American Alliance for Health, Physical Education, and Recreation: Youth Fitness Test Manual. Reston, VA, AAHPER, 1976. Used by permission of AAHPERD.

Table 6–12. ***12-Minute/1½-Mile Run****

Boys, Age 13 and Older Percentile Scores Based on Age/Test Scores in Yards/Time				Girls, Age 13 and Older Percentile Scores Based on Age/Test Scores in Yards/Time			
12-Minute Run	1.5-Mile Run			12-Minute Run	1.5-Mile Run		
Percentile	*Yards*	*Time*	*Percentile*	*Percentile*	*Yards*	*Time*	*Percentile*
100th	3590	7:26	100th	100th	2693	10:20	100th
85th	3037	9:40	85th	85th	2232	14:00	85th
75th	2879	10:19	75th	75th	2100	15:03	75th
50th	2592	11:29	50th	50th	1861	16:57	50th
25th	2305	12:39	25th	25th	1622	18:50	25th

*From American Alliance for Health, Physical Education, and Recreation: Youth Fitness Test Manual. Reston, VA, AAHPER, 1976. Used by permission of AAHPERD.

Bruininks-Oseretsky Test (BOT) of Motor Proficiency (Short Form)[*7]
Test Description by Dr. Janet M. Fisher

Purpose. To assess motor proficiency.

Development. The Complete Battery consists of 46 items; the Short Form has 14 items grouped into 8 subtest areas. Extensive validity and reliability evidence is reported for both the Complete Battery and the Short Form.

Content validity was established by analyzing the relationship between test content and aspects of motor development identified in the research literature. Also analyzed were statistical properties such as the relationship of test scores to chronological age, the internal consistency of the subtests, and the underlying factor structure of the subtests. Construct validity was established using the contrasting groups approach. Normal children were compared to mildly retarded children, to moderately-to-severely retarded children, and to learning disabled children.

Test-retest reliability estimates for the Short Form across a 7- to 12-day period were .87 for Grade 2 and .84 for Grade 6 children. The average standard error of measurement for the Short Form was 4.6.

Interrater reliability, a measure of objectivity, was investigated for the Visual-Motor Control items because scoring of these items requires more judgment than other items. The coefficients for the Short Form items were .80, .84, and .95 for five raters with no formal training.

In a standardization study, the Short Form was found to correlate well with the Complete Battery composite. The correlation for four-year-olds was .80, for eight-year-olds was .93, and for 12-year-olds was .90.

Level and Gender. Boys and girls, aged 4½ to 14½ years.

Uses. As a screening test, to identify children with deficiences in motor functioning.

Equipment. A kit may be purchased from the publisher that has all equipment and materials needed to administer the test—balance beam, target, block, tape measure, ball, test booklet with mazes, and shape cards. The kit comes in a convenient metal carrying case.

Procedures. The 46-item Compete Battery of the BOT takes about 50 to 60 minutes to administer and provides an index of motor proficiency with separate gross and fine motor composites. The 14-item Short Form takes about 15 to 20 minutes to administer and provides only an index of motor proficiency.

The BOT is individually administered. It begins with a pretest to determine the child's arm and leg preference. The items are then to be given in the order that they are listed in the manual—with all gross motor items preceding the fine motor items.

Scoring. Performance scores for each item are converted to point scores on the appropriate scales given in the test manual. The item point scores are then summed. The total points are compared to a norm table and converted to standard scores, percentile rank scores, and stanines.

Comments. The Short Form of the BOT is presently one of the best screening tools available for motor proficiency. The test kit, equipment, and manual are easily used by the general physical educator or adaptive specialist. Although it is labeled as a test of "motor proficiency," one will note that the gross motor items measure the parameters of skill-related physical fitness—speed, agility, balance (both static and dynamic), coordination, and power (labeled as "strength" on the test). There is also a measure of response speed.

Though the BOT is excellent, there are a few cautions that we would like to make about the test:

1. The BOT requires that the gross motor items be completed before the fine motor items; poor performance on early items could negatively influence a child's attitude and performance on later test items.

2. Qualitative processes are not evaluated; the product of each performance is quantitatively scored.

3. Several items require repeated trials. Some of these items are scored using the best performance, while others require the averaging of trial scores. No rationale is given for the different modes of scoring trials.

Subtest 1: Running Speed and Agility

Two lines 16 yards apart are marked; a block is placed on the far line. A short line, the "timing line," is marked 1 yard in front of the first line. The child begins at the first line, runs to the far line, picks up the block, then runs back across the first line as fast as possible. The child is timed to the nearest .2 second between the first and last crossings *of the timing line.* Two trials are taken; the better score is recorded.

Subtest 2: Balance

Standing on the Preferred Leg on Balance Beam. The child stands on the preferred leg on the balance beam, looking at a wall target, with hands on hips, and free leg held with thigh parallel to the floor. The score is the time the child can maintain the balance position to a maximum of 10 seconds. A second trial is given if the child does not score the maximum on the first trial.

Walking Forward Heel-to-Toe on Balance Beam. The child walks forward on the balance beam heel-to-toe, with hands on hips. The recorder keeps track of correct and incorrect steps on six steps, e.g., 1-1-0-1-1-0 = 4. The child must make six consecutive steps correctly to achieve a maximum score. A second trial is given if the child does not score the maximum on the first trial.

Subtest 3: Bilateral Coordination

Tapping Feet Alternately While Making Circles with Fingers. The child sits on a chair and attempts to tap feet alternatively while simultaneously making inward-to-outward circles with the index fingers. This item is scored pass-fail. The child is given 90 seconds to complete 10 consecutive foot taps correctly.

Jumping Up and Clapping Hands. The child jumps as high as possible, clapping his/her hands in front of the face as many times as possible before landing. The score is the number of claps; a maximum score is 5. A second trial is given if a maximum score is not achieved on the first trial.

Subtest 4: Strength

After warming up, the child assumes a bent-knee position, then does a standing long jump. The child's score is the longest of three trials, recorded to the nearest number on the test kit measuring tape.

Subtest 5: Upper-Limb Coordination

Catching a Tossed Ball with Both Hands. The child stands on the test kit mat and, using both hands, catches a tennis ball tossed underhand from 10 feet. The ball should be tossed with a slight arch so it comes down between the child's shoulders and waist. The number of correct catches of five tosses is recorded.

Throwing a Ball at a Target with Preferred Hand. Using the preferred hand, the child throws a tennis ball overhand at a target from a 5-foot distance. One practice throw and five scored throws are given. The score is the number of target hits in the five attempts.

Subtest 6: Response Speed

This item measures the ability of the child to respond quickly to a moving stimulus. The child sits in a chair at arm's distance from a wall. He/she places the preferred hand flat on the wall next to the bottom of the test kit response stick that is held against the wall by the test administrator. The stick is dropped, and the child stops it as quickly as possible with his/her thumb. The score is the response speed number on the stick. One practice and 7 scored trials are given. On the trials, the test administrator follows a specified protocol to vary the number of seconds before releasing the stick. The *median score* of the 7 trials is recorded for this item.

Subtest 7: Visual-Motor Control

Drawing a Line Through a Straight Path with Preferred Hand. The child tries to draw a pencil line within the "road" given in the test booklet. One trial is given, with no time limit. The score is the number of errors, i.e., going outside the boundary lines, up to a maximum of 7.

Copying a Circle with Preferred Hand. The child attempts to trace a circle given in the test booklet. Points (2, 1, or 0) are awarded for the degree of accuracy of the tracing. A good tracing receives 2 points, adequate gets 1 point, and inadequate gets 0 points. One trial is given.

Copying Overlapping Pencils with Preferred Hand. The child attempts to copy a geometric shape of overlapping pencils given in the test booklet. Points (2, 1, or 0) are awarded for good, adequate, or inadequate tracings. One trial is given.

Subtest 8: Upper-Limb Speed and Dexterity

Sorting Shape Cards with Preferred Hand. With the preferred hand, the child sorts a deck of red and blue cards into two piles by color. The score is the number of cards correctly sorted in 15 seconds. One trial is given.

Making Dots in Circles with Preferred Hand. The child makes a pencil dot within each of the series of circles given in the test booklet. The score is the number of circles correctly dotted in 15 seconds. One trial is given.

ADULT HEALTH-RELATED PHYSICAL FITNESS MEASURES

AAHPERD Health-Related Physical Fitness Test (College)*[22]

Purpose. To measure the health-related physical fitness of college students who take classes in physical education and compare their scores to normative data.

---

*Pate, R.R.: Norms for College Students: Health Related Physical Fitness Test. Reston, VA, AAHPERD, 1985. Used by permission of AAHPERD.

Table 6–13.   Percentile Norms for Health Related Physical Fitness Test Items for Male College Students (no age breakdown)

Percentile	Mile Run (min:sec)	9 Min-Run (yards)	Sit-Ups	Sit and Reach (cm)	Sum of SF (mm)	Percent Fat
99	5:06	3035	68	49	10	2.9
75	6:12	2349	50	39	16	6.6
50	6:49	2200	44	34	21	9.4
25	7:32	1945	38	29	26	13.1
5	9:47	1652	30	19	40	20.4

*Reprinted by permission of the American Alliance for Health, Physical Education, Recreation and Dance, 1900 Association Drive, Reston, Virginia 22091.

Development. Normative data were collected on 2177 males and 2981 females at 24 different colleges across the United States. The AAHPERD Health-Related Physical Fitness Test items were administered to all subjects in accordance with specified procedures.[2] Analysis of descriptive data on the recruited subjects suggested that they were representative of young adult college students who took classes in physical education.

Data for each fitness item were analyzed by gender, by gender and 1-year age increments, and by gender and student status (i.e., physical education major, student taking class as a requirement, student taking class as an elective). Means and standard deviations were calculated for each analysis. Additionally, percentile norms were calculated.

Level and Gender. Males and females, ages 18 to 21.

Uses. 1. To determine health-related physical fitness status.

2. To diagnose fitness areas that need improvement.

3. To classify students for further physical activity.

Scoring. Each item score is compared to an appropriate percentile norm table. Tables 6–13 and 6–14 are for males and females, respectively, with no breakdown for age.

Comments. There is no test of upper body muscular endurance in this fitness test battery.

Item 1: Distance Runs

Purpose. To measure maximal functional capacity and cardiorespiratory endurance.

Equipment and Facilities. A 440-yard track, 400-meter track, or any other indoor or outdoor area that is flat and can be easily measured.

Table 6–14.   Percentile Norms for Health Related Physical Fitness Test Items for Female College Students (no age breakdown)

Percentile	Mile Run (min:sec)	9 Min-Run (yards)	Sit-Ups	Sit and Reach (cm)	Sum of SF (mm)	Percent Fat
99	6:04	2640	61	51	11	7.9
75	8:15	1870	42	41	24	19.0
50	9:22	1755	35	37	30	22.8
25	10:41	1460	30	32	37	27.1
5	12:43	1101	21	24	51	33.7

*Reprinted by permission of the American Alliance for Health, Physical Education, Recreation and Dance, 1900 Association Drive, Reston, Virginia 22091.

Test Description. Either a One-Mile Run or a 9-Minute Run may be administered. Procedures for the One-Mile Run are the same as those described for the Physical Best test. Procedures for the 9-Minute Run are to run or walk as much distance as possible in 9 minutes.

Scoring. The One-Mile Run is scored to the nearest second. The 9-Minute Run is scored to the nearest 10 yards or 10 meters.

Comments. Although the test manual suggests that a 1.5 mile distance or a 12-minute run may be used for testing college students, percentile scores are not given for these alternative runs. For most physically active college students, these longer runs would be preferred.

Item 2: Skinfolds

Purpose. To assess body composition.

Equipment. A quality pair of skinfold calipers, as described for the Physical Best test.

Test Description. A skinfold measure is taken at the triceps and subscapular sites, using procedures described for the Physical Best test.

Scoring. The scoring is the same as for the Physical Best. Three measures are taken at each site; the median scores are summed.

Item 3: Modified Sit-ups

Same as Physical Best test.

Item 4: Sit and Reach

Same as Physical Best test.

Queens College Step Test[*20]

Purpose. To assess the cardiovascular capacity of college students.

Development. This test was developed and normed on thousands of male and female college students at Queens College in New York. Validity and reliability data were also studied at Queens College. Concurrent validity was determined using maximal oxygen consumption measured on the treadmill as the criterion. Concurrent validity was estimated at $-.72$ for males and $-.75$ for females; reliability was estimated at .89 for males and .92 for females.[25]

Level and Gender. Males and females of normal college age.

Uses. To screen college students according to cardiorespiratory endurance.

Equipment. A bench that is 16¼ inches high, a metronome to monitor stepping cadence, and a stopwatch.

Test Procedures. The students use an even four-count stepping pattern—up with the left foot, up with the right foot, down with the left foot, down with the right foot. The examinee's legs should be fully extended in the up position on the bench. The metronome is set at 96 counts per minute (24 complete step cycles) for males, and 88 counts per minute (22 complete step cycles) for females.

After 15 seconds of practice, examinees begin stepping and continue for 3 minutes. Examinees are stopped at the end of 3 minutes, but remain standing. They are allowed 5 seconds to find their carotid artery pulse; they then count

*Katch, F.I., and McArdle, W.D.: Nutrition, Weight Control, and Exercise. 3rd Ed. Philadelphia, Lea & Febiger, 1988. Used by permission of the publisher.

Table 6–15. *Percentile Rankings for Recovery Heart Rate and Predicted Oxygen Consumption for Male and Female College Students*

Percentile Ranking	Recovery HR, Female	Predicted Max VO$_2$ (ml/kg·min)	Recovery HR, Male	Predicted Max VO$_2$ (ml/kg·min)
100	128	42.2	120	60.9
95	140	40.0	124	59.3
90	148	38.5	128	57.6
85	152	37.7	136	54.2
80	156	37.0	140	52.5
75	158	36.6	144	50.9
70	160	36.3	148	49.2
65	162	35.9	149	48.8
60	163	35.7	152	47.5
55	164	35.5	154	46.7
50	166	35.1	156	45.8
45	168	34.8	160	44.1
40	170	34.4	162	43.3
35	171	34.2	164	42.5
30	172	34.0	166	41.6
25	176	33.3	168	40.8
20	180	32.6	172	39.1
15	182	32.2	176	37.4
10	184	31.8	178	36.6
5	196	29.6	184	34.1

From Katch, F.I., and McArdle, W.D.: Nutrition, Weight Control, and Exercise. 3rd Ed. Philadelphia, Lea & Febiger, 1988. Used by permission of the publisher.

the pulse for 15 seconds. This value is multiplied by 4 to obtain the "recovery heart rate" in beats per minute.

Scoring. The recovery heart rate is used with Table 6–15 to determine the percentile ranking for each examinee. Also given on Table 6–15 is the maximal oxygen consumption predicted from the recovery heart rate value.

Comments. The procedures must be followed *exactly* in order to have valid comparisons. The bench must be 16¼ inches in height, and the recovery heart rate must be taken between 5 and 20 seconds after the end of stepping.

The carotid artery can be found on either side of the "Adam's apple" at the front of the neck. To palpate it, press lightly on either side of the neck with two or three fingers. After exercise, the carotid pulse can be located easily. Do not press hard, for excess pressure can slow the actual pulse rate.

"Maximal oxygen consumption" refers to the maximal amount of oxygen that the body can take in and use in a minute of time. It is a measure of the efficiency of the circulatory and respiratory systems, but it is also believed to be the single best indicator of overall physical fitness.

Cooper's 12-Minute Walking/Running Test*[10]

Purpose. To assess aerobic capacity.

Development. Cooper reported a concurrent validity coefficient of .897 with a criterion of maximal oxygen consumption from treadmill testing of normal males 17 to 52 years of age.[9] Safrit summarized the results of eight other validation studies that had been performed on different populations of subjects; validity coefficients ranged from .65 for boys aged 11 to 14 to .90 for ninth-grade boys

*Cooper, K.H.: The Aerobics Program for Total Well-Being. New York, Bantam Books, by arrangement with M. Evans & Co., Inc., 1982. Used by permission of M. Evans & Co., Inc.

and college men.[24] Safrit also reported reliability coefficients for six studies that ranged between .75 for boys and girls aged 10 to 12 and .92 for boys aged 11 to 14.[24]

Level and Gender. Cooper reports norms for both genders in categories for ages 13–19, 20–29, 30–39, 40–49, 50–59, and over 60 years of age.

Uses. 1. To determine status of cardiorespiratory function.

2. To classify persons for participation in an aerobic conditioning program.

3. To measure the success of an aerobics program.

Facilities and Equipment. An indoor or outdoor track, or any other flat course that can be measured. Also needed are cones, a stopwatch, and a whistle.

Test Procedures. This test is contraindicated for deconditioned persons over the age of 35 and for younger persons who are symptomatic. At least 6 weeks of training should be engaged in prior to testing.

Cones or other markers should be placed around the track to indicate portions of completed laps—e.g., either every 40 yards or 55 yards. All examinees are started together on a signal. They are instructed to try to cover as much distance as possible in the 12 minutes. They are allowed to walk, but should be encouraged to run at an even pace that can be maintained. Runners are given a signal when 11 minutes have passed. At the end of 12 minutes, the test administrator blows a whistle, and the runner notes the last cone he/she has passed.

Scoring. Distance run in the 12 minutes is converted to hundredths of a mile, then compared to the norm values given in Table 6–16. Six categories of fitness are defined by the score values.

Comments. Partners may help the runners keep track of the number of completed laps, so that scoring is accurate.

The 12-Minute Run Test is popular for use with many different populations. It should be noted, however, that a longer run period may be preferable for assessing the cardiorespiratory endurance of conditioned athletes such as intercollegiate soccer players. A possible alternative would be the 15-minute run test developed by Balke.[5]

Cooper's writings on aerobics are classics that every physical education and sport professional should know. We highly recommend his latest book, *The Aerobics Program for Total Well-Being.*[10]

Alternative Tests. Since development of the original 12-Minute Run Test, Cooper has also developed the 1.5-Mile Run Test, the 3-Mile Walk Test, the 12-Minute Swim Test, and the 12-Minute Cycle Test. The 1.5-Mile Run is administratively easier than the 12-Minute Run. The 3-Mile Walk Test is an excellent alternative for individuals who are deconditioned and should not yet participate in a run test. The 12-Minute Swim and Cycle Tests are appealing alternatives for those individuals who possess sufficient skills to be tested by swimming or cycling. Tables 6–17, 6–18, 6–19, and 6–20 can be used to interpret scores on these tests.

Table 6-16. 12-Minute Walking/Running Test†
Distance (Miles) Covered in 12 Minutes

Fitness Category		13–19	20–29	30–39	40–49	50–59	60 +
				Age (years)			
I. Very Poor	(men)	<1.30*	<1.22	<1.18	<1.14	<1.03	< .87
	(women)	<1.0	< .96	< .94	< .88	< .84	< .78
II. Poor	(men)	1.30–1.37	1.22–1.31	1.18–1.30	1.14–1.24	1.03–1.16	.87–1.02
	(women)	1.00–1.18	.96–1.11	.95–1.05	.88– .98	.84– .93	.78– .86
III. Fair	(men)	1.38–1.56	1.32–1.49	1.31–1.45	1.25–1.39	1.17–1.30	1.03–1.20
	(women)	1.19–1.29	1.12–1.22	1.06–1.18	.99–1.11	.94–1.05	.87– .98
IV. Good	(men)	1.57–1.72	1.50–1.64	1.46–1.56	1.40–1.53	1.31–1.44	1.21–1.32
	(women)	1.30–1.43	1.23–1.34	1.19–1.29	1.12–1.24	1.06–1.18	.99–1.09
V. Excellent	(men)	1.73–1.86	1.65–1.76	1.57–1.69	1.54–1.65	1.45–1.58	1.33–1.55
	(women)	1.44–1.51	1.35–1.45	1.30–1.39	1.25–1.34	1.19–1.30	1.10–1.18
VI. Superior	(men)	>1.87	>1.77	>1.70	>1.66	>1.59	>1.56
	(women)	>1.52	>1.46	>1.40	>1.35	>1.31	>1.19

*< Means "less than"; > means "more than."
†From Cooper, K.H.: The Aerobics Program for Total Well-Being. New York, Bantam Books, by arrangement with M. Evans & Co., Inc., 1982.
Used by permission of M. Evans & Co., Inc.

Table 6–17. 1.5-Mile Run Test†
Time (Minutes)

Fitness Category		Age (years)					
		13–19	20–29	30–39	40–49	50–59	60+
I. Very Poor	(men)	>15:31*	>16:01	>16:31	>17:31	>19:01	>20:01
	(women)	>18:31	>19:01	>19:31	>20:01	>20:31	>21:01
II. Poor	(men)	12:11–15:30	14:01–16:00	14:44–16:30	15:36–17:30	17:01–19:00	19:01–20:00
	(women)	16:55–18:30	18:31–19:00	19:01–19:30	19:31–20:00	20:01–20:30	21:00–21:31
III. Fair	(men)	10:49–12:10	12:01–14:00	12:31–14:45	13:01–15:35	14:31–17:00	16:16–19:00
	(women)	14:31–16:54	15:55–18:30	16:31–19:00	17:31–19:30	19:01–20:00	19:31–20:30
IV. Good	(men)	9:41–10:48	10:46–12:00	11:01–12:30	11:31–13:00	12:31–14:30	14:00–16:15
	(women)	12:30–14:30	13:31–15:54	14:31–16:30	15:56–17:30	16:31–19:00	17:31–19:30
V. Excellent	(men)	8:37– 9:40	9:45–10:45	10:00–11:00	10:30–11:30	11:00–12:30	11:15–13:59
	(women)	11:50–12:29	12:30–13:30	13:00–14:30	13:45–15:55	14:30–16:30	16:30–17:30
VI. Superior	(men)	< 8:37	< 9:45	<10:00	<10:30	<11:00	<11:15
	(women)	<11:50	<12:30	<13:00	<13:45	<14:30	<16:30

*< Means "less than"; > means "more than."

†From Cooper, K.H.: The Aerobics Program for Total Well-Being. New York, Bantam Books, by arrangement with M. Evans & Co., Inc., 1982. Used by permission of M. Evans & Co., Inc.

*Table 6–18. 3-Mile Walking Test (No Running)†
Time (Minutes)*

		Age (years)					
Fitness Category		13–19	20–29	30–39	40–49	50–59	60+
I. Very Poor	(men)	>45:00*	>46:00	>49:00	>52:00	>55:00	>60:00
	(women)	>47:00	>48:00	>51:00	>54:00	>57:00	>63:00
II. Poor	(men)	41:01–45:00	42:01–46:00	44:31–49:00	47:01–52:00	50:01–55:00	54:01–60:00
	(women)	43:01–47:00	44:01–48:00	46:31–51:00	49:01–54:00	52:01–57:00	57:01–63:00
III. Fair	(men)	37:31–41:00	38:31–42:00	40:01–44:30	42:01–47:00	45:01–50:00	48:01–54:00
	(women)	39:31–43:00	40:31–44:00	42:01–46:30	44:01–49:00	47:01–52:00	51:01–57:00
IV. Good	(men)	33:00–37:30	34:00–38:30	35:00–40:00	36:30–42:00	39:00–45:00	41:00–48:00
	(women)	35:00–39:30	36:00–40:30	37:30–42:00	39:00–44:00	42:00–47:00	45:00–51:00
V. Excellent	(men)	<33:00	<34:00	<35:00	<36:30	<39:00	<41:00
	(women)	<35:00	<36:00	<37:30	<39:00	<42:00	<45:00

*< Means "less than"; > means "more than."

The *Walking test*, covering 3 miles in the fastest time possible *without running*, can be done on a track over any accurately measured distance. As with running, take the test after you have been training for at least 6 weeks, when you feel rested, and dress to be comfortable.

†From Cooper, K.H.: The Aerobics Program for Total Well-Being. New York, Bantam Books, by arrangement with M. Evans & Co., Inc., 1982. Used by permission of M. Evans & Co., Inc.

Table 6–19. 12-Minute Swimming Test†
Distance (Yards) Swum in 12 Minutes

Fitness Category		Age (years)					
		13–19	20–29	30–39	40–49	50–59	60+
I. Very Poor	(men)	<500*	<400	<350	<300	<250	<250
	(women)	<400	<300	<250	<200	<150	<150
II. Poor	(men)	500–599	400–499	350–449	300–399	250–349	250–299
	(women)	400–499	300–399	250–349	200–299	150–249	150–199
III. Fair	(men)	600–699	500–599	450–549	400–499	350–449	300–399
	(women)	500–599	400–499	350–449	300–399	250–349	200–299
IV. Good	(men)	700–799	600–699	550–649	500–599	450–549	400–499
	(women)	600–699	500–599	450–549	400–499	350–449	300–399
V. Excellent	(men)	>800	>700	>650	>600	>550	>500
	(women)	>700	>600	>550	>500	>450	>400

*< Means "less than"; > means "more than."

The *Swimming test* requires you to swim as far as you can in 12 minutes, using whatever stroke you prefer and resting as necessary, but trying for a maximum effort. The easiest way to take the test is in a pool with known dimensions, and it helps to have another person record the laps and time. Be sure to use a watch with a sweep second hand.

†From Cooper, K.H.: The Aerobics Program for Total Well-Being. New York, Bantam Books, by arrangement with M. Evans & Co., Inc., 1982. Used by permission of M. Evans & Co., Inc.

Table 6–20. 12-Minute Cycle Test†
(3-Speed or less)
Distance (Miles) Cycled in 12 Minutes

Fitness Category		13–19	20–29	30–39	40–49	50–59	60+
				Age (years)			
I. Very Poor	(men)	<2.75*	<2.5	<2.25	<2.0	<1.75	<1.75
	(women)	<1.75	<1.5	<1.25	<1.0	<0.75	<0.75
II. Poor	(men)	2.75–3.74	2.5–3.49	2.25–3.24	2.0–2.99	1.75–2.49	1.75–2.24
	(women)	1.75–2.74	1.5–2.49	1.25–2.24	1.0–1.99	0.75–1.49	0.75–1.24
III. Fair	(men)	3.75–4.74	3.5–4.49	3.25–4.24	3.0–3.99	2.50–3.49	2.25–2.99
	(women)	2.75–3.74	2.5–3.49	2.25–3.24	2.0–2.99	1.50–2.49	1.25–1.99
IV. Good	(men)	4.75–5.74	4.5–5.49	4.25–5.24	4.0–4.99	3.50–4.49	3.0 –3.99
	(women)	3.75–4.74	3.5–4.49	3.25–4.24	3.0–3.99	2.50–3.49	2.0 –2.99
V. Excellent	(men)	>5.75	>5.5	>5.25	>5.0	>4.5	>4.0
	(women)	>4.75	>4.5	>4.25	>4.0	>3.5	>3.0

*< Means "less than"; > means "more than."

The *Cycling test* can be used as a test of fitness if you are utilizing the cycling program. Cycle as far as you can in 12 minutes in an area where traffic is not a problem. Try to cycle on a hard, flat surface, with the wind (less than 10 mph), and use a bike with no more than 3 gears. If the wind is blowing harder than 10 mph take the test another day. Measure the distance you cycle in 12 minutes by either the speedometer/odometer on the bike (which may not be too accurate) or by another means, such as a car odometer or an engineering wheel.

†From Cooper, K.H.: The Aerobics Program for Total Well-Being. New York, Bantam Books, by arrangement with M. Evans & Co., Inc., 1982. Used by permission of M. Evans & Co., Inc.

YMCA Physical Fitness Test Battery*[14]

Purpose. To assess the physical fitness parameters of body composition, cardiorespiratory endurance, flexibility, and muscular strength and endurance.

Development. Not reported.

Level and Gender. For adults of both genders.

Uses. 1. To assess current fitness levels.

2. To identify training needs.

3. To select training regimes.

4. To evaluate a participant's progress.

5. To evaluate the success of the program in achieving its objectives.

6. To motivate participants.

Scoring. For each test in the fitness battery an individual's score is compared to an age and gender appropriate norm table.

Comments. The complete YMCA Physical Fitness Test Battery consists of measures for body composition, cardiorespiratory endurance, flexibility, and muscular strength and endurance. The body composition and cardiorespiratory endurance tests are fairly sophisticated for field measures of fitness. Presented here are only the tests for flexibility and muscular strength and endurance. Tables 6–21, 6–22, and 6–23 report the values for scoring these tests for adult males and females of varying ages.

Item 1: Flexibility

Purpose. To assess trunk flexion.

Equipment. A yardstick or tape measure is placed on the floor; then the tape is placed across it at the 15-inch mark.

---

*Golding, L.A., Myers, C.R., and Sinning, W.E. (Eds.): The Y's Way to Physical Fitness. Champaign, IL, Human Kinetics Publishers, 1982. Used with permission of the publishers and the YMCA of the USA, 101 N. Wacker Drive, Chicago, IL 60606.

*Table 6–21.   Rating Scale for Males and Females 35 Years and Younger for Trunk Flexion, Bench Press Repetition, and Sit-ups**

Rating	Trunk Flexion (in.)	Bench Press Repetitions	Sit-ups 1 min. Reps
MALES			
Excellent	21	35	45
Good	19	29	41
Above Average	17	24	37
Average	15	20	33
Below Average	12	15	28
Fair	9	11	23
Poor	7	7	18
FEMALES			
Excellent	23	30	39
Good	21	24	34
Above Average	20	20	30
Average	18	16	25
Below Average	15	13	20
Fair	14	10	15
Poor	11	5	10

*From Golding, L.A., Myers, C.R., and Sinning, W.E.: The Y's Way to Physical Fitness. Champaign, IL, Human Kinetics Publishers, 1982. Adapted by permission of the publisher and the YMCA of the USA, 101 N. Wacker Drive, Chicago, IL 60606.

Table 6–22. Rating Scale for Males and Females 36 to 45 Years Old for Trunk Flexion, Bench Press Repetition, and Sit-ups*

Rating	Trunk Flexion (in.)	Bench Press Repetitions	Sit-ups 1 min. Reps
MALES			
Excellent	22	30	42
Good	19	24	38
Above Average	16	19	32
Average	14	17	27
Below Average	12	14	21
Fair	10	10	18
Poor	5	3	11
FEMALES			
Excellent	23	29	39
Good	21	21	29
Above Average	19	18	22
Average	17	15	18
Below Average	14	11	12
Fair	12	7	9
Poor	10	4	4

*From Golding, L.A., Myers, C.R., and Sinning, W.E.: The Y's Way to Physical Fitness. Champaign, IL, Human Kinetics Publishers, 1982. Adapted by permission of the publisher and the YMCA of the USA, 101 N. Wacker Drive, Chicago, IL 60606.

Table 6–23. Rating Scale for Males and Females 46 Years and Older for Trunk Flexion, Bench Press Repetition, and Sit-ups*

Rating	Trunk Flexion (in.)	Bench Press Repetitions	Sit-ups 1 min. Reps
MALES			
Excellent	20	28	38
Good	17	22	33
Above Average	15	19	26
Average	13	16	21
Below Average	11	12	18
Fair	8	8	15
Poor	5	3	10
FEMALES			
Excellent	22	30	24
Good	19	22	20
Above Average	18	18	17
Average	15	14	14
Below Average	14	9	11
Fair	11	5	7
Poor	9	2	2

*From Golding, L.A., Myers, C.R., and Sinning, W.E.: The Y's Way to Physical Fitness. Champaign, IL, Human Kinetics Publishers, 1982. Adapted by permission of the publisher and the YMCA of the USA, 101 N. Wacker Drive, Chicago, IL 60606.

Test Procedures. The examinee should warm up prior to testing. The examinee sits, with shoes removed, with the yardstick between the legs. He/she sits such that the heels are 10 to 12 inches apart and lined up with the taped 15-inch line. The examinee slowly reaches forward with fingertips of both hands along the yardstick, holding the end position momentarily. Hands should stay aligned, with one on top of the other. Knees should stay extended; the test administrator may place a hand across the examinee's knees. The examinee should be encouraged to exhale and drop the head between the arms for a maximal score. Three trials are taken.

Scoring. The score is the most distant point reached in the three trials, recorded to the nearest inch.

Item 2: Muscular Strength and Endurance—Bench Press

Purpose. To assess muscular strength and endurance of the upper body.

Equipment. A 35-pound barbell for women, and a 80-pound barbell for men. Also needed are a conventional weight bench and a metronome set for 60 beats per minute.

Test Procedures. The examinee lies on the bench in a supine position, with knees bent and feet on the floor. The examinee flexes the elbows and prepares to receive the barbell with palms facing upward. The tester (or a spotter) hands the barbell to the examinee, who grips the bar with hands a shoulder width apart. He/she then presses the barbell to a position with full elbow extension. After each extension, the barbell is returned to the original down position. He/she repeats up-down movements in rhythm to the metronome; each click representing either an up or a down movement.

The examinee should be encouraged to breathe regularly during the test. No excessive strain should occur.

Scoring. The score is the number of successful repetitions. The test is terminated when either the examinee is unable to fully extend the elbows or when unable to keep the rhythmic cadence.

Item 3: Muscular Strength and Endurance—Sit-ups

Purpose. To measure muscular strength and endurance of the abdominal muscles.

Equipment. Mat and a stopwatch.

Test Procedure. The examinee lies on his/her back with knees bent at right angles or heels about 18 inches from the hips. Hands should be clasped behind the head. A partner holds the ankles for support.

On "Go," the examinee performs repeated sit-ups, doing as many as possible in one minute. The elbows should alternately touch the opposite knee in the "up" position. After each up movement, the examinee is to return to the back lying position with shoulders touching the mat.

The examinee should be encouraged to breathe regularly during the test.

Scoring. The score is the number of correctly performed sit-ups completed in one minute.

Post 50 Physical Performance Test[*6]

Purpose. To assess stamina (cardiovascular health), strength (muscular strength and endurance), and suppleness (joint flexibility).

Development. Not reported.

Level and Gender. Males and females over 50 years old.

Uses. As a self-measurement test to give information to the examinee on three important areas of physical fitness.

Equipment. This test is designed to be self-administered in the home or neighborhood, so no specialized equipment is needed. A 400-meter (or 440-yard) track is needed for one of the stamina tests.

Test Procedures. Two activities precede the actual test items. First the examinee is to read about the "Body's Traffic Signals" and understand that the Post 50 Test is to be performed within "Your Comfort Zone." Secondly, the examinee is to answer the six questions given in the Physical Activity Readiness Questionnaire (PAR-Q). If answering "Yes" to any of the questions, the subject is asked to see his/her doctor to obtain medical clearance before proceeding with the test. If all questions are answered "No," then the subject may begin the physical test items.

Scoring. Scores for each test item are compared to a gender appropriate table. The examinee is to find his/her age category along the left-hand column of the table, go across that line to the category that includes his/her score, then refer to the top of the column to find his/her evaluation rating.

Comments. The complete Post 50 Test includes seven test items. There are two stamina measures—a 2-Minute Walk-on-the-Spot test and a 400-Meter Brisk Walk. There are also two strength measures— Curl-ups and Modified Push-ups. And, there are three suppleness items—Shoulder Flexion, Lateral Flexion, and a Sit-and-Reach test. Although the entire test is well done and interesting, only two of the seven items will be presented here.

At the end of the test battery, the authors give suggestions about how to get started on an exercise program, explain the concepts of frequency, intensity, and time, and give addresses for agencies that give exercise advice.

---

*Bell, R.D., Collis, M.L., and Hoshizaki, T.B.: The Post 50 Physical Performance Test: A Self-Test for Those Over 50. Draft, 1984. Used by permission of R.D. Bell.

Table 6–24. Scores for 400-Meter Brisk Walk for Males and Females*

Age	Needs Improvement	Below Average	Good	Excellent
		MALES—Time		
50–64	5:09+	5:08–4:12	4:11–3:46	3:45–0
65–74	5:09+	5:08–4:15	4:14–3:46	3:45–0
75–84	5:40+	5:39–4:31	4:30–3:55	3:54–0
85+	8:50+	8:49–5:55	5:54–4:48	4:47–0
		FEMALES—Time		
50–64	5:06+	5:05–4:15	4:14–3:56	3:55–0
65–74	5:43+	5:42–4:37	4:36–4:17	4:16–0
75–84	7:01+	7:00–5:30	5:29–4:57	4:56–0
85+	8:51+	8:50–6:20	6:19–5:10	5:09–0

*From Bell, R.D., Collis, M.L., and Hoshizaki, T.B.: The Post 50 Physical Performance Test: A Self-Test for Those Over 50. Draft, 1984. Adapted by permission of R.D. Bell.

Table 6–25.   Scores for Sit-and-Reach for Males and Females*

Age	Needs Improvement		Below Average		Good		Excellent	
	Male	Female	Male	Female	Male	Female	Male	Female
50–64	B	B	C	C	D	D	E	E
65–74	B	B	C	C	D	D	E	E
75–84	A	B	B	C	C	D	D	E
85+	A	A	B	B	C	C	D	D

*From Bell, R.D., Collis, M.L., and Hoshizaki, T.B.: The Post 50 Physical Performance Test: A Self-Test for Those Over 50. Draft, 1984. Adapted by permission of R.D. Bell.

Item 1: 400-Meter Brisk Walk

Purpose. To measure stamina (cardiovascular health).

Facilities and Equipment. A 400-meter or 440-yard track is ideal. Also needed is a stopwatch or clock with a second sweep hand.

Test Procedures. Using a good arm swing, you are to walk briskly for a distance of 400 meters or 440 yards. Record the time to complete the distance in minutes and seconds.

Scoring. Refer to Table 6–24 to interpret your score.

Item 2: Sit-and-Reach

Purpose. To assess suppleness (of the lower back and hamstring muscles.).

Facilities and Equipment. None.

Test Procedures. Sit on the floor with your knees extended and your feet against the base of a wall. Keeping your feet together and legs as straight as comfortably possible, slide your hands down your legs as far as possible. Note the position of the ends of your fingers in relation to your feet, then return to the starting position.

Scoring. Refer to Table 6–25 to interpret your score. Let A = the fingertips on the top half of shin, B = fingertips on bottom half of shin, C = fingertips beyond the ankle, D = fingertips at toes, and E = fingertips past toes.

REFERENCES

1. American Alliance for Health, Physical Education, and Recreation: Youth Fitness Test Manual. Reston, VA, AAHPER, 1976.
2. American Alliance for Health, Physical Education, Recreation, and Dance: Health related physical fitness: Test manual. Reston, VA, AAHPERD, 1980.
3. American Alliance for Health, Physical Education, Recreation, and Dance: Physical Best: The American Alliance Physical Fitness Education & Assessment Program. Reston, VA, AAHPERD, 1988.
4. American College of Sports Medicine: Guidelines for exercise testing and prescription. 3rd Ed. Philadelphia, Lea & Febiger, 1986.
5. Balke, B.: A simple field test for the assessment of physical fitness. CARI Report 63-18. Oklahoma City, OK, Civil Aeromedical Research Institute, Federal Aviation Agency, April 1963.
6. Bell, R.D., Collis, M.L., and Hoshizaki, T.B.: The Post 50 Physical Performance Test: A Self-Test for Those Over 50. Draft, 1984.
7. Bruininks, R.H.: Bruininks-Oseretsky Test of Motor Proficiency: Short Form. Circle Pines, MN, American Guidance Service, Inc., 1978.
8. Casperson, C., Powell, K., and Christenson, G.: Physical activity, exercise, and physical fitness: Definitions and distinctions of health-related research. Public Health Reports, *100*:126–131, 1985.

9. Cooper, K.H.: A means of assessing maximal oxygen intake. Journal of the American Medical Association, *203*:201–204, 1968.

10. Cooper, K.H.: The Aerobics Program for Total Well-Being. New York, Bantam Books, published by arrangement with M. Evans & Co., Inc., 1982.

11. Fox, K.R., and Biddle, S.J.H.: The use of fitness tests: Educational and psychological considerations. Journal of Physical Education, Recreation, and Dance, *59*(2):47–53, 1988.

12. Gabbard, C., Gibbons, E., and Elledge, J.: Effects of grip and forearm position on flexed-arm hang performance. Research Quarterly for Exercise and Sport, *54*(2):198–199, 1983.

13. Goldberger, M., and Moyer, S.: A schema for classifying educational objectives in the psychomotor domain. Quest, *34*(2):134–142, 1982.

14. Golding, L.A., Myers, C.R., and Sinning, W.E. (Eds.): The Y's Way to Physical Fitness. Champaign, IL, Human Kinetics Publisher, 1982.

15. Harrow, A.: A Taxonomy of the Psychomotor Domain. New York, David McKay, 1972.

16. Hawkins, J.D.: An analysis of selected skinfold measuring instruments. Journal of Physical Education, Recreation, and Dance, *54*(1):25–27, 1983.

17. Jackson, A.S., and Coleman, A.E.: Validation of distance run tests for elementary school children. Research Quarterly, *47*(1):86–95, 1976.

18. Jackson, A.S., and Pollock, M.L.: Practical assessment of body composition. The Physician and Sportsmedicine, *13*(5):76–90, 1985.

19. Jewett, A., Jones, L.S., Luneke, S., and Robinson, S.: Educational change through a taxonomy for writing physical education objectives. Quest, *15*(1):32–38, 1971.

20. Katch, F.I., and McArdle, W.D.: Nutrition, Weight Control, and Exercise. 3rd Ed. Philadelphia, Lea & Febiger, 1988.

21. Mosston, M.: Developmental Movement. Columbus, OH, Charles E. Merrill, 1965.

22. Pate, R.R.: Norms for College Students: Health Related Physical Fitness Test. Reston, VA, AAHPERD, 1985.

23. Pate, R.R., Ross, J.G., Baumgartner, T.A., and Sparks, R.E.: The modified pull-up test. Journal of Physical Education, Recreation, and Dance, *58*(9):71–73, 1987.

24. Safrit, M.J.: Evaluation in Physical Education. 2nd Ed. Englewood Cliffs, NJ, Prentice-Hall, 1981.

25. Safrit, M.J.: Introduction to Measurement in Physical Education and Exercise Science. St. Louis, Times Mirror/Mosby College Publishing, 1986.

26. Seefeldt, V., and Vogel, P.: Children and fitness: A public health perspective. Research Quarterly for Exercise and Sport, *58*(4):331–333, 1987, p. 332.

27. Simpson, E.J.: The classification of educational objectives, psychomotor domain. Illinois Teacher of Home Economics, 1966, pp. 110–114.

28. Smith, J.F., and Miller, C.V.: The effect of head position on sit and reach performance. Research Quarterly for Exercise and Sport, *56*(1):84–85, 1985.

29. Texas Governor's Commission on Physical Fitness: FYT: Fit Youth Today. Austin, Texas Health and Fitness Foundation, 1988.

7

Tests of Specific Sports Skills

7

Tests of Specific Sports Skills*

The skill tests and rating scales included in this chapter approach skill assessment in a variety of ways and are suited to a range of skill levels for either or both sexes. Even though they were developed with subjects of a certain age, gender, and skill level, many tests are suitable for wider applications either with or without modifications.

Often a test is reported in the exact language of its author and is adapted only to fit the general organizational format of this chapter. Usually a physical educator or coach has a use in mind when searching for an appropriate test, so the stated uses are not meant to be restrictive, but merely suggestive.

Norms have been omitted purposely. Often they are outdated, reflect a limited sample, and are inappropriate for interpretations for other than the group used to construct them. Physical educators and coaches should develop norms to fit their own students and players. Except in cases when a national comparison is desired, such as for the AAHPERD fitness test, norms should be established locally.

Each test included in this chapter has been described in sufficient detail to be administered without having to refer to additional sources. The 1978 publication by Collins and Hodges[10] makes a significant contribution by describing in detail many skills tests and by listing a thorough bibliography of tests in each sport.

AEROBICS

Jeffreys Rhythmic Aerobics Rating Scale[28]†

Purpose. To measure knowledge and ability in rhythmic aerobics, especially in grading large classes (30 or more).

Development. No reliability or validity is given. The agreement between the two judges performing the rating was reported to be high. The components to be measured are the (1) quality of movement and body alignment area, (2) the effectiveness of warm-up and stretching exercises, (3) the cardiovascular conditioning phase, and (4) the cool down phase.

Level and Gender. Beginning rhythmic aerobics classes at the college level.

---

*This chapter has been updated and revised by Dr. Andrea Farrow, Professor, Division of Behavioral Sciences, Delta State University, Cleveland, Mississippi.

†From Jeffreys, A.: A rating scale for rhythmic aerobics. Unpublished Paper, University of North Carolina at Greensboro, 1987. Used by permission of the author.

Uses. This scale can be used to measure the knowledge and ability of students in beginning rhythmic aerobics classes or to serve as a content guide for a rhythmic aerobics routine.

Directions. This scale is a group measure. Groups of from 3 to 5 students design a routine that they feel will combine all the elements of the rating scale. They perform this routine before two instructors or judges.

Scoring. Group members will receive one grade based on the combined averaged ratings of the two judges. The scale has 14 elements. Each has the same value and is rated from 1 to 3. There are a possible 42 points.

1—poor	Group shows lack of organization and preference for this activity. Group is not at ease.
2—average	Group is at ease, working together, and sharing the experience by contributing and communicating. All members contribute to the performance.
3—good	Group is very enthusiastic. Bouts are unique, innovative, and creative.

I. Movement and Body Alignment Cues

_____ 1. Move with the music, proper tempo and rhythm.

_____ 2. Correct body positions to reduce compromising positions and injuries.

_____ 3. Transitions and progressions noted by adding/combining several arm works to the same leg movement. Blending of movements smooth, permitting participants to follow with little difficulty.

_____ 4. Eye contact along with verbal, body, and directional cues, singly or in combination.

II. Warm-up and/or Stretches

_____ 5. Static stretches held 10 to 30 seconds. Stretching several muscle groups without compromising body alignment.

_____ 6. Standing and floor stretches appropriate (correct sequencing).

_____ 7. Duration adequate, includes most major muscle groups.

III. Cardiovascular Phase

_____ 8. Interval training combining low, nonimpact aerobics with recovery periods.

_____ 9. Duration and intensity sufficient to reach medium and submaximal rates, gradually increasing, intensifying and decreasing. Follows the aerobic curve.

_____ 10. Heart rate monitored 2 to 3 times with the last count being after a recovery period of 3 minutes.

_____ 11. Bout dense enough to allow most to reach and sustain their targeted heart rate for 15 to 20 minutes without overtaxing and causing strain.

IV. Cool Down Phase

_____ 12. Static stretching of the legs and achilles tendons sufficient.
_____ 13. Relaxation, stretching, walking movements included. Supportive, encouraging and informative.
_____ 14. Time for questions and answers, sharing before departure.

Comments: This scale can be used with smaller groups. It can be used for either men or women, and although it was developed for college classes, it can be used for any age group for whom rhythmic aerobics is appropriate. In many situations using two judges would not be practical, so considering the objectivity reported, it would seem adequate to have the instructor rate the groups. As this scale is set up, each element is of equal value. The user may want to adapt the elements or their values to fit the situation in which it is to be used or the philosophy of the instructor. For some situations it may be appropriate to use the results of this scale along with the results of a routine constructed by the instructor.

ARCHERY

The rounds used in competitive archery are generally too difficult for beginners because the distances from the targets are too great. Consequently, too many students fail to make even minimal scores.

The two factors to be considered in constructing an archery test are the number of trials (arrows shot) needed to assure reliability and the distance appropriate for the group being tested. Ishee and Shannon[27] found that a practice end helps in achieving more reliable scores. One is therefore recommended before testing.

McKenzie-Shifflett Archery Test[32]*

Purpose. To measure the skill level of all students enrolled in beginning classes on the same scale by adjusting the shooting distances.

Development. When 54 male and 54 female beginning archery students all shot from 30 yards, there was a significant difference between the scores of men and women. When 35 male and 13 female beginning archery students shot from varying distances based on bow weight and draw length, no significant differences existed between the genders. The authors concluded that score is a function of strength rather than gender. Reliability was calculated using the best three scores of each student. Reliability coefficients were, respectively, .90, .93, and .93 for females, males, and females and males combined. The test was reviewed by archery experts attending the world archery center to establish logical validity.

Level and Gender. College students enrolled in beginning level coeducational classes.

Uses. This test could be used not only for grading purposes, but also for practice, intramural competition and pretesting and posttesting to show improvement.

Directions. All students shoot at an 80cm F.I.T.A. target face. In the study

_____

*From McKenzie, R. and Shifflett, B.: Skill evaluation in a coeducational beginning archery class. Unpublished Paper, San Diego State University, 1986. Used by permission of the authors.

each student shot one round of 10 arrows on each day during the last third of the course from his or her designated distance. The distance from which students shoot is based on the bow weight (weight written on the bow) plus or minus two pounds for every inch their draw deviates from the 28-inch standard. For example, an archer pulling a 25-pound bow 24 inches would have a draw weight of 17 pounds. Since it is impractical to have everyone at a different distance, the weights are divided into ranges as follows:

Bow Weight	*Distance*
Under 20 lb.	25 yd.
20–23 lb.	30 yd.
24–29 lb.	35 yd.
30 lb. or more	40 yd.

Scoring. The average of the three best scores is taken. All students are graded on the same scale.

Comments. Some caution needs to be used in interpreting the results of this study because of the small number of women in the sample, 13. However, this seems to be a better method than having all students shoot from the same distance, since 7 of the 13 women qualified to shoot from the least distance, 25 yards, and about two thirds of the men shot from the two longest distances, 35 or 40 yards. Additional work is needed to determine the best distance for shooting for each bow weight/draw length. Also the appropriateness of using this method with younger students needs investigation. The authors suggest that when classes are being held indoors in limited space, the instructor might experiment with using different sized targets rather than different distances.

AAHPER Archery Test for Boys and Girls[4]*

Purpose. To help students evaluate their performances in the fundamental skills of archery and to provide an incentive for improvement.

Development. From 600 to 900 scores were used for each gender and for each age. The test was considered to have logical validity, since the test was nearly identical to the skill. The test-retest reliability was at least .70.

Level and Gender. Boys and girls aged 12 to 18 enrolled in beginning archery classes.

Uses. The results can be used for grading, practice, pretesting, and posttesting to indicate improvement, intramurals, and classification.

Directions. A standard 48-inch target is used. Each student shoots two ends of six arrows each from each distance for which he or she qualifies. Girls shoot from 10 and 20 yards and boys shoot from 10, 20, and 30 yards. Students are allowed to take four practice shots from each distance. Both ends from one distance are shot before the students proceed to a longer distance.

Scoring. Each arrow shot is scored according to standard scoring procedures. From the center outward, the scoring areas are 9, 7, 5, 3, and 1. Arrows touching two colors are given the higher score, and arrows hitting the target and falling to the ground count 7. The totals for each distance as well as the combined distances are computed. The maximum score for each distance is 108 points.

---

*From Skills Test Manual—Archery for Boys and Girls. Washington, D.C., AAHPER, 1967. Used by permission of the AAHPERD.

The maximum score for girls shooting the two distances is 216 and for boys shooting the three distances is 324.

Comments. National norms are available for this test. However, they should be used with caution because of their age. The equipment being used today could be considerably improved from that used when these norms were constructed. The distances for boys and girls are different because in the testing it was found that from 65% of girls aged 12 and 13 to 35% of girls aged 17 and 18 scored zero at the 30 yard distance. Consequently, this distance was dropped from the test for girls. These findings seem to agree with the McKenzie and Shifflett[32] study indicating that score is indeed a function of strength.

BADMINTON

French Short Serve Test[37]*

Purpose. To measure ability to serve accurately and low.

Development. A validity coefficient of .66 was reported using a criterion of tournament rankings. The test-retest reliability was .96.

Level and Gender. Players who have developed skill in the short serve.

Uses. This test may be used to increase awareness that the short serve must be low, as a self-testing device for motivation, and to indicate "touch."

Court Markings. Four concentric quarter circles are drawn on the right service court, as illustrated in Figure 7–1. The circular lines are 1½ inches wide and the width of them is included in the amount of each radius. The use of different colors for the circles makes scoring more objective. A rope is stretched 20 inches above the net and parallel to it.

Directions. The player stands in the regulation right court for serving and serves 20 times into the opposite right service court for the doubles game. The shuttlecock must go under the rope placed 20 inches above the net and parallel to it and must otherwise be a legal serve. The serves should be taken in groups of at least 5 and preferably 10 if there are a sufficient number of shuttlecocks.

Scoring. Score each serve by the numerical value of the area in which it first lands. Shuttlecocks that land on a line will score the higher value. Serves that fail to go between the rope and net, that are out of the bounds of the right service court for doubles, and that are not executed legally, will score zero. The final score is the total of the values made on 20 serves.

Comments. The reliability will not hold up for beginning players. A rating of the serve might be a better measure of serving skill for beginning players. This test is appropriate for intermediate and advanced players.

GSC Badminton Clear Test[11]†

Purpose. To measure the skill of beginning level players in hitting the deep clear shot.

Development. The test was given to 61 male and 65 female students enrolled in seven beginning badminton classes at Georgia Southern College. A badminton

---

*From Scott, M.G., Carpenter, A., French, E., and Kuhl, L.: Achievement examinations in badminton. Research Quarterly, *12*:242–253, May 1941. Used by permission of the AAHPER.

†From Cotten, D.J., Cobb, P.R., and Fleming, J.: Development and validation of a badminton clear test. Abstract of Research Paper 1987, AAHPERD National Convention and Exposition, Las Vegas, Nevada, April 13–17, 1987, p. 168. Used by permission of the authors and the AAHPERD.

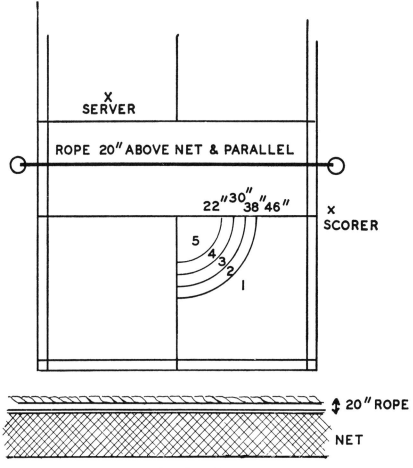

Fig. 7–1. Specifications for the Short Serve Test.

expert and the instructor for each class independently ranked each student on his or her ability to hit a deep clear. The validity of this test was .85 for both males and females using a combination of judge's and teacher's ratings as the criterion. Intraclass reliability for 10 trials was found to be .87 for males and .89 for females.

Level and Gender. College men and women enrolled in beginning level classes.

Uses. This test can be used to measure clearing ability, ability to use wrist action, and as part of a battery to measure skill in playing badminton.

Administrative Considerations. A player or instructor who can consistently serve a high deep long serve is essential for the administration of this test if every student is to have an equal chance at making his or her best score.

Court Markings. A badminton court is marked as shown in Figure 7–2. The scoring area is on the right side of the diagram and the receiving areas for men and women are shown on the left side of the diagram. Note that the area for women is two feet closer to the net than the area for men. A rope is stretched across the court at a height of 8 feet and a distance of 13½ feet from the net.

Directions. An adequate warm-up period should be provided on a nearby

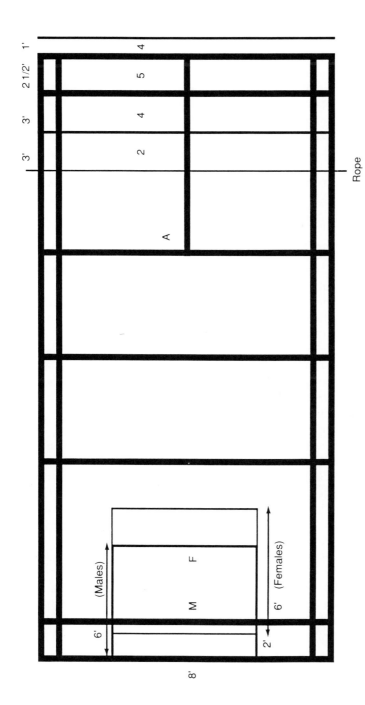

Fig. 7–2. Court markings for the GSC Badminton Clear Test.

court. The test administrator stands at point A on the court and serves to the subject standing in the appropriate receiving area. The administrator attempts to serve the shuttle to the midpoint of the appropriate receiving area. The subject does not have to play any poorly placed serve, but any swing is considered a trial. The test consists of ten trials.

Scoring. The zone in which the shuttle lands is recorded as the score. The value of the zones from the net, respectively, are 2, 4, 5, and 4. No points are awarded for any shuttle failing to clear the rope or land in the scoring zones. A shuttle landing on a line receives the higher point value. The score is the total points for the ten trials. Separate scoring scales for men and women should be developed.

Comments. This test has been shown to measure only clearing ability, so it should be used cautiously for any other purpose, such as measuring playing ability. However, this is not to say that further study might not show that it can be equated with playing ability.

Bobrich Badminton Observational Rating Scale[8]*

Purpose. To measure development in the basic skills as a student participates in a regulation doubles badminton game.

Development. This scale was adapted from the original Bobrich scale, which included several additional skills as well as strategies and knowledges. The parts of the scale presented here are the ones most frequently taught in beginning badminton classes. The tool was developed using 2 classes of 67 girls enrolled in a high school beginning badminton course. The reliability was estimated on a test-retest basis using 3 qualified judges. Both Pearson r and analysis of variance techniques were used to determine the reliability of the testing tool. The coefficients ranged from .77 to .87.

Level and Gender. High school girls.

Uses. The rating scale can be used for grading purposes, for classification into tournament groupings, and for measuring individual achievement. Parts of it can be used to focus on specific aspects of the game. It can also be used by players to make peer evaluations.

Administrative Considerations. A trained student leader and a qualified physical education teacher can administer the test. A 20-minute time period is needed for 1 evaluator to rate 4 students engaged in a doubles match.

Directions. Below are listed criteria to be used when evaluating individuals as they participate in doubles badminton games. A score should be based on consistency in form and execution, rather than the frequency of items or skills. There must be a score for each item or skill for each participant being rated. The rating scale is worded for right-handed players.

Scoring. Scores can range from 0 to 21.

Point values for each item are:

0   Skill not observed or not attempted
1   Fair ability
2   Good ability
3   Excellent ability

---

*From Bobrich, M.N.: Reliability of an Evaluative Tool Used to Measure Badminton Skill. Master's Thesis, George Williams College, 1972. Used by permission of the author.

Long Serve

1 point— If the shuttle height is medium or low; if there is no direction of the shuttle to the opposite court; or if the shuttle falls out of bounds or close to the short service line of the opposite court.

2 points—If the shuttle is hit to travel high and lands in the middle of the opposite service court.

3 points—If the shuttle is hit to travel high and deep to land on the back service line or is directed to land in either corner of the opposite service court.

Long Serve Return

1 point— If the attempt made shows slow footwork in a backward direction causing the body to become off balance and results in a poor return or a failure of the shuttle to cross the net.

2 points—If quick footwork is used in moving backward; some body balance is observed as the shuttle is successfully returned over the net.

3 points—If the receiver uses quick footwork in moving backward to get behind the shuttle; body balance is in good control; and the shuttle is returned by any overhead stroke, preferably the smash.

Short Serve

1 point— If the shuttle is hit more than 3 feet over the top of the net, lands more than 4 feet beyond the front service line, or lands out of bounds.

2 points—If the shuttle is hit to cross the net within 1 to 3 feet over the top of the net and lands within 4 feet of the front service line.

3 points—If the shuttle is hit to skim the top of the net, loses height immediately, and lands along the front service line or near the corner of the opposite service court.

Short Serve Return

1 point— If the shuttle is returned out of bounds, or in the attempt to return the shuttle the footwork is slow, causing the body to become off balance, resulting in a poor return.

2 points—If the receiver moves forward to meet the shuttle and successfully returns it into the opponent's court.

3 points—If the receiver moves forward to meet the shuttle and makes an effective return.

Clear

1 point— If the body is off balance or the shuttle is improperly contacted, causing a poor return or a fault.

2 points—If the body is aligned with the shuttle so contact is made overhead and shuttle flight is high so that it lands in the opponent's mid-court.

3 points—If the body is aligned so that contact with the shuttle is made over-head with a full swing, and the return is high into the opponent's backcourt landing just inside the baseline.

Smash

1 point— If the body is off balance, no wrist snap is present, or the shuttle is hit over the net as in any return with no aim or direction present.

2 points—If the body is aligned with the oncoming shuttle; or contact is made but the wrist snap is weak and the shuttle is moved downward without the necessary speed for a successful stroke.

3 points—If the body is aligned with the oncoming shuttle so that contact is made high and on top of the shuttle; there is a definite wrist snap at point of contact so that shuttle is forced downward with great speed aimed at opponent's body, his left side, to baseline, or to sidelines.

Drop

1 point— If the body is not aligned with the shuttle for proper execution of the stroke, a forward drive is used instead of an overhead stroke, or the shuttle does not fall in bounds.

2 points—If the body is aligned with the shuttle for contact overhead but is hit behind the short-service line with either too much arc or too much speed.

3 points—If the body is aligned with the shuttle so contact is made in front of the body, the shuttle is "patted" down so it falls in a steep angle just over the net in front of the short-service line, and the swing is overhead but slow so as to deceive the opponent.

BASKETBALL

AAHPERD Basketball Test for Boys and Girls[25]*

Purpose. To measure the four essential skills in basketball in two class periods to an average size class.

Development. Six test items were administered in developing this battery. The four presented here are the items chosen for the final AAHPERD basketball battery. It was felt that these covered the essential skills and could be administered to an average-sized class in two class periods.

Reliability and validity coefficients for each test item for each gender and academic level were established by the administration of the test battery in the school setting at the conclusion of a basketball unit. Fifty students per gender per grade level were administered multiple trials of the test items. Intraclass stability reliability estimates ranged from .82 to .98. Concurrent validity coefficients were determined by correlating subjective ratings for both the specific skill and game performance with each test. The minimum acceptable coefficient for correlation between the test and the specific skill was set at .70 but was not met for both genders across all grade levels; it ranged from .37 to .91. Those

*From Skills Test Manual—Basketball for Boys and Girls. Washington, D.C., AAHPERD, 1984. Used by permission of the AAHPERD.

falling below the accepted criterion were for males and females at the college level and for females at the elementary and junior high level. These low coefficients could have been affected by a lack of agreement among the raters, and the college age coefficients may also have been affected by the homogeneity of the sample due to the testing of elective physical education classes. Validity estimates for the entire test battery ranged from .65 to .95. The degree of agreement among raters was much greater for overall performance than for specific skills. Degree of agreement of raters for overall game performance ranged from .62 to .90. Construct validity estimates were determined by identifying test performance differences between groups of varsity and non-varsity players. The minimum accepted significance level of .01 was met in all cases.

Level and Gender. Boys and girls ages 10 through college.

Uses. The test battery can be used for measuring playing ability for the purposes of grading, grouping, practice, diagnosis, classification, and showing improvement. It could aid in team selections. Individual items can be used for the same purposes relative to that specific skill.

Scoring. In the Skill Test Manual norms are given for males and females separately for ages 10 through college. Both percentile and T-score scales are listed. The scales may be used if they are appropriate, or local norms may be developed. A total score for playing ability can be found by converting the raw scores for each of the four tests to T-scores and then totaling these T-scores.

Item 1: Speed Spot Shooting

Purpose. To measure skill in rapidly shooting from specified positions and, to a certain extent, agility and ball handling.

Court Markings. Five floor markers 2 feet long and 1 inch wide are placed on the floor. For grades 5 and 6, the markers are 9 feet from the backboard, for grades 7, 8, and 9, 12 feet from the backboard, and for grades 10, 11, 12, and college, 15 feet from the backboard (Fig. 7–3). The distances for spots B, C, and D must be measured from the center of the backboard; those for spots A and E must be measured from the center of the basket.

Directions. There will be three trials of 60 seconds each. The first is a practice trial and the next two are recorded. The performer stands behind any marker designated for his or her age level. On the signal "Ready, Go!" the performer shoots, retrieves the ball, dribbles to, and shoots from another designated spot. One foot must be behind the marker during each attempt. A maximum of four lay-up shots may be attempted during each trial, but no two may be in succession. The performer must attempt at least one shot from each designated spot. The player continues until "Stop!" is called.

Scoring. Two points are awarded for each shot made. One point is awarded for an unsuccessful shot that hits the rim from above either initially or after rebounding from the backboard. If a ball handling infraction (traveling, double dribbling) occurs, the shot following the violation will be scored as zero points. If two lay-ups in succession occur, the second lay-up shall be scored as zero. If more than four lay-ups are attempted, the excessive ones will be scored as zeros. If the performer does not shoot from all the designated spots, the trial will be repeated. The final score is the total of the two trials.

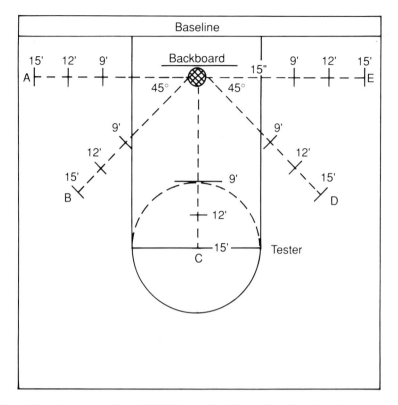

Fig. 7–3. Markings for the AAHPERD Basketball Speed Spot Shooting Test.

Item 2: Passing

Purpose. To measure skill in passing and recovering the ball accurately while moving.

Court Markings. Six squares of 2 feet each are marked on the wall so that the base of the square is either 3 or 5 feet from the floor. All adjacent squares are 2 feet apart. A restraining line is marked on the floor at a distance of 8 feet from the wall and parallel to it (Fig. 7–4).

Directions. A total of three trials of 30 seconds each. The first is a practice trial and the last two are recorded. The performer with a ball stands behind the restraining line and faces the target on the far left. On the signal "Ready, Go!" the performer chest passes to the first target, recovers the rebound while moving to a location behind the second target and behind the restraining line, and chest passes at target B. This pattern continues until target F is reached, where two chest passes are executed, following which the performer then passes to E, repeating the sequence by moving to the left.

Scoring. Each pass that hits the target or the boundary lines of the target counts two points. Each pass hitting the intervening spaces on the wall counts one point. If a pass is made from a point in front of the restraining line, no points are awarded for the pass. If passes are made at targets B, C, D, or E twice in succession, no points are scored for the second pass. If the pass is not a chest pass, no points are awarded for the pass. The final score is the total of the two trials.

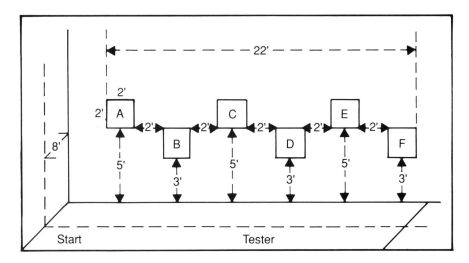

Fig. 7–4.   Markings for the AAHPERD Basketball Passing Test.

Item 3: Control Dribble

Purpose. To measure skill in handling the ball while the body is moving.

Court Set-up. An obstacle course marked by six cones is set up in the free throw lane as shown in Figure 7–5.

Directions. Three timed trials are given. The first is a practice trial, and the last two are scored for the record. With the ball, the performer starts on his or her nondominant hand side of cone A. On the signal, "Ready, Go!" the performer dribbles with the nondominant hand to the nondominant hand side of cone B. The performer will then proceed to follow the course using the preferred hand, changing hands as deemed appropriate until the finish line is crossed by both feet. If there is a ball handling infraction (traveling, double dribble), the performer or the ball remains outside the cone, or the performer fails to begin at the point in the course where control was lost, the trial is stopped, the performer returns to the start, and the trial timing begins again.

Scoring. The score for each trial is the elapsed time required to legally complete the course. Scores are recorded to the nearest tenth of a second for each trial, and the final score is the sum of the two trials.

Item 4: Defensive Movement

Purpose. To measure performance of basic defensive movement.

Court Markings. The test perimeters are marked by the free throw line, the boundary line behind the basket, and the rebound lane lines, which are marked into sections by a square and two lines. Only the middle line (rebound lane marker) is a target point for this test. Additional spots outside the four corners of the area should be marked with tape at points A, B, D, and E (Fig. 7–6).

Directions. There are three trials to the test. The first is a practice trial, and the last two are scored for the record. The performer starts at A facing away from the basket. On the signal, "Ready, Go!" the performer slides to the left without crossing feet and continues to marker B, touches the floor outside the lane with the left hand, executes a dropstep (Fig. 7–7), slides to point C, and

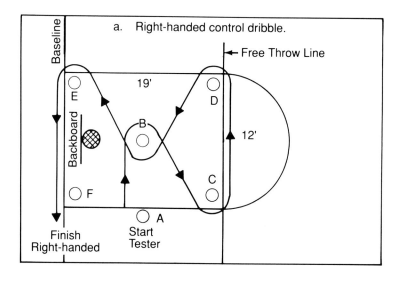

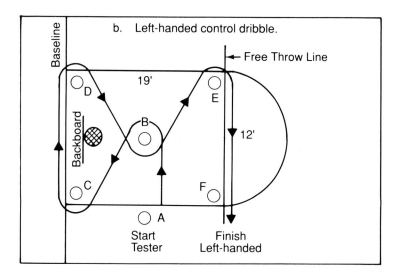

Fig. 7–5. Set-up for AAHPERD Basketball Control Dribble Test.

touches the floor outside the lane with the right hand. The performer continues the course as diagrammed. Completion of the course occurs when both feet have crossed the finish line. If the performer crosses his or her feet during the slide or turns and runs, or fails to touch the floor outside the lane with the hand, or executes the dropstep before the hand touches the floor, the trial is stopped, the performer returns to the start, and the trial timing begins again.

Scoring. The score for each trial is the elapsed time required to legally complete the course. Scores are recorded to the nearest tenth of a second for each trial, and the score is the sum of the two trials.

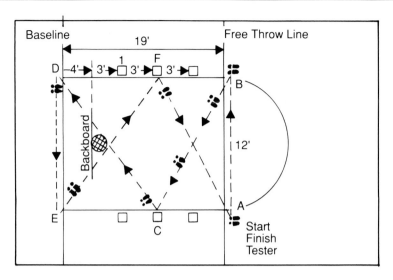

Fig. 7–6. Court markings for AAHPERD Basketball Defensive Movement Test.

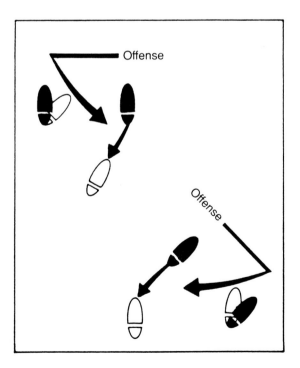

Fig. 7–7. Footwork pattern for the Dropstep.

Boetel Basketball Rating Scale[3]*

Purpose. To evaluate the physical performance of female basketball players in a game situation.

Development. A 96-item rating scale was designed, which purportedly represented seven categories of basketball performance: shooting ability and offensive moves, defensive moves and tactics, ball handling, rebounding, speed and quickness, body control and balance, and general floor play. These categories were determined by investigation into the literature and interviews with basketball coaches and players and physical education teachers. The scale was used to evaluate 38 interscholastic and intercollegiate female basketball players. Means and standard deviations were calculated for each of the 96 items, and a correlation matrix for each category was formed. From this matrix, each of the seven categories was factor analyzed independently of the remaining six categories. Based on the factor structure after rotation, an abbreviated rating scale was developed. The original seven categories were retained and 17 items were developed and selected to represent the original 96. This scale was used to evaluate 34 high school girls playing in a state "B" tournament. The interjudge reliability using Kendall's Coefficient of Concordance was .86, significant at the .01 level. The degree of relationship between the total scores of players on the scale and a subjective ranking of the players was .65, significant at the .01 level.

Level and Gender. High school females engaged in competitive basketball.

Uses. This scale can be used to evaluate players engaged in competitive basketball and to aid in selecting players for competition. It might also be helpful in diagnosing a player's weaknesses.

Directions. Raters should judge each of the 17 items on the scale according to the following key:

HA *Highly Agree* the statement is descriptive of the player.
A *Slightly Agree* the statement is descriptive of the player.
NN *Neither Disagree nor Agree* the statement is descriptive of the player.
D *Slightly Disagree* the statement is descriptive of the player.
HD *Highly Disagree* the statement is descriptive of the player.

Judges should attempt to answer each item and choose only one response for each item. A check should be marked in the space that corresponds to the judge's response. An *N* in front of an item indicates a negative statement.

Shooting Ability and Offensive Moves

	HA	A	NN	D	HD
1. Player is accurate in shooting with the proper alignment of the body and shooting arm.					
2. When shooting, the player has a smooth balanced hand release and follow-through.					
3. The player gains an offensive advantage by using evasive moves (fakes, cuts, pivots, and dribbles).					
N4. The shooter takes shots when he/she is off balance and has *not* squared his/her body toward the basket.					

*From Boetel, N.A.: Factorial approach in the development of a basketball rating scale to evaluate players in a game situation. Dissertation, University of North Carolina Greensboro, 1976. Used by permission of the author.

5. Player uses a variety of shots.

6. The shooter can go both left and right to successfully get the shot started from the dribble.

Defensive Moves and Tactics

7. The player uses the appropriate defense stance to counteract the opponents' movements on offense.

8. The player works efficiently as part of the total defense team plan by being alert for possible interceptions and aiding teammates on defense.

9. The player blocks attempted shots by his/her opponents.

Ball Handling

10. The player executes the dribble with the head and shoulders up and keeps the ball from bouncing too high.

11. When dribbling the ball the player uses either hand to change directions and pace efficiently.

12. Passes are accurate and relative (lob, bounce, straight) to each situation.

Rebounding (Offensive and Defensive)

N13. When rebounding, the player consistently jumps over a positioned defender.

14. The player is consistent in acquiring the rebound.

Speed and Quickness

15. The player maintains his/her weight on the balls of the feet enabling quick movement.

Body Control and Balance

16. The player maintains body control and balance through the execution of proper footwork.

General Floor Play

17. The player is at the right place at the right time consistently.

Scoring. Values for the categories used on the scale are: HA = 5, A = 4, NN = 3, D = 2, and HD = 1, except on negative items which are scored by reversing the scale. The total number of points is the player's score.

Comments. Although this scale was developed for high school women, it could be used for men and for other age groups who are at a relatively beginning level of competitive play. It should be noted that each item on the scale is equal in value. Consequently, categories contribute different proportions to the total score. For example, Shooting Ability and Offensive Moves with 6 items contributes twice as heavily in the overall scoring as Defensive Moves and Tactics, which has only 3 items. The scoring could be adjusted to meet the philosophy and needs of the teacher or coach.

FIELD HOCKEY

Henry-Friedel Field Hockey Test[22]*

Purpose. To measure general field hockey skill.

Development. Henry's[22] test was tested on 31 college and high-school hockey players ranging in experience from 2 weeks to 6 years. The players were given the Strait Field Hockey Test[41] and Henry modification of the Friedel Field Hockey Test.[18]

Two judges rated the players on general abilities such as footwork, stickwork, and body control while they were performing 20 trials of the modified test and 6 trials of Strait's test. The agreement between the judges was reported with a coefficient of .97.

Using the results of the Strait Test, the validity coefficient was .75 for raw speed scores and .70 for speed and accuracy scores combined by T-scores. The ratings of the judges yielded coefficients of .89 for the raw speed scores and .83 for the speed and accuracy scores combined by T-scores. Test-retest and ANOVA were used to calculate the test reliability. For 10 trials, the mean speed scores were .81 and .77, respectively, and the total test scores were .71 and .67, respectively.

Level and Gender. College and high school hockey players of varying abilities.

Uses. The test can be used as a partial measure of field hockey playing ability. It can also be used for practice.

Field Markings. The area needed is 25 yards by 10 yards, with one 10-yard line marked off along the goal line, so that the goal area is in the middle of that line. See Figure 7–8 for field markings.

Administrative Considerations. Two trained individuals are needed to administer the test. A trained person rolls the balls to the students. He or she must be proficient enough to roll the ball so that it passes diagonally through the target, within a foot in either direction of both corners, and comes to a stop within 1 foot inside the sideline of the testing area.

Directions. The player stands behind the starting line, inside the goal cage, with hockey stick in hand, and ready to run. At the signal, "Ready, Go!" the clock is started as the player runs forward toward the target area. As the player crosses the 7-yard mark, the ball is rolled in from the 10-yard mark, either on the left or right side line. The player fields the ball on the run and within the 2-yard square target area, dribbles toward the person standing in the dodge square, and does a right dodge around her. As soon as the stationary person is dodged, she moves out of the testing area so that she will not obstruct the player on her return. The player continues dribbling up to the line, goes around the obstacle as if doing a circular tackle, and dribbles back downfield, moving within the 1½-yard lane. Before getting to the restraining line, but within the lane, the player drives the ball, aiming for the goal area. The clock is stopped as soon as the ball crosses the starting line, or the sideline if inaccurately driven, or when the ball comes to a stop within the testing area if it does not cross the starting line or a sideline.

A trial is discounted and repeated only if the ball is inaccurately rolled so that it does not pass through the target area.

---

*From Henry, M.E.: The Validation of a Test of Field Hockey Skill. Master's Thesis, Temple University, 1970. Used by permission of the author.

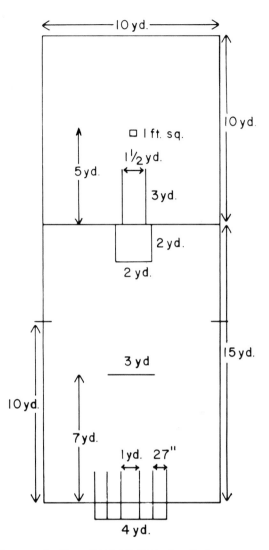

Fig. 7–8. Testing area for Henry-Friedel Field Hockey Test.

Each player has 10 scored trials, 5 of them with the ball rolled in from the left side and the other 5 with the ball rolled in from the right side. One practice trial from each side is given.

Scoring. The time for a trial is the elapsed time in seconds and tenths of seconds from the word "Go!" until the driven ball crosses the starting line or the sideline or comes to a stop within the testing area plus:

1. One second for an incorrect right dodge or for omitting the dodge
2. One second for 'sticks' on the drive
3. One second for using reverse sticks during the circular tackle
4. One second for the driven ball going over the sideline or not reaching the starting line
5. One second for not fielding an accurately rolled ball within the target area

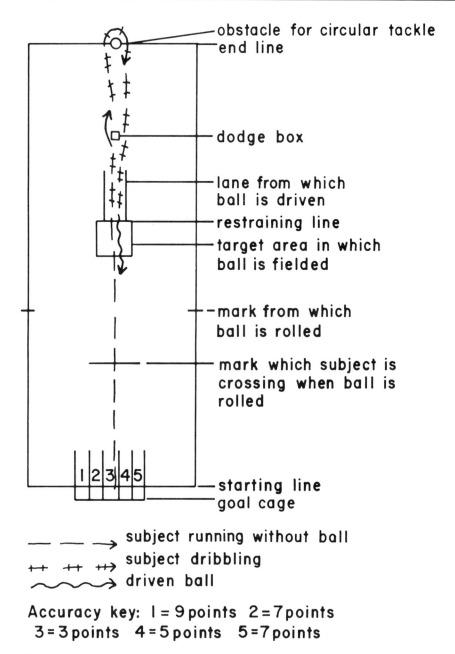

obstacle for circular tackle

end line

dodge box

lane from which ball is driven

restraining line

target area in which ball is fielded

mark from which ball is rolled

mark which subject is crossing when ball is rolled

1 2 3 4 5

starting line

goal cage

— — → subject running without ball

+ + ++ ++→ subject dribbling

∿∿∿∿→ driven ball

Accuracy key: 1 = 9 points 2 = 7 points
3 = 3 points 4 = 5 points 5 = 7 points

Fig. 7–9. Testing procedures for Henry-Friedel Field Hockey Test.

The lower score is the better score. The speed score for the test is the total of the times for all 10 trials.

The accuracy score on the trial is determined by the division on the starting line through which the ball passes. Areas 1 through 5, as shown in Figure 7–9, score respectively 9, 7, 3, 5, 7. Any area on the starting line outside of the goal cage scores 1. The score is 0 if the ball goes over the sideline or if it does not reach the starting line. The higher score is the better score. The accuracy score for the test is the total of the accuracy scores for all 10 trials.

Comments. This study was conducted in the off-season for hockey, and this is one explanation Henry makes for the borderline reliability coefficients. The speed scores proved to be as good an indicator of hockey skill as speed and accuracy scores combined. The accuracy score, however, adds a motivational factor. Henry purposely used players with wide range of ability in field hockey. The test is capable of reflecting a wide range of scores. Field hockey has been played by girls and women primarily, but the test would be suitable for students in coeducational classes and on coeducational teams.

Chapman Ball Control Test[8]*

Purpose. To measure ball control skills in field hockey, and more specifically, the subject's ability to combine quickness in wrist and hand movements needed to manipulate the stick with ability to control the force element when contacting the ball.

Development. The test was administered to 11 varsity and 12 junior varsity intercollegiate women field hockey players at Illinois State University. Their years of experience ranged from 1 to 7. To find the test reliability a one-way ANOVA was used on the scores of the three first day trials and from that an estimate of reliability of the sum of the trials was made using an intraclass correlation. Reliability equalled .89. Validity was established in two ways. First day trial scores were subjected to a *t* test and revealed a statistical difference between the means of scores of members on the two teams, significant at the .01 level. Before the test, players on each team were asked to rank the first three players on their team. The scores were treated by a Pearson Product-Moment technique. The correlations between the varsity team and test scores and the junior varsity and test scores were both .63.

The test was then given to 106 high school, college, and adult-aged women field hockey players who were trying out for the United States Olympic women's field hockey team. The players were rated subjectively by a panel of coaches appointed by the United States Field Hockey Association. Players were classified into Levels A, B, or C, according to their potential for selection as participants on the U.S. Team. The test accurately classified players 58.49% of the time. The weakest part of this evaluation was the differentiation between members of the B and A levels. This might have been affected by the fact that many B level players were experienced players, but were not selected for the A level because of their age.

Level and Gender. High school through adult aged women playing at the competitive level.

Uses. This test can be used to aid in the selection of competitive teams or to help in classifying advanced players. It could also be used for practice by players who wish to improve their ball handling skills.

Floor Markings. The target is placed on a gymnasium floor. The pattern, made of self-adhesive plastic, measures $9\frac{1}{2}$ inches in diameter, with an inner circle measuring $4\frac{1}{2}$ inches in diameter (Fig. 7–10). The larger circle is divided into

---

*From Chapman, N.L.: Chapman ball control test—field hockey. Research Quarterly for Exercise and Sport, 53(1):239–42, 1982. Used by permission of the author and the AAHPERD.

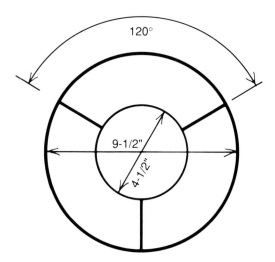

Fig. 7–10. Chapman Ball Control Test target measurements.

three equal segments of 120 degrees. Lines ⅛ inch in width originating in the center of the circle and extending to its outer edge are marked on the target to define the boundaries of the segments. The color of the ring-like pattern should contrast with the color of the floor.

Administrative Considerations. The movement is so quick that a test administrator and a timekeeper are needed for the test.

Directions. The test is a timed test in which the subject is required to send the ball into and out of the center circle by tapping it with the stick. Examples of basic scoring techniques are shown in Figure 7–11.

Scoring. A point is scored each time the ball is clearly tapped into or through the center circle, and each time it is tapped from the center, outside the larger circle, provided it is sent out through a segment other than that through which it entered. No point is awarded for a ball that is tapped while it is in the area between the two circles or with the rounded side of the stick. A total of the

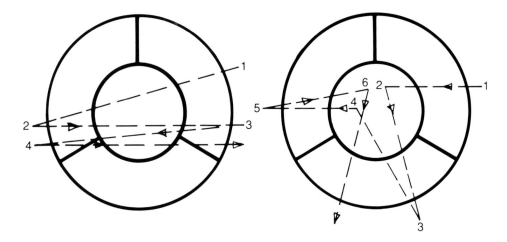

Fig. 7–11. Basic scoring techniques for the Chapman Ball Control Test.

points scored on three 15-second trials is the subject's score. A brief practice period and rest between each trial should be provided.

Comments. This test measures ball control for skilled players. It has not been tested on lesser skilled groups. It measures to some degree field hockey playing ability, but should not be used as the sole measure for determining playing ability. Although most field hockey has been played by women, there appears to be no reason why this test could not also be used with skilled male players.

GOLF

Rowlands Golf Skills Test Battery[36]*

Purpose. To measure the golf skills of experienced male golfers.

Development. Most skill tests in various sports have been developed for beginning level performers. In this battery, however, Rowlands[36] has used golfers with established handicaps. Even those with handicaps that would classify them as below average golfers are still beyond the beginning level of golfing performance. Ninety-two experienced male golfers with USGA handicaps and membership in the Glenview, Illinois Men's Golf Club served as subjects. Twenty-nine excellent golfers had handicaps between 0 and 12 strokes and usually scored 18 holes of golf between 70 and 80. The 43 average golfers had handicaps between 13 and 18 strokes and shot 18 holes of golf with a score in the 81 to 89 range. The 20 below average golfers had handicaps of 19 strokes and over and played 18 holes of golf scoring 90 or above.

The test results indicated that the battery mean score of each ability level subgroup was significantly better than the subgroup of the next lower level of skill. This gives credence to the construct validity of the battery.

Rowlands investigated four items. Only two are given here, the 5-iron test and the pitch test. Intercorrelations among items showed that the 5-iron and pitch tests had low intercorrelations and high correlations with the criterion measure, thus making the most significant contributions to the battery. The results of these tests items when correlated to the handicaps of the players were −.756 for the 5-iron test and −.627 for the pitch test.

Level and Gender. Adult male golfers with handicaps from 0 to over 19.

Uses. To evaluate 5-iron and pitch shot achievement and improvement of students in intermediate and advanced golf classes. To use as a partial basis for a unit grade. To study shot patterning.

Comments. The pitch test is appropriate for both men and women. Because of the strength factor involved in the 5-iron test, shorter distances would be used for women golfers. The concepts of the two tests, however, are equally appropriate for men and women golfers who are beyond the beginning levels of instruction.

Item 1: 5-Iron Test

Directions. The object of the test is to hit the ball as far and straight in the air as possible. Each student hits 14 shots to a target area.

Scoring. Each shot is scored on a distance minus direction deviation basis. For

*From Rowlands, D.J.: A Golf Skills Test Battery, Ph.D. Dissertation, University of Utah, 1974. Used by permission of the author.

example, a 5-iron shot that first hits at 140, but is 30 yards to the right, would be scored 110. The shot is measured at the point where it first hits the ground. Scores are measured to the nearest 5-yard marker. The sum of the 14 net scores for the shots is the test score. Any misses count as zero. Figure 7–12 shows the field markings.

Item 2: Short Pitch Test

Field Markings. Markings require 4 concentric circles located 65 feet from the student to the center of the circles. The radii of the circles are 3, 7.5, 15, and 22.5 feet from the center (Fig. 7–13).

Directions. Each student hits 14 shots to a target area.

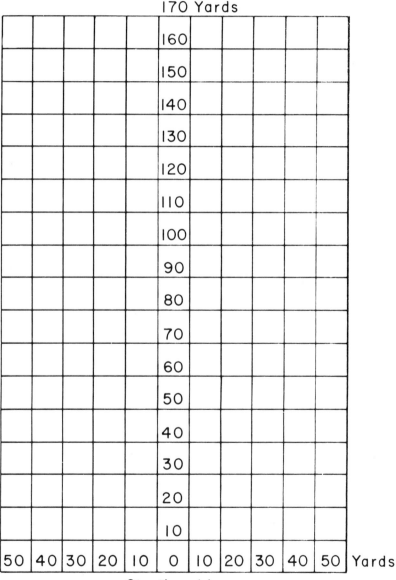

Fig. 7–12. The 5-Iron Test area.

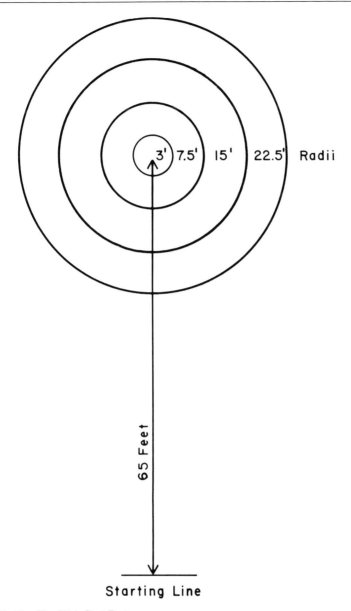

3' 7.5' 15' 22.5' Radii

65 Feet

Starting Line

Fig. 7–13. The Pitch Shot Test area.

Scoring. Shots are scored on a 4, 3, 2, and 1 basis, with 4 points for the inner circle. Missed shots or those not landing within any circle are given a zero value. Shots are measured at the point where they first hit the ground. A shot landing on a line is given the higher of the 2 values.

Shick-Berg Indoor Golf Skill Test[39]*

Purpose. To measure golf skills of junior high school boys.

Development. Subjects were 63 junior high school boys who had just completed a unit in golf. The reliability coefficient for 10 and 20 trials, respectively,

*From Shick, J. and Berg, N.G.: Indoor golf skill test for junior high school boys. Research Quarterly for Exercise and Sport, 54:1:75–78, 1983. Used by permission of the authors and the AAHPERD.

were .90 and .97. The scores from three rounds of 9 holes each were used as the criterion measure for establishing validity. The reliability coefficient for the play of these rounds was .91. Validity coefficients were calculated for the best of the three rounds and the total of the three rounds for both 10 and 20 trials on the test. They ranged from −.79 to −.84 (note the best score for the test was the highest and the best score for the rounds was the lowest).

Level and Gender. Junior high school boys.

Uses. This test can be used for grading, pretesting, and posttesting to show improvement, practice, and classification.

Course Layout. The target area is shown in Figure 7–14. The authors found that it was not necessary to draw the target on the floor. They marked the intersection of the scoring areas with small, colored flags. Two stations are recommended. If space is a problem, the target areas can be overlapped, using the same outside area (1, 1, 2, 4) for both targets.

Directions. The student stands on a mat and, using a 5-iron, hits the plastic ball off a driving mat positioned so that the front edge is 1 foot from the target line. The student is told to try to hit the ball as far and as straight as possible, aiming for the cone. The student takes 2 practice trials and then 20 consecutive test trials. Considering the reliability and validity coefficients found for 10 trials, teachers could give the shorter test if time or facilities are a problem.

Scoring. The score for each trial is the point value of the area where the ball first hits. Balls landing on a line are given the higher or highest value. Balls traveling beyond the target area but in line with it are awarded either a 4 or 6 as if those areas were extended. A topped ball which enters the scoring area is

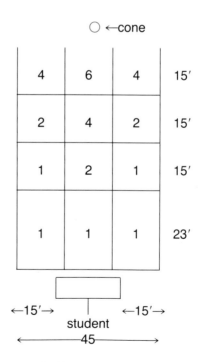

Fig. 7–14. Markings for Indoor Golf Test.

awarded 1 point. A whiff scores zero as does a ball landing outside the target. The final score is the sum of the 20 trials.

Comments. The primary reason this test is included in addition to the Rowlands[36] Test is that it is given indoors. Frequently, golf instructors find they need to give a test, but the weather is not cooperative. This test could be used for beginning groups other than junior high school boys. The distance of the mat from the target area may need adjustment if the players are considerably weaker or stronger than the test group. Neal,[34] as reported by Shick and Berg, found that when driving a plastic ball the golfer achieves a distance about 10% of that for a regulation ball. Using these data, the target could be adjusted to fit the group being tested. A strong aspect of the test is that both distance and deviation are taken into consideration in determining the point values of the target area.

GYMNASTICS AND TUMBLING

Ellenbrand Gymnastics Skills Test[14]*

Purpose. To measure gymnastics skills in the four official gymnastics events for women: balance beam, floor exercise, uneven parallel bars, and vaulting.

Development. Fifty-six college women were used in the development of this test. From a list of available skills for each event, students selected the one stunt of highest difficulty value which they could perform with the best execution score. Intraclass reliabilities ranged from .94 to .99 for the four items. Using judges' ratings, the validity coefficients ranged from .88 to .99. The agreement of the judges and examiners ranged from .97 to .99. Since all of these are high, they are not reported separately for each test item.

Intracorrelations between events ranged from .44 to .70. Since they were not extremely high, it was determined that the events were measuring different aspects of women's gymnastics.

Level and Gender. Beginners to advanced level college women. Since the student makes the choice of item within each event, the difficulty can be suited to the ability.

Uses. This battery can be used to classify students in gymnastics skills and to diagnose specific strengths and weaknesses within particular events.

Administrative Considerations. Familiarity with the test items and procedures will expedite the administration. To this end, a copy of the test in its entirety should be distributed to the students prior to the testing time. The students will need practice in selecting the proper skills to match their ability and, in some instances, to combine the selected skills into a gymnastics routine. For example, the balance beam has 5 test items, but several skills are listed within each item from which the student selects the one she wishes to perform.

Scoring. The score for each test item is the product of the difficulty value and the execution rating for the skill selected. The sum of all test items in each event is the score for that event and the final test score is the sum of all events or all test items.

*From Ellenbrand, D.A.: Gymnastics Skills Test for College Women. Master's Thesis, Indiana University, 1973. Used by permission of the author. Published in Review and Resource Manual. *Measurement and Evaluation in Physical Education,* by T.A. Baumgartner and A.S. Jackson. Boston, Houghton Mifflin Co., 1975. Used by permission of the publishers.

If a student is not capable of performing any skill listed for a test item, a difficulty value of zero is recorded.

Execution ratings for the selected skills must be recorded on the score sheet during or immediately following the performance. The ratings are based upon the proper execution of each skill and the characteristics for each basic movement pattern. The following is a general description of the rating scale:

3 points—Correct performance; proper mechanics; executed in good form. Performer shows balance, control, and amplitude in movements.

2 points—Average performance; errors evident in either mechanics or form; may show some lack of balance, control, or amplitude in movements.

1 point —Poor performance; errors in both mechanics and form. Performer shows little balance, control, or amplitude in movements.

0 points—Improper or no performance; incorrect mechanics or complete lack of form; no display of balance, control, or amplitude in movements.

There is no deduction for falls or repeated skills. However, a stunt that is excecuted with assistance is given a rating of zero.

Comments. The student's selection of skills to perfect, made several days before testing time, and the combination of difficulty and execution values contribute unique and positive factors to this package of gymnastics tests.

Section 1: Balance Beam Event

A Reuther board may be used to mount, and the beam may be approached from any direction. Positioning of arms is optional. However, arm movements are considered part of the form, and may add or detract from the execution rating. Select one skill from each test item.

TEST ITEM 1: MOUNTS

Difficulty	Skills
1.0	a. Front support mount
2.0	b. Single knee mount
3.0	c. Single leg squat on
3.0	d. Straddle on
4.0	e. Forward roll mount
5.0	f. Single leg step on (to stand)
6.0	g. Handstand mount

TEST ITEM 2: LOCOMOTOR SKILLS

Difficulty	Skills
.5	a. Slide forward or sideward
1.0	b. Walk forward
2.0	c. Plié walk (dip step) forward
3.0	d. Step-hop forward (skip step)
4.0	e. Walk backward
5.0	f. Run forward
6.0	g. Cross-step sideward

TEST ITEM 3: HEIGHTS

Difficulty	Skills
.5	a. Hop on 1 foot
1.0	b. Two-foot jump
2.0	c. Jump with change of legs
3.0	d. Hitch kick forward

3.0	e. Cat leap
4.0	f. Stride leap
4.0	g. Tuck or arch jump
5.0	h. Stag or split leap
6.0	i. Series of leaps or jumps

TEST ITEM 4: TURNS

Difficulty	Skills
.5	a. Half turn standing (2 feet)
1.0	b. Half turn squat
2.0	c. Half turn on 1 foot
3.0	d. Full turn on 2 feet (walking turn)
4.0	e. Full turn on 1 foot
5.0	f. Jump with half turn
5.0	g. One-and-one-half turn on 1 foot
6.0	h. Leap with half turn

TEST ITEM 5: TUMBLING SKILLS (ON BEAM)

Difficulty	Skills
.5	a. Back lying position
1.0	b. Roll backward to touch toes over head and return
2.0	c. Back shoulder roll
2.0	d. Forward shoulder roll
3.0	e. Forward head roll to back lying
4.0	f. Shoulder stand
4.0	g. Forward head roll to feet
4.0	h. Bridge position (push to a back arch position)
4.0	i. Cartwheel off or walkover off
4.5	j. Handstand one-quarter turn dismount
5.0	k. Cartwheel on
5.0	l. Back walkover on
5.5	m. Handstand forward roll
5.5	n. Front walkover on
5.5	o. Free forward roll
6.0	p. Series of cartwheels or walkovers
6.0	q. One-handed cartwheel or walkover
6.0	r. Handspring on (forward or backward)
7.0	s. Aerials on

Section II: Floor Exercise Event

Perform skills on the length of mats provided. A return trip may be used if necessary. Connecting skills may be added if needed for preparation of a selected skill (e.g., round-off to prepare for a back handspring). However, extra steps and runs should be avoided as they will detract from the execution rating.

TEST ITEM 6: TUMBLING SKILLS—ROLLS

Difficulty	Skills
.5	a. Foward roll to stand
.5	b. Backward roll to knees
1.0	c. Back roll to stand
2.0	d. Pike forward or backward roll
2.0	e. Straddle roll (forward or backward)
3.0	f. Dive forward roll (pike)
4.0	g. Handstand forward roll
4.0	h. Back roll to headstand
4.5	i. Back extension
5.0	j. Dive forward roll (layout)
6.0	k. Back tuck somersault (aerial)
6.5	l. Back pike somersault

6.5	m. Forward tuck somersault
7.0	n. Back layout somersault
8.0	o. Somersault with a twist

TEST ITEM 7: TUMBLING SKILLS—SPRINGS

Difficulty	*Skills*
1.0	a. Handstand snap-down
2.0	b. Round-off
2.5	c. Neck spring (kip)
3.0	d. Headspring
3.5	e. Front handspring to squat
4.0	f. Front handspring arch to stand
4.5	g. Front handspring walk-out
5.0	h. Back handspring
5.0	i. Front handspring on 1 hand or with a change of legs
5.5	j. Series of front handsprings
6.0	k. Series of back handsprings
6.5	l. Back handspring to kip (cradle)
6.5	m. Back handspring with twist

TEST ITEM 8: ACROBATIC SKILLS

Difficulty	*Skills*
1.0	a. Mule kick (three-quarter handstand)
1.0	b. Bridge (back arch position)
2.0	c. Handstand
2.0	d. Cartwheel
2.5	e. Backbend from standing
3.0	f. Front limber
3.0	g. One-handed cartwheel
4.0	h. Walkovers (forward and backward)
4.0	i. Dive cartwheel
4.0	j. Tinsica
4.5	k. Dive walkover
5.0	l. Handstand with half turn or straddle-down to a sit
5.0	m. One-handed walkovers
6.0	n. Butterfly (side aerial)
7.0	o. Aerial cartwheel or walkover

TEST ITEM 9: DANCE SKILLS

Difficulty	*Skills*
1.0	a. Half turn (1 foot), run, leap
2.0	b. Half turn, step, hitch kick forward, step, leap
3.0	c. Half turn, slide, tour jeté, hitch kick
4.0	d. Full turn (1 foot), step, leap, step, leap
5.0	e. Full turn, tour jeté, cabriole (beat kick forward)
6.0	f. One-and-one-half turn, step, leap, step, leap with a change of legs

Section III: Uneven Parallel Bars Event

Connecting stunts may be added as preparation for selected skills (e.g., back hip circle as preparation for eagle catch). Dismounting between items is allowed, but is not necessary.

TEST ITEM 10: KIPS

Difficulty	*Skills*
1.0	a. Single knee swing-up
2.0	b. Double leg stem rise to high bar
3.0	c. Single leg stem rise to high bar
4.0	d. Kip between bars from sit on low bar
4.5	e. Glide kip with single leg shoot-through

5.0	f. Glide kip
5.5	g. Glide, kip, regrasp high bar
5.5	h. Drop, glide kip
6.0	i. Kip from long hang
6.5	j. Rear or reverse kip

TEST ITEM 11: CASTS

Difficulty	Skills
.5	a. Cast rearward off low bar to stand
1.0	b. Cast and return to bar
2.0	c. Cast to squat (1 hand on low bar, 1 hand on high bar)
3.0	d. Cast, single leg shoot-through
4.0	e. Cast to long hand (from high bar)
4.5	f. Cast to squat, stoop, or straddle stand on either bar
5.0	g. Cast, half-turn to catch high bar
5.0	h. Eagle catch
5.5	i. From front support on high bar facing low bar, cast to handstand on low bar
6.0	j. Cast, full turn to regrasp either bar

TEST ITEM 12: HIP CIRCLES

Difficulty	Skills
1.0	a. Forward somersault over high bar to a hang
2.0	b. Back pull-over high bar or low bar
3.0	c. Back hip circle
4.0	d. Forward hip circle
5.0	e. Forward hip circle, regrasp high bar
5.0	f. Flying back hip circle (hands on high bar, circle low bar)
6.0	g. Free back hip circle to hang
6.0	h. Forward hip circle directly to a handstand

TEST ITEM 13: SEAT CIRCLES

Difficulty	Skills
1.0	a. Half seat circle backward (skin-the-cat)
2.0	b. Single knee circle backward
3.0	c. Single knee circle forward (modified split leg circle)
4.0	d. Split leg circle forward (straight legs)
4.0	e. From straddle or rear sit, circle backward and release to a rear stand
5.0	f. Seat circle forward or backward
6.0	g. Seat circle forward to straddle cut-and-catch
6.0	h. From a seat circle backward on high bar, release to a front support on low bar

TEST ITEM 14: UNDERSWINGS

Difficulty	Skills
1.0	a. From sit on low bar, facing high bar, underswing dismount
2.0	b. From front support, half hip circle backward (underswing)
3.0	c. Half sole circle backward to dismount
3.5	d. Underswing on high bar to dismount over low bar
4.0	e. Sole circle backward or forward to regrasp high bar
4.5	f. Underswing on high bar to dismount over low bar with half twist
5.0	g. Straddle or sole circle backward, half turn to regrasp high bar in a hang
5.5	h. Straddle or flank cut on return swing of half seat circle backward
6.0	i. Straddle cut-and-catch

Section IV: Vaulting Event

Two different vaults with varying difficulty values must be selected for performance. The Reuther board should be used for takeoff and may be adjusted to any distance from the horse.

TEST ITEM 15: VAULT #1

Difficulty	Skills		Difficulty	Skills
1.0	a. Knee mount		9.0	m. Horizontal squat
2.0	b. Squat mount		9.5	n. Horizontal straddle
2.5	c. Straddle mount		10.0	o. Horizontal stoop
3.0	d. Squat vault		11.0	p. Layout squat
3.5	e. Flank vault		11.5	q. Layout straddle
4.0	f. Straddle vault		12.0	r. Layout stoop
4.0	g. Wolf vault		13.0	s. Handspring vault
4.5	h. Rear vault		13.0	t. Giant cartwheel
5.0	i. Front vault		14.0	u. Hecht vault
6.0	j. Thief vault		15.0	v. Yamashita
6.5	k. Headspring vault		15.0	w. Handspring with half twist (on or off)
7.0	l. Straddle half twist			

TEST ITEM 16: VAULT #2 (Select from previous list)

SCORE SHEET

Ellenbrand Gymnastics Skills Test for College Women

Name: _____ Class period: _____ Date: _____

Balance Beam Event

Item	Difficulty		Execution	
1.	_____	×	_____	= _____
2.	_____	×	_____	= _____
3.	_____	×	_____	= _____
4.	_____	×	_____	= _____
5.	_____	×	_____	= _____

B.B. Total _____

Uneven Parallel Bars Event

Item	Difficulty		Execution	
10.	_____	×	_____	= _____
11.	_____	×	_____	= _____
12.	_____	×	_____	= _____
13.	_____	×	_____	= _____
14.	_____	×	_____	= _____

Bars Total _____

Floor Exercise Event

Item	Difficulty		Execution	
6.	_____	×	_____	= _____
7.	_____	×	_____	= _____
8.	_____	×	_____	= _____
9.	_____	×	_____	= _____

F.X. Total _____

Vaulting Event

Item	Difficulty		Execution	
15.	_____	×	_____	= _____
16.	_____	×	_____	= _____

Vault Total _____

Event Totals
B.B. _____
F.X. _____
Bars _____
Vault _____

Final Test Score _____

Harris Tumbling and Apparatus Proficiency Test[20]*

Purpose. To measure proficiency in tumbling and apparatus.

Evaluation. Harris[20] started with a battery of 22 items which he narrowed to 6. His work was accomplished using students at the University of North Dakota. The test-retest reliability was satisfactory, and the 6-item battery discriminated well between high, medium, and low skills as judged by raters.

---

*From Harris, J.P.: A Design for a Proposed Skill Proficiency Test in Tumbling and Apparatus for Male Physical Education Majors at the University of North Dakota. M.S. in Ed., University of North Dakota, Grand Forks, 1966. Used by permission of the University of North Dakota and the author.

The Test

Name:	Judge:		Class: Date:

Directions: Circle the number which indicates the performer's score in areas of form and execution respectively. Leave the totals until all testing has been completed.

Tumbling
1. Forward roll to head stand.

	form:	1 2	
	execution:	1 2 3 4 5	Total _____

Parallel Bars
2. Back uprise, shoulder balance, front roll.

	form:	1 2	
	execution:	1 2 3 4 5	Total _____

3. Shoulder kip from arm support, swing, front dismount.

	form:	1 2	
	execution:	1 2 3 4 5 6	Total _____

Horizontal Bar
4. Cast to kip up.

	form:	1 2	
	execution:	1 2 3 4 5 6	Total _____

5. Front pull-over, cast, back hip circle.

	form:	1 2	
	execution:	1 2 3 4 5	Total _____

Trampoline
6. Back, front, seat, feet.

	form:	1 2	
	execution:	1 2 3 4 5	Total _____

Total Points ____

Scoring. Form and execution scores are summed for all six events. A score of 44 points is possible. The total point value was divided into form points and execution points to help lessen the possibility of scoring confusion with regard to beauty of performance as compared to beauty of the performer. For example, a student could receive maximum execution points and a zero score for form. However, the form score should in no way influence the performer's execution points.

LACROSSE

Ennis Multi-Skill Test in Lacrosse[15]*

Purpose. A task-oriented test to measure skill and knowledge of lacrosse technique and the flexibility to adapt skills to new situations.

Development. Ennis[15] developed a one-item multi-skill test to resemble the game situation. Test directions do not require specific skills, but encourage the completion of the total task as quickly and as skillfully as possible. One hundred and five players from five Virginia colleges participated in the study. Varsity lacrosse coaches from each college rated their players into five categories using a revision of the Hodges Rating Scale.[24] These ratings were completed in two weeks prior to the testing. The timed scores and subjective ratings for 95 players were used in the analysis. The coefficients of reliability between levels and between trials were $R = .89$ and $R = .78$, respectively. A validity coefficient using Kendall's rank correlation coefficient, tau, between coaches' ratings and

*From Ennis, C.D.: The Development of a Multi-Skill Test in Lacrosse for College Women. Master's Thesis. The University of North Carolina at Greensboro, 1977. Used by permission of the author.

mean time scores was r = .66. The test had construct validity as well owing to its power to discriminate significantly between player performance at different levels.

Level and Gender. Women lacrosse players beyond the beginning level of skill.

Uses. This test can be used to measure the basic skills in lacrosse for beginning through advanced players.

Field Markings. Measurements and field markings are shown in Figure 7–15. Note that the lines are not drawn on the field; only the circles are drawn on the field. The X's mark spots for cone placements (Fig. 7–16).

Directions. The examiner leads the students through the test, repeating key words for each task. There is no demonstration and no reference is made to specific ways to perform the various tasks.

A group of 8 students follows the examiner through the complete test. The examiner repeats the word cues for each task and explains there are many movement and skill shortcuts that may be used to cut seconds from the time. The students should try to discover ways to move as quickly and skillfully as possible. The group of 8 students completes the second practice trial as the examiner repeats the word cues when necessary.

Instructions for Players. Explanation occurs simultaneously with demonstration (Fig. 7–16).

1. Begin in the area of cone 3.

2. Run forward to pick up a stationary ball. Time begins as you touch the ball.

3. Turn to your left, around cone 1. Run to the right of cone 2, to the left of cone 3, and to the right of cone 4.

4. Once past cone 4, continue running and toss and catch the ball twice above your head. The examiner must be able to see the ball above your head for each toss. If the ball is not above your head, the examiner will call, "Repeat."

5. After tossing and catching the ball twice, shoot for goal. There is no penalty if you miss, but if you are successful, 1 second will be deducted from your time. You may shoot from anywhere; there is no restraining line.

6. Without the ball, run goal side of cone 5. Turn and run backward to cone 6, and then forward to pick up a ball beside cone 7.

7. Run around cone 7 and throw the ball beyond cone 8. You may throw from anywhere; there is no restraining line. The ball may bounce. If the ball stops before passing cone 8, you must use your stick to propel it again. Time will be recorded as the ball passes cone 8.

Instructions for Examiner. A. Allow students to begin when ready.

B. Begin time when student touches stationary ball, even if pick-up is unsuccessful.

C. Observe that tosses are above student's head. If not, call "Repeat." Student should repeat only unsuccessful tosses.

D. Record success of shot on goal.

E. Backward running: Observe if player's back is square with cone 8. If not, call "Backward." No penalty is given.

F. Move opposite cone 8. If throw is unsuccessful, encourage player to propel ball again. Record time as the ball passes cone 8.

G. Time is recorded to the nearest tenth of a second. Score is time for trials minus a 1-second deduction for successful goal. Final score is sum of 3 trials.

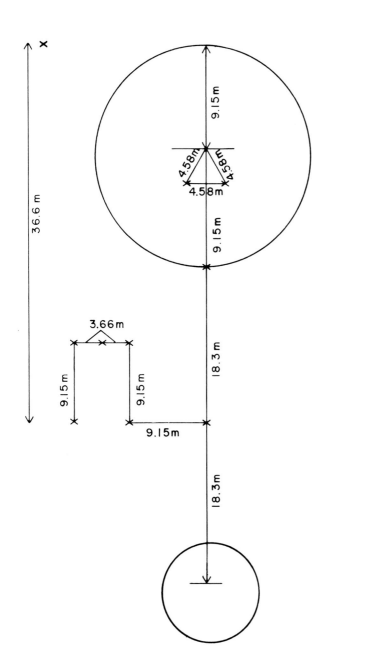

Fig. 7–15.   Field markings for Ennis Lacrosse Test.

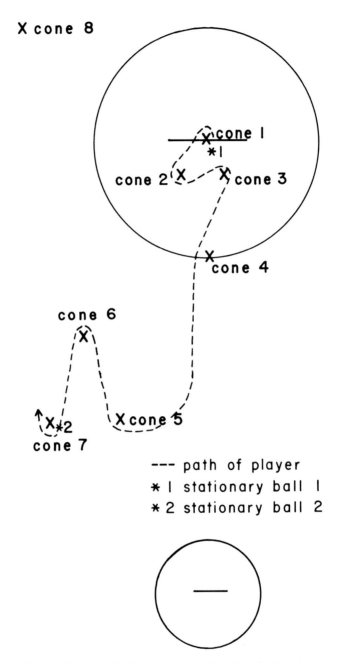

Fig. 7–16. Cone positioning, ball placement, and path of player for Ennis Lacrosse Test.

Comments. The directions for this test are extremely complex. Care must be taken to be assured that the players understand what they are supposed to do and can go from one part of the test to the next smoothly.

RACQUETBALL

Valcourt Racquetball Skills Test Battery[42]*

Purpose. To measure the racquetball playing ability of adult male and female beginner and intermediate racquetball players.

Development. The subjects in this study were beginning and intermediate men and women racquetball players. The beginners were volunteers from beginning racquetball skills classes, and the intermediates were volunteers from the Empire One Racquetball Club, Chicopee, Massachusetts. The testing period for beginners took place after 4 or 5 weeks of instruction. Intermediate players were tested during the same time period. Subjects were required to play two games with a minimum of five different opponents of the same gender and skill level. Subjects reported only the scores resulting from the first match with any one opponent. The scores from these matches were used to determine the criteria for this study. The total number of wins and losses (winning percentage) and the total number of points scored and lost by a player (point differential) were computed for each subject.

Three tests were investigated in this study. However, only the two recommended by the author as the final battery are presented here. These tests are the Buschner Ceiling Shot Placement Test[7] and a slight variation of the Long Wall Volley Test of Hensley, East and Stillwell.[23] For beginner males the Ceiling Shot Placement Test had the highest correlation with the criteria of winning percentage, r = .82, and point differential, r = .75. For beginner females, the Long Wall Volley Test provided the highest correlation with winning percentage, r = .75. The Ceiling Shot Placement Test had the highest correlation for beginner females for point differential, r = .64. For male intermediate players the Long Wall Volley Test had the highest correlation for both winning percentage, r = .83 and point differential, r = .78. The Long Wall Volley Test had the highest correlation with winning percentage, r = .77, for female intermediate players. The Ceiling Shot Placement Test reported the highest correlation, r = .60, with the point differential for female intermediate players. Reliability coefficients were not given.

Level and Gender. Beginning and intermediate adult men and women racquetball players.

Uses. This test or test battery with the appropriate equation can be used for grading both beginning and intermediate adult players. It could also be used to classify players for different level classes or to rank players for a challenge or ladder type of tournament. The test items could be used for practice.

Scoring. Multiple correlation and stepwise regression analyses were computed. Based on these results seven different prediction equations were developed for the prediction of winning percentage and point differential. The winning percentage and point differential equations for the same group could be used separately or together for grading purposes.

*From Valcourt, D.F.: Development of a racquetball skills test battery for male and female beginner and intermediate players. Thesis, Springfield College, 1982. Used by permission of the author.

1. Winning percentage for Male Beginners = .014 (Ceiling Shot Placement Test score) + .011 (Long Wall Volley Test score) + .092.
2. Point Differential for Male Beginners = .023 (Ceiling Shot Placement Test score) + .794.
3. Winning Percentage for Female Beginners = .028 (Long Wall Volley Test score) + .019 (Ceiling Shot Placement Test score) − .260.
4. Point Differential for Female Beginners = .068 (Ceiling Shot Placement Test score) + .648.
5. Winning Percentage for Male Intermediates = .569 (Long Wall Volley Test score) − 1.0172.
6. Point Differential for Male Intermediates = .156 (Long Wall Volley Test score) − 3.202.
7. Winning Percentage for Female Intermediates = .031 (Long Wall Volley Test score) + .013 (Ceiling Shot Placement Test score) − .549.
8. Point Differential for Female Intermediates. None of the variables was able to predict point differential for female intermediate players.

Comments. This test may be appropriate for younger players. At this time it has not been tested on this group. A player must be able to hit an adquate lob serve to score on the Ceiling Shot Placement Test. This could be a problem for some beginners.

Item 1: Ceiling Shot Placement Test

Purpose. To measure the defensive abilities of a player.

Court Markings. Two lines are drawn across the back wall, 2.5 feet and 5.0 feet above the floor and parallel to it. Three lines are drawn on the floor 2 feet, 4 feet, and 6 feet from the back wall and parallel to it (Fig. 7–17).

Directions. The player stands behind the short line and strokes the ball, using a lob serve to the front wall. When the ball rebounds, the player positions his or her body to attempt a ceiling shot. Ideally, the ball should come off the ceiling, rebound near the middle court, then rebound again in the back court. When the ball hits the floor a second time upon rebounding from the ceiling, the appropriate point value is awarded. Ten trials are given.

Scoring. The point values from the short line to the upper area on the back wall are, respectively, 0, 1, 2, 4, 5, 3, 0. If the ball does not strike any of the zones, zero will be recorded for that particular trial. The subject must attempt to hit the ball following each of his or her set-ups for the ten trials. No extra trials will be allowed. The ball must hit the ceiling first, then the front wall on the initial return. A ball hitting a line receives the higher value. The total of the ten trials is the score for the test. Fifty points are possible.

Item 2: The Long Wall Volley Test

Purpose. To measure the speed and power components of the game of racquetball.

Court Markings. A line is drawn across the court 12 feet behind the short line and parallel to it (Fig. 7–18).

Directions. The test item is explained and demonstrated. The subject is permitted a 5-minute warm-up on an adjacent court and 1-minute warm-up on the testing court. The test consists of two 30-second trials. Trial 2 should begin immediately after trial 1. The student begins the test holding two racquetballs.

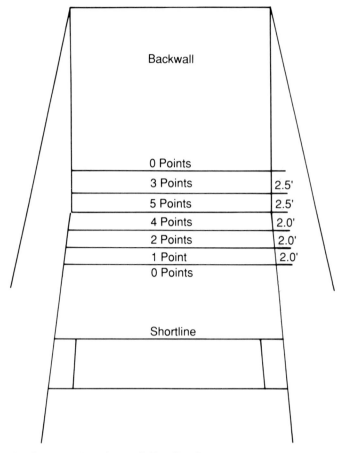

Fig. 7–17. Court markings for the Ceiling Shot Placement Test.

The student stands behind the restraining line (line drawn on the court), drops a ball and volleys it against the front wall for 30 seconds. The trial begins the instant the student drops the ball. The student should hit strokes from behind the restraining line. The ball may be hit in the air after rebounding from the front wall or may be hit after bouncing. There is no restriction on the number of bounces the ball may take before being hit. In case the ball fails to return past the restraining line, the student is allowed to step into the front court to retrieve the ball, but must return behind the restraining line for the succeeding stroke. If the student should miss the ball, a second ball may be put into play in the same manner as the first, or the student may retrieve the first ball and continue to volley it. If both balls are missed, the player may retrieve either ball and put it in play in the same manner. Any stroke may be used to keep the ball in play.

Scoring. One point is scored each time the ball legally hits the front wall. A legal hit requires that the ball travel from the face of the racquet and hit the front wall prior to hitting the floor during the 30-second trial. The total score is the sum of all legal hits for the two trials. No points are scored when the student steps over the restraining line to volley the ball or when the ball hits the floor on the way to the front wall.

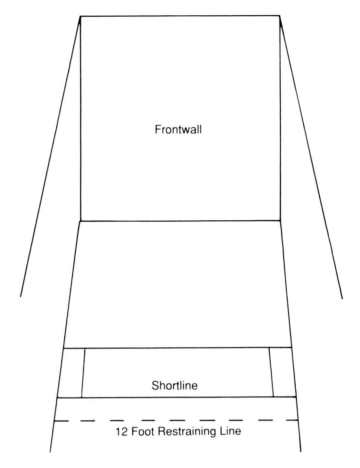

Fig. 7–18.   Court markings for the Long Wall Volley Test.

SOCCER

Mor-Christian General Soccer Ability Skill Test Battery[33]*

Purpose. To measure overall soccer playing ability.

Development. Forty-five male college students participated in this study. They were classified into three groups: varsity team players, intramural divisional championship players, and physical education soccer class players.

Five tests were investigated in this study. The three presented here make up a battery with acceptable reliability and validity. The other two tests required special equipment that would rarely be found in schools and added little to the overall battery. The criterion measure was a rating scale developed and used by three soccer experts. Each subject was evaluated during actual matches played. Each test was correlated with the criterion measure. The coefficients obtained were: Dribbling, .731; Passing, .776; and Shooting, .912. Using the test-retest method, the reliability coefficients were: Dribbling, .795; Passing, .961; and

*From Mor, D., and Christian, V.: The development of a skill test battery to measure general soccer ability. North Carolina Journal of Health and Physical Education, *15*(1):30–39. Spring, 1979. Used by permission of the authors and the NCAHPERD.

Shooting, .984. The objectivity coefficients were: Dribbling, .998; Passing, 1.0; and Shooting, .999. A multiple correlation analysis was used to select the test battery. The following multiple correlation coefficients were obtained for the various test battery combinations: Passing, .776; Passing + Dribbling, .790; and Passing + Dribbling + Shooting, .913. The latter is recommended for use.

Level and Gender. College men at the varsity, intramural championship, or physical education activity class level.

Uses. This test battery could be used for grading, classification, and practice and to aid in varsity team selection.

Scoring. The scores from any or all of the tests can be used separately. However, if a battery or overall playing ability score is desirable, scores from each test should be converted to T-scores. The T-scores from the three tests can then be combined to make up a test battery score.

Comments. Since the male subjects in this study represented three levels of playing ability, this test could probably be used with other age groups and with females. If the Passing Test proved too difficult, the line might be moved closer to the target or the target might be enlarged. For the Shooting Test, giving some score for going through the designated area, but not one of the circular targets might be considered.

Item 1: Dribbling

Field Markings. A circular course 20 yards in diameter is drawn. The starting line is a 3-foot line drawn perpendicular to the outside of the circle (Fig. 7–19). Plastic cones 18 inches high are placed at 5-yard intervals around the circle.

Directions. The ball is placed on the starting line. On the signal, "Ready, Go!"

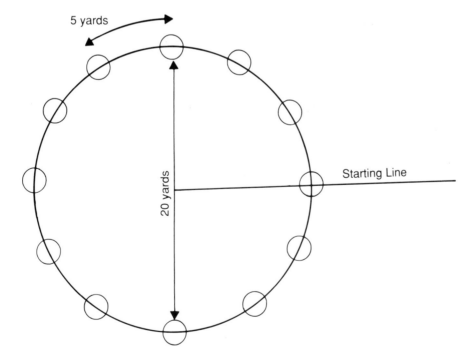

Fig. 7–19. Field markings for the Soccer Dribbling Test.

the subject dribbles the ball around the circular course by weaving among the plastic cones until getting back to the starting line. The dribble should be performed in the least time possible. Three trials are given. The first trial is performed in a clockwise direction, the second in a counterclockwise direction, and the third in the direction of the subject's choice.

Scoring. The combined best two of the three trials is the test score.

Item 2: Passing

Field Markings. A small goal marked 1 yard in width and 18 inches in height is constructed by utilizing two plastic cones as goal posts, and a 4-foot rope as the crossbar. Three plastic cones located 15 yards from the goal line are placed at angles of 90 degrees and 45 degrees (Fig. 7–20).

Directions. Students pass a stationary ball with their preferred foot into the small goal from the three angles marked by the cones. Four trials are taken from each angle for a total of 12 trials. Two practice trials from each angle are allowed.

Scoring. A score of one point is given for each successful pass. Balls that rebound from the goal post (plastic cones) are considered successful trials. The score is the total of the 12 trials.

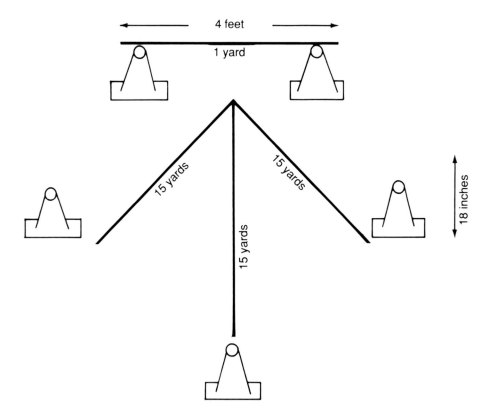

Fig. 7–20. Field markings for Soccer Passing Test.

Item 3: Shooting

Field Markings. The soccer goal is divided into two scoring areas by two ropes suspended from the crossbar 4 feet from each goal post. In addition, each scoring area is divided into two circular targets by two circular hoops 4 feet in diameter. A line is drawn 16 yards from the designated target area and parallel to it (Fig. 7–21).

Directions. The student shoots a stationary ball with the preferred foot from the 16-yard line. The student may place the ball at any point along the line. Four practice trials are given, and then four consecutive balls are attempted at each of the four target areas. There is a total of 16 trials.

Scoring. When aiming toward the upper right target, the subject receives a score of 10 points each time the ball is shot through the upper target; a score of 4 points is scored if the ball is shot through the lower right target when aiming at the upper right target. The scoring procedure is identical when the student is aiming at the lower target, 10 points for the lower and 4 for the upper. The targets on the left side are scored the same way. Balls that rebound from the circular targets are considered as successful trials. No points are given for balls that roll or bounce through the target area.

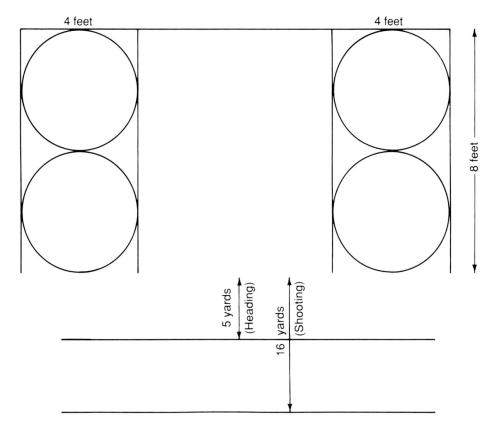

Fig. 7–21. Field markings and target for the Soccer Shooting Test.

SOFTBALL

Maver Softball Skills Test Battery[31]*

Purpose. To measure the major skills of softball and softball playing ability.

Development. Maver's study included five tests of softball playing ability. Only the four recommended for the final battery are presented here.

The tests were administered to 60 female subjects of high school and college age. There were four subgroups of 15 subjects each. Level 1 was composed of college varsity softball players, level 2 college students, level 3 high school varsity softball players, and level 4 high school students. An additional 10 college students were administered the tests while two individuals scored and recorded to assess inter-scorer agreement.

The subjects on level 1 participated in a test-retest administered to provide data for estimation of the stability of the tests. The Pearson product-moment correlation produced the following results: Distance Throw, .87; Baserunning, .64; and Batting, .42. A comparison of the means of the four levels showed a significant difference between athletes and students in baserunning and distance throwing. Athletes, as a group, scored better than students on all tests. High school and college groups were significantly different in the baserunning and distance throw. The intercorrelations for the test items were low, ranging from −.33 to .06, so, for the most part, the tests measured different skills.

A battery of the distance throw, baserunning, and batting is recommended for use by the physical educator and/or coach. Batting is included as a part of the battery even though its reliability is low. To have a softball battery without batting would be ungamelike. Batting did have a high predictive value. The problem with the results of the batting test may have been that the students were tested in terms of slow or fast pitch according to the type of game they were playing. Three of the groups were playing slow pitch; only the college athletes were playing fast pitch. In essence, two different batting tests were given that did not combine well into one.

Scoring. The scores from each of the tests must be converted to T-scores. A discriminant analysis yielded the following equation for combining the three tests scores into a battery score: − .5 (T-score for baserunning) + .7 (T-score for distance throw) + .10 (T-score for batting).

Administrative Considerations. The tests designed are efficient and economical to administer and practical for use outdoors on a softball diamond. They are game-like, require limited equipment, do not entail excessive preparation, and can be completed in the time frame of two class periods if two tests are run simultaneously. The battery, however, requires a large number of test administrators if the tests are to be administered accurately and efficiently.

Item 1: Distance Throw

Purpose. To measure the distance a softball can be thrown with accuracy.

Field Markings. A throwing zone is marked off at one end of the field, $6\frac{1}{2}$ feet wide and $6\frac{1}{2}$ feet deep, from which the throw is made (Fig. 7–22). A 50-foot tape measure is laid out from A to B, and a longer tape, 100 to 200 feet, is laid out from B to C. The first tape marks the 50-foot line from which right angle

*From Maver, D.J.: Maver softball skills test battery. Unpublished Paper, University of North Carolina at Greensboro, 1986. Used by permission of the author.

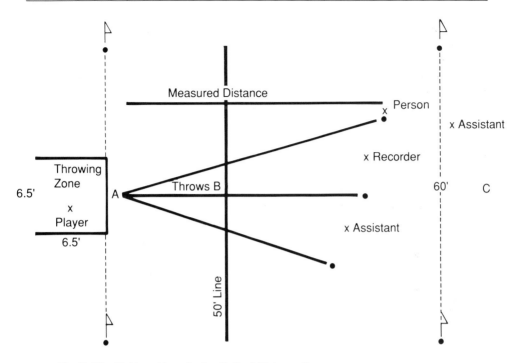

Fig. 7–22. Field markings for the Softball Distance Throw.

measures must be made. Two markers are placed 60 feet apart on either side of the throwing zone, and two more are placed 60 feet apart approximately 150 feet from the throwing zone.

Directions. The player takes a position in the throwing zone with a softball in hand and throws as far as possible within the 60-foot width. The player may throw with either hand. Players must stretch their arm prior to throwing. The player makes three throws.

Scoring. A testing assistant stands where the first throw hits. If the second or third throw is longer, the assistant moves to the new point. The best of the three throws is the score, so only the longest throw is measured. The score is the distance of the farthest throw, measured, to the nearest foot, at a right angle from the throwing line. If the student is outside the throwing zone when the ball is released or the throw hits outside the 60-foot wide area, the throw counts as one of the three trials, but is not scored.

Item 2: Baserunning

Purpose. To measure the speed with which a player can run to first base after hitting a ball from a tee.

Directions. In the study, the batter began the test by swinging at an imaginary ball. After administering the test, however, the author suggests it be administered as follows. A batting tee is placed on home plate. The player stands in the right hand batter's box, holding the bat as if ready to swing at a pitch. On the signal "Go," the player hits the ball off the tee, drops the bat, and runs to first base. If the player does not contact the ball on the swing, the trial begins again. A practice trial is allowed. The player then runs two trials. A rest is given between each trial. See Figure 7–23 for field markings.

Scoring. Trials are timed in seconds and tenths of seconds from the signal "Go," to the instant the runner touches first base. The score for the test is the better of the two trial scores. A zero is recorded for a trial if the bat is thrown, if the player runs outside the base path, or if the player does not touch first base.

Item 3: Batting

Purpose. To measure the skill with which a player can hit a pitched ball.

Administrative Considerations. This test uses a pitcher. This person must be skilled at delivering a pitch consistent in speed for fast pitch and consistent in arc for slow pitch. The pitcher must also be able to get the ball over the plate a high percentage of the time. The same pitcher should be used throughout the test. A trained observer is needed to administer this test. The observer judges the type of hit made by the batter. This needs to be the same person throughout the test. The umpire also needs to be the same person throughout the test.

Directions. The batter must wear a protective helmet. The batter stands in the

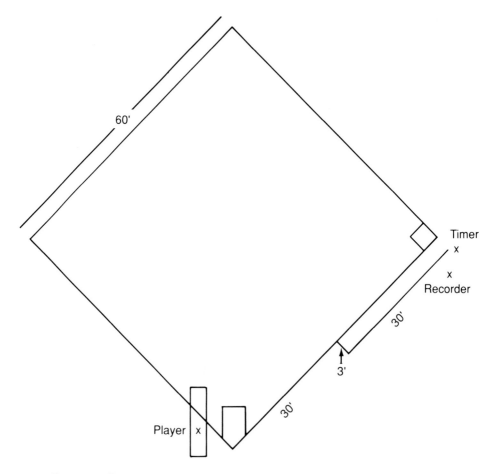

Fig. 7–23. Field markings for the Softball Baserunning Test.

batter's box (right or left to remain consistent once the test begins) and receives nine opportunities to hit a pitched ball. The player's primary objective is to hit a line drive because it has the highest scoring value. An umpire behind the catcher calls each pitch a ball or strike. The test administrator says "pitch" prior to each pitch. If the batter does not swing and the umpire calls it a ball, it does not count as one of the nine attempts; if a strike is called, it counts as an attempt. If the batter swings, regardless of the umpire's decision, it counts as a trial. The pitcher throws a fast ball or arc depending on whether the test is fast pitch or slow pitch. Two practice trials are allowed. See Figure 7–24 for field markings.

Scoring. The score is the sum of the points scored on the nine hits or strikes. A swing and miss counts zero. Zero is scored if the batter does not swing and a strike is called. If the batter steps out of the box or on home plate while swinging, the score is zero. A foul or fly ball counts one. A grounder counts two, and a line drive counts three. A line drive is a ball hit in virtually a straight line from the point of contact with the bat.

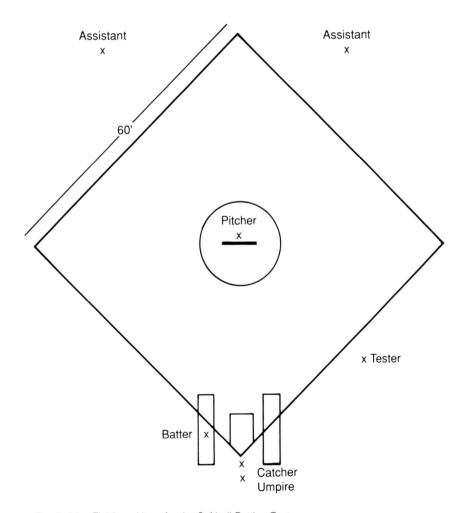

Fig. 7–24.   Field markings for the Softball Batting Test.

SWIMMING

Rosentswieg Revision of the Fox Swimming Power Test[35]*

Purpose. To evaluate five basic swimming strokes on form and power.

Development. Rosentswieg revised the Fox[17] test by changing the starting procedures, by adding a form rating, and by testing five strokes. He used 184 college women for the analysis. The reliability coefficients are computed on two trials. They ranged from .89 to .96. The form rating was correlated with the better of the power scores, not as a validity measure, but to show the relationship of the two components. These coefficients were .72 for the Front Crawl, .81 for the Side Crawl, .83 for the Elementary Back Stroke, .63 for the Back Crawl and .74 for the Breast Stroke.

Level and Gender. College women.

Uses. These tests can be used for grading the five basic strokes, for practice, and to show improvement.

Administrative Considerations. Students can help each other with starting procedures and power scoring, but an instructor will probably need to rate the form. This means individual testing, which is time-consuming.

Markings. The pool deck is marked off in 1-foot intervals beginning 8 feet from the shallow end to designate the starting line.

Directions. The test is started by having a student stand to the side of the swimmer being tested. She uses her forearms as a cradle, holding the legs of the swimmer to the surface of the water. The student sculls or floats in the appropriate position with her shoulders parallel to the starting line. All measurements are taken at the shoulders. When the student is ready, she swims away from the helper by using an arm stroke first. If a kick is made prior to the arm stroke, the trial is immediately stopped. Twelve arm strokes or 6 cycles are allowed, depending upon the stroke. Two trials are allowed.

Scoring. The better distance is accepted as the score. A subjective rating of the swimmer's form is made at the same time the distance factor is being measured. A 5-point scale is used for the rating. Both scores are considered in the final grade.

Burris Speed-Stroke Test of the Crawl[6]†

Purpose. To measure crawl stroking ability.

Development. Five tests of crawl stroking ability were administered to 69 college men and women. The scores were converted to T-Scores and added to get a composite criterion. Reliabilities were computed on a test-retest basis. They were .910 for men and .902 for women. The validity coefficients were .887 for men and .864 for women.

Chapman[9] compared three methods of measuring stroke proficiency:
1. Number of strokes constant; time and distance vary.
2. Time constant; number of strokes and distance vary.
3. Distance constant; time and number of strokes vary.

---

*From Rosentswieg, J.: A Revision of the Power Swimming Test. Research Quarterly, *39*:818–819, Ocxtober, 1968. Used by permission of the AAHPER.

†From Burris, B.J.: A Study of the Speed-Stroke Test of Crawl Stroking Ability and Its Relationship to Other Selected Tests of Crawl Stroking Ability. M.Ed., Temple University, Philadelphia, 1964. Used by permission of the author.

The third method proved most satisfactory. This supports the method used by Burris: the 25-yard distance was constant, and the time and number of strokes varied with the swimmer.[6]

Level and Gender. Men and women swimmers at the intermediate level or above.

Uses. This test can be used for grading, for practice, and to show improvement.

Directions. This is a test of crawl stroking ability. The student swims as fast as he or she can, at the same time using as few strokes as possible. The student has to get as much power as possible from the kick and from the arm pull. The regular crawl stroke is used with the flutter kick and with rhythmic breathing on every second or third stroke. The student starts in the deep water with one hand grasping the gutter, and with the feet vertical in the water and away from the wall. On the signal, "Ready, go!" the student begins swimming without pushing off from the wall and stops when touching the far wall.

Scoring. On the signal, "Go," the watch is started. The watch stops when any part of the student's body touches the wall at the 25-yard distance. Time is recorded to the nearest tenth of a second.

Each time either hand enters the water for a pull, 1 stroke is counted. The touch to the wall is counted as a stroke if part of the arm pull has occurred. The first stroke is counted when the hand that had been touching the wall on the start enters the water for the first time.

Local norms will need to be developed. The speed scores and stroke scores are each converted to T-scores. The T-scores are combined for the test score.

An interesting method of combining T-scores for this test is presented in Tables 7–1 and 7–2. This method may be useful, but the norms are probably not useful.

TENNIS

Sherman Untimed Consecutive Rally Test[38]*

Purpose. To measure rallying ability.

Development. Sherman used 113 college women enrolled in 6 sections of a 7-week beginning tennis unit to investigate several tennis test items. Following experimentations in a pilot study, she proposed a rally, a volley, and a serve test. The Untimed Consecutive Rally Test is reported here because it was found to be the best single index of tennis playing ability and could be used if time were not available to administer the full battery. The test reliability was .88. Validity was calculated by comparing the test to the Scott Modified Dyer Wall-board Test. The concurrent validity coefficient was .60.

Level and Gender. College women enrolled in beginning classes.

Uses. This test can be used to evaluate a student's progress, to compare achievement in relation to others, to diagnose strengths and weaknesses, to classify the students for ability groupings in tennis, to classify the students for tournament pairings and seedings, to evaluate the instructor's teaching methods, to challenge the student to improve, and to promote further skill development through participation in the test.

Court Markings. A backboard or a smooth wall surface at least 10 feet high

---

*From Sherman, P.A.: A Selected Battery of Tennis Skill Tests. Ph.D. Dissertation, University of Iowa, 1972. Used by permission of the author.

Table 7–1. Scoring Table for Men for 25 Yards of Speed-Stroke Test of the Crawl

	Seconds																							
	10	11	12	13	14	15	16	17	18	19	20	21	22	23	24	25	26	27	28	29	30	31	32	33 34
	90	85	80	75	70	65	61	58	55	52	50	47	45	42	40	38	36	35	33	31	29	28	27	26 25

T-Scores

Strokes	T-Scores
10	92
11	89
12	85
13	83
14	80
15	77
16	75
17	72
18	70
19	68
20	66
21	64
22	62
23	60
24	58
25	56
26	54
27	52
28	50
29	48
30	46
31	44
32	42
33	40
34	38
35	36
36	34
37	32
38	31
39	30
40	28
41	27
42	25

DIRECTIONS

Place the corner of the score sheet in the angle between the 2 sets of conversion scores. Round the time score to the nearest second and look for the appropriate number along the top row of figures marked seconds. Immediately below the score in seconds is the T-Score equivalent of that score. Look up the raw score in strokes in the left-hand column marked "Strokes." Just to the right of the stroke score is the T-Score equivalent for strokes. Add the T-Score for strokes to the T-Score for seconds for the combined speed-stroke score.

and 20 feet wide is required for the test. A court or floor area is required that extends outward from the board at least 30 feet. A net line running parallel to the floor is located on the board 3 feet above the floor area. A 7-foot by 18-foot target is placed on the board. It extends 7 feet above the net line and is 18 feet wide. A restraining line is located on the floor 21 feet from the board and parallel to it. Figure 7–25 shows the test dimensions and the placement of the testing personnel.

Directions. Each student is allowed one warm-up trial consisting of 3 balls. All students in each group are to take their warm-up trial prior to the beginning of the first test trials.

The student attempts to achieve the greatest number of consecutive rallies into the target with each ball of each trial. In starting the ball for the rally, the student drops the ball and hits it on the first bounce into the target area. All balls are to be contacted on or prior to the first bounce throughout the consecutive rally. Each student has a total of 3 trials which are scored. Each trial consists of 3 balls. All students in a group are to finish the first trial before the second trial is taken. Failure to accomplish the following items ends the consecutive rally for a particular ball of a particular trial:

Table 7–2.   Scoring Table for Women for 25 Yards of Speed-Stroke Test of the Crawl

	Seconds																									
	16	17	18	19	20	21	22	23	24	25	26	27	28	29	30	31	32	33	34	35	36	37	38	39	40	41
	91	85	80	75	70	66	62	58	55	53	51	49	48	46	44	43	42	40	39	38	36	34	33	31	30	27

T-Scores

Strokes	T-Scores
14	89
15	85
16	82
17	80
18	78
19	75
20	73
21	71
22	68
23	66
24	64
25	62
26	60
27	57
28	55
29	53
30	51
31	49
32	47
33	45
34	44
35	42
36	41
37	40
38	39
39	37
40	36
41	35
42	34
43	33
44	31
45	30
46	28
47	26
48	25

DIRECTIONS

Place the corner of the score sheet in the angle between the 2 sets of conversion scores. Round the time score to the nearest second and look for the appropriate number along the top row of figures marked seconds. Immediately below the score in seconds is the T-Score equivalent of that score. Look up the raw score in strokes in the left-hand column marked "Strokes." Just to the right of the stroke score is the T-Score equivalent for strokes. Add the T-Score for strokes to the T-Score for seconds for the combined speed-stroke score.

1. To rally or volley the ball into the designated target area.
2. To contact the ball on the first bounce when starting the rally.
3. To contact the ball on the first bounce or prior to the bounce throughout the consecutive rally.
4. To have at least one foot behind the restraining line.

Scoring. The score for each trial is the number of consecutive good rallies for each ball in each trial. (Three trials—3 balls per trial.) The final score for the test is the sum of all balls on each of the 3 trials.

Comments. This test seems suitable for both men and women players incorporating an even wider range of tennis skill. It will take longer to administer for more advanced players because their number of consecutive hits with each ball will be higher. For this reason, the test is uniquely suited for beginning level players.

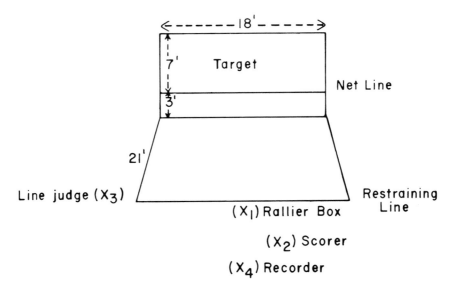

Fig. 7-25.   Diagram for the Untimed Consecutive Rally Test.

Hamer "Mini-Match" of Tennis Ability[19]*

Purpose. To measure playing ability of beginning women tennis players with a test that simulates actual game play.

Development. Hamer used four beginning tennis classes to investigate the appropriateness of a "mini-match" tournament as an indication of tennis playing ability. The official rules of the USLTA 7-out-of-12 tie break were used for the mini-match round robin tournament in each class. The rules for this particular tie break were used because the service rotation and open-ended scoring were believed to allow the fairest opportunity for each player. The mini-match tournament was conducted during the fifth and sixth weeks of instruction. At the same time, two judges rated each student once each week. Each student was assigned a rank within her class according to the number of wins and losses recorded. Each student also received a rank from the average of the four subjective ratings by the two judges.

The reliability and validity coefficients were calculated for each of the four classes. The validity coefficients ranged from .72 to .81, using Spearman-Rho. The reliability coefficients were based on test-retest, using the Chi Square statistics. They were .43, .50, .50, and .75. The reliability of the judges' ratings was calculated using ANOVA. Reliability estimates ranged from .87 to .93.

Hamer concluded that the mini-match was a valid measure of tennis playing ability. Since three of the four reliability coefficients were significant at the .05 or better level of significance, she also concluded that the mini-match was a reliable measure.

Level and Gender. Beginning college women players.

Uses. This test can be used as a motivational technique, as an assessment of playing improvement during the unit, and as a partial measure of achievement in overall tennis playing ability.

---

*From Hamer, D.R.: The "Mini-Match" as a Measurement of the Ability of Beginning Tennis Players. PED Dissertation, Indiana University, 1974. Used by permission of the author.

Directions. A class plays a round robin tournament using the mini-match format. Player A serves Points 1 and 2, right court and left court. Player B serves Points 3 and 4. A serves Points 5 and 6. The players then change sides. B serves Points 7 and 8. A serves Points 9 and 10. B serves Points 11 and 12. If a player wins 7 points, and is at least 2 points ahead, the player wins the match. If the score reaches 6 points all, the players change sides and play continues with serve alternating on every point until one player establishes a margin of 2 points, as follows:

A serves Point 13 (right court). B serves Point 14 (right). A serves Point 15 (left). B serves Point 16 (left). If the score is still tied, the players change sides every 4 points and repeat this procedure.

Comments. Ideally, the reliability coefficients should be higher. This might be possible with a double round robin tournament or a tournament conducted later in the unit when skill performance is more stable.

Wisconsin Wall Test for Serve[13]*

Purpose. To measure the effectiveness of the serve as reflected by force and height.

Development. The Serve Test is reported to be reliable and to be valid logically. The time scores had a reliability of .978 using 20 trials on 2 days determined by the analysis of variance statistic. Using only 10 trials on 1 day, the reliability of the velocity score was .942. The final score combining speed and placement values had a reliability of .957 using 20 trials on 2 days and .912 using 10 trials on 1 day. The test also validated well with subjective ratings.

The Wisconsin Wall Test for Serve correlated .62 with tournament rankings in 9 classes (229 students) at Memphis State University.[16]

Level and Gender. College women.

Uses. This test can be used to measure improvement in service ability, to measure achievement in service ability, to use as a partial basis for a grade, and to diagnose individual needs.

Markings. The test can be administered either indoors or outdoors using a wall or a fence. The wall target is 42½ feet away from the serving line. The wall is marked off in 1-foot intervals from the floor to the height of 12 feet. The 3-foot line, designating the height of the net, should be a thicker line. No limit is set on the width of the target.

Directions. The student serves at the wall target 10 times. The student aims at area 4 on the wall, just above the thick line marking the net height. All serves that do not reach the wall before hitting the floor are repeated. The student holds two balls in his/her tossing hand for each serve. Three practice serves are allowed.

Scoring. The area where the ball lands and the time it takes the ball to travel from the racquet to the target are both recorded. The score is the total number of point values for velocity and vertical placement that are made with 10 serves. The velocity measures for the total of 10 trials should be added and then converted to the point values from Table 7–3.[16] The placement conversions will need to be made from Table 7–3 for each of the 10 serves and then added.

---

*From Edwards, J.: A Study of Three Measures of the Tennis Serve. MSPE, University of Wisconsin, Madison, 1965. Used by permission of the Department of Physical Education for Women of the University of Wisconsin and the author.

Table 7–3. Wisconsin Wall Conversion Tables

| Vertical Placement | | Velocity* | |
Wall Area	Point Values	Time	Point Values
11'	1	4.00	300
10'	2	4.25	290
9'	4	4.50	280
8'	6	4.75	270
7'	7	5.00	260
6'	8	5.25	250
5'	9	5.50	240
<u>4' Net</u>	10	5.75	230
3'	6	6.00	220
2'	4	6.25	210
1'	2	6.50	200
		6.75	190
		7.00	180
		7.25	170
		7.50	160
		7.75	150
		8.00	140
		8.25	130
		8.50	120
		8.75	110
		9.00	100
		9.50	90
		10.00	80
		10.50	70
		11.00	60
		11.50	50
		12.00	40
		12.50	30
		13.00	20
		13.50	10
		13.51 +	0

*Velocity scores treated in terms of 10 serves, not in terms of individual serves, as suggested by Farrow, A.C.: Skill and Knowledge Proficiencies for Selected Activities in the Required Program at Memphis State University. Ed. D., University of North Carolina at Greensboro, 1971, and used by permission of the author.[16]

Comments. Hulbert[26] used these same conversion values to apply to a forehand drive test. The wall markings and the 42½-foot restraining line are identical to the service test. The player puts the ball into play with a self-toss and uses 10 trials. Content validity is claimed and a reliability of .78 for 10 trials on 1 day, using the analysis of variance statistic, is reported.

VOLLEYBALL

Helmen Volleyball Tests[21]*

Purpose. To measure the volleyball skills necessary in the modern power volleyball game.

Development. The responses of 31 volleyball experts indicated that the forearm pass, the overhead volley, and the spike were the three most important skills to be tested. Consequently, Helmen developed tests for these three skills crucial

*From Helmen, R.: Development of Volleyball Skill Tests for College Women. Volleyball Guide—1971–1973. Washington, D.C., AAHPER, 1971, pp 47–53. Used by permission of the AAHPER and the author.

to power volleyball. Seventy-six college women who were enrolled in volleyball classes served as subjects. Four pilot studies were used to establish the face validity of the items. The final battery selected from the experimental tests included the overhead volley test (face pass), the bump-to-self test (forearm pass), and the wall spike test. Three experienced volleyball players rated the 76 students on their general playing ability using a 9-point rating scale. Helmen reported a sufficient degree of consistency among the ratings of the 3 judges to consider their scores as criterion measures. The validity coefficients were .50 for the bump-to-self, .56 for the wall spike, .69 for the overhead volley, and .73 for the battery.

The test-retest method was used to estimate reliability. The coefficients were .66 for the wall spike, .76 for the overhead volley and bump-to-self, and .84 for the test battery.

The Overhead Volley Test is the best single item if time does not permit the use of all three items.

Level and Gender. College women.

Uses. This test battery can be used to measure volleyball playing ability. Its items can also be used for practice.

Court Markings. Each area is 15 feet wide. On two of the items, the restraining line is 15 feet, and it is 13 feet on the third item. Both restraining lines could be indicated on the floor using different colors for each line. Two items use a line on the wall 12 feet high. This line can be disregarded for the third item (Figs. 7–26 and 7–27).

Comments. Helmen suggested that further study needs to be done on different age groups and with male players. Modifications in wall and floor markings and the length and number of trials could be determined. The essential ideas of the test items, however, seem to be universally appropriate to all who play volleyball.

Item 1: Overhead Volley Test

Purpose. To test the player's ability to set, pass, and control the ball with the finger pads of both hands.

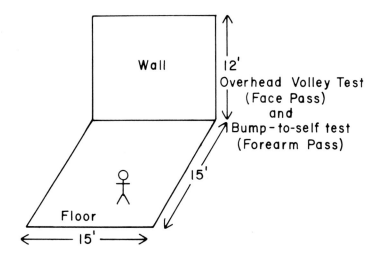

Fig. 7–26. Markings for Helmen Overhead Volley Test and Bump-to-Self test.

Directions. The student tosses the ball up to begin each trial and volleys the ball above the head with two hands, with finger tip control, and with a full extension of the arms. To score, the ball has to reach or go above the 12-foot height, and the player has to remain in the area with at least 1 foot. Each time that control is lost, the player recovers his or her own ball with the count restarting at zero. Dropping the ball, catching the ball, using one hand, bumping the ball, or using an open underhand hit, constitute loss of control. A student who permits the ball to come to a visible rest in his or her hands is warned the first time and called on a loss of control the second time. If the ball hits the wall, or is below the 12-foot height, or both of the student's feet are out of the area, the volley is disallowed. This does not return the count to zero, however.

Scoring. Note that the 12-foot line on the wall is used by the scorer to judge the height of the volley. The ball is *not* rebounded off the wall. Two nonconsecutive 30-second trials are given to each student. The score for a trial is the highest number of consecutive volleys. The score for the test is the total of the two trials.

Item 2: Bump-to-Self Test (forearm pass)

Purpose. To test the player's ability to control the ball with the forearm pass.

Directions. The test markings and scoring are the same as for the Overhead Volley Test. The test directions are also the same, with the exception that the forearm pass is used rather than the face pass. The players are instructed to execute the forearm pass by joining both hands and receiving the ball on the forearms for the best control. Dropping the ball, catching the ball, using only one arm, using open hands, or using the face pass constitute loss of control.

Scoring. The scoring is the same as for the Overhead Volley Test.

Item 3: Wall Spike Test

Purpose. To measure the performer's ability to hit the ball repeatedly with controlled power and accuracy against the wall.

Directions. The spiking hand is open and the ball is contacted from a height above the shoulder. The ball is started with a toss to self. As the player spikes it, the ball hits the floor and, after making contact with the wall, rebounds directly to the player. The student repeats the action each time the ball returns. If control is lost, the ball is restarted and the spikes are added to the score. The ball must be spiked as it returns from the wall; it cannot legally be spiked from

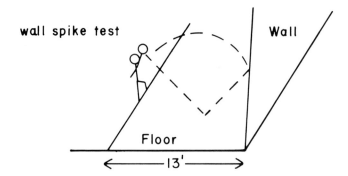

Fig. 7–27. Markings for Helmen Wall Spike Test.

a bounce off the floor. The student is instructed to catch the ball and restart it with a toss to self.

Scoring. Three nonconsecutive 20-second trials are administered. The total number of times the ball legally hits the wall during each trial is totaled for the final score.

Modified Brady Volleyball Test[30]*

Purpose. To indicate overall volleyball playing ability.

Development. Kronqvist and Brumbach[29] revised the Brady[5] test, which had been developed for college men, to fit secondary school boys. Seventy-one tenth- and eleventh-grade boys were involved. Three judges used the rating scale suggested by Laveaga[30] to form the validity criterion. Their intercorrelations were .776, .804, and .903. The validity coefficient was .767 and the reliability, established by the test-retest method, was .817.

Level and Gender. Secondary school boys.

Uses. To aid in determining grades, as a screening device for grouping students, and as a motivation for individual practice.

Markings. A target area is a line 5 feet long placed on the wall 11 feet above the floor. From both ends of this line, lines extend toward the ceiling for at least 4 feet. No restraining lines are on the floor.

Directions. The test is composed of three 20-second trials. To start the test, the student throws the ball against the wall within the rebound area. The student continues to volley the ball until "Stop" is called. If the student loses control of the ball or the ball hits the floor, the ball should be caught, thrown against the wall as at the beginning of the test, and the test continues.

Scoring. The score is the number of legal volleys executed in three 20-second trials. In order for a volley to be counted, the ball must hit in or above the target area, and the ball must be clearly hit. When, in the opinion of the scorer, the ball visibly comes to rest at contact, the volley will not be counted.

Comments. Cunningham and Garrison[12] report the results of a similar test for college women. The target area is lower, 10 feet, and smaller, 3 feet wide. Two 30-second trials are given, with the better score being used for the test score. The tosses to begin the test do not count as part of the score.

Allen Volleyball Diagnostic Instrument[1]†

Purpose. To qualitatively assess a player's ability in executing the basic skills of volleyball.

Development. This instrument assesses the player's performance in terms of techniques and mechanics. The techniques illustrated have been advocated by the authorities and by the jury members that completed a survey instrument.

Level and Gender. Males and females of any age or skill level.

Uses. This test was developed to help teachers and coaches diagnose the technical and mechanical problems that affect student performance.

Directions. This instrument consists of sequences of pictures. When the in-

*From Kronqvist, R.A., and Brumbach, W.B.: A Modification of the Brady Volleyball Skill Test for High School Boys. Research Quarterly, 39:116–120, March, 1968. Used by permission of the AAHPER.

†From Allen, D.W.: Volleyball skill guide and diagnostic instrument for coaches and players. Dissertation, Indiana University, Bloomington, Indiana, 1983. Used by permission of the author.

THE SERVE

1. Ready Position   **2**. Stride Forward   **3**. Toss Ball Cock arm with elbow back.   **4**. Swing arm forward, rotate about vertical axis.   **5**. Shift weight to lead foot.

6. Extend elbow rapidly before contact.   **7.** Contact through center of ball in front of body.   **8.** Punch ball with low trajectory.   **9.** Smooth follow-through with no wrist.

List all of the faults in the appropriate sections.

Legs	Arms	Body-Ball Relation	Other

Fig. 7–28.   The volleyball serve.

THE FOREARM PASS

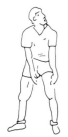    

1. Assume a ready, relaxed position.

2. Knees flexed, elbows extended.

3. Clasp hands, shift weight to meet ball.

4. Line ball up with the midline of the body.

5. Watch ball onto the arm. Begin knee extension.

6. Swing arms gently to proper contact angle. Shrug shoulders at contact.

7. Arms straight, lift through the ball.

8. Leg and arm lift continue in follow through.

9. Weight shifted forward in direction of desired pass.

Fig. 7–29.   The volleyball forearm pass.

THE FRONT SET

1. Ready position, hands up.

2. Cock wrists back, hands open but relaxed.

3. Hands contact the sides of the ball.

4. Hands give to absorb force of ball, wrists radial flex.

5. Wrists ulnar flex, fingers push the ball out of the hands.

6. Follow through with hands and arms up and out.

1. Knees flexed hands up.

2. Hands up, watch ball thru triangle of hands.

3. Line ball with midline of body. Hands on sides of ball.

4. Simultaneous extension of knees and elbows.

5. Hands pronate after release of the ball.

6. Step in direction of set.

Fig. 7–30.   The volleyball front set.

THE SPIKE

 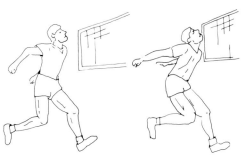  

1. Begin approach at an angle to the net.

2. Build up horizontal momentum.

3. Plant heels to achieve heel-to-toe motion with the feet.

4. Knees flexed 90° COG behind heels.

   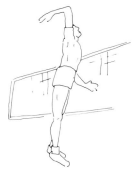

5. Push off from toes. Thrust arms upward for added height.

6. Assume "drawn-bow" position, legs under body, trunk torqued and arm raised behind head.

7. Cock hitting arm behind head. Thrust non-hitting arm downward.

8. Extend legs, begin arm extension and trunk rotation.

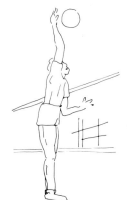  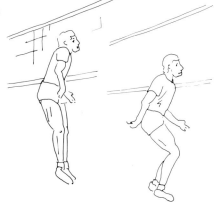

9. Contact the ball with heel of open hand. Keep the ball in front of the hitting shoulder.

10. Snap the wrist for top spin on the ball. The body pikes (flexion of the trunk).

11. Follow through with arm across the body (laterally).

12. Cushion the landing by flexing the knees and ankles.

Fig. 7–31.   The volleyball spike.

THE BLOCK

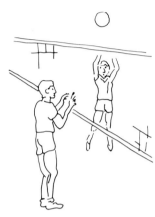

1. Ready Position: arms up, stand close to the net, watch set and spiker.

2. Crouch (flex at knees) in preparation of jump. Keep eyes on hitter.

3. Line up with the midline of blockers' body on the shoulder of spiker's hitting arm. Jump after the spiker leaves the ground.

4. Jump straight up. Time the jump to meet the ball while over the plane of the net.

5. Press block from shoulders. Snap the wrists down upon contact with the ball.

6. Cushion the landing by flexing the ankles and knees. Withdraw the hands and arms from the net.

Fig. 7–32. The volleyball block.

structor or coach observes a player executing a particular technique, he or she compares the player's technique with that of the model in the Diagnostic Instrument. A mark on the body part on the instrument that corresponds with the body part being observed indicates an error during performance. Beneath the illustrations are four columns labeled "Legs," "Arms," "Ball-Body Relation," and "Other." These four columns are intended to be used by the instructor or coach to make remarks pertaining to the specific error or proper execution of a skill (Figs. 7–28 to 7–32).

WRESTLING

Sickel Amateur Wrestling Ability Rating Form[40]*

Purpose. To measure wrestling ability.

Development. This scale was formulated on the basis of the performance of 129 high-school boys who participated in interscholastic competition and in physical education classes.

Uses. This test can be used for grading and classification.

The Rating Form

AMATEUR WRESTLING ABILITY RATING FORM		
Name _____Weight Class _____Date _____		
Rating Scale: 7—Superior 6—Excellent 5—Good 4—Average 3—Poor 2—Very Poor 1—Ineffective		
I. WRESTLING ON FEET	A. Balance	1 2 3 4 5 6 7
	B. Timing and speed	1 2 3 4 5 6 7
	C. Strategy	1 2 3 4 5 6 7
	D. Aggressiveness	1 2 3 4 5 6 7
II. WRESTLING ON MAT		
1. Top Position	A. Balance	1 2 3 4 5 6 7
	B. Timing and speed	1 2 3 4 5 6 7
	C. Wrestling skills	1 2 3 4 5 6 7
2. Botton Position	A. Balance	1 2 3 4 5 6 7
	B. Timing and speed	1 2 3 4 5 6 7
	C. Wrestling skills	1 2 3 4 5 6 7
	TOTAL POINTS _____	

Scoring. The scores range from a maximum of 70 points to a minimum of 10 points.

REFERENCES

1. Allen, D.W.: Volleyball skill guide and diagnostic instrument for coaches and players. Dissertation, Indiana University, Bloomington, Indiana, 1983.
2. Bobrich, M.N.: Reliability of an evaluative tool used to measure badminton skill. Thesis, George Williams College, 1972.
3. Boetel, N.A.: Factorial approach in the development of a basketball rating scale to evaluate players in a game situation. Dissertation, University of North Carolina at Greensboro, 1976.

*From Sickels, W.L.: A Rating Test for Amateur Wrestling Ability. MSPE, San Jose State College, San Jose, California, 1967. Used by permission of the author.

4. Brace, D.K. (Consultant): Skills Test Manual—Archery for Boys and Girls. Washington, D.C., AAHPER, 1967.

5. Brady, G.F.: Preliminary investigation of volleyball playing ability. Research Quarterly, 16:14–17, March, 1945.

6. Burris, B.J.: A study of the speed-stroke test of crawl stroking ability and its relationship to other selected tests of crawl stroking ability. Thesis, Temple University, 1964.

7. Buschner, C.A.: The validation of a racquetball skills test for college men. Dissertation, Oklahoma State University, Stillwater, 1976.

8. Chapman, N.L.: Chapman ball control test—field hockey. Research Quarterly for Exercise and Sport, 53:1:239–42, 1982.

9. Chapman, P.: A comparison of three methods of measuring swimming stroke proficiency. Thesis, University of Wisconsin, Madison, 1965.

10. Collins, D.R. and Hodges, P.B.: A Comprehensive Guide to Sports Skills Tests and Measurement. Springfield, IL, Charles C Thomas Publishers, 1978.

11. Cotten, D.J., Cobb, P.R., and Fleming, J.: Development and validation of a badminton clear test. Abstract of Research Paper 1987, AAHPERD National Convention and Exposition, Las Vegas, Nevada, April 13–17, 1987, p. 168.

12. Cunningham, P. and Garrison J.: High wall volley test for women's volleyball. Research Quarterly, 39:486–490, October, 1968.

13. Edwards, J.: A study of three measures of the tennis serve. Thesis, University of Wisconsin, Madison, 1965.

14. Ellenbrand, D.A.: Gymnastics skills test for college women. Thesis, Indiana University, 1973.

15. Ennis, C.D.: The development of a multi-skill test in lacrosse for college women. Thesis, University of North Carolina at Greensboro, 1977.

16. Farrow, A.: Skill and knowledge proficiencies for selected activities in the required program at Memphis State University. Dissertation, University of North Carolina at Greensboro, 1971.

17. Fox, M.G.: Swimming power test. Research Quarterly, 28:233–238, October, 1957.

18. Friedel, J.F.: The development of a field hockey test for high school girls. Thesis, Illinois State University, 1956.

19. Hamer, D.R.: The "mini-match" as a measurement of the ability of beginning tennis players. Dissertation, Indiana University, 1974.

20. Harris, J.P.: A design for a proposed skill proficiency test in tumbling and apparatus for male physical education majors at the University of North Dakota. Thesis, University of North Dakota, Grand Forks, 1966.

21. Helmen, R.: Development of volleyball skill tests for college women. Volleyball Guide—1971–1973. Washington, D.C., AAHPER, 1971.

22. Henry, M.E.: The validation of a test of field hockey skill. Thesis, Temple University, 1970.

23. Hensley, L.D., East, W.B., and Stillwell, J.L.: A racquetball skills test. Research Quarterly, 50:114–118, March, 1979.

24. Hodges, D.R.: Construction of an objective knowledge test and skills tests in lacrosse for college women. Thesis, University of North Carolina at Greensboro, 1967.

25. Hopkins, D.R., Shick, J. and Plack, J.J.: Skills Test Manual—Basketball for Boys and Girls. Washington, D.C., AAPHERD, 1984.

26. Hulbert, B.A.: A study of tests for the forehand drive in tennis. Thesis, University of Wisconsin, Madison, 1966.

27. Ishee, J.H. and Shannon, J.L.: Scoring collegiate archery. Perceptual and Motor Skills, 57:525–526, 1983.

28. Jeffreys, A.: A rating scale for rhythmic aerobics. Unpublished Paper, University of North Carolina at Greensboro, 1987.

29. Kronqvist, R.A. and Brumbach, W.B.: A modification of the Brady volleyball skill test for high school boys. Research Quarterly, 39:116–120, March, 1968.

30. Laveaga, R.C.: Volleyball. 2nd Ed. New York: Ronald Press Co., 1960.

31. Maver, D.J.: Maver softball skills test battery. Unpublished Paper, University of North Carolina at Greensboro, 1986.

32. McKenzie, R. and Shifflett, B.: Skill evaluation in a coeducational beginning archery class. Unpublished Paper, San Diego State University, 1986.

33. Mor, D. and Christian, V.: The development of a skill test battery to measure general soccer ability. North Carolina Journal of Health and Physical Education, 15(1):30–39. Spring, 1979.

34. Neal, C.: The value of variation in grip in selected sports for women in compensating factors for sex difference in strength. Thesis, University of Iowa, Iowa City, 1951.
35. Rosentwieg, J.: A revision of the power swimming test. Research Quarterly, *39*:818–819, October, 1968.
36. Rowlands, D.J.: A golf skill test battery. Dissertation, University of Utah, 1974.
37. Scott, M.G., Carpenter, A., French, E. and Kuhl, L.: Achievement examinations in badminton. Research Quarterly, *12*:242–253, May, 1941.
38. Sherman, P.A.: A selected battery of tennis skill tests. Dissertation, University of Iowa, 1972.
39. Shick, J. and Berg, N.G.: Indoor golf skill test for junior high school boys. Research Quarterly for Exercise and Sport, *54*:1:75–78, 1983.
40. Sickels, W.L.: A rating test for amateur wrestling ability. Thesis, San Jose State College, San Jose, California, 1967.
41. Strait, C.J.: The construction and evaluation of a field hockey skills test. Thesis, Smith College, 1960.
42. Valcourt, D.F.: Development of a racquetball skills test battery for male and female beginner and intermediate players. Thesis, Springfield College, 1982.

8

Knowledge Testing

The measurement of knowledges and understandings has become justified as the fuller definition of physical education and sport has evolved. No longer is physical development enough. The meanings behind the performance are now considered a vital part of the total program. The background "hows" and "whys" enhance the performance and consequently justify the teaching/coaching and the assessments of knowledge and understanding. If they are important to the physically educated person, then they must be a part of the instructional program and so a phase of the measurement program. Students/players are no longer expected to accept at face value anything the teacher/coach decides to present. The deeper meanings, the explanations, the causes, and the possible results are explained as well. This richness and fullness of content should be reflected in the measurement program.

Tests of knowledge imply at least an involvement with the facts. Tests requiring higher cognition demand, in addition, analysis, synthesis, and enough facility with the facts to make judgments and decisions. Traditionally, written tests in physical education and sport have emphasized only the minor factual aspects, such as rules and scoring, of the various sports. Tests that include items to assess some of the higher cognitive levels, such as analysis and synthesis, are more difficult to construct. They provide, however, a more valuable instrument to assess the students'/players' grasp of the subject.

USES

Traditionally, written tests have been a part of schooling. It is true, unfortunately, that nearly all tests are given in school situations and so the materials presented in this chapter will focus on the school setting. It is recommended, however, that they be used in athletics and fitness/spa settings, and in such other places where movement skill acquisition and fitness are emphasized such as YM/YWCAs.

Written tests, or "paper and pencil" tests, serve several functions. The most prevalent use is the one of *assessing achievement*. At the completion of a unit, the students are tested to see how much information and meaning they have assimilated. The grade made on the test usually becomes a part of the overall grade for the unit. A unit test should follow the unit plan in its points of emphasis and its general content. If 50% of the unit was spent on skill techniques, then approximately 50% of the questions should investigate information about the

213

execution of the techniques. In more advanced units, more time frequently is spent on strategy, and this emphasis should be reflected in the content of the test.

Tests should be learning experiences. Too often there is little or no follow-up of tests, resulting in the loss of learning opportunities. The teacher may have the students check the papers immediately with a discussion to follow. A check of the number of students who miss each question may give the teacher direction for a follow-up discussion of the test during the next class period. False information and misconceptions can be clarified if the students have the opportunity to study their incorrect answers along with the correct ones. Knowledge of the correct information is the ultimate objective even if it has to be learned after the test.

Tests also serve as *motivational devices*. Unit tests are motivational if the students realize the uses to be made of the final results. They should know the weighting of the test in the overall grade, the type of test, and the content areas. Plans should be made to go over the test papers to discuss questions and misunderstandings. Such follow-up discussions are helpful to the instructor when test revisions are made. If the test and its results are used in meaningful ways, the students are motivated to learn.

Once or twice during a unit a short test could be given to stimulate the students to keep up with the content of the unit. Short tests on scoring in tennis, on positions and marking in soccer, on the physiological aspects of weight training, or on terminology in golf are some examples of this application. This serves a diagnostic purpose as well as a motivational one and tends to keep the participants "on their toes." This type of test usually covers only one aspect of the content of the activity and consequently plays a small part in the overall unit grade.

Whether for grading, for encouraging, for learning, for detecting weak areas, or whatever, it is well for the physical activity teacher to remember that knowledge tests help to complete the total measurement program. Skill assessments are not enough, just as information about strategy, techniques, and rules alone is inadequate. The physical educator is teaching the total person and must be concerned with mental as well as physical and social accomplishments.

QUALITIES OF TESTS

The six types of tests presented have various qualities that are not mutually exclusive. For example, a criterion-referenced test can be either standardized or teacher-made. Knowing the qualities and characteristics attributed to each kind of test will enable the reader to better evaluate and construct tests.

Standardized Tests

Tests that have been scientifically constructed and that *may* be accompanied by norms are called standardized tests. The validity and reliability of standardized tests have been established. The norms are of questionable value except for gross comparisons because each must be computed in light of a particular unit of a certain length with a specific content presented to a certain age group. These factors vary so greatly that norms for knowledge tests are seldom appropriate. Standardized tests are carefully developed and usually can be made available. Few knowledge tests in physical education are available commercially, but this is one area in which, undoubtedly, measurement progress will be made. Standardized test have several characteristics:

1. They usually provide more psychometrically sound measures.
2. They evaluate the content areas and cognitive levels reflected in the test as well as the degree of difficulty applied to various groups.
3. They provide good tests when teachers do not have the time or skill to construct them.
4. They provide tests for a great variety of activities.
5. They serve as examples for format and content balance.
6. They are in print somewhere for distribution. Not all tests in print, however, have been standardized. The sample tests in college activities handbooks, courses of study, and state syllabi usually are not standardized.

Teacher-Made Tests

More prevalent are teacher-made tests. They are the work of teachers for their local purposes. They also have certain characteristics:

1. They fit the unit for which they are planned in content and difficulty.
2. They may or may not be scientifically constructed, depending on whether the teacher has ascertained their psychometric qualities. The fact that a test has not been analyzed does not mean that it has no validity. If the test coincides with the unit of instruction, it automatically has curricular validity.
3. They may or may not be accompanied by local norms, depending on whether the instructor has collected the scores year after year and prepared norms.
4. They usually are prepared quickly and, consequently, probably are not as well-constructed as standardized tests.
5. They generally are not available to others. They are used only locally.

Essay Tests

These tests require a written answer by the student that involves the organization of information to be presented in logical paragraph form. Essay questions are usually general and test the ability of the student to write the material to be covered. Numerous factors are characteristic of essay tests:

1. They usually involve only five or six questions and thus test a limited sample of the subject content.
2. They may be constructed quickly.
3. They are difficult to grade objectively and reliably.
4. They usually require more time to answer than objective tests.
5. They may test general explanations, interpretations, and problem-solving concepts that may be difficult to measure in isolated questions of an objective test.
6. They test ability to compose in prose, which may *not* be one of the purposes of the test.
7. They are usually good for creative and exploratory testing.
8. They are more efficient for small-scale testing.
9. They favor the verbally inclined student.[15]
10. They promote good study habits.[15]
11. Traditionally they have been considered more scholarly than objective

tests because they enable the student to focus and elaborate on a particular question, thus promoting critical thinking and development.

12. They are inappropriate for testing simple knowledge and comprehension levels of cognition, but are more suitable for questions that require synthesis and judgments.

13. Essay items could be used to provide the students with the opportunity to express their feelings about their physical activity experiences. These responses, however, should not be used in assigning grades.

14. The answer must be supplied by the student.

15. The student's time is spent thinking and then writing the response.

Objective Tests

Objective tests require a brief response to questions encompassing smaller pieces of information. They have certain characteristics:

1. Good objective tests are difficult and time-consuming to prepare.

2. They may be quickly, efficiently, and objectively graded.

3. They can be validated and revised.

4. They are reliable.[15]

5. They may test for several types of information, such as rules, strategy techniques, terminology, and history of any activity.

6. They lend themselves to follow-up lessons to correct errors and misconceptions.

7. They too frequently measure only superficial and trivial facts.

8. They should rank the students rather accurately according to their overall knowledge of the content.

9. They encourage guessing.[15]

10. They usually cover an extensive amount of the subject content.

11. They eliminate bluffing or evasion of an issue.[15]

12. They clearly define the task to be done.

13. The answer must be selected by the student from those given on the test.

14. The student's time is spent reading, thinking, and then selecting the desired response.

Some critics state that objective tests examine only superficial information. If well-constructed, however, an objective test can be a challenging mental exercise that measures insights, understandings, interpretations, and judgments. Too frequently, objective tests are prepared quickly and contain questions on rules almost exclusively. Such tests are criticized justifiably, and it is hoped they are being used less frequently in measurement programs. The trend is for the physical education teacher to prepare objective knowledge tests carefully and to continue to analyze and revise them into refined standardized measurement tools worthy of confidence.

The vast majority of knowledge testing in physical education activities uses the objective test format. It is to the advantage of the student, however, if both objective and essay formats can be used from time to time. Some students test better on the essay format, and some seem to respond better to the objective format. Alternating and/or mixing the formats would probably provide a fairer assessment of the student. With care, both kinds can be constructed to reap a valid and reliable measure even though they serve somewhat different functions.

Norm-Referenced Tests

To interpret a student's score by comparing it with scores of other students, norm-referenced tests are used.[21] They are used and characterized in various ways:

1. They reflect individual differences in the amount learned.
2. They are used when the amount of content learned varies, but the amount of time allotted for learning is set.
3. They are useful for testing complex material and a broad coverage of content.
4. They tend to encourage open, divergent thinking.
5. They reveal maximum achievement in a content area.
6. They reflect the proportion of students who learned less than each other student (percentiles).
7. They require a wide range of scores in order to make the proper statistical applications and interpretations.
8. They are often used for summative evaluation at the completion of a unit of instruction.
9. They produce a scale of scores anchored in the middle of the distribution. Interpretations are made in relation to achievement above and below the average.
10. They are useful when fixed quotas have been set and decisions have to be made about who is to be admitted to the next level, for example, or to the team.

Criterion-Referenced Tests

To interpret a student's score by comparing it to some predetermined standard, criterion-referenced tests are used.[21] They are unique in various aspects of function and construction:

1. They are applicable for individualized instruction and help identify the kinds of learning activities to be prescribed.
2. They are used when the amount of content to be learned is set, but the amount of time needed to learn it varies from student to student.
3. They are useful for testing a high degree of comprehension on limited content.
4. They tend to encourage closed, convergent thinking.
5. They establish minimum acceptable learning essentials in a content area.
6. They reflect the proportion of what could (should) have been learned (percentages).
7. The scores cluster within a small range toward the top of the distribution. Consequently, the statistical analyses used for norm-referenced tests are not appropriate for criterion-referenced tests.
8. They are used in formative evaluation settings so subsequent learning can be achieved to meet mastery standards.
9. The scores are anchored at the top of the distribution and indicate mastery. Scores below the "cutting level" indicate nonmastery.
10. They indicate if specific areas of the curriculum have been learned to the level of mastery.
11. They are prevalent in elementary-school programs and in certification programs such as in sports officials training.

12. They are usually confined to relatively small units of instruction. [16]

13. They require a more detailed statement of objectives. That, in itself, enhances the precision of the measurement.

14. They are useful for assessing hierarchic learning.

15. They are also known as mastery tests, domain-referenced tests, and universe-defined measurements.

An increase in the use of criterion-referenced measures has been stimulated by individualized instruction and other humanistic educational trends. Measurement theorists consider criterion-referenced measures a supplement to and not a substitute for norm-referenced measures.[9,21] The establishment of the criterion standard is crucial, and this standard must be based partially on what students can logically be expected to attain. Experience, conventional wisdom, and norm-referenced information must be used to help decide on the cutting point indicative of mastery. It may not be possible to distinguish between test items used in norm-referenced tests and those used in criterion-referenced tests. The difference comes in judging the performance of the students—one by comparing the score to an ideal criterion and the other by comparing the score to scores of other similar students.[10] Ideally, both norm- and criterion-referenced measures could and should be used because they are both related to the decisions that are made about the education of students.

COGNITIVE TAXONOMIES

The test maker should be able to show the content area, to be discussed later, and the cognitive levels that comprise a test. Otherwise no clear-cut information will be available about whether the test is either a very beginning level tool assessing only the basic knowledges of an activity or a more advanced instrument covering some of the higher levels of the cognitive taxonomy, such as the analysis and synthesis concepts of a sport activity.

Two cognitive systems will be presented so that the student can compare them and apply whichever one is appropriate to a given testing situation.

Bloom's Taxonomy

Bloom et al. have classified the cognitive domain into the following six levels: *knowledge, comprehension, application, analysis, synthesis,* and *evaluation.*[4] Knowledge and comprehension are the bases for cognition, and beyond these parameters are the higher intellectual abilities and skills. A hierarchical arrangement from the simple to the more complex in these cognitive processes is shown in Figure 8–1.[4]

1. *Knowledge* is defined as an awareness of specific facts, universals, and information and involves remembering and the ability to recall. The most common knowledges in the cognitive domain of sports, exercise, dance, and related activities are: (1) terminology; (2) rules governing the activity; (3) techniques involved in performing the activity; (4) historical background; (5) strategy; (6) equipment and facilities; and (7) game courtesies and etiquette.

2. *Comprehension* is the lower level of understanding and implies the abilities to interpret knowledge and to determine its implications, consequences, and effects. An example would be knowing the facts and principles concerning the

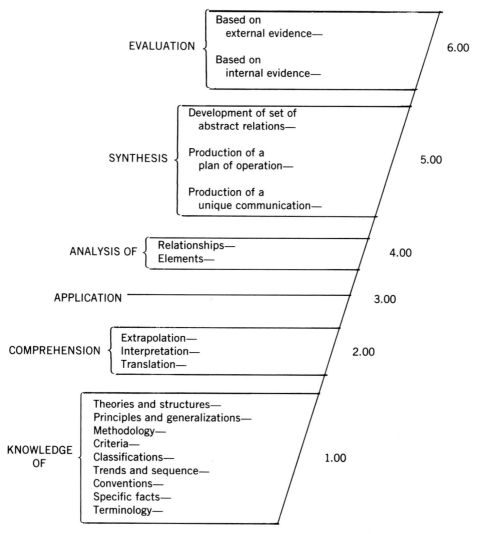

Fig. 8–1. Bloom's taxonomy continuum for the cognitive domain. (Adapted by permission from Bloom, B.S., et al.: *Taxonomy of Educational Objectives: The Classification of Educational Goals. Handbook I: Cognitive Domain.* New York, David McKay Company, Inc., 1956.)

effect of exercise on the heart and circulatory systems and understanding the necessity of exercise for survival.

3. *Application* is a higher level cognitive process that enables the learner to use knowledge and understanding in a particular concrete situation. It is possible to know and understand the facts, but still not be able to apply them.

4. *Analysis* involves a higher level cognitive process than application. It is based on knowledge and understanding, but implies the ability to identify the elements or parts of the whole, to see their relationships, and to structure them into some systematic arrangement or organization.

5. *Synthesis* involves a process similar to that of analysis, but is a reverse procedure. As a process it moves from the specific elements or parts to form

the whole. Once again knowing and understanding become the basis out of which facts and information are combined into wholes or some patterns that are different and larger than any part.

6. *Evaluation* is the highest level of the cognitive domain because it is used to form judgments with respect to the value of information made available through the other cognitive processes.

Each of the six levels will be illustrated by appropriate infinitives and sample multiple-choice items in the content area of court-coverage systems in badminton.

Knowledge. Ability to bring to mind small pieces of material. Very little, if any, alteration in the material is required.

Infinitives. To recognize, to recall, to identify, to define.

Sample Item. Which set of terms can be most closely identified with court-coverage systems in badminton?

1. up and back, parallel, rotation
2. horizontal, random, ad lib
3. right-left, front face, rotation
4. side-by-side, diagonal, freelance

Comprehension. Ability to redefine literal meaning, but not just rote memory.

Infinitives. To translate, to interpret, to extrapolate, to summarize, to paraphrase, to transform, to give in own words, to illustrate, to represent, to rephrase, to restate, to reorder, to extend.

Sample Item. What is another term that relates closely to the rotation system of court coverage?

1. circular
2. counterclockwise
3. clockwise
4. round

Application. Ability to use abstractions such as general ideas, rules, and principles.

Infinitives. To apply, to use, to generalize, to relate, to employ, to transfer.

Sample Item. When is the rotation system used most advantageously?

1. when the partners are of equal ability
2. when the players are quick
3. when the partners are playing mixed doubles
4. when the opposition is using an up-and-back system

Analysis. Ability to break down material into its parts so the relationships among the components can be seen.

Infinitives. To classify, to identify elements, to detect (parts), to distinguish, to discriminate, to categorize, to compare, to contrast, to analyze, to separate into parts, to draw relationships.

Sample Item. Which factor seems most crucial to the success of the rotation plan of court coverage?

1. quickness
2. communication
3. backhand strength
4. stamina

Synthesis. Ability to put together the parts to make a whole. The process may result in a new whole.

Infinitives. To design, to integrate, to formulate, to propose, to plan, to produce, to originate, to synthesize, to develop, to modify, to combine, to structure.

Sample Item. Which set of combined elements seems most important to the successful use of the rotation plan of court coverage?

1. strong forehand, short serve, and clear
2. quick movements, talking, and execution
3. good footwork, backhand, and hairpin dropshot
4. lasting stamina, practice, and perseverance

Evaluation. Ability to make judgments and decisions.

Infinitives. To judge, to decide, to compare (with a standard), to assess, to argue, to validate, to appraise.

Sample Item. You are accepting a challenge for a mixed-doubles match with the city champions. They are well-known for their dexterity, shrewdness, and "thinking" type of game. Which kind of court coverage would you be wise to select for the best defense?

1. parallel
2. up-and-back
3. rotation
4. diagonal

It is hoped that the test writer can now see how the content can be used to tap various levels of cognition by the students. Probably the test should include a range of items assessing facility with the content at various levels of the content at various levels of the taxonomy. It is usual, however, that beginning level tests include items predominantly at the knowledge, comprehension, and application levels. Intermediate and advanced level tests have a minimum of items at these levels and concentrate on items at the analysis, synthesis, and evaluation levels. The higher the item is on the taxonomy scale, the more difficult it is to construct. The payoff, however, is a better knowledge test on which to assess the cognition of the students.

Table 8–1 shows the use of Bloom's taxonomy for an intermediate tennis test. A few items from the intermediate test are included for illustrative purposes. The numbers of the items can be located on the two-way table to see the placement of items on content and taxonomic axes. A careful view of Table 8–1 shows that 39% and 26% of the points on the test covered skill/techniques and strategy, which seems appropriate for an intermediate level test. Likewise, the horizontal line on the table for Percent of Points shows that only 13% of the test items were judged to be at the two lowest levels of the cognitive taxonomy. This provides further evidence that the designation of the test as an intermediate test is fitting. The two-way table gives a picture of the test both as to content emphasis and cognitive taxonomic placement.

ETS Taxonomy

The second taxonomy was developed by the Educational Testing Service, Princeton, New Jersey, an institution well known for its expertise in test construction.[6] The Educational Testing Service recommends this taxonomy for classroom teachers who are developing their own knowledge tests. The taxonomy has a simplicity that is beneficial and yet also has a graduated precision that reveals a clear picture of the cognitive levels included in a test. Some similarity to the Bloom scheme will be noticed.

Table 8–1. Two-Way Table Using Bloom's Taxonomy: Intermediate Tennis Test*

Content Area	Knowledge†	Comprehension	Application	Analysis	Synthesis	Evaluation	Totals		
							Number of Items	Number of Points	Percent of Points
Rules	3, 36, 39, 41, 42		25, 26, 27, 28, 29, 30, 31, 32, 33, 34				10	20	23%
History		5					5	6	7%
Skill and Technique			1	8, 9, 10, 23, 24, 43, 44	17, 18, 21, 22	13	14	34	39%
Equipment and Facilities	35, 38, 40	37					4	4	5%
Strategy			4, 11, 15, 20			2, 6, 7, 12, 14, 16, 19	11	22	26%
TOTALS Number of Items	8	2	15	7	4	8	44		
Number of Points	9	3	30	20	8	16		86	
Percent of Points	10%	3%	35%	23%	9%	19%			100%

*Prepared by Pamela A. Reynolds, George Washington High School, Danville, Virginia, to fit her Objective Knowledge Test for Intermediate Tennis.

†From Bloom's Taxonomy.[4]

Point Breakdown

Questions 1–34 (2 points each)
Questions 35–42 (1 point each)
Questions 43–44 (5 points each)

Table 8–2.   Two-Way Table Using ETS Taxonomy: Intermediate Tennis Test*

Content Area	Remembering†	Understanding	Thinking	Total		
				Number of Items	Number of Points	Percent of Points
Rules		25, 26, 27, 28, 29, 30, 31, 32, 33, 34		10	20	23%
History	3, 36, 39, 41, 42			5	6	7%
Skill and Technique		1, 5, 8, 9, 10, 23, 24, 43, 44	13, 17, 18, 21, 22	14	34	39%
Equipment and Facilities	35, 38, 40	37		4	4	5%
Strategy		4, 11, 15, 20	2, 6, 7, 12, 14, 16, 19	11	22	26%
TOTALS Number of Items	8	24	12	44		
Number of Points	9	53	24		86	
Percent of Points	10%	62%	28%			100%

*Prepared by Pamela A. Reynolds, George Washington High School, Danville, Virginia, to reflect her Objective Knowledge Test for Intermediate Tennis.

†From Educational Testing Service's Taxonomy.[6]

Point Breakdown
  Questions 1–34 (2 points each)
  Questions 35–42 (1 point each)
  Questions 43–44 (5 points each)

REMEMBERING	UNDERSTANDING	THINKING
Recall of facts, rules, procedures	Classification	Analysis
Routine manipulation	Application	Generalization
Reproduction	Translation	Evaluation

The Educational Testing Service uses the three major categories and uses the secondary words for clarification. No hierarchic meanings, vertically, are claimed. There is, however, value in the horizontal development of levels. For example, a student who can reproduce something should next be able to translate it, and finally to evaluate it in some way. A description of a test, however, would be reported only according to the number of items in the remembering, under-standing, and thinking levels, respectively. Table 8–2 illustrates the use of the ETS taxonomy for the same intermediate tennis test used with the Bloom tax-onomy in Table 8–1.

EXCERPTS FROM AN INTERMEDIATE TENNIS TEST*
High-School Level

PART I—MULTIPLE CHOICE. (2 points each)

DIRECTIONS: Read each of the following items and select the best response. Place an X beside the number on the answer sheet under the letter you choose. All of the items refer to right-handed players.

1. What is the best return of service in doubles?
   *A. Cross-court shot
   B. Drop shot
   C. Lob
   D. Alley shot
2. What is the best serve to use when serving to someone with a weak backhand?
   A. Topspin
   B. Reverse twist
   C. Flat
   *D. American twist

   . . .
   . . .
   . . .

4. What is the best shot to make against a player at the net?
   A. Drop shot
   *B. Deep lob
   C. Down the line
   D. Shot to backhand of player
5. Which forehand grip is the best and why?
   A. Continental—because the open-racket face allows one to lift the ball
   B. Continental—because one may use this same grip for the backhand also
   *C. Eastern—because this position of the hand is more natural
   D. Eastern—because the closed-racket face allows one to handle the high bounce of the ball

*Used by permission of Pamela A. Reynolds, George Washington High School, Danville, Virginia.

6. What is the advantage of playing an Australian formation in doubles?
   *A. Prevents cross-court shots
   B. Allows for better net coverage
   C. Forces the opponents to lob
   D. Intimidates the opponents
7. What is the best strategy against a player with a good serve and volley game?
   *A. Force your opponent back by hitting deep lobs
   B. Go to the net after receiving the ball
   C. Hit drop shots
   D. Hit strong forehand drives
8. What path will the ball take if one uses an open-racket face?
   A. The ball will go directly into the net
   B. The ball will go in a straight path just clearing the net
   *C. The ball will go high
   D. The ball will barely clear the net and then immediately drop
9. What correction should be made if your serve consistently goes long?
   A. Allow your weight to remain on your back foot
   B. Contact the ball at a higher point
   C. Delay the toss and begin the motion of the racket first
   *D. Toss the ball lower
17. What corrections should you consider if your serve consistently goes into the net?
   (1) Toss the ball higher
   (2) Extend your racket arm more
   (3) Toss the ball closer to your body
   (4) Keep your weight on your back foot
   (5) Contact the ball at a higher point
       A. 2, 3
       B. 1, 5
       C. 2, 3, 4
       *D. 1, 3, 5
18. What causes the majority of the errors in serving?
   (1) Toss of the ball
   (2) Footwork
   (3) Extension of the racket
   (4) Power of the hit
   (5) Timing of the toss with contact
       *A. 1, 5
       B. 2, 4
       C. 1, 3, 5
       D. 2, 3, 4
19. What are the advantages of serving to a player's backhand in doubles?
   (1) Causes a weaker return
   (2) Reduces down-the-alley percentage shots
   (3) Pulls the player out of position in the ad court
   (4) Allows the server to approach the net sooner
   (5) Prevents the receiver from hitting effective lobs
       A. 1, 3, 4
       B. 2, 4, 5
       *C. 1, 2, 3
       D. 3, 4, 5
         . . .
         . . .
         . . .

21. What are the advantages of using a topspin stroke?
    (1) It allows you to hit the ball harder and keep it in bounds
    (2) It bounces toward your opponent causing her to back up
    (3) It will not bounce as high, thus throwing your opponent off balance
    (4) It allows you to use either a forehand or backhand grip and still be able to make
        the shot
    (5) It bounces away from your opponent off the court
         A. 2, 3, 4
         B. 1, 2, 3
         C. 1, 4
        *D. 1, 5
          . . .
          . . .
          . . .

23. Which diagram below shows the path of your forehand drive if you are swinging
    your racket late?

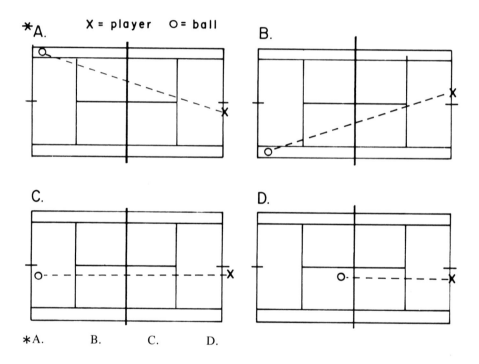

*A.   B.   C.   D.

24. Which diagram below shows the path of the ball for the American twist serve?

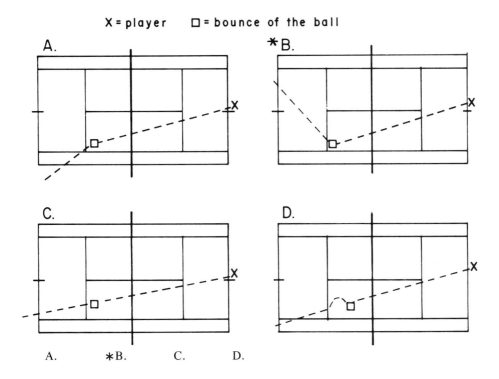

X = player   □ = bounce of the ball

A.   *B.

C.   D.

A.   *B.   C.   D.

PART II—CLASSIFICATION. (2 points each)

DIRECTIONS: Read each of the situations and decide what the ruling would be from the selection of choices below. Place an X beside the number on the answer sheet under the letter you choose.

Rulings
A. Point receiver
B. Point server
C. Let

(A) 25. Player A serves the ball and comes to the net. Player B returns the ball and remains at the baseline. After several hits, player B accidentally hits player A in the eye with the ball. What is the decision?

(A) 26. Player A and player B are playing a match. Player A serves. In the middle of a rather long point, a string breaks in the racket of player A. Immediately, player A walks off the court for another racket. Player B puts the ball away with a drop shot. What is the decision?

(B) 27. Team A and team B are playing doubles. Team A is serving. After several hits, a player on team A contacts the ball so that it passes on the outside of the net posts and much below the top of the net, but somehow lands good down the alley. Team B fails to return the ball. What is the decision?

· · ·

· · ·

· · ·

(C) 29. Player A and player B are playing a singles match in a local tournament. Player A is serving. In the middle of a very long point, a dog walks onto player B's side of the court. This obviously distracts both players. Player B stops the play and requests a let. What is the decision?

. . .

. . .

. . .

PART III—TRUE-FALSE. (1 point each)

DIRECTIONS: Read each statement below and decide whether it is true or false. If the statement is *true,* mark an X beside the number under column A on the answer sheet. If the statement is *false,* mark an X beside the number under column B on the answer sheet.

(A) 35. Composition-surfaced courts cause the ball to bounce more slowly than hard-surfaced courts.

(B) 36. Wightman Cup competition is principally for men.

(B) 37. Beginning players should string their rackets at about 65 pounds of pressure.

. . .

. . .

. . .

(A) 42. The International Tennis Hall of Fame is located in Newport, Rhode Island.

CONSTRUCTION OF OBJECTIVE KNOWLEDGE TESTS

Physical education knowledge tests are rare in the literature, so they must be developed locally. The acquisition of cognitive abilities is one of the objectives of physical education. Consequently, the measurement related to this objective should be as accurate as possible. The physical education teacher is charged with the responsibility of developing knowledge tests that are valid, reliable, and patterned to fit certain units of instruction. Once such professional skills are acquired, the teacher will build a collection of good knowledge tests. Soon a nucleus of tests, in which the instructor has some confidence, will be available. Revisions will need to be made from time to time, but the basic structure of the tests will remain the same.

Two pitfalls in test construction seem to have plagued the teacher in the past. One is the quickly constructed test that is either essay in type or composed of a short collection of ambiguous true-false statements. The other weakness has been the great emphasis placed on the inclusion of questions on rules to the exclusion of questions on technique and strategy. Good tests should reflect the content of the unit of instruction, should be prepared carefully, and should be restudied continually.

In addition, attention should be given to the reading level of the test. The vocabulary level should coincide with the reading level of the group taking the test. There are formulas and computer programs available to help determine reading levels of tests and test questions.[14]

Table 8–3. *Example of Content Balance for a Beginning Level Test*

Content Area	Percentage
Rules and terminology	25
Etiquette and procedures	10
Techniques and skills	30
Strategy and tactics	25
History and equipment	5
Safety	5
	100%

Content Balance

The constructor of the test should itemize the areas of information to be covered and assign them certain proportional weightings in the overall content (Table 8–3). These weightings should parallel the weighting each area received in the instructional work.

The suggested content balance will change from unit to unit and from sport to sport. Essentially, however, rules and terminology probably should never cover more than one-quarter of the value of the total test and preferably less. Emphasis should be on the execution of the skills and how to apply them in a game situation. Some basic facts concerning the equipment, the historical background of the sport, and some of the special terms seem appropriate. In some sports, safety is an important aspect of the game and is worthy of some emphasis in a test.

Questions of fact and definition covering rules and terminology are rather simple to construct. They measure the lower levels of understanding. Questions covering the application, analysis, and synthesis of skills and strategies are more difficult to construct. How well a student is able to "know" a game is better measured by how well he/she can apply his/her understanding of the game than by how well he/she can recall facts about the game. Thus, the precision of the test instrument and the skill required to construct it are a reflection of how well the teacher is able to test for the depth of concepts about a particular activity.

Sources of Items

Good test questions can be gleaned from several sources. The teacher should be alert for such questions and collect them as they appear. The ideas for the questions must come first and then be developed. The teacher's own creativeness and intellectual endeavors provide many questions. Textbooks, rule books, and sports books are good sources. The questions that the students ask during classes often bring out excellent ideas and their wording is also worthy of note for future application to test questions. Sample tests from books and research reports supply good ideas for questions and formats. Colleagues can be helpful by sharing written tests. And collections of test questions for activities are available both in hard copy and on computer diskettes.[20,29] Whenever a teacher has the use of a test, it is seldom possible to use the test exactly as it appears. Usually it has to be adapted to fit a particular unit in content, difficulty, format, and the like. Although it is seldom possible to use a test as it appears, it does give the teacher a beginning on which to build.

Types of Items

Questions for objective tests are of several types. They each have certain applications and some rules for construction.

Alternate-Response:

a. Examples of alternate-response questions are true-false, yes-no, right-wrong, and same-opposite.

b. True-false is the most prevalent of this style of question.

c. True-false questions permit a wide range of content coverage in limited space and time.

d. They are usually constructed quickly, although good true-false questions may require a good deal of time to design.

e. They encourage guessing. Guessing can be minimized if the students are told that the questions will be scored by deducting the number wrong from the number answered correctly. Guessing can also be minimized by using other scoring methods: Subtract the percentage wrong from the number right, or subtract one-half the number wrong from the number right. The selection of the scoring method depends on how severely the teacher wants to penalize for guessing.

f. They frequently test for trivial information.

Example of a poor question: The lines on a tennis court may be no more than 2 inches in width.

g. They are applicable when only two responses are possible.

h. They should involve only one concept to be judged.

Example of a poor question: The maximum number of sets in a match shall be 5, or when women take part, 3.

i. They should be stated in positive terms unless the negative word is emphasized by underlining of the word.

Example of a poor question. A freestyle swimmer should not do more than 3 strokes without taking a breath.

j. They should be stated in quantitative instead of qualitative terms.

Example of a poor question: There are several (instead of 4) recognized systems of court coverage related to badminton.

k. There should be approximately the same number of true questions as there are false questions.

l. They should not be constructed as trick questions.

Example of a poor question: The object rallied in badminton is called a "birdie."

m. No cue words should reveal the correct answer.

Example of a poor question: The side stroke is *always* used as a speed style of swimming.

n. Questions of opinion should be avoided unless the authority is stated.

o. The answers should follow no pattern or sequence.

p. False statements should not be stated in negative terms.

Example of a poor question: A person engaged in strenuous activity should refrain from drinking water.

The *True-False format has several variations* that can be used to advantage to help the teacher achieve testing objectives:

a. True or false and tell why.

b. True or false and correct if wrong.

c. True or false or sometimes choices.

Examples of True-False Questions:

1. Golfers who have holed out may repeat their putts for practice.

2. Trimming a canoe is a matter of balancing the weight of occupants and duffle.

3. One of the chief causes of accidents in rowboats and canoes involves occupants exchanging positions.

*4. Left-handed players may hit ball on the rounded part of the stick.

*5. A goal may *not* be scored off the stick of a defense player unless it was first touched by the stick of an attacker within the striking circle.

†6. It is best to rest a sore muscle until the soreness is gone.

Examples of Alternative-Response Questions:

Knowledge Test-First Grade‡

Movement Exploration

The teacher will give the directions, read each question, and wait for each child to make the appropriate mark or response on his paper.

1. Draw a circle around the children who are in a scattered formation.

2. Draw a cross mark on the child who is landing softly from a jump.

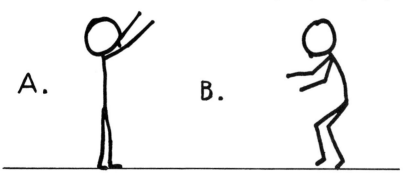

*Used by permission of Miss Paula Drake, Cape Elizabeth High School, Cape Elizabeth, Maine.
†Used by permission of Ms. Cindy Kennedy, Sandhills Community College, Southern Pines, North Carolina.
‡Used by permission of Dr. Virginia Hart, Mars Hill College, Mars Hill, North Carolina.

Multiple-Choice

The multiple-choice style of question is held in high esteem by test constructors. They consider it capable of measuring the application of facts and the higher cognitive levels that the teacher hopes to assess. The question or preliminary statement is known as the stem or the problem. The alternatives listed are known as choices; the incorrect ones are known either as distractors or foils.

a. Multiple-choice questions are the most difficult to construct.

b. The multiple-choice format is inappropriate if only two choices are possible.

c. Skill is required to develop plausible yet incorrect choices.

d. Multiple-choice questions require some discriminatory thinking.

e. They may be very easy or very difficult, depending on the closeness or homogeneity of the choices.

f. They require no adjustment in scoring for guessing.

g. The stem should be a complete statement or question.

h. Each possible choice should be plausible.

i. All choices should follow a parallel structure which is grammatically consistent.

j. All choices should be about the same length.

k. The placement of the correct answers among the choices should follow no pattern.

l. Four plausible choices seem adequate.

m. Each question should have the same number of choices if possible. However, having few choices that function is better than having more just for the sake of consistency in format.

n. Each choice should be listed separately.

o. Questions are usually stated in the third person. The use of the second person "You" is sometimes advantageous because it puts the test taker in the setting of the question.

p. The problem should be simply and concisely presented in the stem.

q. Multiple-choice questions sometimes have as the fourth choice either "Any of these," "All of these," or "None of them." Great care should be taken when using such a choice. These choices are overused. If one of these is used at all, it must also be included when that choice is not the correct one.

r. The terminology used in the stem should not be repeated in the choices.

s. Negatively stated questions should be minimal, and care should be taken to emphasize the negative words by underlining them.

t. Care should be taken that a question does not give a clue to the answer of some other question in the test. Each item should be independent.

The Multiple-Choice format has several variations:

Correct Answer. One answer is correct and the others, while plausible, are definitely incorrect. Questions on rules are of this format because they are statements of facts and thus not debatable.

*Example (volleyball): Team A serves at the beginning of the match. Team B serves at the beginning of the next match. The score is tied 1 game to 1 game. Which team serves first in the final game of the match?

*Used by permission of Ms. Carolyn Littlejohn, Mecklenberg County Schools, Charlotte, North Carolina.

1. The team that served first in the game will serve first in the final game
2. The team that won the second game will serve first in the third game
3. The first serve in the final game is decided by a coin toss
4. The visiting team will serve first in the final game

Example: Which condition causes a person to drown?
1. Unconsciousness
2. Shock
3. Panic
4. Suffocation

Best Answer. One answer is definitely preferable. Other choices have a degree of correctness but are not the best possible response. Questions on strategy and skill technique are suitable for this format because judgments are made in selecting the one best response.

Example (golf): What is the most important factor in determining the height and distance of the flight of the ball?
1. the length of the shaft of the club
2. the angle of the clubface
3. the weight of the clubhead
4. the strength of the player

*Example (racquetball): You are positioned behind your doubles partner who swings at the ball and misses. Both of your opponents are in front court. Which shot should you use?
1. Kill shot
2. Cross-court pass
3. Back-wall shot to either corner
4. Ceiling shot

The cluster format is a variation of the best answer format and is useful for analysis and synthesis questions that involve combinations of factors.

†Example: Which combination of elements *should* a person have to be considered a conditioned person?

a.	Agility	1.	a, b, c, d
b.	Strength	2.	b, d, f, g
c.	Flexibility	3.	c, e, f, h
d.	Weight loss	4.	d, e, g, h
e.	Muscular endurance		
f.	Fast recovery rate		
g.	Increased muscle bulk		
h.	Decreased heart rate		

Multiple Response or Multiple Answer. There is at least one correct answer and there may be more. Two keys are necessary—one to see if all correct answers were selected and another to see that no incorrect answers were selected. Each statement is scored. It is a mistake to choose an incorrect answer just as it is to omit a correct one.

---

*Used by permission of Mr. Byron Petrakis, University of North Carolina at Charlotte, Charlotte, North Carolina.

†Used by permission of Ms. Cindy Kennedy, Sandhills Community College, Southern Pines, North Carolina.

*Example: What are the functions of the round-the-head stroke?
1. To keep the court well-covered
2. To cover the weak backhand
3. To retain the attack for the hitter
4. To provide deception when returning

Example: Which square dance calls are examples of the "couple visitor" figure?
1. Birdie in the Cage
2. Texas Star
3. Rip and Snort
4. Form a Star with a Right-hand Cross
5. Inside Arch and Outside Under

Poor examples of multiple choice items and suggestions for revisions:
   a. If a ball touches a boundary line
     1. It is out-of-bounds
     2. Is played over
     3. Is good
     4. Neither team scores

Complete the stem and make the choices parallel in structure.
  What decision is made when the ball touches a boundary line?
     1. It is out-of-bounds
     2. It is replayed
     3. It is good
     4. It is dead
   b. Safety factors for bathing places do <u>not</u> include
     1. Good bottom
     2. Clear runways and decks
     3. Swimming areas should be large

Note that the negative word is underlined for emphasis. Make the choices parallel in structure and grammar, and make the stem a complete statement.
  Which factor is <u>not</u> essential to a safe bathing place?
     1. Good bottoms
     2. Clear runways and decks
     3. Spaciousness
     4. Marked areas

General Examples of Multiple-Choice Questions:

a. Tennis   Why is it important to toss the ball high enough to serve with the arm fully extended?
     1. Enables the server to hit the ball either to the right or left of the receiver
     2. Enables the server to use the entire body as a lever, thus getting more power behind the ball
     3. Eliminates the possibility of hitting the ball into the net
     4. Assures the server greater accuracy

---

*Used by permission of Ms. Gwendolyn Davis, Hickory, North Carolina.

*b. Lacrosse   What causes the rocking motion of the crosse that is nec-
                      essary in cradling?
                      1. Twisting the shoulders
                      2. Keeping both elbows bent
                      3. Flexing and extending the wrists
                      4. Keeping the left elbow bent

 c. Badminton   What is the advantage of the rotation system over the parallel
                      system of doubles play?
                      1. Eliminates many backhand shots
                      2. Confuses the opponents
                      3. Provides opportunity for players to see a greater variety
                         of strokes
                      4. Encourages more cooperation between partners

†d. Volleyball   In which skills will a player increase efficiency by jumping?
                      A. Spike
                      B. Offensive volley
                      C. Bump
                      D. Overhand serve
                      E. Block
                      1. A, B, D, E,
                      2. B, C, D
                      3. A, B, E
                      4. A, B
                      What provides the majority of force for the bump?
                      1. The quick armlift and follow-through
                      2. The redirected force from the incoming ball
                      3. The contracting arm and shoulder muscles
                      4. The finger and wrist flexion

‡e. Bowling   Which principle best relates to the starting position?
                      1. First ball delivery, distance from foul line is constant,
                         position from side to side varies
                      2. First ball delivery, distance from foul line varies, po-
                         sition from side to side constant
                      3. First or second ball delivery, distance from foul line is
                         constant, position from side to side varies
                      4. First or second ball delivery, distance from foul line
                         varies, position from side to side is constant

Matching

Matching statements are applicable for definitions, personality identifications,
and rules.

a. Matching questions should be homogeneous in content. Terms should not
be mixed with personalities in the same question. It is better to have two short
matching sections than one longer one containing a mixture of content.

---

*Used by permission of Dr. Dorothy Harris, Pennsylvania State Univ., University Park, Pennsyl-
vania.

†Used by permission of Miss Beth Kerr, University of Oregon, Eugene, Oregon.

‡Used by permission of Dr. Roberta Howells, State Department of Public Instruction, Hartford,
Connecticut.

b. They are likely to measure only memory in contrast to comprehension and understanding.

c. They are likely to include clues to the correct response.

d. The response column should be arranged in some systematic order, such as alphabetically or chronologically.[30]

e. All of the parts of the question should be on one page.[30]

f. Matching questions should probably include at least 5 and probably not more than 15 items.[30]

g. More responses should be listed than items to be matched.

h. Responses should be in the right-hand column.

i. At least two plausible answers for each question should be included in the response column.[30]

Several variations are possible on matching questions:

a. Perfect. The same number of responses is listed as there are items to be matched. This practice is not recommended because some answers can be determined by the process of elimination.

b. Imperfect. There are more choices than are needed. At least two extra choices should be included.

c. Multiple. There are two columns of responses and each item to be matched must be answered by one response from each column.

Example of a Matching Question:

Match the term with the definition. Indicate the letter of the correct response in the first set of brackets on the answer sheet.

34. Down	*a.* a stroke that makes a return impossible
35. In	*b.* lost service for the first server in doubles
36. Kill	*c.* the receiving side
37. One down	*d.* a fault
38. Out	*e.* a stroke that initiates each rally
39. Serve	*f.* a toss
	g. shuttlecock
	h. the serving side
	i. the long service area
	j. loss of service through failure of the serving side to score

Classification

Classification is a kind of matching question. There are fewer choices from which to select. The choice may be used more than once. Classification questions lend themselves to measuring the organization of information and the relationship of small items to larger concepts.

a. The content should cover material of similar nature.

b. The format is opposite from the matching categories. The short list of classifications is usually given either at the top or on the right-hand side. The situations are listed in the left-hand column.

*Example:

Situations	Rulings
1. Team B serves the ball. The center forwards on both teams jump up to get the ball, and the ball is held simultaneously. What is the correct ruling?	1. Point 2. Side-out 3. Double fault 4. Play continues

. . . . .

. . . . .

10. . . .

†Another example:

Activity	Type of Activity
1. Swimming	a. Aerobic
2. Gymnastics	b. Anaerobic
3. Tennis	
4. Jogging	
5. Softball	
6. Weight training	
7. Sprint	
8. Cycling	

c. Care should be taken to be sure each entry fits into one of the categories.

Rearrangement

Rearrangement questions place emphasis on the order of things. Sequence of a skill execution and chronological order of sporting events are examples. Questions on history and progression of skill are possible with this format.

a. The order provided should be well-scrambled.

b. The unraveled order of each question should follow no pattern.

c. Care should be taken in scoring decisions because an incorrect choice of the first answer may make the succeeding answers incorrect even though in logical order.

d. Probably each question should have only a single value. Any error in the sequence would mean a missed question. If a sequence question with 5 parts is allotted 5 points, the weightings in the content balance would most likely become distorted.

Examples of Rearrangement Questions:

Arrange in logical order the following steps in learning to dive.

1. One-leg dive
2. Crouched dive
3. Standing dive
4. Sitting dive
5. Kneeling dive

---

*Used by permission of Ms. Carolyn Littlejohn, Mecklenberg County Schools, Charlotte, North Carolina.

†Used by permission of Ms. Cindy Kennedy, Sandhills Community College, Southern Pines, North Carolina.

Special Formats

Sometimes a higher cognitive level can be measured better if diagrams, charts, stick figures, symbols, and the like are used in the format of the questions. Examples may be seen in the sample intermediate tennis test and in the section on item writing. A diagram could be referred to for the answers to several questions. Strategy questions on court placements are appropriate to this format. Musical symbols and baseball scoring symbols have been used effectively in tests. Stick figures are effective for stunts, tumbling and sports technique questions. Scoring lines in bowling and in golf are examples of the use of graphics in the construction of test questions. Often rules questions can be placed at the application level instead of the basic knowledge level by using diagrams of various kinds. Special formats permit a type of question that might otherwise be difficult to structure. They also add variety to the test, and they are challenging to construct.

Final Format

1. The test should be typed carefully, proofread, and duplicated. A double column of questions saves space.

2. Directions for answering the questions should be stated carefully and thoroughly on the test paper.

True-False. Read each question carefully. If the statement is entirely true, put an X in the first set of brackets; if the statement is wholly or partially false, put an X in the second set of brackets on the answer sheet.

Multiple-Choice. Read each statement carefully. The questions are worded for right-handed players. Decide which is the one *best* answer and place an X in the brackets on the answer sheet corresponding to the number of the response.

Matching. Indicate the letter of the correct response in the first set of brackets on the answer sheet.

Rearrangement. Arrange in logical sequence the correct order for each statement. Place the number representing the first factor in the first set of brackets on the answer sheet, the number of the second point in the sequence in the second set of brackets, and so forth.

3. A double space should be between questions.

4. All parts of a question should be on the same page of the test.

5. The test should be titled.

Length

The number of questions in a test should be sufficient to assure some degree of reliability, but not so many that few students are able to complete it. Fifty questions is a good "rule of thumb," especially if most of them are multiple-choice items.

Test writers seem to be enamored with a test value of 100 points. They arrive at this number either by writing 100 questions or by assigning each question a certain numerical value. For example, multiple-choice questions might be worth 2 points each and true-false questions worth only 1 point. This practice is questionable because it distorts the content emphasis intended for the test. If the rules area is to cover only one-fourth of the test, but each rules question is given a double value, then it is possible, depending on the weightings given the other questions, to put undue stress on this area of the content. Tests of 43 questions or of 61 questions, for example, are quite acceptable. Scale the final scores in relation to the total number of points on the test. There is no magic in the 100-point test except that it may be a little easier to handle mathematically. A test composed of 54 good questions is a far better measuring tool than one containing 100 questions that is prepared less thoughtfully.

Answer Sheets and Keys (Fig. 8–2)

The use of answer sheets is recommended for several reasons:
1. They permit the reuse of the test papers.
2. They facilitate scoring the papers.
3. They permit a mark showing the correct answer for later study of the test by the students.
4. They are economical in time and in money.
5. They are convenient to use when doing an item analysis of the test.

Students should be taught how to use an answer sheet. For example, a form answer sheet may provide space for 5 possible responses while a test question may have only 4 choices. Deciding the correct answer is the last one, the student

EXAMPLE OF ANSWER SHEET FOR 90 QUESTIONS

Name_____ Course_____ Date_____

	1 2 3 4 5		1 2 3 4 5		1 2 3 4 5
1.	( )( )( )(X)( )	31.	( )( )( )( )( )	61.	( )( )( )( )( )
2.	( )( )( )( )( )	32.	( )( )( )( )( )	62.	( )( )( )( )( )
3.	( )( )( )( )( )	33.	( )( )( )( )( )	63.	( )( )( )( )( )
4.	( )( )( )( )( )	34.	( )( )( )( )( )	64.	( )( )( )( )( )
5.	( )( )( )( )( )	35.	( )( )( )( )( )	65.	( )( )( )( )( )

30. ( )( )( )( )( )   60. ( )( )( )( )( )   90. ( )( )( )( )( )

EXAMPLE OF ANSWER SHEET FOR 60 QUESTIONS

Name_____ Activity_____ Date_____

1.	1 2 3 4	16.	1 2 3 4	31.	1 2 3 4	46.	1 2 3 4
	" " " "		" " " "		" " " "		" " " "
	" " " "		" " " "		" " " "		" " " "
	" " " "		" " " "		" " " "		" " " "
2.	1 2 3 4	17.	1 2 3 4	32.	1 2 3 4	47.	1 2 3 4
	" " " "		" " " "		" " " "		" " " "
	" " " "		" " " "		" " " "		" " " "
	" " " "		" " " "		" " " "		" " " "
15.	1 2 3 4	30.	1 2 3 4	45.	1 2 3 4	60.	1 2 3 4
	" " " "		" " " "		" " " "		" " " "
	" " " "		" " " "		" " " "		" " " "
	" " " "		" " " "		" " " "		" " " "

Fig. 8–2. Sample answer sheets.

marks the fifth spot on the answer sheet and misses the question. The student should be cautioned about such practices. The use of the answer sheet may take a little more time because the student's attention must be shifted back and forth from the test paper to the answer sheet.

Most types of questions can be answered on an answer sheet. The form should provide for about 60 to 90 questions so it can accommodate a test of almost any length.

Scoring keys for efficient grading can be made. Stencil keys are the type that are superimposed on the answer sheet and have the correct answer cut out. The grader is able to mark the correct answer, if not already indicated, so the student knows what it should have been when going over the test paper later. Strip keys are placed adjacent to the answers. Comparisons are necessary as the grader works down the column. The grader should designate the correct answers for any questions missed.

Computerized answer sheets can be read, scored, and analyzed electronically by various types of optical scanners.[31] If such equipment is available in the school or school system, it should be used. Technology is available for taking a test via computer.[19] The paper and pencil test will become an out-dated procedure as more computers become available.

CONSTRUCTION OF ESSAY KNOWLEDGE TESTS[3,21,28,32]

Essay tests are criticized for their low reliability and the inordinate amount of time necessary for reading and grading. These disadvantages can be minimized if steps are taken to prepare the essay test carefully.

Content

The content balance of an essay test should be similar to that for an objective test. It should parallel the emphasis given to various aspects of the content during instruction. It is likely, however, that the content at the knowledge, comprehension, application, and analysis levels can be more efficiently measured by an objective format. At the higher cognitive levels of the taxonomy, the essay format is useful.

Types of Items

Three types of items are related to the essay test format, each varying in the length of the response the student needs to write.

Completion

The completion question requires a response of either one word or perhaps two to three words at the most. Longer responses result in less objective and more time-consuming grading.
  a. Omit only key significant words.
  b. Include only one or two blanks in any one statement.
  c. Locate the blank(s) toward the end of the statement.
  d. All acceptable answers should be noted on the key before the test is given. Acceptance of only one certain word promotes rote learning which may be accompanied by very little understanding.

Poor Example: _____ and _____ are two important concepts in the definition of _____.

Improved Example: Two important concepts in the definition of first aid are _____ and _____.

*Example: Racquetball is more closely related to handball than to _____.

Short Answer

This format is used for answers to questions requiring only one or two sentences. It is useful when a restatement of a rule or a brief explanation of some point is desired. The answers can be graded rather objectively because the key points are evident.

†Examples: 1. Explain how the factor of distance influences the application of the obstruction rule.

2. Write in your own words the rule for a foot fault.

Long Answer (Essay)

The response to the essay item, traditionally titled, can vary in length from a paragraph to several pages.

a. Clearly define the aim of the question by using specific verbs. To discuss is too general and does not help the student know the exact treatment desired of the information. Some helpful verbs are: define, describe, outline, select, illustrate, compare, contrast, classify, summarize, give the reasons for, explain how, what factors have contributed to, differentiate, criticize, predict what would happen if, give original examples of.

b. Indicate the value of each question to help the student understand the depth of treatment desired.

c. Prepare the key carefully before administering the test. Sometimes the key helps the test writer identify exactly the type of response expected (e.g., comparison or explanation), and this assists the writer in refining the essay item.

d. Include several questions of shorter length instead of only one or two lengthy items.

e. Give all the students the same items. There should be no choices if the grades are used to compare the performance of the students, that is, if they are to be norm-referenced instead of criterion-referenced.

f. State the ground rules for the essay test. Approximate length is helpful to know and is usually correlated with the point value of the item. For instance, "In no more than one paragraph . . .," or "Use a half page to . . . ." Indicate if spelling, handwriting, and grammar will be considered in grading the paper.

g. Try to grade the papers anonymously, if possible.

h. Score all the students on one question and then proceed to another item.

Examples:

‡1. Outline the factors you would consider in analyzing your serve if it consistently goes long. Include at least 5 factors. (15 points)

---

*Used by permission of Mr. Byron Petrakis, University of North Carolina at Charlotte, Charlotte, North Carolina.

†Used by permission of Ms. Linda Turkovich, Physical Education Instructor, J.F. Luther Junior High School, Fort Atkinson, Wisconsin.

‡Used by permission of Ms. Pamela A. Reynolds, George Washington High School, Danville, Virginia.

*2. Explain how composition-surfaced courts and hard-surfaced courts differ in relation to the play of the ball, specifically, and to the overall game, in general. Include at least 4 factors related to each type of surface. (16 points)

†3. Summarize the major differences in the principles of strategy which should be used in the singles and the doubles games of badminton. Indicate at least 5 points for each type of game. (20 points)

‡4. Contrast interchange "flow" playing and position playing. Cite at least 4 differences. (10 points)

EVALUATION OF OBJECTIVE KNOWLEDGE TESTS

The evaluation of objective knowledge tests is a procedure that the teacher can learn and apply. As the teacher builds a collection of written tests, revisions will be underway continually: some only minor and some major in scope. The revision of only one or two tests per year would be feasible. The work involved in test revision would prevent such a practice for every test administered. Other phases of teaching and of testing would suffer from such overemphasis on written tests. The teacher learns to save and label sets of answer sheets so they will be available whenever a test revision is anticipated.

Editing

Editing revisions come from close scrutiny of a test. Reading and rereading each question will suggest changes in the structure of the item, in the choices, in the word order, and in the statements that changes in rules and strategy have altered.

A study of the unit outline will suggest ideas for new questions and the deletion of others. The comments of the students will suggest word changes for better clarity of questions. A review of the test by a colleague will be helpful. The study of other tests will suggest changes in question format that will improve the question. A growing knowledge of test construction and awareness of the fine points of item construction will make the teacher more and more confident to edit his/her tests.

There are some differences in the validity and reliability procedures appropriate for norm-referenced and criterion-referenced tests. The former rely on a spread of scores and the latter depend on a clustering of scores at the top. Consequently, different statistical procedures are indicated. The validity and reliability of each type of test will be discussed separately.

Validity of Norm-Referenced Tests

The validity of a written test is the same in concept as the validity of a performance test. A measure of the truthfulness and honesty of the test is indicated. At least 2 types of validity should be considered.

---

*Used by permission of Ms. Pamela A. Reynolds, George Washington High School, Danville, Virginia.

†Used by permission of Ms. Gwendolyn Davis, Hickory, North Carolina.

‡Used by permission of Ms. Linda Turkovich, Physical Education Instructor, J.F. Luther Junior High School, Fort Atkinson, Wisconsin.

1. *Content validity* is achieved if the content of the test is in agreement with the unit of instruction. The test may be studied by several "authorities" who consider its contents in relation to what they consider such a unit should include. The test constructor alone may do this. The test can be compared in content with the content of books covering the activity. The test can be compared in content balance with similar tests. The test content can be compared with the content of a specific unit it is designed to fit. If approximately parallel emphasis is evident in some or all of these methods, validity is usually built into the test as it is being constructed. Once administered, however, and once answer sheets are available for analysis, a further validity check of the test can be made that utilizes statistical procedures.

2. *Statistical validity* is a more involved process and answers the more technical question of the internal ability of the test to distinguish between those who "know" and those who "do not know." The process is known as *item analysis* and operates on the premise that each test question should meet certain standards. An item is retained in a test only if it is a quality item. The inference is that if each item is "good" then the total test will be valid.

The Flanagan Method[2,12,13]

The Flanagan Method of item analysis is the best known and most widely used. An item analysis reveals three qualities about each item on a test: (1) the difficulty of each item, (2) the power of each item to discriminate between the students who know the most about the subject and those who know the least, and (3) the amount that each possible response functions by noting the frequency with which each response is chosen.

The *Difficulty Rating* shows the proportion of students who answered each test question correctly.

The higher the percent, the easier the question. If the question is answered correctly by over 90% of the students, it is considered too easy. If answered correctly by fewer than 10% of the students, it is considered too difficult. Revisions are indicated for such questions.

Items with Difficulty Ratings of 50% are most desirable because they also discriminate maximally. The average Difficulty Rating for the entire test should be around 50 to 60%.

The *Index of Discrimination* is reported as a correlation coefficient and shows the relationship between answering an item either right or wrong and scoring either high or low on the total test. This index is considered acceptable if over .20. If the coefficient for an item is between .15 and .19, it is deemed questionable, and if below .15, the question should be deleted or revised. The average Index of Discrimination for all the items on the test will probably fall between .30 and .40. If the index for a particular item is negative, i.e., $-.38$, more of the students who scored at the low end on the total test than at the high end answered this particular question correctly. Negative coefficients indicate items that definitely should be eliminated from the test or reviewed for clarification.

Function is the third characteristic of an item that is checked. Each choice should be appealing enough to be chosen by some of the students. Some authors indicate that at least 3% of the students should use each response. Others list 2%.

If no one selects a choice, it cannot help the item or the total test to make a distinction between the students who know the most and the ones who know the least about the topic. Revision of nonfunctioning or inactive choices is indicated.

Revisions. Once all three pieces of information are known about each item, revisions can be made. The process of constructing, administering, analyzing, and revising tests then starts over. This process continues in order to refine tests and to strengthen the evidence of validity.

Whereas formerly such analysis was done by tediously hand-tallying every response to every question, the practice now is to process item analyses on a computer. TESTAN is one example of a computer program for item analysis.[31] The use of computer programs for item analysis is recommended. The process has been described here to make the computer printout more understandable and to assist the person who needs to use the hand-tally method of item analysis.[2]

The Educational Testing Service Method[6,8]

The Educational Testing Service method proposes an item analysis scheme that requires limited computational work because it makes use of only the top 10 answer sheets and the bottom 10 answer sheets for a class. It is recommended for use by teachers. Obviously, at least 20 answer sheets are needed. The procedures are the same if 100 answer sheets are available. The ETS method of item analysis reveals the Index of Difficulty and the Index of Discrimination of the correct response for each multiple-choice term. It gives no information about the functioning of choices, information that would be helpful if revisions are indicated. It is usually true, however, that if the item is too easy, there will be choices not functioning.

The Educational Testing Service system also investigates the "speededness" of the test. The discrimination and difficulty reports can be distorted if some of the students did not have time to complete the test. However, in most physical education settings, the test length is designed to be completed within 1 class period.

Step 1. Prepare the data collection form. An answer sheet will suffice or another form that provides space for recording 5 columns of numbers.

Item Number	H	L	H + L	H − L
	(10 papers)	*(10 papers)*	*(Difficulty 7–17)*	*(Discrimination 3 +)*
1.	6	3	9	3
2.				

Step 2. Spread out the 10 high-answer sheets so the number of students in the high group who answered each question correctly can be counted. Record the number right for each item on the test in the H column. Error is possible, so care should be taken that the answer sheets are properly aligned when they are displayed. A recounting is a good double check for accuracy.

Step 3. Repeat the same process using the 10 answer sheets in the low group. Record the number of students getting each question right in the L column.

Step 4. Add the numbers in the H and L columns to complete the H + L column. This number will reflect the difficulty of the item. ETS suggest a standard of acceptance between 7 and 17. If more than 17 of the 20 students responded correctly, the item is probably too easy. If fewer than 7 in the combined groups answered an item correctly, the item is too difficult. Since there are 20 papers, this range of 7 to 17 could be interpreted as equivalent to 35 to 75% as a satisfactory standard for accepting an item on the basis of difficulty level alone.

Step 5. Subtract the H and L columns and place the resulting number in the H − L column. It is possible to have negative numbers and this is important to know. The numbers in this last column represent the discriminating ability of the item. Ideally, more students in the high group than in the low group should get an item correct. ETS suggests a standard of 3 and above as an acceptable criterion for accepting the discrimination power of an item. If lower, the item needs revising, and if falling low enough to reach the negative range (i.e., −2), the item is definitely in need of revising. Each item should contribute to the mission of the whole test. If an item has a negative index of discrimination, it is contributing to the total test the opposite quality an item is supposed to furnish.

Step 6. Summarize the results of the tally and identify the items that are satisfactory, those that should be revised, and those that should be discarded.

There is some reluctance about using this system because it uses only 20 answer sheets. Depending upon the number of answer sheets available, this could be a substantial number. At any rate, the results provide the teacher with a good estimate of the worth of each test item as well as some information needed to proceed with revisions.

Some teachers like to involve students in the item analysis procedures. If anonymity of answer sheets can be assured, this is an efficient process and can be a worthwhile educational experience. Proceeding item by item, students are asked to raise their hands so the appropriate numbers can be recorded for the number of correct responses shown on the top ten papers and on the bottom ten papers. The class members become aware of the questions that caused trouble and become participants in the discussion of content that needs clarifying.[8]

Reliability of Norm-Referenced Tests

The *reliability* indicates the *consistency* with which a test can rank the students from good to poor. It is influenced in written tests by several factors. The length of the test, or the number of items, determines the reliability to a great extent. The more items, the greater the reliability, excluding such factors as fatigue, boredom, and the like. The reliability is also affected by the ability of the items to discriminate. The testing situation plays an influencing role. The more closely the items measure knowledge in one area of information, the more likely that the reliability will be high.

If the test is too easy, the reliability will be lowered. For example, if a 50-item test has a mean score of 43, the reliability will be low because all the students cluster toward the top of the scale, preventing a normal distribution and a greater range of the scores. The average difficulty level of an entire test should be approximately 50 to 60% of the number of items. When this is the case, the reliability coefficient gives a truer picture of the test consistency.

Assumed Reliability

Many authors believe that a valid test will automatically produce a reliable one. They see no need for estimating statistical reliability. If the test has sufficient items, if its content is homogeneous, if its difficulty level is stabilized around 50 to 60%, and if its scores have a good range, then it is probably safe to assume adequate test reliability.

Test-Retest

This method requires two administrations of the complete test to the same group. The two scores for each student are correlated and a reliability coefficient is the outcome. A coefficient indicative of the *stability* of the test results.

Sometimes substantial memory and learning factors have undue influence on the coefficient. At times the students are bored with the second administration. They fail to be motivated to perform at their best because they consider the second testing senseless. The test-retest method of establishing reliability is probably more appropriate to various motor tests than it is to written tests. In any case, very careful administrative considerations have to be made concerning the time element and the motivation of the students.

It is generally accepted that the square root of a reliability coefficient will estimate the upper limit of a validity coefficient. It is evident, therefore, that the two concepts are interrelated.

Parallel Forms

The test constructor prepares two tests covering the same topic that are similar in content balance, length, difficulty, and discriminating power. Both forms are administered to the same group, and the two scores for each person are correlated to obtain the reliability. The coefficient indicates the *equivalency* of the two forms. This method rests on the assumption that the two forms are actually parallel. Such a quality is difficult to achieve.

Parallel forms of a test are more prevalent in written tests than in motor tests. Officials' ratings exams are often prepared in two forms so a person may have a second chance if unsuccessful on the first attempt. Parallel forms could be used to measure progress from the beginning to the end of a unit. If the tests are measuring the same thing to the same degree, comparison of the two test scores is reasonable. These applications, however, are not suitable for obtaining reliability estimates.

The use of parallel forms of written tests by the average classroom teacher is rare. As more commercially standardized tests become available, this application of tests will be possible.

Kuder-Richardson Formula[24]

Many variations of this formula have been designed especially for use with written tests. Only one administration of the test is required. The test does not need to be split into odd-even or first and second halves, for example. Therefore, the different results caused by different methods of dividing the test are eliminated. This method does not require the correlation and so reduces the amount of the computational work. It does, however, operate on the same assumptions as the Spearman-Brown Prophecy formula with regard to item difficulty and discrimination. The Kuder-Richardson formula is considered to estimate the lower limit of what the real reliability of a test may be.

$$r_{tt} = \frac{n\sigma_t^2 - M(n-M)}{(n-1)\sigma_t^2}$$

r_{tt} = Reliability of total test
n = Number of items in test
M = Mean of the scores
σ_t^2 = Standard deviation of the test scores squared

Example: n = 55 items
M = 30
SD = 8

$$r_{tt} = \frac{(55)\,(64) - 30\,(55-30)}{(55-1)\,(64)}$$

$$= \frac{3520 - 30\,(25)}{3456}$$

$$= \frac{3520 - 750}{3456}$$

$$= \frac{2770}{3456}$$

$$= .802 \text{ or } .80$$

The teacher will want to know the mean and standard deviation of the test scores anyway. With this information available, the teacher can apply the Kuder-Richardson formula to estimate the reliability of the test.

None of the methods discussed for arriving at test reliability should be used for speed tests. The introduction of the speed factor is not compatible with the assumptions of the various formulas.

Figure 8–3 shows a form on which an item analysis by the Flanagan Method can be summarized. A similar form could be designed for use with an ETS analysis. This summary information should be filed with the analysis materials, a copy of the test, and the key, so it is available for reference when revisions are made.

Validity of Criterion-Referenced Tests[7,25]

The usual types of item analysis are not appropriate for evaluating criterion-referenced items because the test constructor is hoping that all the students can answer all the items correctly. Two methods have been proposed for establishing the validity of criterion-referenced knowledge tests. One is similar to the content validity discussed with norm-referenced tests. In this case, however, the behavioral objectives are stated more clearly and more definitely, and encompass smaller segments of the unit of instruction. Many objectives are stated and the questions on the test parallel the behavioral objectives previously established for the unit. The test might contain several items to accommodate each behavioral objective. This would be possible considering that criterion-referenced tests us-

Summary Table

Name of test _____ Groups tested _____ Dates _____

Number of answer sheets used in analysis _____.

Content   *Scores*

    Total number of items_____   Mean_____
        Multiple Choice   _____   Standard Deviation _____
        True-False   _____
        Matching   _____
        Classification   _____
        Rearrangement   _____
        Completion   _____

Validity

	Number	*Percent*	*Judgment*
Difficulty Rating **(Between 10% and 90%)**			
Above 90%	_____	_____	_____
Between 11% and 90%	_____	_____	_____
Below 10%	_____	_____	_____
Index of Discrimination (Above .19)			
Above .19	_____	_____	_____
Between .16 and .19	_____	_____	_____
Below .16	_____	_____	_____
Functioning of Responses (3%)			
All responses function	_____	_____	_____
1 response fails to function	_____	_____	_____
2 responses fail to function	_____	_____	_____
More than 2 fail to function	_____	_____	_____

Reliability

  Method Used   _____
  Coefficient   _____   _____

Comments

Date of Report _____

Test Analyzer _____

Fig. 8–3. Suggested form: summary table for analysis of norm-referenced written tests using the Flanagan Method.

ually cover short units of instruction. A series of short tests might be used instead of only one long test.

The second method reflects construct validity. The test is administered prior to instruction and again following instruction. Validity is claimed if there is significant improvement in the scores or if the predetermined level of mastery is achieved by a sufficient number of the class members. An estimate about the performance of subsequent groups on just the final test could be made on the basis of this information.

Crucial to the whole realm of criterion-referenced testing is the setting of the cutting point indicative of mastery. It should be set high enough to enable the student to learn effectively the next stage of instruction. It should be a realistic standard. Usually, a cutting score of 80 to 85% is mentioned as reasonable. This allows for some measurement error and still assures enough mastery to indicate with some confidence that the student is ready to proceed. If, indeed, the student does perform successfully on related tasks in the future, a validity can be inferred.

Reliability of Criterion-Referenced Tests[18,21,22,25,28,32]

Classic test theory does not apply to criterion-referenced reliability estimates because of the lack of variability in the scores. Perhaps the best way to insure reliability of a criterion-referenced test is to be sure the items are closely parallel to the detailed objectives and that there are a sufficient number of items (3 to 5) to measure each objective.

Lovett[18] has worked with an ANOVA statistic to estimate the reliability of criterion-referenced tests. Safrit[25] proposes the use of a kappa coefficient; she considers it superior to the ANOVA approach because it uses a contigency table similar to the chi square concept and corrects for the chance factors that influence the placement of students into the cells of the contingency table. Even so, measurement theorists are not yet satisfied with the statistical methods available to estimate criterion-referenced reliability and are continuing to refine these procedures.

Thorndike and Hagen[32] have suggested a procedure that could be utilized by the classroom teacher without a high degree of statistical sophistication. They refer to a "percentage of consistent decisions." Two forms of a criterion-referenced test are administered to a group of students within a short time interval of several days following a unit of instruction. Decisions about the proportion of students who achieved mastery and those who did not should be in fairly high agreement between the two administrations. In other words, there is a consistency of agreement on the two administrations about the proportion of students who achieved the designated cutting point of mastery and the proportion who did not meet mastery. Thorndike and Hagen illustrate the method using two standards of mastery: a severe one (100%), and more lenient one (75%). The idea is to have a high proportion of students receiving the same decision on both tests, whether it is mastery or nonmastery. Reliability is lowered when a student is successful in meeting the standard on one test and unsuccessful on the other. Higher percentages of consistent agreement are possible when using the less severe criterion standard. When the decision of mastery is not a consistent one from test to test, a reversal results. This means either that students are being incorrectly advanced because they are really "nonmasters" who happen to score in the mastery level, or that students are being incorrectly retained because they are really "masters" who happen to score at a nonmastery level. Either reversal means an incorrect decision has been made about a student. The test was not consistent enough to enable the teacher to make reliable decisions about student mastery levels. Thorndike and Hagen report that percentages of consistent agreement between test administrations from 70 to 85% are about as high as can be expected. They also remind us that the shorter the test and the more severe the standard, the more reversals that can be expected. In addition, however, the less crucial the decision (for example, to proceed to intermediate level golf lessons or to be certified as a lifeguard), the more reversals that can be tolerated. The appropriate cutoff is established at the level that reduces the number of incorrect decisions in either direction.

Revising

The information gained from procedures to establish the validity and reliability of tests, whether they are norm-referenced or criterion-referenced, provides the direction for revisions. Tests must be continually examined, polished, and revised, in order to have them become more and more accountable instruments for both teachers and students.

REFERENCES

1. AAHPER: *Knowledge and Understanding in Physical Education.* Washington, D.C., AAHPER, 1969.
2. Barrow, Harold M. and Rosemary McGee: *A Practical Approach to Measurement in Physical Education.* 3rd Ed. Philadelphia: Lea & Febiger, 1979.
3. Baumgartner, T.A., and A.S. Jackson: Measurement for Evaluation in Physical Education. Boston, Houghton Mifflin Co., 1987.
4. Bloom, B.S. (Ed.), et al: Taxonomy of Educational Objectives Handbook I Cognitive Domain. New York, David McKay Co., 1956.
5. Chiodo, J.J.: The effects of exam anxiety on grandma's health. The Chronicle of Higher Education. August 6, 1986. p. 68.
6. Cooperative Test Division: Making Your Own Tests. Princeton, N.J., Educational Testing Service, undated. Mimeographed.
7. Cronbach, L.J.: Test Validation. In Educational Measurement. 2nd Edition. Edited by R.L. Thorndike. Washington, D.C., American Council on Education, 1971.
8. Diederich, P.B.: Short-Cut Statistics for Teacher-Made Tests. Princeton, N.J. Educational Testing Service, 1973.
9. Ebel, R.L.: Essentials of Educational Measurement. Englewood Cliffs, Prentice-Hall, 1972.
10. Ebel, R.A.: The Paradox of Testing. Measurement in Education, 7, Fall, 1976.
11. Educational Testing Service, Making the Classroom Test: A Guide for Teachers. Princeton, N.J. Educational Testing Service, 1973.
12. Flanagan, J.C.: Calculating Correlation Coefficients. Pittsburgh, American Institute of Research and University of Pittsburgh, 1962.
13. Flanagan, J.C.: Statistical method related to a test construction. Review of Educational Research, *11*:109, February, 1941.
14. Fry, E.: Graph for Estimating Readability. In Zenger and Zenger, (Eds.) Handbook for Evaluating and Selecting Textbooks. Belmont, California. Fearon. n.d.
15. Green, J.A.: Teacher-made Tests. New York, Harper & Row, 1963.
16. Gronlund, N.E.: Preparing Criterion-Referenced Tests for Classroom Instruction. New York, Macmillan Co., 1973.
17. Haney, W.: Making testing more educational. Educational Leadership. October, 1985. p. 4–13.
18. Lovett, H.T.: Criterion-referenced reliability estimated by ANOVA. Educational and Psychological Measurement, *37*:21–29, 1977.
19. McBride, J.R.: Computerized adaptive testing. Educational Leadership. October 1985, p. 25–28.

20. McGee, R., and A.C. Farrow: *Test Questions for Physical Education Activities.* Champaign, IL.: Human Kinetics, 1987.
21. Mehrens, W.A., and I.J. Lehmann: Measurement and Evaluation in Education and Psychology. New York, Holt, Rinehart and Winston, Inc., 1973.
22. Meskauskas, J.A.: Evaluation Models for Criterion-Referenced Testing: Views Regarding Mastery and Standard-Setting. Review of Educational Research, 46:133–159, Winter, 1976.
23. Popham, W.J.: Criterion-Referenced Measurement. Englewood Cliffs, Educational Technology Publications, 1971.
24. Richardson, M.M., and G.F. Kuder: The calculation of test reliability coefficients based on the method of rational equivalence. Journal of Educational Psychology, 30:681, December, 1939.
25. Safrit, M.J.: *Introduction to Measurement in Physical Education and Exercise* Science. St. Louis: Times Mirror/Mosby, 1986.
26. Safrit, M.J.: Validity and Reliability as Concerns in the Assessment of Motor Behavior. In Psychology of Motor Behavior and Sport. Edited by D.M. Landers and R.W. Christina. Champaign, Illinois, Human Kinetics Pub., 1977.
27. Salganik, L.H.: Why testing reforms are so popular and how they are changing education. Phi Delta Kappan. *66*(9): May 607–617, 1985.
28. Sax, G.: Principles of Educational Measurement and Evaluation. Belmont, California, Wadsworth Publishing Co., Inc., 1974.
29. Shick, J.: Written tests in activity classes. Journal of Physical Education and Recreation. April 21–22, 83, 1981.
30. Stanley, J.C., and K.D. Hopkins: Educational and Psychological Measurement and Evaluation. Englewood Cliffs, Prentice-Hall, 1972.
31. TESTAN, (1983) VAX-DOC1, University of North Carolina at Greensboro, Academic Computer Center. Greensboro, North Carolina.
32. Thorndike, R.L., and E.P. Hagen: Measurement and Evaluation in Psychology and Education. 4th Edition, New York, John Wiley and Sons, 1977.
33. Trimble, R.T.: Strike three—you're in. Redemptive opportunities in written exams. Journal of Physical Education and Recreation, February 1983, p. 59–60.

9

Affective Measures

A person is not physically educated by simply developing psychomotor skills. Another aspect of learning is inherent in the acquisition of physical activities. This is the *affective* domain which includes *interests, appreciations, attitudes, values, and adjustments.*[17] These sociopsychological patterns are inevitably present in physical education and sport settings regardless of whether direct attention is called to them in the objectives of a program. Affective learnings often take place in an indirect casual manner without the intent to learn because they are inexorably a part of the psychomotor and cognitive learnings. However, these learnings may also be planned for and taught in a more direct way as an essential part of the physical education curriculum.

The affective domain continuum is structured in a hierarchy of simple to more complex patterns. As shown on the continuum in Figure 9–1, the parts are *receiving, responding, valuing, organizing, and characterizing by a value complex.*[17] It is obvious from the continuum that some of the accompanying elements run concurrently; others (interest and adjustment) occupy some space on the scale alone. As individuals ascend the social and emotional continuum through the levels of receiving, responding, valuing, organizing, and characterizing by value complex, they use the elements of interest, appreciation, attitude, value, and adaptation to achieve psychosocial maturity. This process may be similar to what the sociologist calls *socialization* or the cultural anthropologist calls *enculturation.* Krathwohl et al.[17] identify the process as *internalization.*

Internalization starts with receiving and responding. Unless individuals become fixated at these levels, however, they establish values and move to a hierarchy or cluster of values through conceptualization into a value system. They ultimately behave consistently with this value system, which becomes their philosophy of life, or perhaps on a higher level they behave as autonomous, self-actualizing persons.

The affective domain is a permeating force in the physical education/sport matrix as shown by its objectives. It is clear the teacher/coach not only has an opportunity, but also a compelling obligation to teach these constructs such as attitudes and values. If such psychosocial objectives are to be a part of the physical education/sport program, they should be evaluated. It would be inexact and misleading to imply that these aspects can be measured with the same scientific techniques that are somewhat freely used in the domains of the cognitive and psychomotor. Measurement becomes exceedingly difficult in this area

253

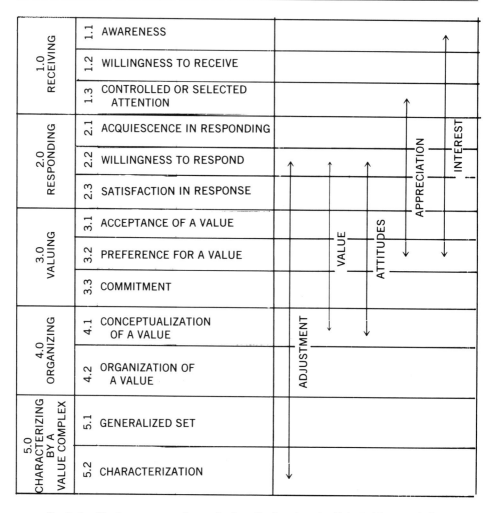

Fig. 9–1. The taxonomy continuum for the affective domain. (Adapted by permission from Krathwohl, D.R. et al.: *Taxonomy of Educational Objectives: The Classification of Educational Goals. Handbook II: Affective Domain.* New York, David McKay Company, Inc., 1964.)

because of the complexity of the factors and the sparcity of reliable measurement techniques.

The professional student should be aware of some of the pitfalls with the use of and interpretation of affective evaluation techniques. Many of them are in the form of a questionnaire or checklist, either requiring a response from the student/athlete or a response about him/her from a teacher/coach/rater. If the students/athletes answer the response themselves, they may choose the answers that will bring them the tacit rewards of acceptance and positive sanctions of their reference groups. However, they may really behave in a different way in practice. On the other hand, if teachers/coaches make the response, they must bear in mind that modern culture brings certain rewards to those who keep their feelings to themselves. To evaluate the sometimes deep underlying emotion is difficult to do through observing behavior. This becomes more of a problem as the one who is being observed achieves higher levels on the internalization scale. Krathwohl et al.[17] seem to think that it is possible in a school situation to evaluate the changes that take place at the lower end of the continuum, but much more difficult to assess those at the top. Changes come about over a long period of time and typically no one teacher/coach would have access to students/ athletes long enough to observe and measure such changes.

Physical educators and coaches have tried to use the holistic approach to the teaching of children and youth. They have concentrated on physical development, realizing that mental and social development must accompany it. The psychomotor, cognitive, and affective areas all interrelate, react, and influence one another. A learner does not move without thinking and feeling, or think without moving and feeling, or feel without moving or thinking. The measures included in this chapter are related to the sociopsychological area or to affective behavior. They are listed in the three categories of Social Measures, Attitude Measures, and Self-Concept Measures as an organizational necessity and not because persons develop these concepts in isolation.

Physical educators and coaches have been reluctant to state objectives in the affective domain even though they give lip service to hopeful achievements in this area. The measuring tools are less precise than those in the psychomotor and cognitive domains, and there is less confidence in interpreting results. In addition, there is the belief that the statement of an objective and the resultant measure of it must be a part of the grading system. This belief is unfortunate because purposes of heightening awareness and discovering changes are then restricted. The attitudes, interests, self-concept, and values of students/players should be personal and free of value judgment by others. It is appropriate, however, for instructors and coaches to help students/players become more aware of and develop their interests, appreciations, and other facets of their affective selves.

SOCIAL MEASURES

The measures of social factors include such constructs as behavior, leadership, acceptance, and character. These instruments may be used in three ways. First, some scales call for the student/player to make a response about himself/herself. When the student/player makes a response about his/her own behavior, habits, and conduct, he or she becomes aware of some social values worthy of attaining and is more cognizant of them as they occur in physical education and sport situations. Second, some scales call for a coach or teacher to make a response about the performer. The scales used by teachers/coaches, and classmates/team members also delve into the concepts of behavior, habits, and acceptance, but they are assessments of someone else. They differ from the scales filled out by the persons themselves because these scales use an observer who makes the judgment about the other person. A third application is to note any discrepancy between the perception of the self-assessment and the perceptions that have been assessed by someone else about the same student/player.

Horrocks Prosocial Play Behavior Inventory (HPPBI)*

Purpose. To measure the prosocial play behavior of fifth- and sixth-grade boys and girls in recreational play situations.

Development. Working with teachers, Horrocks[15] developed a set of behavioral attributes associated with successful and cooperative recreational games playing. Ten fifth- and sixth-grade teachers and six elementary school physical education teachers observed the students in recreational settings, which consisted of both high and low organizational games, and under conditions that provided extensive, moderate, and limited supervision. The teachers looked for 35 prosocial and antisocial play behaviors that had been identified by Horrocks. The behaviors were rated as either easily observable, at times difficult to observe, or very difficult to observe. Only statements on which the teachers could achieve 80% agreement as "easily observable" were retained in the inventory. Content validity can be claimed because the scale reflects easily identifiable behaviors. Horrocks used a split-half method for estimating the internal consistency reliability of the inventory. The coefficient was .98 for 1 group of 63 fifth- and sixth-grade students, and was .96 on a random sampling of 50 children from the total population of 245.

Prosocial Play Behavior Inventory

Child's Name _____   Teacher _____

INSTRUCTIONS

Please describe as accurately as possible the above student's behavior during recreational game playing activities by circling one of the 4 responses to each statement. Give a response to every item and BASE YOUR RESPONSES UPON YOUR PERSONAL OBSERVATIONS AND EXPERIENCES.

	THE STATEMENT IS:			
THE CHILD:	*Not at all* like the child	*Very little* like the child	*Somewhat* like the child	*Very much* like the child
1. Avoids arguments	1	2	3	4
2. Wins without "gloating"	1	2	3	4
3. Accepts defeat without complaining	1	2	3	4
4. Offers consolation when a group member makes a mistake	1	2	3	4
5. Shares equipment readily	1	2	3	4
6. Abides by the rules of the game	1	2	3	4
7. Shares the game activities (Does not "hog" the ball)	1	2	3	4
8. Accepts referee's decisions	1	2	3	4
9. Takes turns readily	1	2	3	4
10. Accepts constructive criticism and suggestions from peers	1	2	3	4

Level and Gender. The inventory is appropriate for use with children in the fifth and sixth grades.

Uses. To assess prosocial behavior in recreational game settings. To identify

---

*From Horrocks, R.N.: Relationship of Selected Prosocial Play Behaviors in Children to Moral Reasoning, Youth Sports Participation, and Perception of Sportsmanship. Dissertation, The University of North Carolina at Greensboro, 1979. Used by permission of the author.

students who need some assistance with moral reasoning and perceptions of the concept of sportsmanship.

Scoring. A student's prosocial play behavior score is determined by totaling the points circled for each of the 10 behavior statements. Those children who display prosocial play behaviors receive more points than those who do not display the prosocial behaviors. The score can range from 10 to 40 points. Horrocks identified the following levels within the score range and reported statistically significant differences on both moral reasoning and perceptions of sportsmanship for those students in the upper and low groups:

Upper	37–40
Average	26–36
Low	10–25

Comments. This behaviorally anchored rating scale (BARS) approach to scale development has achieved acclaim because it restricts the behaviors to those that can actually be observed.

Adams Prosocial Behavior Inventory*[1]

Purpose. To measure the prosocial behaviors distinctive to students participating in high school physical education classes.

Development. Two criteria for content validation were met by establishing a pool of 106 behavior statements from a number of sources and by using competent judges to rate the observability of each behavior. In addition, videotape sequences were staged to enact the 12 final prosocial behaviors. In the final judging by six physical educators who viewed the tape, 11 behaviors were correctly identified. Those 11 behaviors constitute the Adams inventory.

Level and Gender. The Inventory is suitable for use with high school age girls and boys.

Uses. The Inventory has the potential to assist teachers observe prosocial behavior while students are engaged in physical education classes. It could be used as part of a behavioral contract. In addition, "the identification of prosocial behaviors associated with sports participation might help students more closely understand what kind of behaviors are desirable social responses."[1]

Adams Prosocial Behavior Inventory

	Yes	No
1. Helps opponent up after a fall.	____	____
2. Uses school equipment properly.	____	____
3. Attentive to help a partner for safety reasons. Example, a spotter in gymnastics or weight training.	____	____
4. Acknowledges a single effort by a teammate. Example, a good lay-up shot in basketball or a teammate who wins a high jump event.	____	____
5. Helps another student with a new skill.	____	____
6. Gives another student instruction and encouragement.	____	____

*From Adams, D.L.: The Development of a Prosocial Behavior Inventory Related to Participation in High School Physical Education Classes. Thesis, California State University, Long Beach, 1982. Used by permission of the author.

7. Accidentally injures an opponent—helps the player up, apologizes, goes to get aid, or shows some kind of concern for the hurt player.   ____ ____
8. Participates each day if not ill.   ____ ____
9. Leaves the game quietly after asked to by the official. Example, receiving a fifth foul in basketball.   ____ ____
10. Volunteers to take out or pick up equipment.   ____ ____
11. Praises a teammate who makes a good play.   ____ ____

Scoring. Not every behavior can be observed in any one class period or game because they will not all occur. The teacher may wish to keep a running tally of how the student responds to behaviors as they occur. Over time, a pattern of behavior should emerge.

Comments. The Adams inventory is similar to the one developed by Horrocks[15] and appears to have strong validity credentials.

Nelson Leadership Questionnaire*

Purpose. To identify the leaders as perceived by coaches and by teammates.

Development. A "guess who" kind of questionnaire, as suggested by Cattell and Eber,[5] was developed by Nelson to be used by coaches and team members.[25]

Level and Gender. High school varsity male basketball players.

Uses. To identify leaders and nonleaders on basketball teams according to coaches' opinions and teammates' opinions. To study the agreement of two groups in identifying leaders. To discuss factors of leadership. To foster individual counseling.

INSTRUCTIONS—COACH'S QUESTIONNAIRE*

The same names can be used any number of times and in all cases give your first and second choice for each question.

1. Who are the most popular men on your squad?
    1. _____   2. _____
2. Which players on the team know the most basketball, in terms of strategy or team play?
    1. _____   2. _____
3. Of all the players on your team, who exhibits the most poise on the floor during the crucial parts of the game?
    1. _____   2. _____
4. Who are the "take charge" men on your squad?
    1. _____   2. _____
5. Who are the most consistent ball handlers on your squad?
    1. _____   2. _____
6. Who are the most consistent shooters on your squad?
    1. _____   2. _____
7. Who are the most valuable players on your squad?
    1. _____   2. _____
8. Who are the 2 players who play most "for the team"?
    1. _____   2. _____
9. Which players have the most overall ability on the squad?
    1. _____   2. _____

*From Nelson, D.O.: Leadership in sports. Research Quarterly, 37:268–275, 1966. Used by permission of the AAHPER and the author.

10. Who are the most likable players on the squad?
    1. _____   2. _____
11. Which players do you think would make the best coaches?
    1. _____   2. _____
12. If you were not present for practice, which players would you place in charge of the practice?
    1. _____   2. _____
13. Who are the players endowed with leadership qualities?
    1. _____   2. _____
14. Who are the players least endowed with leadership ability?
    1. _____   2. _____

INSTRUCTIONS—PLAYER'S QUESTIONNAIRE

Do not sign your name to the questionnaire. Fill in the name or names of the squad members who, in your opinion, best fit the question. Give your first and second choice in all cases. *Do not use your own name* on any of the answers. The names of the same players can be used any number of times and your answers will be kept confidential.

1. If you were on a trip and had a choice of the players you would share the hotel room with, who would they be?
   1. _____   2. _____
2. Who are the most popular men on the squad?
   1. _____   2. _____
3. Who are the best scholars on the squad?
   1. _____   2. _____
4. Which players on the team know the most basketball, in terms of strategy or team play?
   1. _____   2. _____
5. If the coach were not present for a workout, which players would be the most likely to take charge of the practice?
   1. _____   2. _____
6. Which players would you listen to first if the team appeared to be disorganized during a crucial game?
   1. _____   2. _____
7. Your team is behind 1 point with 10 seconds remaining in the game and you could pass to anyone on the squad. Who would it be?
   1. _____   2. _____
8. Of all the players on your team, who exhibits the most poise on the floor during the crucial parts of the game?
   1. _____   2. _____
9. Who are the "take charge" men on your team?
   1. _____   2. _____
10. Who are the most consistent ball handlers on your squad?
    1. _____   2. _____
11. Who are the most consistent shooters on your squad?
    1. _____   2. _____
12. Who are the most valuable players on your squad?
    1. _____   2. _____
13. Who are the most unselfish players who are interested most in the team as a whole and who play most "for the team"?
    1. _____   2. _____
14. Which players have the most overall ability on the squad?
    1. _____   2. _____

15. Who are the most likable players on the squad?
    1. _____ 2. _____
16. Which players on your team have influenced you the most?
    1. _____ 2. _____
17. Which players have actually helped you the most?
    1. _____ 2. _____
18. Which players do you think would make the best coaches?
    1. _____ 2. _____
19. Which players do you most often look to for leadership?
    1. _____ 2. _____
20. Who are the hardest workers on the squad?
    1. _____ 2. _____

Scoring. No particular scoring method is recommended. Probably the frequency with which various players are listed would be one way to summarize the information.

Comments. Coaches often believe they can identify leaders without the help of assistant coaches and the players. This additional input from coaches and players serves to verify the coach's perceptions about the leadership structure of a team. In addition, use of the scale gives the coaches and players a feeling of involvement in the identification process. The questionnaire may be used with female basketball players by substituting "player" for "men."

Cowell Personal Distance Scale*

Purpose. To measure a student's degree of harmony within a social group and his or her social growth from year to year. To ascertain an index of acceptance.

Development. The validity, judged by using a "who's who in my group" test as the criterion, was .84. The reliability was reported to be around .90.[7]

Level and Gender. Developed for use with a class of high school age boys and girls.

Scoring. The maximum distance is valued 7 and the minimum 1. The index of acceptance is determined by adding all of the weighted scores and dividing this sum by the number of ratings, e.g., if all 50 students checked a given student in the first column (into my family as a brother or sister), his index would be 50 × 1 = 50 ÷ 50 or 1.00. Dropping the decimal, his index would be 100. The lower the index, the greater the degree of acceptance by the group. When referring to girls, the "him" would be changed to "her," and "brother" to "sister."

Comments. Usually this scale is given to measure the closeness of a group such as a team or a scout troop. If the group does not trust the person administering the scale and understand how the results are to be used and protected, there is considerable doubt that the results will be valid. The Cowell scale can reveal the index by which each individual is accepted by the group as well as the index by which an individual accepts the group. The former piece of information is especially sensitive and must be handled confidentially by the person administering the scale.

*From Cowell, C.C.: Validating an Index of Social Adjustment for High School Use. Research Quarterly, 29:7–18, March, 1958. Used by permission of the AAHPER.

The Scale

Cowell Personal Distance Scale

I would be willing to accept him/her:

What to do If you had full power to treat each student in this group as you feel, just how would you consider him/her? Just how near would you like to have him/her to your family? Every student should be checked in some one column. Circle your own name and be sure you check every student in 1 column only.	Into my family as a brother/sister	As very close pal	As a member of my gang or club	On my street as a next-door neighbor	Into my class at school	Into my school	Into my city
	1	2	3	4	5	6	7
1. Stanley Whitaker							
2. James Southerlin							
3. Alice Porsche							
.							
.							
15.							

ATTITUDES MEASURES

Attitudes are predispositions to actions, so their proper development is important to the total development of the individual. They are acquired concurrently with activity and often have tremendous influence on performance. Not every person can be a championship performer, but each can develop a favorable attitude toward activity.

McKethan Student Attitude Inventory—Instructional Processes in Secondary Physical Education (SAI-IPSPE)*[20]

Purpose. To assess student attitudes about the instructional processes used in secondary physical education instructional settings. These processes include teachers' verbal behavior, the nature of the activities in the class, patterns of class organization, and rules and regulations governing the physical education environment.

Development. McKethan[20] used Bain's[2] value dimensions as the theoretical base on which to build the items in the inventory. Criteria for retaining statements in the final inventory were factor loadings on the value dimensions and estimates of communality for statements within each factor. The Bain value dimensions were autonomy, privacy, orderliness, universalism, competitive achievement, instructional achievement, and specificity. McKethan's final 15 factors included all of Bain's factors except Privacy. The 75-statement pool was reduced to 46 statements based on each statement's estimate of communality being less than .65 or factor loadings less than .50. The original pool of 75 statements was administered to 278 randomly selected male and female tenth grade physical education students.

Test-retest reliability, using 54 students randomly drawn from the first sample, was estimated to be .72 on the 46 items in the final version of the inventory.

Level and Gender. The inventory is appropriate for use with male and female students in secondary physical education instructional settings.

Uses. To assess the attitudes of students about the way the physical education class is conducted. Comparisons by gender, type of class, amount of participation, and class grades are possible.

Directions. This is *not a test*. This inventory will not be used for grading purposes. The SAI-IPSPE will not in any way affect the way you are treated in this class. You are being asked to indicate your feelings about a number of things that are commonly done in physical education classes. Read the following directions carefully. For each statement, go to the corresponding number on the answer sheet and darken the circle which best represents your feelings about the statement.

> A = Strongly Agree
> B = Agree
> C = Undecided
> D = Disagree
> E = Strongly Disagree

Example: If you agree with statement one, you would darken the circle in the

---

*From McKethan, J.R.: Students Attitudes Toward Instructional Processes in Secondary Physical Education. Dissertation, The University of North Carolina at Greensboro, 1979. Used by permission of the author.

column headed by "B." Should you change your mind, then "X" out that circle and then darken the circle for your answer. Your answers to these statements will not require a lot of thought. Your first impression will usually represent best your feelings about the statement. It is very important that you answer *all* statements.

The Inventory

SAI-IPSPE

1. I do not like having my grade based on how well I do sports skills.
2. My teacher's clothing for P.E. class should be appropriate for participating in the class activity.
3. I do not like it when my teacher spends a lot of time talking to the whole class.
4. Students should decide whether or not to take P.E.
5. I should not have to stay quiet when I am not participating in my gym class.
6. It does not make any difference to me whether a man or a woman is teaching such activities as dance or gymnastics.
7. I should make the decision to shower.
8. It is a waste of time for a teacher to spend a lot of time talking about sport skills.
9. My teacher does not have the right to question or talk with me about things not concerned with school.
10. I believe that more than one activity should be going on at the same time in my physical education class.
11. I do not think class time should be taken up with matters such as giving out equipment.
12. I like it when my teacher praises me.
13. I do not mind showering if private stalls are in the shower room.
14. It is a waste of time to have to wait in order to participate. (Example: standing in line to do layups.)
15. I like doing gymnastics and tumbling when the class has both boys and girls participating.
16. I like making the decision whether or not to shower after gym class.
17. I get a lot out of class when my teacher talks about sports skills.
18. I like being introduced to new skills by having a skilled student demonstrate the skill.
19. I should be excused when I am not going to participate in class.
20. My teacher should see me as different from my classmates.
21. I like games in which there are no losers.
22. My teacher should expect that students will perform in different ways.
23. I do not like class activities that emphasize staying in one place.
24. I enjoy my P.E. class more when everyone is participating.
25. Standards for grading should be determined separately for each student.
26. I should be corrected for my mistakes individually.
27. I do not like to give my excuse for not dressing for gym when the teacher checks the roll.
28. My grade for P.E. should not be determined by how well I do sports skills.

29. When I am dressed for participating, it is reasonable to expect my teacher to be dressed for activity too.
30. I do not like gym class when my teacher uses a lot of time discussing game strategy.
31. I should have a choice whether or not to take P.E.
32. I like the freedom of moving about the gym when I am not actively involved in an activity.
33. It does not make any difference to me whether a man or a woman is teaching such things as basketball or football.
34. The activities that I like the most are those in which there are no rewards. (Example: winners do not have to run extra laps.)
35. I do not believe that I should be penalized for not participating in the class.
36. My personal life should be of no concern to my teacher.
37. I like my class when there are a number of activities going on at the same time.
38. I think it is a waste of time when a lot of my time is taken up by matters such as roll check.
39. Activities such as football and baseball should be taught with boys and girls in the same class.
40. Classes in which my teacher talks about game rules bore me.
41. I do not believe that I should be required to take P.E.
42. When I do not participate, I like to be free to move about.
43. It does not matter to me whether my teacher is a man or a woman.
44. I do not believe the teacher should check to see if I have showered.
45. The teacher should not check to see if I am wearing my gym uniform.
46. I like not having class time taken up by matters such as the giving out of equipment.

Scoring. McKethan purposely made the statements unipolar in nature to simplify scoring and interpretations.

A = Strongly Agree	= 5 points
B = Agree	= 4 points
C = Undecided	= 3 points
D = Disagree	= 2 points
E = Strongly Disagree	= 1 point

A maximum score of 230 is possible and a minimum score of 46. The following range of scores provides an approximate estimate of feelings about class procedures:

207–230	Very favorable attitude about the way class is conducted.
161–206	Favorable attitude about the way class is conducted.
115–160	Undecided feelings about the conduct of the class.
69–114	Unfavorable attitudes about instructional processes used in the class.
46– 68	Very unfavorable attitudes about the way the class is conducted.

Comments. Not many scales are available that relate to the manner in which a class is conducted as opposed to what content is offered. The McKethan scale addresses the process issue, which has such a viable impact on the attitudes that students are developing about physical education and active life styles. This scale may be used as part of the overall physical education program evaluation.

Toulmin Elementary Physical Education Attitude Scale (TEPEAS)*

Purpose. To measure expressed attitudes of elementary school children toward the physical education program.

Development. Toulmin[37] conducted both a preliminary and final study to measure the careful construction of this attitude assessment tool. For the preliminary study 365 students from 9 to 12 years of age were used. Revisions in the scale were made and then another group of 315 students was administered the final form of the scale. For analysis, data on 300 students were used. Concurrent validity was determined by correlating scores on the 50-item attitude scale with self-ratings on a 10-point graphic rating scale with respect to their general attitudes toward the physical education program. The coefficient was .29. Construct validity was ascertained in 2 ways. An item analysis was applied to each item on the scale using the 27% highest and lowest scores. Those items that had indices of discrimination between .40 and .66 were considered for retention. Fifty of the 110 original items were retained because they were able to discriminate between the students who enjoyed physical education and those who did not. The final 50 items were also selected to insure coverage of the content areas in the scale: program content, outcomes of program content, self-concept and level of aspiration, peer group relations, teacher, and scheduling and time. In addition, construct validity was studied by ranking 65 students on the track and field team who had the highest scores on the AAHPER fitness test with an equal number of students who had the lowest fitness scores and were not on the track and field team. The analysis of variance F was significant beyond the .01 level. The reliability coefficient was estimated to be .91 after using the Spearman Brown Prophecy formula on the split-halves technique for 300 fourth-, fifth-, and sixth-grade students. The scale may be considered to have construct validity and internal consistency.

Level and Gender. The scale is appropriate for both boys and girls in grades four, five, and six. Analysis of variance showed no differences in scores by gender or by grade.

Uses. To measure status of attitude toward program. To evaluate changes in attitudes about the program.

Directions. Please read carefully! Below you will find some statements about physical education. We would like to know exactly how you feel about each statement. You are asked to think about physical education as it concerns you during your regular physical education class period. Do not consider the statements as after-school activities. Students are not all alike in their feelings. There are no right or wrong answers.

You have been given a separate answer sheet on which to write your feelings to each statement. After reading a statement you will know at once, in most cases, whether you agree or disagree with the statement. If you agree, then decide whether to place an "X" under *strongly agree, agree,* or *slightly agree.* If you do not agree, then place an "X" under *slightly disagree, disagree,* or *strongly disagree.*

Wherever possible, let your own experience affect your answer. Work rapidly. Do not spend much time on any statement. This is not a test, but is simply a

*From Toulmin, M.L.B.: The Development of an Original Instrument to Measure the Expressed Attitudes of Children Toward the Elementary School Program of Physical Education. Thesis, Texas Woman's University, 1973.

way to find out how students feel about physical education. Your answers will not affect your grade. We will keep your answers secret, so please answer each statement exactly the way you feel it. Be sure to answer every statement.

The Scale

TEPEAS

1. I would like to have physical education every day.
2. We do not get to play what we want in physical education.
3. Because physical skills are important to youth, it is important for a person to be helped to learn and improve those skills.
4. Physical education teaches you to get along with others better.
5. I am afraid of getting hurt in physical education.
6. Many of the games we play in physical education are a waste of time.
7. Physical education should be only for those who are good at it.
8. Time for physical education is too short.
9. I like to play games in physical education.
10. I never get to be "it" when we play games in physical education.
11. I get enough exercise without physical education.
12. Boys and girls laugh at me in physical education when I cannot do things.
13. Students learn to understand each other better after playing together in physical education.
14. Too often we must go outside in cold weather when we should stay inside.
15. Most of the things I learn in physical education, I can use after school.
16. Our physical education teacher likes children.
17. A person could better control his feelings if he did not have to take physical education.
18. When I get older, I plan to take band instead of physical education.
19. Physical education teaches us to respect others' rights.
20. Physical education skills bring more enjoyment to life.
21. I get tired in physical education before others do.
22. My parents do not think physical education is very important.
23. Physical education does not help me learn to control my feelings, such as anger.
24. Our physical education teacher knows his/her job well.
25. I like to run.
26. Arguments in physical education have caused me to lose friends.
27. Physical education has helped me set goals to improve my physical fitness.
28. When I grow up I will continue to exercise.
29. My parents often scold me for ruining my clothing in physical education.
30. Physical education teaches you good sportsmanship.
31. I feel so out-of-place in a physical education class.
32. Physical education helps me to relax.
33. Our teacher makes us do dumb things.
34. Physical education has taught me to appreciate the things my body can do.
35. Physical education is a waste of time in improving health.
36. Physical education does not help you to make friends.
37. I learn something new nearly every time I have physical education.
38. I look forward to physical education regardless of the weather.
39. Fat students should not have to take physical education.
40. Physical education encourages boys and girls to cheat.
41. Physical education is just as important for girls as it is for boys.
42. Many physical education activities make me feel clumsy.
43. I would rather not play in physical education if I cannot be on my best friend's team.

44. Physical education activity gets one interested in good health habits.
45. Our grading system in physical education is fair.
46. Physical education is too rough.
47. Tests should not be given in physical education.
48. Most of my friends like physical education.
49. I like to do exercises.
50. There is not enough good coming from physical education class to give it so much time.

Scoring. Toulmin stated that the maximum score possible is 300. Those students scoring 150 and above have expressed a favorable attitude toward the physical education program and those scoring below 150 have indicated attitudes that are unfavorable toward the elementary physical education program.

The 24 positive statements are item numbers 1, 3, 4, 8, 9, 13, 15, 16, 19, 20, 24, 25, 27, 28, 30, 32, 34, 37, 38, 41, 44, 45, 48, and 49. The other 26 statements are negative statements and the scoring values need to be reversed, i.e., a "strongly agree" response to a negative statement is worth 1 point instead of 6 points.

	Positive Statements	*Negative Statements*
Strongly Agree	6	1
Agree	5	2
Slightly Agree	4	3
Slightly Disagree	3	4
Disagree	2	5
Strongly Disagree	1	6

Unlike most scales designed on the Likert format, there is no provision for a neutral response. A range of scores from 50 to 300 is possible. If intermediate interpretations are desired, they could be designated as follows:

50– 74	Strongly unfavorable attitude
75–124	Unfavorable attitude
125–150	Slightly unfavorable attitude
151–224	Slightly favorable attitude
225–274	Favorable attitude
275–300	Strongly favorable attitude

Shortened Physical Estimation Scale*

Purpose. To measure the self perceptions of college students about their estimation of physical ability in sports and physical activity.

Development. Sonstroem[35] originally developed a Physical Estimation and Attraction Scale (PEAS), which contained 100 items. Subsequently the scale was shortened to 33 items. Since that time Safrit, Wood, and Dishman[31] have used factor analysis to recommend a 12-item estimation scale. In addition, Fox, Corbin, and Couldry[9,10] used an item analysis approach to suggest that still another shortened scale of 13 items may be as powerful as the full scale. Fox, Corbin, and Couldry undertook four studies over several years to investigate the validity

*From Fox, K.R., Corbin, C.B., and Couldry, W.H.: The validity and reliability of shortened physical estimation scales. Paper presented at the Centennial Convention of AAHPERD. Atlanta, GA, 1985. Used by permission of the authors.

and reliability of the shortened form. It is shown to exhibit exceptional internal consistency (Kuder-Richardson 20 coefficients ranging from .80 to .93) as well as good discriminatory power. Correlations reported by Fox, Corbin, and Couldry[10] among the three versions of the scale ranged from .90 to .93. In addition, they changed the response format from true-false to a 4-point Likert scale.

Level and Gender. The research studies by Fox, Corbin, and Couldry[9,10] have involved both male and female undergraduate college students. The scale seems appropriate for the collegiate age group and perhaps as well for senior high school students. Sonstroem used high school students, college students, and middle-aged men to do his original research. This shortened form is a descendent of that original scale.

Uses. To measure self-confidence, self-efficacy, and perceived competence in a physical setting. This scale could be used in both in-school and out-of-school settings with various types of groups involved with physical activities.

Directions. Please circle the response which is most appropriate for you.

> SA = Strongly agree
> A = Agree
> D = Disagree
> SD = Strongly disagree

The Scale

Shortened Physical Estimation Scale

1. My body is strong and muscular compared to other men (women) my age.	SA A D SD
2. I am quite limber and agile compared to other men (women) my age.	SA A D SD
3. I am better coordinated than most people I know.	SA A D SD
4. I am a good deal stronger than most of my friends.	SA A D SD
5. Most people I know think I have very good physical skills.	SA A D SD
6. I exhibit a fair amount of leadership in a sports situation.	SA A D SD
7. I am a natural athlete.	SA A D SD
8. I am stronger than a good many of my friends.	SA A D SD
9. I am in better physical condition than most people my age.	SA A D SD
10. I have a strong throwing arm for baseball or softball.	SA A D SD
11. I am well-equipped to excel at physical activities.	SA A D SD
12. Probably I could get into physical condition faster than most people my age.	SA A D SD
13. I am a natural leader in sports activities.	SA A D SD

Scoring. All items are scored: SA = 4; A = 3; D = 2; SD = 1. The authors do not provide for a neutral or undecided response. The score can range from 13 to 52 with 33.5 being the middle point. Scores that are above 34 can be interpreted to reflect positive feelings about physical abilities.

Comment. The shortened forms of the PEAS by Safrit, Wood, and Dishman[31] and by Fox, Corbin, and Couldry[10] seem to be equally effective. They include some of the same items.

Building on Sonstroem's work and the scale presented here, Fox has constructed an instrument called the Physical Self-Perception Profile.* It is a 5 sub-scale multidimensional instrument designed to tap the salient content of the physical domain for young adults.

Feelings About Physical Activity†[6,13,26,27,28]

Purpose. To provide information about commitment to physical activity in general.

Development. This scale is an adaptation by Corbin of a Commitment to Running scale developed by Carmack and Martens[3] with the intent of providing a more global measure. Its reliability was estimated to range from .88 to .91 using Cronbach's Alpha and 859 subjects. Split halves coefficients ranged from .90 to .92. Validity, examined using discrimination indexes of item analysis, averaged .45. Construct validity was also investigated using the "known group" approach and added further credence to the scale. Factor analysis showed all items loading to one factor, explaining 52% of the variance.[27] This scale provides a valid and reliable method for looking at commitment to physical activity in a general sense.

Level and Gender. The original scale, related to running, was developed with respondents who were ages 12 to 60. This scale seems appropriate for a wide age range and for both genders.

Uses. The popularity of physical fitness has prompted new interest in how people feel about physical activity. This scale could be used in a variety of in-school and out-of-school settings.

Directions. The following statements may or may not describe your feelings about physical activity. Physical activity is interpreted to include all individual/dual sports, all team sports, and all individual exercises. Examples of these activities are tennis, badminton, yoga, racquetball, football, basketball, cycling, dance, running, swimming, weight training, and fitness calisthenics. Please *CIRCLE* the appropriate letter or letters to indicate how well the statement describes *your feelings most of the time.* There are no right or wrong answers. Do not spend too much time on any one item, but give the answer that seems to describe how you *generally feel* about physical activity.

SD = STRONGLY DISAGREE
D = DISAGREE
U = UNCERTAIN
A = AGREE
SA = STRONGLY AGREE

The Scale

FEELINGS ABOUT PHYSICAL ACTIVITY

1. I look forward to physical activity.	SD D U A SA
2. I wish there were a more enjoyable way to stay fit than vigorous physical activity.	SD D U A SA
3. Physical activity is drudgery.	SD D U A SA
4. I do not enjoy physical activity.	SD D U A SA
5. Physical activity is vitally important to me.	SD D U A SA

*Further information about the Physical Self-Perception Profile can be obtained from Dr. Kenneth R. Fox at Northern Illinois University, DeKalb, IL.

†From Nielsen, A.B., and Corbin, C.B.: Physical Activity Commitment. Conference Abstracts, North American Society for the Psychology of Sport and Physical Activity Conference. Scottsdale, AR, p. 93. June, 1986. Used by permission of the authors.

6. Life is so much richer as a result of physical activity.　　SD D U A SA
7. Physical activity is pleasant.　　SD D U A SA
8. I dislike the thought of doing regular physical activity.　　SD D U A SA
9. I would arrange or change my schedule to participate in physical activity.　　SD D U A SA
10. I have to force myself to participate in physical activity.　　SD D U A SA
11. To miss a day of physical activity is sheer relief.　　SD D U A SA
12. Physical activity is the high point in my day.　　SD D U A SA

Scoring. Items 1, 5, 6, 7, 9, and 12 are scored 1 to 5; items 2, 3, 4, 8, 10, and 11 are scored 5 to 1. Thirty-six is the middle score. The following scale gives some interpretative information:

54–60　　Very favorable feelings about physical activity
42–53　　Favorable feelings
30–41　　Neutral feelings
18–29　　Unfavorable feelings
12–17　　Very unfavorable feelings about physical activity

Children's Attitudes Toward Physical Activity—Revised (CATPA)*[32]

Purpose. To assess the meanings that physical activity has to elementary, middle, and high school age students.

Development. Originally a multidimensional semantic differential scale based on Kenyon's conceptual model for physical activity was constructed (Kenyon;[16] Simon and Smoll;[34] Schultz, Smoll, and Wood;[33] and Wood[40]). Subsequently, Schultz, Smoll, Carre, and Mosher[32] restructured the inventory, making it shorter and psychometrically superior. The revised inventory inquires into subdomains of social growth, social continuation, health and fitness, vertigo, aesthetic, catharsis, and ascetic. The semantic differential format will show the meaning that each of these subdomains has for students. For example, physical activity may be more meaningful as a social experience than as a fitness motive. Carre, Mosher, and Schutz,[4] reporting on the British Columbia Physical Education Assessment project, found the revised inventory to include item analysis correlations and internal consistencies equally as good as and sometimes better than those reported for the original inventory. The eight bipolar adjective pairs have been reduced to 5, and the 7-point response scale for each set of bipolar adjectives has been reduced to a 5-point scale.

Level and Gender. The CATPA is suitable for use with boys and girls from fourth grade through high school.

Uses. The inventory can be used in both school and out-of-school settings in which attitudinal dispositions toward the 7 subdomains would be of interest. Rather than using the inventory to measure change in attitude, the authors recommend its use to detect abnormally low attitudes toward physical activity related to each of the subdomains.

Directions. To be read aloud by the administrator of the inventory.

"This questionnaire is designed to find out how you feel about physical activity. Physical activities are games, sports, and dance such as tag, soccer, hockey, ballet and figure skating on ice.

*From Schutz, R.W., Smoll, F.L., Carre, F.A., and Mosher, R.E.: Inventories and norms for children's attitudes toward physical activity. Research Quarterly for Exercise and Sport, *56*:3, 256–265, 1985. Reprinted by permission of the authors and the American Alliance for Physical Education, Recreation, and Dance, 1900 Association Drive, Reston, VA 22091.

"Each one of you has a booklet. Do not open it yet. Please listen carefully to the instructions. (Refer to visual aid: The visual aid consists of a sample page with the single word REFEREE in the box followed by the five bipolar adjectives. It may be drawn on the blackboard or a large piece of paper, or presented as an overhead projection, so the entire group can see it.)

"At the top of each page in your booklet there is a box, and in the box there is an idea. Down below the box are five different pairs of words. You will be marking these word pairs to show how you feel about the idea. This is not a test, so there are no right or wrong answers. Read the idea in the box, for example, REFEREE. Now go down to the first pair of words—Good-Bad. How do you feel about Referees? If you think they are very good, you would put a "√" here (mark at the end of the scale by good) or, if you think that they are very bad, you would put a "√" here (mark at the end of the scale by bad). If you think that referees are pretty good but not super good you would put a "√" here (indicate) or if you think that referees are sort of bad but not really bad you would put a "√" here (indicate). If you think that referees are neither good nor bad (i.e., a neutral feeling) then put a "√" in the middle. If you do not understand the idea in the box put a "√" in the *do not understand box* on the middle of the page. Then go to the next page. If you understand the idea in the box but not the word pair, leave the word pair line blank and go on to the next word pair. Do you have any questions?

"It is important for you to remember several things. First of all, put your "√" right in the middle of the space—not on the top of the dots. Second, there are five pairs of words on each page, so how many "√"s will you have on each page? (Five).

"When I tell you to begin, go through the booklet page by page. Read the idea in the box at the top of the page and fill in how you feel about all of the word pairs before you go on to the next page. Don't go back to a page after you have finished it; and don't try to remember how you answered the other pages. Think about each word pair by itself. As you go through the booklet go fairly quickly; don't worry or think too long about any word pair. Mark the first thing that comes into your mind, but don't be careless. Remember, the idea in the box at the top of each page is a new idea, so think only about that idea. When you are finished, put down your pencil and go back through the booklet to make sure that you haven't left anything out by mistake. After you have finished checking, turn your booklet over and wait until everyone is finished. If you have any questions raise your hand and I will come around to help you. You may begin."[32]

The Inventory (CATPA)

Sample page for Test Administration:
How do you feel about the idea in the box?

REFEREE

Always think about the idea in the Box.

1.	good	——:——:——:——:——	bad
2.	of no use	——:——:——:——:——	useful
3.	not pleasant	——:——:——:——:——	pleasant
4.	nice	——:——:——:——:——	awful
5.	happy	——:——:——:——:——	sad

First page of CATPA Instrument

How do you feel about the idea in the box?

> ### PHYSICAL ACTIVITY FOR SOCIAL GROWTH
> Taking part in physical activities which give you
> a chance to meet new people

Always think about the idea in the Box.

If you do not understand this idea, mark this box ☐ and go to the next page.

1. good ———:———:———:———:——— bad
2. of no use ———:———:———:———:——— useful
3. not pleasant ———:———:———:———:——— pleasant
4. nice ———:———:———:———:——— awful
5. happy ———:———:———:———:——— sad

Idea to go in box on second page of booklet:

> ### PHYSICAL ACTIVITY TO CONTINUE SOCIAL RELATIONS
> Taking part in physical activities which give you a chance
> to be with your friends

Idea to go in box on third page of booklet:

> ### PHYSICAL ACTIVITY FOR HEALTH AND FITNESS
> Taking part in physical activities to make your health
> better and to get your body in better condition

Idea to go in box on fourth page of booklet:

> ### PHYSICAL ACTIVITY AS A THRILL BUT INVOLVING SOME RISK
> Taking part in physical activities that could be
> dangerous because you move very fast and must
> change directions quickly

Idea to go in box on fifth page of booklet:

> ### PHYSICAL ACTIVITY AS THE BEAUTY IN MOVEMENT
> Taking part in physical activities which have beautiful
> and graceful movements

Idea to go in box on sixth page of booklet:

> ### PHYSICAL ACTIVITY FOR THE RELEASE OF TENSION
> Taking part in physical activities to reduce stress or to
> get away from problems you might have.

Idea to go in box on seventh page of booklet:

> ### PHYSICAL ACTIVITY AS LONG AND HARD TRAINING
> Taking part in physical activities that have long and
> hard practices. To spend time in practice you need to
> give up other things you like to do.

Scoring. The more positive end of the semantic space is switched in the listing of the polar adjectives so the students will not respond in a pattern.

"The items are scored using a 5-point scale, with 5 always being associated with the positive adjective and 1 with the negative adjective of the word pair. It should be noted that in the Revised CATPA inventory word pairs 1, 4, and 5 are reverse ordered in comparison to word pairs 2 and 3. For the Revised CAPTA inventory, the scores are added to yield a total score out of 25 for all subdomains except Health and Fitness. This subdomain is scored as Health and Fitness: Value (with a maximum score of 10, based on the word pairs *good–bad* and *no use–useful,* and as Health and Fitness: Enjoyment (with a maximum score of 15, based on the remaining three word pairs, *not pleasant–pleasant, nice–awful, happy–sad.* For intersubdomain comparisons, these two Health and Fitness components should be rescaled to a value out of 25 by multiplying the scores by 2.5 and 1.67. It is recommended that such rescaling be the standard procedure."[32]

Key

	5	4	3	2	1	
good						bad
of no use	1	2	3	4	5	useful
not pleasant	1	2	3	4	5	pleasant
nice	5	4	3	2	1	awful
happy	5	4	3	2	1	sad

Scoring Table for CATPA Instrument

Score by Word	Range of Scores by Idea of Subdomain	Interpretation
5	23–25	Very good
4	18–22	Kind of good
3	13–17	Neither good nor bad
2	8–12	Kind of bad
1	5–7	Very bad

A score of 19 on one idea would indicate that the student would feel kind of good about it. No total score for all 7 subdomains is indicated. In fact, the idea of the CATPA is to permit comparison of meanings among the subdomains.

Willis Sports Attitudes Inventory—Form C*[38,39]

Purpose. To measure competitive related motives in sport: (1) power motive (POW), (2) motive of achieve success (MAS), and (3) motive to avoid failure (MAF).

Development. An original pool of 140 items was reduced to 40 items using factor analysis and jury procedures. Subsequently test-retest reliability, using college age athletes, ranged from .69 to .75 over an 8-week period. Content validity was claimed from measures of internal consistency using coefficient alpha. The coefficients ranged from .76 to .78 and provided a conservative indication that the items have something in common. Relationship of the scales

*From Willis, J.D.: Three scales to measure competition-related motives in sport. Journal of Sport Psychology, 4:3, 338–353, 1982. Used by permission of the author.

to the Sports Competition Anxiety Test,[19] the Mehrabian Measure of Achieving Tendency,[22] and the Dominance Scale of the California Psychological Inventory[12] was determined as convergent measures of motives to achieve success and the power motive. Construct validity is an accumulation of many studies that Willis has begun to assemble. The use of the scales should be confined to the study of group differences.

Level and Gender. The scale is appropriate for use with junior high school through college age male and female athletes.

Uses. Coaches will find this scale useful to analyze the competitive motives of their teams as well as changes in motives that might occur over time.

Directions. This questionnaire is designed to assess your reactions to situations that often arise in the sport setting. Please answer all questions on the separate answer sheet. Do not mark on the questionnaire. There are no right or wrong answers. Please use the following scale to indicate your agreement or disagreement with each statement:

> A — Strongly Agree
> B — Agree
> C — Neither Agree nor Disagree
> D — Disagree
> E — Strongly Disagree

The Inventory

Sports Attitudes Inventory

Form C

1. I have the ability to get my teammates "fired up" to play.
2. Before a game I don't worry too much about what is going to happen.
3. Teammates respect the way I hustle.
4. The night before a game, I don't find it difficult to sleep.
5. Recognition from the coach makes a hard practice seem worthwhile.
6. I do not enjoy being a team leader.
7. It is hard work rather than luck that leads to success.
8. I often take a loss harder than I should.
9. Winning a game gives me great satisfaction.
10. Others do not see me as an outstanding competitor.
11. I would be willing to work all year around in order to be a success in my sport.
12. I am nervous and fidgety right before a game.
13. I enjoy thinking about my past successes in sports.
14. I don't seem to be as tough as most of my teammates.
15. I seem to play better when spectators are present.
16. Teammates respect my leadership ability.
17. I admire athletes who are willing to put in extra practice time to improve their skills.
18. I seem to play best against highly skilled opponents.
19. I work hard at my sport in the hope of gaining recognition.
20. After losing a game, I find it difficult to sleep.
21. I am not pleased with my athletic ability.
22. Sometimes when I lose it bothers me for several days.
23. Making a "big play" gives me a thrill.

24. Teammates admire my persistence and determination.
25. I usually feel butterflies in my stomach just before a game.
26. My goal is to become outstanding in some sport.
27. In head-to-head competition with someone of my own ability, I lose more often than I win.
28. I get excited just talking to someone about a game.
29. I try very hard to be the best.
30. During a game if I blow a play it takes a while for me to shake it off.
31. I like to forget my sport in the off season.
32. I enjoy having people see me perform.
33. I try to get other players to train hard.
34. When I play I get so caught up in a game I temporarily lose contact with reality.
35. I enjoy any assignment which others find difficult.
36. Being a good athlete is not important to me.
37. I enjoy making suggestions which will help a teammate's play.
38. When I make a mistake, it bothers me the rest of the game.
39. I have a very strong desire to be successful in sports.
40. It is hard for me to stay calm before a game.

Scoring. A. Power—Items numbered 1, 3, 6, 10, 14, 16, 18, 21, 24, 27, 33, 37 comprise POW Scale.

B. Motive to Achieve Success—Items numbered 5, 7, 9, 11, 13, 15, 17, 19, 23, 26, 28, 29, 31, 32, 35, 36, 39 make up the MAS Scale.

C. Motive to Avoid Failure—Items numbered 2, 4, 8, 12, 20, 22, 25, 30, 34, 38, 40 make up the MAF Scale.

Items 1, 3, 5, 7, 8, 9, 11, 12, 13, 15, 16, 17, 18, 19, 20, 22, 23, 24, 25, 26, 28, 29, 30, 32, 33, 34, 35, 37, 38, 39, 40 should be scored as follows:

A – Strongly agree	=	5
B – Agree	=	4
C – Neither agree nor disagree	=	3
D – Disagree	=	2
E – Strongly disagree	=	1

For items 2, 4, 6, 10, 14, 21, 27, 31, 36 score in the opposite direction, i.e., A—Strongly agree = 1, etc.

Norms. Willis reports the following norms for males and females and from junior high school to college level athletes. In addition, he shows norms for 11 different sports.

Sample	N	POW Scale		MAS Scale		MAF Scale	
		Mean	SD	Mean	SD	Mean	SD
Females	251	41.43	6.20	66.99	7.90	34.23	7.09
Males	741	43.54	5.77	69.77	6.85	33.39	6.91

Comment. Willis cautions against using these three scales for individual analysis but thinks they are sufficiently sound for use with groups.

Sport Orientation Questionnaire—Form B*[11]

Purpose. To measure competitiveness and achievement behavior in sport and exercise settings.

*From Gill, D.L., and Deeter, T.E.: Development of the sport orientation questionnaire. Research Quarterly for Exercise and Sport, 59:3, 191–202, September, 1988. Used by permission of the authors and the AAHPERD.

Development. Two samples of undergraduate students and one sample of high school students were used to help establish credentials of the Sport Orientation Questionnaire. The Work and Family Orientation Questionnaire by Helmreich and Spence[14] was used as one validity check since it includes a measure of general achievement orientation. Items in the Sport Orientation Questionnaire originally numbered 58 and were reduced subsequently to 32 and finally to 25 items by factor analysis procedures. Factor 1, labeled competitiveness, reflects a desire to enter sport achievement situations, to strive for success, to work hard, and to master skills and an eagerness to meet competitive challenges. The other two factors, win orientation and goal orientation, "seem to reflect an orientation to the two major types of outcomes in sport achievement situations, specifically the desire to win in interpersonal competition in sport, and the desire to reach personal goals in sport."[11]

Internal consistency coefficients ranged from .70 to .95 over the three factors using the three samples. In addition, test–retest reliability was .89 for competitiveness, .82 for win orientation, and .73 for goal orientation. Gill and Deeter believe they have sufficient evidence of reliability and validity to warrant the use of this sport achievement orientation measure of individuals in sport and exercise settings.

Level and Gender. The Sport Orientation Questionnaire was developed using high school and college age men and women and would be appropriate to use with similar groups.

Uses. Coaches will find this questionnaire helpful as they explore the competitiveness, win, and goal orientations of their players.

Directions. The following statements describe reactions to sport situations. We want to know how you *usually* feel about sports and competition. Read each statement and circle the letter that indicates how much you agree or disagree with each statement on the scale: A, B, C, D or E. There are no right or wrong answers; simply answer as you honestly feel. Do not spend too much time on any one statement. Remember, choose the letter that describes how you *usually* feel about sports and competition.

The Questionnaire

SPORT ORIENTATION QUESTIONNAIRE—FORM B

	Strongly agree	Slightly agree	Neither agree nor disagree	Slightly disagree	Strongly disagree
1. I am a determined competitor.	A	B	C	D	E
2. Winning is important.	A	B	C	D	E
3. I am a competitive person.	A	B	C	D	E
4. I set goals for myself when I compete.	A	B	C	D	E
5. I try my hardest to win.	A	B	C	D	E
6. Scoring more points than my opponent is very important to me.	A	B	C	D	E
7. I look forward to competing.	A	B	C	D	E
8. I am most competitive when I try to achieve personal goals.	A	B	C	D	E

9. I enjoy competing against others.	A	B	C	D	E
10. I hate to lose.	A	B	C	D	E
11. I thrive on competition.	A	B	C	D	E
12. I try hardest when I have a specific goal.	A	B	C	D	E
13. My goal is to be the best athlete possible.	A	B	C	D	E
14. The only time I am satisfied is when I win.	A	B	C	D	E
15. I want to be successful in sports.	A	B	C	D	E
16. Performing to the best of my ability is very important to me.	A	B	C	D	E
17. I work hard to be successful in sports.	A	B	C	D	E
18. Losing upsets me.	A	B	C	D	E
19. The best test of my ability is competing against others.	A	B	C	D	E
20. Reaching personal performance goals is very important to me.	A	B	C	D	E
21. I look forward to the opportunity to test my skills in competition.	A	B	C	D	E
22. I have the most fun when I win.	A	B	C	D	E
23. I perform my best when I am competing against an opponent.	A	B	C	D	E
24. The best way to determine my ability is to set a goal and try to reach it.	A	B	C	D	E
25. I want to be the best every time I compete.	A	B	C	D	E

Scoring. The Sport Orientation Questionnaire yields three scores: Competitiveness, Win orientation, and Goal orientation. Each item is scored from 1 to 5 (A = 5, B = 4, C = 3, D = 2, E = 1). To obtain the three scores total the responses as follows:

Competitiveness — Total items 1, 3, 5, 7, 9, 11, 13, 15, 17, 19, 21, 23, 25.
Win Orientation — Total items 2, 6, 10, 14, 18, 22.
Goal Orientation — Total items 4, 8, 12, 16, 20, 24.

It would be inappropriate to total the three separate scores. The Competitiveness factor is the strongest and includes the 13 odd-numbered items on the SOQ. If a single score is needed, probably this one would be the most useful.

McMahan Sportsmanship Questionnaire*

Purpose. To assess sportsmanship attitudes of high school students.

Development. McMahan[21] had 667 male and female high school students re-

---

*From McMahan, R.: The Development of an Instrument for Assessing Sportsmanship Attitudes. Doctoral Dissertation, University of Tennessee, Knoxville, 1978. Used by permission of the author.

spond to 48 statements involving both positive and negative behavior in baseball, basketball, football, golf, tennis, and a universal category of behavior that was not specific to a sport. Content validity was established by using a definitionally based set of constructs gleaned from high school students and later verified by a panel of judges. Internal consistency reliability (split-halves) was shown to be .91. Construct validity was obtained through a factor analytic technique. Honesty and fair play were two constructs definitely identified. A combination of self-control and courtesy comprised a third construct.

Administrative Considerations. Each student should be provided with a copy of the questionnaire and an answer sheet. Names may or may not be placed on the answer sheets depending on the use of the results and the need to maintain the anonymity of the students.

Sportsmanship Questionnaire

Directions. Listed below are 48 statements describing events that take place in games and sporting events. Read each statement carefully and decide whether you agree or disagree with the action taken by those involved in the situation.

Place the number that describes the way you feel about the statement in the blank on the answer sheet corresponding with the number of the statement.

Please complete *every* item, and make all numbers clear on the answer sheet. Do not sign your name to the answer sheet or paper.

Strongly agree	−5
Agree	−4
Undecided	−3
Disagree	−2
Strongly disagree	−1

Please follow all directions on the answer sheet.

Key		BASEBALL
−	1.	When running into home, the base runner pushed the catcher off balance in an effort to make him/her drop the ball.
−	2.	A baseball player blamed the sun for his/her error in the field.
+	3.	A player told the umpire that he/she trapped a fly ball hit by the opponent.
−	4.	After striking out, the player threw his/her bat toward the dugout.
+	5.	A runner was called out when he/she admitted that he/she did not touch second base.
+	6.	The left fielder told the umpire that a ball hit by an opposing batter was fair.
−	7.	Players in the dugout heckled the opposing pitcher.
−	8.	In order to distract the opposing pitcher, a batter faked something in his/her eye. The umpire called time-out.
+	9.	The first baseman told the umpire that his/her foot left the bag before the ball was caught.

BASKETBALL

+	10.	A basketball player told the official he/she touched the ball as it went out of bounds.
+	11.	A basketball player moved quietly toward the bench when he/she fouled out of the game.
+	12.	A member of the home basketball team told the official that the shot which apparently won the game was released after the buzzer sounded.

− 13. A basketball player questioned an official about a previous call in order to stop the clock.

+ 14. Following a very close basketball game, opposing teams shook hands as they left the court.

+ 15. A basketball player admitted touching the rim of the basket in a controversial goal-tending call.

− 16. When talking with members of the press, a basketball player blamed the loss on the officiating.

− 17. A guard continually tagged his/her opponent in order to distract him/her.

FOOTBALL

− 18. Football players refused to shake hands at the end of the game.

− 19. A football player grabbed a face mask in order to get the opposing player down.

− 20. A football player threw his/her helmet to the ground following a penalty.

+ 21. A defensive back admitted to the official that he/she hit an opposing split end before the split end attempted to catch the pass.

+ 22. A football player told the official that he/she stepped out of bounds on an apparent touchdown run.

− 23. With no time-outs remaining, the quarterback on the losing football team faked an injury in order to stop the clock.

− 24. A football player threw dirt in the opposing player's eyes just as the ball was snapped.

GOLF

+ 25. A golfer stood very quietly as his/her opponent analyzed his/her putting strategy.

+ 26. The gallery applauded a tremendous sand shot by a visiting golfer.

− 27. A group of golfers recorded their scores before leaving the green.

+ 28. A golfer helped an opponent search for a lost ball.

+ 29. A golfer displayed no emotion after missing the short putt.

− 30. When placing his/her ball on the green to putt, a golfer moved the ball closer to the hole than it was originally.

− 31. While searching for a lost ball, a golfer refused to wave the group behind to pass.

TENNIS

+ 32. A tennis player was applauded for his/her honesty involving a particular call.

+ 33. On a match point, a tennis player called a ball good that hit close to the baseline. This call gave the match to the opponent.

+ 34. A tennis player asked to replay a point that the opponent lost due to a wind gust.

+ 35. A tennis player told his/her opponent he/she hit the net with the racket, thus giving a point to the opponent.

− 36. In order to distract the opponent, a tennis player took excessive time in serving the ball.

− 37. In a game of doubles, a tennis player blamed his/her partner for the loss.

+ 38. A tennis player admitted losing the match because he/she played poorly.

+ 39. A tennis player lost a point by telling his/her opponent that he/she committed a foot fault.

+ 40. A tennis player congratulated his/her opponent when the opponent made an exceptional return.

− 41. In a display of anger, the spectators threw paper cups onto the tennis court.

+   42. A tennis player insisted on replaying a point when his/her opponent fell during a rally.

UNIVERSAL

−   43. The spectators threatened the referee after the game because their team lost.
+   44. The fans were very quiet as a player prepared for a difficult shot.
+   45. The player displayed an even temper throughout the heated contest.
−   46. A player attempted to trip an opponent when the referee was not looking.
+   47. A coach congratulated an opposing player for his/her fine effort in the game.
−   48. A player blamed his/her loss on poor officiating.

Scoring. The statements have been keyed in the left margin, but the plus and minus signs would not appear on the copies used by the students.

	Positive Statements	Negative Statements
Strongly Agree	5	1
Agree	4	2
Undecided	3	3
Disagree	2	4
Strongly Disagree	1	5

The possible range of scores is from 48 to 240.

48– 72   Strong negative sportsmanship attitude
73–120   Negative sportsmanship attitude
121–168   Neutral attitude range
169–216   Positive sportsmanship attitude
217–240   Strong positive sportsmanship attitude

A score of 144 is at the exact middle of the range and scores on either side could be interpreted as being toward either the negative or positive sides of the scale.

SELF-CONCEPT MEASURES

Self-concept measures relate to the person's perception of self. They are ascertained indirectly, sometimes by comparing the way a person thinks about himself or herself with the way he or she would like to be. These scales represent some of the more recent measurement tools developed for use in physical education and sport. Their implementation reflects the trend of using movement experiences as one avenue of self-understanding.

Cratty Adaptation of Piers-Harris Self-Concept Scale*

Purpose. To estimate how children feel about their physical appearance and their ability to perform physical skills.

Development. The Piers-Harris[29,30] scale is based on a compilation of statements made by children concerning their likes and dislikes about themselves. In 1967, Cratty,[8] working at the UCLA Perceptual Motor Learning Laboratory, con-

---

*From Cratty, B., et al.: Movement Activities, Motor Ability, and the Education of Children. Springfield, Illinois, Charles C Thomas, 1970. Used by permission of Charles C Thomas and the author.

structed a scale adapted from the Piers-Harris scale which could concentrate more on physical ability and appearance. The statement questions are classified into five categories: feelings about general well-being, social competence, physical ability, physical appearance, and social achievement. Using 288 children, a test-retest reliability coefficient of .82 was obtained. Internal validity was established using an item analysis approach. All 20 statements were found to be valid because each one discriminated between the children with high scores and those with low scores on the scale. The 20-item scale involves a Yes-No response by the child. It can be read to the children if reading ability is a factor.

Level and Gender. Cratty designed the test for use with children in kindergarten through grade 6. His research showed no significant differences for age or gender.

Uses. To encourage children to talk about their physical abilities and appearance. To identify the children who have low self-concept scores so they can be helped.

Directions. You have a questionnaire that will determine how you feel about yourself. Each question will be read and you should then immediately decide how you feel and circle yes *or* no to answer. Ready?

The first question is —. Now circle "Yes" or "No." (The question is repeated and the instruction to circle yes or no given again.) The second question is —. (Continue through the twenty items.)

The Scale

SELF-CONCEPT SCALE

NAME _____ DATE _____ GRADE _____ M _____ F _____

Scoring
Key*

+	1. Are you good at making things with your hands?	Yes	No
+	2. Can you draw well?	Yes	No
+	3. Are you strong?	Yes	No
+	4. Do you like the way you look?	Yes	No
	5. Do your friends make fun of you?	Yes	No
+	6. Are you handsome/pretty?	Yes	No
	7. Do you have trouble making friends?	Yes	No
+	8. Do you like school?	Yes	No
	9. Do you wish you were different?	Yes	No
	10. Are you sad most of the time?	Yes	No
	11. Are you the last to be chosen in games?	Yes	No
+	12. Do girls like you?	Yes	No
+	13. Are you a good leader in games and sports?	Yes	No
	14. Are you clumsy?	Yes	No
	15. In games do you watch instead of play?	Yes	No
+	16. Do boys like you?	Yes	No
+	17. Are you happy most of the time?	Yes	No
+	18. Do you have nice hair?	Yes	No
	19. Do you play with younger children a lot?	Yes	No
+	20. Is reading easy to you?	Yes	No

Scoring. The Scoring Key has been included with the Self-Concept Scale but should not be printed on the copy of the answer sheet used by the children.

*Questions to which a positive response is expected.

Score 1 point for each response expected. Deduct 1 point for each positive expected answer which was circled No and each negative expected answer which was circled Yes. The score is the number of expected responses given for the 20 items.

Merkley Measure of Actual Physical Self*[23]

Purpose. To measure perception of the physical self related to exercise and physical activity.

Development. College students in tennis, racquetball, and fitness classes were used as subjects. They took the Tennessee Self Concept Scale and Budge's Self-Description and Evaluation Scale as criterion measures. Correlation coefficients ranged from .68 to .81 among the measures. All were significant at the .001 level. Merkley claimed strong predictability for use in measuring physical self-image due to the high coefficients. Preliminary construction of the measure reflected use of factor analysis which resulted in the identification of six factors which accounted for 72.8% of the total variance:

Factor 1: Confidence-Cognitive
Factor 2: Endurance
Factor 3: Skill
Factor 4: Strength
Factor 5: Weight and Body Fat
Factor 6: Flexibility

No reliability information was located.

Level and Gender. This scale was developed using collegiate age males and females. It appears suitable as well for upper level secondary school students and for adults.

Uses. To measure physical self-image and the effects of different types of physical activity on the psychological aspects of personality involving self-image.

Directions. The purpose of this test is to measure the meanings and feelings of various people about their physical selves and their physical activity by having them make judgments against a series of descriptive scales. In rating your actual physical self, rate yourself as you are now, not how you wish you were or how you feel you should be. *Rate yourself within the framework of your physical self or your experience in physical activity only.*

Here is how you are to use these scales: if you feel your physical self is *very closely related* to the term at one end of the scale, circle the number at the extreme end, i.e., 1 or 7.

Strong 1 2 3 4 5 6 7 Weak

If you feel it is *quite closely related*, circle 2 or 6. If you feel it is *only slightly related*, circle 3 or 5. If you feel it is *neutral*, equally associated or irrelevant, circle 4.

---

*From Merkley, L.R.: Physical self-image and physical activity: the development and testing of an evaluative instrument to measure the effects of physical activity on changes in physical self-image. Dissertation, Brigham Young University, 1981. Used by permission of the author.

Measure of Actual Physical Self

1 or 7	Very closely related
2 or 6	Quite closely related
3 or 5	Only slightly related
4	Neutral, equal or irrelevant

1.	Coached	1	2	3	4	5	6	7	Uncoached
2.	Tired	1	2	3	4	5	6	7	Fresh
3.	Fat	1	2	3	4	5	6	7	Lean
4.	Unskilled	1	2	3	4	5	6	7	Skilled
5.	Important	1	2	3	4	5	6	7	Unimportant
6.	Agile	1	2	3	4	5	6	7	Awkward
7.	Ignorant	1	2	3	4	5	6	7	Knowledgeable
8.	Ungraceful	1	2	3	4	5	6	7	Graceful
9.	Educated	1	2	3	4	5	6	7	Uneducated
10.	Enjoyable	1	2	3	4	5	6	7	Loathsome
11.	Fleshy	1	2	3	4	5	6	7	Skinny
12.	Sure	1	2	3	4	5	6	7	Unsure
13.	Refreshed	1	2	3	4	5	6	7	Exhausted
14.	Muscular	1	2	3	4	5	6	7	Unendowed
15.	Rigid	1	2	3	4	5	6	7	Supple
16.	Weak	1	2	3	4	5	6	7	Strong
17.	Untrained	1	2	3	4	5	6	7	Trained
18.	Unfavorable	1	2	3	4	5	6	7	Favorable
19.	Difficult	1	2	3	4	5	6	7	Easy
20.	Informed	1	2	3	4	5	6	7	Uninformed
21.	Obese	1	2	3	4	5	6	7	Slender
22.	Flexible	1	2	3	4	5	6	7	Inflexible
23.	Powerful	1	2	3	4	5	6	7	Powerless
24.	Fatigued	1	2	3	4	5	6	7	Energetic
25.	Stiff	1	2	3	4	5	6	7	Limber
26.	Certain	1	2	3	4	5	6	7	Uncertain
27.	Coordinated	1	2	3	4	5	6	7	Uncoordinated

Scoring. Merkley's measure of Actual Physical Self uses a semantic differential format of bipolar adjectives. Items 2, 3, 4, 7, 8, 15, 16, 17, 18, 19, 21, 24, and 25 are scored 1 to 7 as shown on the response sheet. Items 1, 5, 6, 9, 10, 11, 12, 13, 14, 20, 22, 23, 26, and 27 are scored in reverse, i.e., 7-6-5-4-3-2-1. For example, if a person marks 5 on the coached–uncoached continuum, it would be scored as a 3 instead of a 5. A maximum score of 189 is possible. Persons who score around 108 have a neutral, equal, or irrelevant feeling about their physical selves in an activity context. Higher scores reflect a more positive feeling about the physical self just as lower scores show more negative feelings.

Nelson-Allen Movement Satisfaction Scale*

Purpose. To assess movement satisfaction.

Development. Nelson and Allen[24] noted that most scales of body image and self-concept have not considered the person as a moving entity. An initial list of 129 items was reduced to 75 by a jury of eight experts and administered to 176 men and women between 18 and 21 years of age. Item analysis and reliability

*From Nelson, B.A., and Allen, D.J.: Scale for the appraisal of movement satisfaction. Perceptual and Motor Skills, *31*:795–800, December, 1970. Used by permission of the authors and the publisher.

information was obtained which enabled the authors to reduce the scale to 50 items. Subsequent administrations of the scale to over 800 men and women produced a reliability coefficient of .95 using a Kuder-Richardson formula.

Level and Gender. Nelson and Allen purposely designed the scale for both men and women to avoid the shortcomings of previous instruments. Their data were collected on several different groups, but within the 14 to 21 year age group.

Uses. To become aware of movement satisfaction status and changes. To investigate the relationship between self-concept and movement satisfaction. To compare movement satisfaction between men and women and between younger and older people.

FORM A

Name _____ Sex _____ Age _____ School _____
Year in school _____ Activity _____ Date _____

On the following pages are listed a number of statements concerning human movement which are related to your ability to move. Consider each item listed and encircle the number after each item which best represents your feelings according to the following scale:

1. Have STRONG NEGATIVE feelings
   Encircle a 1 for those aspects of your movement about which you are unhappy, feel uncomfortable, or inadequate, and wish change could be made. For example, if you feel inadequate about your skill in jumping for height and wish change could be made, encircle the 1 after the item "jumping for height."
2. Have MODERATE NEGATIVE feelings
   Encircle a 2 for those aspects of your movement about which you have some negative feeling but not as strong as that in category 1 (see previous paragraph).
3. Have NO feeling one way or the other
   Encircle a 3 for those aspects of your movement about which you have no feeling at all. For example, if you have no feeling at all about your ability to move rapidly whenever you wish to, encircle a 3 after that item.
4. Have MODERATE POSITIVE feelings
   Encircle a 4 for those aspects of your movement about which you have some positive feeling but not as strong as that in category 5 (see next paragraph).
5. Have STRONG POSITIVE feelings
   Encircle a 5 for those aspects of your movement about which you feel proud, happy, fortunate, or which give you a pleasant feeling when you think about them. For example, if you are proud of your physical activity, encircle the 5 after the item.

1. Have strong negative feelings
2. Have moderate negative feelings
3. Have no feeling one way or the other
4. Have moderate positive feelings
5. Have strong positive feelings

ITEM	SCALE
1. Pride in physical activity.	1 2 3 4 5
2. Other peoples' opinions about my ability to move well.	1 2 3 4 5
3. Ability to learn physical skills easily.	1 2 3 4 5
4. Ability to maintain my balance when moving.	1 2 3 4 5
5. Ability to participate in sport activity on a varsity level.	1 2 3 4 5
6. Ability to jump for height.	1 2 3 4 5
7. Ability to run with speed.	1 2 3 4 5
8. Ability to arise from a chair without feeling awkward or clumsy.	1 2 3 4 5

9. Ability to move freely without being inhibited. 1 2 3 4 5
10. Ability to pick up or carry things without dropping them. 1 2 3 4 5
11. Ability to move rapidly whenever I wish to. 1 2 3 4 5
12. Ability to run in a relaxed manner. 1 2 3 4 5
13. Ability to move the total body effectively in almost everything I 1 2 3 4 5
    do.
14. Ability to do cartwheels and gymnastic stunts. 1 2 3 4 5
15. Ability to learn new movements without becoming discouraged. 1 2 3 4 5
16. Confidence in moving well in almost all situations. 1 2 3 4 5
17. Ability to maintain my balance when stationary. 1 2 3 4 5
18. Ability to move with a feeling of lightness. 1 2 3 4 5
19. Ability to throw overarm for distance. 1 2 3 4 5
20. Ability to walk with poise. 1 2 3 4 5
21. Ability to sit down in a chair without being awkward. 1 2 3 4 5
22. Ability to balance on one leg. 1 2 3 4 5
23. Ability to move quickly around obstacles. 1 2 3 4 5
24. The way I move in general. 1 2 3 4 5
25. Ability to recover from an unbalanced position. 1 2 3 4 5
26. Ability to move in a direct manner when necessary. 1 2 3 4 5
27. Ability to participate in movement activities without fear of falling. 1 2 3 4 5
28. Ability to move to music. 1 2 3 4 5
29. Ability to stretch my body. 1 2 3 4 5
30. Ability to perform movements smoothly in most physical tasks I 1 2 3 4 5
    undertake.
31. Ability to do dance movements. 1 2 3 4 5
32. Ability to make graceful movements whenever I wish. 1 2 3 4 5
33. Ability to move better than my friends in most situations. 1 2 3 4 5
34. Ability to do as well as others on a sports item. 1 2 3 4 5
35. Ability to produce sudden movement. 1 2 3 4 5
36. Ability to perform physical skills effectively without unnecessary 1 2 3 4 5
    movements.
37. Carriage of my body when walking. 1 2 3 4 5
38. Ability to kick a stationary ball for distance. 1 2 3 4 5
39. Ability to express my feelings with movement. 1 2 3 4 5
40. Ability to judge distances between myself and others or myself and 1 2 3 4 5
    objects when we are moving.
41. Ability to reduce muscular tension at will. 1 2 3 4 5
42. Ability to reproduce a rhythmical beat with bodily movements. 1 2 3 4 5
43. Grace in performing everyday movement activities. 1 2 3 4 5
44. Ability to relax at will. 1 2 3 4 5
45. Ability to stay on beat with the music when I dance. 1 2 3 4 5
46. Ability to get my arms and legs to work together when appropriate. 1 2 3 4 5
47. Ability to control slow movement whenever necessary. 1 2 3 4 5
48. Ability to perform very vigorous physical activities. 1 2 3 4 5
49. Ability to meet the physical demands of everyday living. 1 2 3 4 5
50. My skill in swimming. 1 2 3 4 5

Scoring. Total all the point values encircled. There are 50 items and each can be weighted as much as 5 points, so 250 is the maximum possible score. The following ranges will help the instructor interpret the scores:

    50– 74   Strong negative feelings
    75–124   Moderate negative feelings
    125–174 No feelings one way or the other—neutral

175–224   Moderate positive feelings
225–250   Strong positive feelings

Tanner Movement Satisfaction Scale*

Purpose. To measure the degree of satisfaction or dissatisfaction a child feels with his or her own movement.

Development. This scale was revised by Tanner[36] from the Nelson and Allen Movement Satisfaction Scale[24] to make it appropriate for primary-grade children. A jury of five elementary physical education authorities judged 55 of the statements from the Nelson-Allen scale for relevance and appropriateness for measurement of feeling of movement satisfaction/dissatisfaction of primary-age children. Fifty items were included in the final version with a simulated Likert 5-point answer scale. Reliabilities were established in a pilot of 99 subjects in first and second grades (r = .875). An item analysis was conducted and reliability for each item was computed. The 20 least reliable items were eliminated. The final instrument was composed of 30 items.

Level and Gender. For primary-grade children.

Directions. The teacher should prepare a series of face drawings, showing reactions from very happy to very sad, to pin to the board.

Instructions to the Children for the Movement Satisfaction Scale. Do you recognize these pictures? (Point to the wall chart of faces. Responses from children.) Yes, of course you do. Do you notice anything about the faces in these drawings? Yes, in some the face is very happy, and in some it is sad, either looking as though the face feels good about things, or bad about them. How does it look here? (Point to the first drawing.) Yes, very happy indeed; and here? (Point to the second drawing.) Yes, still happy, but not *very* happy like the last one. In this one? (Point to the last drawing.) Oh yes, this face is *very unhappy,* isn't it, very sad looking; and here? (Point to the next-to-last drawing.) This face is still sad. Is it as unhappy as the one before? No, it isn't, is it? Now look at this drawing in the middle. (Point to the middle drawing.) The face is not happy or sad, is it? In fact it looks as though the face is not quite sure *how* it feels about things. This face really doesn't know how to feel about it all.

Can you really tell how the faces feel by these pictures? Yes, I think you can now. So now you are going to use them in a fun way; you are going to use them to show me how *you* feel about some of the things that you do.

You see the papers in front of you; they have faces drawn on them just like these on the board. I am going to ask you some questions about things that you do, and you are to color the face which best shows how *you feel* about doing them.

Let's have a little practice with one or two questions before you start coloring on your paper. If I ask you, "How do you feel about eating ice cream?" which one would you color? Yes, nearly all of you would color the very happy one; some might not feel quite so pleased about it and might color just the happy one, but I don't suppose anyone would color the very sad one. Let's try another, "How do you feel about playing the piano?" Some of you may never have had

---

*From Tanner, P.W.: The Relationship of Selected Measures of Body Image and Movement Concept of Two Types of Programs of Physical Education in the Primary Grades. Dissertation, Ohio State University, 1969. Used by permission of the author. Reprinted from Logsdon[18] with permission of Lea & Febiger.

the chance to try this, and so have no idea how you would feel about it. If that is the case, which one would you color? Yes, this one in the middle, the one which is not really sure what to think about how it feels. One more: "How do you feel about having to sit down all day long?" Most of you feel very unhappy when you have to sit still for a long time, don't you?

I think you know how to do this now, don't you? Just remember, you don't have to try to please anyone by your answer; there is no right or wrong answer; you are just showing how *you* feel about the question.

Is your name at the top of your paper? Put your marker pencil beside number one, and listen—now color the face which best shows how you feel about that. Now put your marker beside number two. . . .

Scale Items

MOVEMENT SATISFACTION SCALE ITEMS:
1. How do you feel about bouncing a ball many times without stopping?
2. How do you feel about jumping very high?
3. How do you feel about picking very big things up and carrying them?
4. How do you feel about moving and stopping very suddenly?
5. How so you feel about climbing on very high things?
6. How do you feel about tagging games?
7. How do you feel about playing hard and using lots of energy?
8. How do you feel about stretching your body as far as you can?
9. How do you feel about balancing on one leg?
10. How do you feel about running very fast?
11. How do you feel about jumping over something about as high as your knee?
12. How do you feel about rolling over and over and over?
13. How do you feel about moving in a big space?
14. How do you feel about moving quickly around chairs, tables, or people when you have to?
15. How do you feel about kicking a ball a long way?
16. How do you feel about having to move slowly all the time?
17. How do you feel about running for a very long time?
18. How do you feel about moving to music?
19. How do you feel about running backwards?
20. How do you feel about bouncing a ball quickly lots of times?
21. How do you feel about hanging from things?
22. How do you feel about throwing a ball for someone else to catch?
23. How do you feel about moving when your friends are watching you?
24. How do you feel about playing hard and fast?
25. How do you feel about jumping onto something about as high as your knee?
26. How do you feel about moving very heavy things?
27. How do you feel about throwing and catching a ball?
28. How do you feel about moving sideways?
29. How do you feel about changing directions quickly when you are moving?
30. How do you feel about jumping a long way, when you get to run before you jump?

Scoring. An answer sheet accommodating 30 sets of face figures should be prepared and given to the student. There are 30 items, each receiving a possible 5 points for a Very Happy response, 4 points for Happy, 3 for Undecided, and so on. The range of scores would be from 30 to 150 with the larger number representing the more positive attitude about a child's own movement.

$$135–150 \text{ points} = \text{Very Happy}$$
$$105–134 \text{ points} = \text{Happy}$$
$$75–104 \text{ points} = \text{Undecided}$$
$$45–\ 74 \text{ points} = \text{Sad}$$
$$30–\ 44 \text{ points} = \text{Very Sad}$$

Comments. The scale is printed in the book by Logsdon et al.[18] on physical education for children, and is reprinted here because of its unique application for primary age children.

REFERENCES

1. Adams, D.L.: The development of a prosocial behavior inventory related to participation in high school physical education classes. Thesis, California State University, Long Beach, 1982.
2. Bain, L.L.: Differences in values implicit in teaching and coaching behaviors. Research Quarterly, *49*:1, 5–11, 1978.
3. Carmack, M.A., and Martens, R.: Measuring commitment to running: A survey of runners' attitudes and mental states. Journal of Sports Psychology, *1*:25–42, 1979.
4. Carre, F.A., Mosher, R.E., and Schutz, R.W.: British Columbia Physical Education Assessment: General Report. Victoria: British Columbia Ministry of Education, 1980.
5. Cattell, R.B., and Eber, H.W.: Handbook for the Sixteen Personality Factor Questionnaire. Champaign, IL, The Institute for Personality and Ability Testing, 1957.
6. Corbin, C.B., Nielsen, A.B., Borsdorf, L.L., and Laurie, D.R.: Commitment to physical activity. International Journal of Sport Psychology, *18*:215–222, 1987.
7. Cowell, C.C.: Validating an index of social adjustment for high school use. Research Quarterly, *29*:7–18, March, 1958.
8. Cratty, B., et al.: Movement Activities, Motor Ability, and the Education of Children. Springfield, IL: Charles C Thomas, 1970.
9. Fox, K.R., Corbin, C.B., and Couldry, W.H.: Female physical estimation and attraction to physical activity. Journal of Sport Psychology, *7*:2, 125–136, 1985.
10. Fox, K.R., Corbin, C.B., and Couldry, W.H.: The validity and reliability of shortened physical estimation scales. Paper presented at the Centennial Convention of AAHPERD. Atlanta, GA. April, 1985. Abstract located in Abstracts of Research Papers, 138, 1985. AAHPERD.
11. Gill, D.L., and Deeter, T.E.: Development of the sport orientation questionnaire. Research Quarterly for Exercise and Sport, *59*:3, 191–202, September, 1988.
12. Gough, H.G.: California Psychological Inventory Manual. Palo Alto, CA: Consulting Psychologists Press, 1969.
13. Gruger, C.C., Corbin, C.B., and Nielsen, A.B.: General commitment to physical activity. *In* C.O. Dotson (Ed.), Exercise Physiology, Current Selected Research, 2:1–9, 1986. New York, AMS Press.
14. Helmreich, R.I., and Spence, J.T.: The work and family orientation questionnaire: An objective instrument to assess components of achievement motivation and attitudes toward family and career. Catalog of Selected Documents in Psychology, *8*:2 (Document # 1677), 1978.
15. Horrocks, R.N.: Relationship of selected prosocial play behaviors in children to moral reasoning, youth sports participation, and perception of sportsmanship. Dissertation, The University of North Carolina at Greensboro, 1979.
16. Kenyon, S.G.: A conceptual model for characterizing physical activity. Research Quarterly, *39*:96–104, 1968.
17. Krathwohl, D.R., Bloom, B.S., and Masia, B.B.: Taxonomy of Educational Objectives: The Classification of Educational Goals. Handbook II. Affective Domain. New York, David McKay Company, 1964.
18. Logsdon, B.J., et al: Physical education for children: A focus on the teaching process. 2nd Ed. Philadelphia, Lea & Febiger, 1984.
19. Martens, R.: Sport Competition Anxiety Test. Champaign, IL, Human Kinetics, 1977.
20. McKethan, J.R.: Students attitudes toward instructional processes in secondary physical education. Dissertation, The University of North Carolina at Greensboro, 1979.
21. McMahan, R.: The development of an instrument for assessing sportsmanship attitudes. Dissertation, University of Tennessee, Knoxville, 1978.

22. Mehrabian, A., and Bank, L.: A Manual for the Mehrabian Measure of Achieving Tendency. University of California, Los Angeles: A. Mehrabian, 1975.
23. Merkley, L.R.: Physical self-image and physical activity: The development and testing of an evaluative instrument to measure the effects of physical activity on changes in physical self-image. Dissertation, Brigham Young University, 1981.
24. Nelson, B.A., and Allen, D.J.: Scale for the appraisal of movement satisfaction. Perceptual and Motor Skills, 31:795–800, December, 1970.
25. Nelson, D.O.: Leadership in sports. Research Quarterly, 37:2, 268–275, 1966.
26. Nielsen, A.B.: Commitment to physical activity. Dissertation, Arizona State University, Tempe, 1985.
27. Nielsen, A.B.: Letter to R. McGee, June 25, 1986.
28. Nielsen, A.B., and Corbin, C.B.: Physical activity commitment. Conference Abstracts, North American Society for the Psychology of Sport and Physical Activity Conference. Scottsdale, AR, p. 93, June, 1986.
29. Piers, E.V., and Harris, D.B.: Age and other correlates of self-concept in children. Journal of Educational Psychology, 55:91–95, 1964.
30. Piers-Harris Children's Self-Concept Scale: "The Way I Feel About Myself." Counselor Recording and Tests, Box 6186 Acklan Station, Nashville, Tennessee, 37212, 1969.
31. Safrit, M.J., Wood, T.M., and Dishman, R.K.: The factorial validity of the physical estimation and attraction scales. Journal of Sport Psychology, 7:2, 166–190, 1985.
32. Schutz, R.W., Smoll, F.L., Carre, F.A., and Mosher, R.E: Inventories and norms for children's attitudes toward physical activity. Research Quarterly for Exercise and Sport, 56:3, 256–265, 1985.
33. Schutz, R.W., Smoll, F.L., and Wood, T.W.: A psychometric analysis of the inventory for assessing children's attitudes toward physical activity. Journal of Sport Psychology, 4:321–344, 1981.
34. Simon, J.A., and Smoll, F.L.: An instrument for assessing children's attitudes toward physical activity. Research Quarterly, 45:407–415, 1974.
35. Sonstroem, R.J.: Physical estimation and attraction scales; research and rationale. Medicine and Science in Sports, 10:2, 97–102, 1978.
36. Tanner, P.W.: The relationship of selected measures of body image and movement concept of two types of programs of physical education in the primary grades. Dissertation, The Ohio State University, 1969.
37. Toulmin, M.L.B.: The development of the original instrument to measure the expressed attitudes of children toward the elementary school program of physical education. Thesis, Texas Woman's University, 1973.
38. Willis, J.D.: Three scales to measure competition-related motives in sport. Journal of Sport Psychology, 4:4, 338–353, 1982.
39. Willis, J.D.: Letter to R. McGee, July 17, 1986.
40. Wood, T.M.: A psychometric analysis of the Simon and Smoll children's attitude toward physical activity inventory. Thesis, University of British Columbia, Vancouver, 1979.

10

Measurement for Program Evaluation

The primary purpose for evaluating any program is to improve it, so it can better serve the people for whom it is designed. "If there is no desire or motivation to ask the tough questions about what can be done to make programs better, then no program evaluation needs to occur."[5] This is true whether the inspiration for program evaluation is required (e.g., for accreditation or funding) or whether you have voluntarily elected to conduct a program evaluation (e.g., as part of program or faculty/staff development).

The practice of program evaluation involves measurement of the degree to which the program's stated goals are being attained. Thus the first step in program evaluation is always to review the existing goals or objectives of the program. If the program does not have stated goals, then your first task will be to draft a statement of goals. Step two requires development of a total evaluation plan that guarantees that pertinent data will be collected. Step three is the implementation of the evaluation plan, i.e., the collection of data. This step is followed by evaluation of the data results. Data are, of course, evaluated in terms of the stated goals. And finally, one must make appropriate adjustments to the program in an attempt to move the program closer to its stated goals.

Process in Relation to the Product

Physical education and sport programs may be evaluated in one of two ways, but a total evaluation program employs both approaches. First, programs may be evaluated by applying measurement techniques directly to program components; this is often referred to as measurement of the *process*. In general, process measurement is directed toward the ways in which the program environment is structured and utilized. The checklists for the evaluation of elementary and secondary physical education programs included in this chapter are examples of process measures. The aspects of the process measured by these instruments include the content of the instructional program, administration of the instructional program, qualifications of the instructional staff, scheduling, facilities, equipment, and financing.

The second way in which program evaluation may occur is by measuring the status and progress of the *product* of the program. This method is clearly more indirect but perhaps more valid than the direct process measurement of programs. In this approach, physical performance tests, knowledge tests, and affective inventories are used to measure the physical education student, the youth sport athlete, and the fitness spa client. Such measurement attempts to answer the questions related to accountability, by trying to determine the extent to which a program actually accomplishes what it sets out to do. In this chapter you will find two examples of instruments that can be used for this type of program evaluation; these are the Scale to Measure Attitudes toward Intramural Sports and the Nebraska Youth Sport Inventory.[10,11] Many other such instruments will be found in Chapters 6, 7, 8, and 9.

Since all facets of the process are means to the end product, evaluation of the process through the measurement of the product could be the ultimate test of the effectiveness of the process. However, it is not always easy to relate positive, or even negative, performance of the product to the process components. When student or athlete performance does not measure up to specific standards in fitness, skill, knowledge, and attitudes, the inadequacy is apparent, but the cause is still undetermined. Such measurement data may serve as a basis for study and discussion by staff members, but ultimately the data must be interpreted in terms of strengths, weaknesses, and needs of the process. This interpretation usually becomes a subjective process based on judgment of the evaluators. The more data available, and the more accurate the data are, the more likely the judgments will have validity. Therefore, the measurement of both the process and the product should complement and supplement each other when programs are being evaluated. In general, the ultimate result of program evaluation is based on judgment and is highly subjective. Such judgments, however, must be based on as much quantified data as possible.

Uses of Program Evaluation

Although the immediate end of program evaluation is improvement of the program, there are a number of other specific uses for the results of program evaluation.

Measurement of Status and Progress. The basic use of measurement is to secure data that are necessary to *reveal the status of the program:* its relative quality and effectiveness. If reevaluation is done and comparisons are made with previous measurements, *there is an identification of progress.* The measurement of this rate of progress or improvement is an important outcome of evaluation. If measurement is made annually and a profile, graph, or chart is constructed of the findings, a graphic picture is available to show how some aspects of the process have moved closer to the standards that have been established.

Comparisons. Evaluation always involves comparisons made in relation to certain criteria with well-established standards. Probably the most basic use in this area is to make comparisons with established standards in order to show how present programs stand with respect to the ideal program or with a previous measurement of the same program to show progress and achievement. Other frequent uses are to compare the effectiveness of an existing program with another program and the program in one locale with programs in another. In any event, it is essential that comparisons be made with acceptable educational standards if the program outcomes are to be effectively evaluated. When the process is evaluated through the product, client progress and achievement can be compared with either criterion-referenced or norm-referenced standards.

Identification of Strengths and Weaknesses. When measurement results are compared with norms or standards, certain aspects of the process are revealed. Such comparisons basically reveal two conditions: First, they may show in what aspect or aspects the standards are met or surpassed. Second, they may show needs and weaknesses. Both approaches have great value. In some cases, a profile is used to summarize measurement data and to indicate needs in a graphic and quantitative manner. Probably the most practical result of comparisons is the uncovering of weaknesses, which, when identified, can furnish the focal point of the follow-up. This follow-up is most important because what happens to the program after measurement is far more important than the measurement itself or its results. On the basis of significant weaknesses that are revealed by measurement, the process can be modified and strengthened. Some results can be used to show a need in the factors of personnel and facilities. On the basis of these revealed needs, requests can be made for additional staff members or equipment and facilities to carry on the program in an effective manner. Measurement results may also be used to gather material and supporting evidence to justify an existing program that has already been in operation, a pilot project, or a particular technique in use at the present time. Also, they may be used to indicate the needs for new strategies or the use of new materials.

Indication of Teacher/Coach Effectiveness. In addition to the appraisal of the program and tools, it is frequently important to find out how good the teachers/coaches are in bringing about changes that are stated in the objectives. How effective are their methods and teaching/coaching skills? How effective are the materials that they use? Do they have good teaching/coaching personalities? Are their students/players motivated to scale greater heights? Do they lead others into assuming greater responsibility and self-analysis? Are they developing leadership and citizenship? Can they teach skills and do they inculcate a desire on the part of the student/athlete to participate and to be fit? Most of these questions can be answered through a good evaluation program.

A measure of the product may be used to reveal teacher/coach effectiveness. However, care must be exercised in evaluating the product because the teacher/coach does not always have control of all the pertinent facets bearing on the student's or athlete's capacity and motivation to learn or perform. Accountability in terms of client achievement must be limited only to those things over which teachers/coaches and perhaps administrators have control.

Motivation. One of the uses of program evaluation is motivation. Such self-evaluation and self-analysis, which are necessary in program and personnel evaluation, inevitably lead to stimulating effects. Evaluation should encourage staff members individually and as a group to strive for greater efficiency and to exert greater effort. Program evaluation results will furnish them with knowledge that has the potential to inspire self-improvement. This, in turn, should enhance the upgrading of other factors of the process and eventually should have a positive effect in producing a better product.

Contribution to Research. Many times program evaluation is carried out as a part of a research project. These studies naturally make contributions to the field in numerous ways. Results of studies have many uses in themselves, including interpretation of the program, justification for more emphasis, serving as a basis for curriculum construction, and serving as a basis for making general and specific recommendations to administrators.

Administrative Understanding and Support. It is no secret that in the field of physical education one of the weak areas has been public relations. The very nature of its activities and the climate in which it operates have led to misunderstandings and false beliefs. In addition, the leadership in the past has not always been of the best quality, and the conduct of many programs has not been conducive to a universal appreciation and acceptance of the field. This lack of appreciation for the needs and outcomes of physical education and the misunderstanding of its program frequently are shared by school administrators. Along with other media, the results of program evaluation can be used to interpret the program to the school administrators and to gain their understanding and support. If program objectives are to be achieved, not only must the understanding and support of the school administrator be available, but also that of the community.

MEASURES FOR PHYSICAL EDUCATION PROGRAMS

Illinois Criteria for Evaluating Elementary Physical Education*[3]
Purpose. To provide a basis for improving the quality of physical education programs in grades K–6. Also to stimulate self-study and self-evaluation to ascertain the strengths and weaknesses of a school physical education program.

Development. None reported.

Level. Grades K–6.

Uses. For program evaluation. For research, to assess the effectiveness of curricular and/or methodological innovations.

Directions. Each "Evaluative Criteria" statement may be answered "yes," "no," or "partially." If the situation can be answered as mostly yes or mostly no, then check the appropriate column; otherwise, check the "partial" column. If an item does not apply to your situation or if an explanation would clarify your response, please write in the "comments" section. It is also recommended that the evaluator write comments when responding "no" or "partially."

The use of the "Evaluative Criteria" will require interpretation of the checklist items. The evaluator may alter or modify an item through explanation, if deemed necessary. The evaluator may also eliminate items deemed inappropriate to the situation.

The Instrument

1980 Criteria for Evaluating Elementary Physical Education in Illinois Schools†

School _____ School Population _____

Address _____ Telephone _____

Name _____ Position at School _____

Teaching Level _____

Provision for Physical Education : Minutes per week _____

Days per week _____

Number of Teachers: _____ Average Class Size _____

The responder is using the form as:

Administrator _____ Physical Education Specialist _____

Classroom Teacher _____ Other—Identify _____

*Illinois Association for Health, Physical Education and Recreation: 1980 Criteria for evaluating elementary physical education in Illinois schools. Illinois Journal, Fall 1984, 39–43. Used by permission of Illinois-AHPER.

†From Illinois Association for Health, Physical Education and Recreation: 1980 Criteria for evaluating elementary physical education in Illinois schools. Illinois Journal, Fall 1984, 39–43. Used by permission of Illinois-AHPER.

A. INSTRUCTIONAL

	Yes	No	Part.	Percent of Time	Comments
1. The program provides for the development of skills, and attitudes related to:					
a. Basic Movement Skills					
Locomotor					
Non Locomotor					
Body Awareness					
Spatial Awareness					
Perceptual Motor Skills					
Object Handling					
b. Rhythmic Activities					
Basic Fundamental Rhythms					
Creative/Interpretive					
Singing Games					
Folk/Square Dance					
c. Fitness and Conditioning					
Cardio Vascular Fitness					
Muscular Strength and Endurance					
d. Stunts/Tumbling					
e. Gymnastics					
f. Combatives					
g. Posture and Body Mechanics					
h. Games and Relays					
i. Sport Skills and Lead up Games					
Softball					
Basketball					
Flag Football					
Soccer					
Track and Field					
Volleyball					
j. Modified and Adaptive Programs					
k. Outdoor Education					
l. Aquatics					
2. Knowledges:					
a. Cardio-respiratory fitness					
b. Strength development					
c. Body mechanics					
d. Movement concepts					
e. Game rules					
f. Rhythmic concepts					

B. ADMINISTRATION OF INSTRUCTIONAL PROGRAM

	Yes	No	Part.	Comments
1. A daily program of instructional physical activity is provided.				
2. A written curriculum or course of study is available which allows for unit and yearly plans.				
3. Curriculum is relevant to the student interests, needs, and facilities.				
4. Provisions are made for progression in the program.				
5. Available audio-visual aids are used.				
6. Provisions are made for continuous review of the program.				
7. Provisions are made for individual needs.				
8. All classes are coeducational.				
9. Students are grouped by ability for competitive activities.				

C. ENRICHMENT PROGRAM

	Yes	No	Part.	Comments
1. Qualified teachers are provided to lead the enrichment program.				
2. Some free play and free choice periods are provided which encourage self-improvement of skills.				
3. Participation in the enrichment program is in addition to, not a substitute for, the required physical education program.				
4. The activities offered in the enrichment program are well organized and efficiently conducted.				
5. The program is arranged to correlate with the class work in physical education.				
6. Intramurals in a variety of activities are provided for students in upper grades.				
7. Intramural programs provide for voluntary participation for all students.				
8. If interscholastic activities are provided, provisions are made for: a. Teams of varying abilities, sizes, or weights.				
b. Activities appropriate to the level of maturity, skills and interest of participants.				
c. A variety of individual, dual, and team activities.				
d. A program for all students in the upper grades.				

D. EVALUATION PROGRAM

	Yes	No	Part.	Comments

1. Provisions are made within the program for the following devices:
  a. Fitness tests
  b. Motor skill evaluation
  c. Self-testing activities				

2. Provisions are made for pre-testing to identify learning disorders and/or other problems related to effective learning.				
3. Students and parents are kept apprised of the students' progress.				
4. Records are kept on the physical fitness, motor skill and growth accomplishments of the students.				

E. MISCELLANEOUS

	Yes	No	Part.	Comments
1. Gymnasium shoes are worn during most physical education classes. Bare feet are appropriate for some activities.				
2. Appropriate activities are substituted if religious objections are raised to specific activities.				

F. INSTRUCTIONAL STAFF QUALIFICATION

	Yes	No	Part.	Comments
1. Teachers are properly certified, having either a major or minor in physical education from an accredited institution including preparation at the elementary level.				
2. Physical education specialists, either teachers or consultants, serve all grade levels in the school.				
3. All persons engaged in the physical education and enrichment programs are members of the faculty.				
4. Staff members have access to qualified supervisory personnel who can assist them in determining their effectiveness with respect to:				
a. Planning and organizing class work.				
b. Establishing and maintaining acceptable teacher-student relations.				
c. Knowledge of the curriculum of physical education.				
d. Methods of teaching.				
e. Relationship with other teachers.				
f. Relationship with administration.				
g. Participating in community life.				
5. Staff members follow a plan for personal and professional growth through participation in:				
a. Graduate work.				
b. Physical education workshops, conventions and conferences.				
c. Professional meetings and committee work.				
d. Independent study including current literature.				
e. Membership in professional organizations.				

G. RESPONSIBILITIES

	Yes	No	Part.	Comments
1. Whenever possible, teaching assignments are based on interests, training and experience.				
2. There is a positive working relationship among superintendents, principals, curriculum coordinators, department chairmen, teachers, and students toward learning.				
3. Leadership responsibilities in the enrichment program are considered in the total teaching load, or additional compensation is made to those participating teachers.				

H. ADMINISTRATION OF INSTRUCTIONAL AND ENRICHMENT PROBLEMS

	Yes	No	Part.	Comments
1. The program fulfills the School Code of Illinois, Section 27–6, regarding daily participation in physical education instruction.				
2. All enrichment activites are conducted under the standards supported by the American Alliance for Health, Physical Education, Recreation and Dance.				
3. All students are enrolled in a physical education class.				

I. ORGANIZATION AND SCHEDULING

	Yes	No	Part.	Comments
1. Time is not deleted from the basic physical education program for: a. Musical activities.				
b. Unrelated activities such as picture taking.				
c. Lunch time activity programs.				
d. Enrichment programs.				
e. Recess.				
2. Class size of any given physical education class is not in excess of that of any other classroom in the building.				
3. The needs of the various grade levels are considered in the scheduling of physical education classes.				
4. The total work load is comparable to any other teacher in the building.				
5. The physical education teacher is not on duty any more than other teachers in the building.				

J. FACILITIES, EQUIPMENT AND FINANCING

	Yes	No	Part.	Comments
1. Indoor facilities provide reasonably good stations to adequately accommodate all curriculum needs for effective teaching.				
2. Outdoor facilities provide reasonably good stations to adequately accommodate all classes.				
3. Indoor and outdoor facilities are used and maintained under basic safety conditions.				
4. A swimming pool is available.				
5. Facilities are designed for community as well as school purposes.				
6. Ceiling height in the gymnasium from the floor to the nearest overhead obstruction is at least 20 feet.				
7. Lights and windows are covered with protective devices.				
8. Teaching areas, indoor and outdoor, are appropriately laid out, marked and free of hazards.				
9. The outdoor area is suitably surfaced and has adequate drainage.				
10. A separate office is available for instructors.				
11. Appropriate bulletin board space is provided and maintained to supplement the program.				
12. The school facilities are made available for after school activities.				
13. Proper equipment and supplies are in sufficient quantity to permit each child to participate fully in the program.				
14. There is adequate storage space available for equipment.				
15. Storage space is adjacent to or near activity space.				
16. Students are made aware of their responsibility for the preservation of equipment.				
17. An inventory list of all equipment is available.				
18. First aid supplies are readily available.				
19. The Board of Education provides funds, through the same medium as other phases of education, for personnel, supplies and other equipment essential for an effective physical education program.				
a. Adequate equipment for maximum participation.				
b. Appropriate equipment for age and ability of children.				
20. The enrichment program is completely financed by school (or district) funds other than physical education allotments.				

K. MEDICAL REQUIREMENTS AND CONSENTS

	Yes	No	Part.	Comments
1. A medical record for each child is on file at the school before a student is permitted to participate in physical education activity.				
2. When a student has been absent from school as a result of severe illness or injury, he must be medically cleared before participating in activity.				
3. Students who are unable to participate in the more vigorous forms of activity are assigned to a modified program. Assignment is based on a physician's recommendation.				
4. All students participating in interscholastic activities are properly insured.				
5. Parental permission and physical examinations are required for participation of students in interscholastic sports.				
6. Appropriate medical and first aid procedures are developed for class, intramural and interscholastic activities.				
7. Students exempted from required physical examinations because of religious or constitutional grounds are required to participate fully in the physical education program.				

Comments: _____

Recommendations: _____

Scoring. Upon completion of the checklist, the evaluator should identify and summarize the apparent weaknesses by checklist sections. The weaknesses should be ranked by priority, from greatest to least, in order to serve as a guide for developing a master plan for improving those areas where weaknesses exist.

Comments. The authors of the checklist suggest that a physical education department may decide to utilize only certain sections of the "Evaluative Criteria" in order to evaluate suspected areas of weakness. They also recommend progressive implementation of a master plan to make the corrections that will improve your program.

If assistance in developing improvement plans is needed by persons in Illinois public schools, the Illinois-AHPER will send a visiting team of consultants to your school. Persons in other states might get similar help from their state association or from an elementary school specialist at a local college or university.

Illinois Criteria for Evaluating Physical Education Programs in Grades 7–12*[4]

Purpose. To provide a basis for improving the quality of physical education programs in grades 7–12. Also to stimulate self-study and self-evaluation to ascertain the strengths and weaknesses of a school physical education program.

Development. None reported.

Level. Grades 7–12.

Uses. Same as elementary school checklist.

Directions. Same as elementary school checklist.

The Instrument

Criteria for Evaluating Physical Education Programs in Illinois Schools (Form: 7–12) April, 1984†

School _____ School Population _____

Address _____ Zip _____ Telephone _____

Name _____Position at school _____

Grade Level Teaching _____

Provision for Physical Education: Hours per week _____

Days per week _____

Number of Teachers: Men _____ Women _____

Average Class Size _____

The responder is using the form as:

Administrator _____ Department Chairperson _____

Physical Education Instructor _____ Other _____

_____

*Illinois Association for Health, Physical Education and Recreation: Criteria for evaluating physical education programs in Illinois schools (Form: 7–12), April, 1984. Illinois Journal, Fall 1984, 34–38. Used by permission of Illinois-AHPER.

†From Illinois Association for Health, Physical Education and Recreation: Criteria for evaluating physical education programs in Illinois schools (Form: 7–12), April, 1984. Illinois Journal, Fall 1984, 34–38. Used by permission of Illinois-AHPER.

A. INSTRUCTIONAL PROGRAM

	Yes	No	Part.	Comments
1. Provides for the development of skill, knowledge and attitude related to:				
a. Rhythms and dance				
b. Physical fitness				
c. Sports (balance of)				
Dual				
Individual				
Lifetime				
Team				
d. Aquatics				
2. Provides for the development of competency in the following:				
a. Dual				
Individual				
Lifetime				
Team				
b. Dance and/or rhythmic movements				
c. Basic swimming and water safety				
3. Provides for the gaining of knowledge of rules, techniques and concepts required for effective participation in sports and activities common to our culture.				
4. Provides for elective activities.				
5. Provides for a modified or adaptive program.				
6. Provides evidence of a written curriculum which allows for daily, unit and yearly plans.				
7. Provides audio-visual aids.				
8. Provides supplementary books for students.				
9. Provides for use of community resources when appropriate (people/facilities).				
10. Provides for individual progression in program.				
11. Provides for handicapped participation as outlined in PL 94-142.				
12. Provides for opportunities to achieve the goals of physical education.				

B. ENRICHMENT PROGRAM

	Yes	No	Part.	Comments
1. Provides for an intramural program.				
2. The intramural program provides for: a. A variety of activities for all students				
b. Voluntary participation for all students				
c. Student leadership of the program with effective faculty guidance				
3. The Interscholastic program provides for: a. A variety of activities for all students				
b. Activities appropriate to the level of maturity, skills and interest of students (no tackle football below 9th)				
4. Provides for other enrichment opportunities (dance/water ballet).				
5. Provides for recreational clubs within the school.				
6. A student is not exempt from the required physical education program regardless of participation in the enrichment program.				
7. The activities offered in the program are well organized, efficiently conducted, and closely supervised.				
8. Provides for successful and enjoyable experience for all students regardless of competency level.				
9. Provides transportation for those who must ride buses.				

C. EVALUATION OF STUDENTS

	Yes	No	Part.	Comments
1. Physical status is periodically reviewed (i.e., exam, evaluation, fitness to participate).				
2. The following pupil evaluation devices are used: a. Skill tests				
b. Fitness tests				
c. Knowledge tests				
d. Self-evaluation				
e. Attitude evaluation				
3. Criteria for evaluation are based upon the objectives of the physical education program.				
4. Credit comparable to that given other phases of the school program is provided for physical education.				
5. Credit in Physical Education is required for graduation.				
6. Annual provision is made for student evaluation of the program.				

D. MISCELLANEOUS

	Yes	No	Part.	Comments
1. Showers are provided.				
2. Students appropriately dressed for physical education.				
3. Provides for student input in the planning of the instructional program.				
4. Provides for development of leadership among students with the instructional and enrichment programs.				

E. LEADERSHIP QUALIFICATIONS

	Yes	No	Part.	Comments
1. The instructors in the physical education program have a major or minor in the field from an accredited institution.				
2. Certified teachers are in charge of the physical education program.				
3. All coaches are members of the faculty.				
4. All coaches are certified.				
5. Staff members effectively demonstrate: a. Planning and organizing classwork.				
b. Establishing and maintaining acceptable teacher-student relations.				
c. Knowledge of the curriculum area of physical education.				
d. A variety of teaching methods.				
e. Good working relationships with other teachers.				
f. An understanding of student needs.				
6. Demonstrates usage of supplementary teaching aids, books and materials.				
7. Staff members follow a plan for personal and professional growth through participation in: a. Graduate work				
b. Workshops, conventions and conferences.				
c. Professional meetings and committee work.				
d. Independent study and current literature.				

F. ADMINISTRATION OF INSTRUCTIONS AND ENRICHMENT PROGRAMS

	Yes	No	Part.	Comments
1. Fulfills School Code of Illinois, Section 27-6 regarding daily participation in physical education.				
2. Fulfills Title IX regulations regarding non-sex discrimination in physical education.				
3. Fulfills PL 94-142 regulations regarding handicapped participation in physical education.				
4. State eligibility standards for students in interscholastic activities are subscribed and enforced.				
5. All students are enrolled in a physical education class.				
6. There is provision for written evaluation of the physical education program based upon the objectives of the program.				

G. ORGANIZATION AND SCHEDULING

	Yes	No	Part.	Comments
1. Time is not deleted from the basic physical education instructional program for:				
a. Driver education				
b. Musical activities				
c. Intramural programs				
d. Interscholastic programs				
e. Cheerleaders or marching activities				
f. Medical self-help and related type activities				
g. Unrelated activities				
h. Lunch time activity programs				
2. Daily instructional periods are comparable to all regular periods in the school day.				
3. Classes are grouped homogeneously by:				
Level				
Chronological age				
Physical ability				
4. Classes are of a size to permit effective instruction.				
5. Facilities are assigned fairly to both sexes.				
6. The enrichment program is completely administered by school personnel.				
7. The total responsibility for the physical education program is equally shared among the physical education staff.				
8. Whenever possible, teaching assignments are based on interests and qualifications.				

H. FACILITIES, EQUIPMENT AND FINANCING

	Yes	No	Part.	Comments
1. Indoor and outdoor facilities provide reasonably good stations to adequately accommodate all classes.				
2. Indoor and outdoor facilities are properly maintained to make them as safe as possible.				
3. Facilities are designed for community as well as school purposes.				
4. Activity room ceiling should be adequate to accommodate the activity.				
5. Lights and windows are covered with protective devices.				
6. The outdoor area is suitably surfaced and has adequate drainage.				
7. A swimming pool is available for class use.				
8. The facilities are made available for after school activities.				
9. Locker and shower rooms are provided.				
10. Adequate towel and soap services are provided.				
11. Separate office, shower and dressing facilities are available for instructor.				
12. Appropriate bulletin board space is provided and maintained to supplement program.				
13. Supplies and equipment are available for the most efficient and optimum use.				
14. Adequate storage space is available for equipment.				
15. Storage space is adjacent to or near activity areas.				
16. Care of equipment is the responsibility of the school personnel and students.				
17. Adequate first aid equipment and supplies are readily available.				
18. Proper protective equipment is provided for all activities.				
19. Funds essential for an effective physical education program are provided through the same medium as other educational programs.				
20. The enrichment program is completely financed by school funds.				

I. MEDICAL PROCEDURES AND CONSENTS

	Yes	No	Part.	Comments
1. A medical record for each pupil is on file at the school before a student is permitted to participate in physical activities.				
2. A medical or parental permit is required upon re-entry to the physical education program following severe illness or injury.				
3. Students who are unable to participate in the more vigorous forms of activity are assigned to a modified program. The assignment is based on a physician's recommendation.				
4. A medical permit is on the file at the school prior to involvement in interscholastic activities.				
5. Insurance is required for each student participating in interscholastic activities.				
6. Insurance is available for each student.				
7. A parental permit is on file at the school prior to involvement in strenuous competitive activities.				
8. Trained medical personnel are available during all phases of the instructional and enrichment programs.				
9. An alternative program is provided for students with religious convictions pertaining to any particular aspect of the program.				
10. Medical screening is available annually for vision, hearing, and postural defects.				

Scoring. Same as elementary school checklist.

Comments. Same as elementary school checklist.

A curricular area that has been overlooked in the section on Instructional Program is outdoor education activities.

Lifetime Sports Course Evaluation Form*[6,7]

Purpose. To evaluate instructional effectiveness in lifetime sports and physical activity classes.

Development. A two-part form was developed after a review of literature related to student evaluation of different aspects of teaching effectiveness and course outcomes. One part addressed dimensions of instructional effectiveness; the other addressed course outcomes. Modifications to the original form were made as a result of feedback from faculty and graduate students in the physical education department at Kansas State University, and from the administration of the instrument to three classes of lifetime sports. The revised form was then used with all lifetime sports classes for seven semesters.

Coefficient alpha, used to estimate the internal consistency of the instructor evaluation items, ranged from .68 to .83 for five of the six dimensions. After eliminating one negatively stated item, coefficient alpha improved from .27 to .70 for the other dimension. Test-retest reliability was estimated at over .70 for one class using a one-week retest interval. Split-half reliabilities of the six dimensions were equal or better than .79 for all dimensions except Preparation and Organization ($r = .60$). Reliabilities of the eight outcome items were all above .70, except Item 20 ($r = .41$) and Item 22 ($r = .59$).

Validity evidence was demonstrated by comparing class mean scores on each of the six instructional dimensions with the perceived course outcomes. All six dimensions correlated highly with satisfaction with the course (Item 25) and satisfaction with the instructor (Item 26). Further evidence of validity was claimed based upon the comparison of follow-up questionnaire results from students who had been in the highest and lowest rated classes.

Level. The instrument is appropriate for evaluating university or college instructors of lifetime sports classes. It may also be appropriate for use in high school and selected non-school instructional settings involving group physical activity classes.[7]

Uses. The primary use is to provide feedback to the instructor to help him/her become a better teacher. The authors emphasize that it should not be used for administrative purposes such as awarding of merit raises.

The Instrument

Lifetime Sports Course Evaluation Form

Your thoughtful answers to these questions will provide helpful information to your instructor.

Part I. Describe your instructor in terms of the following items by blackening a number between "1" and "5." Use this code:

1—Rarely or	3—Sometimes	5—Almost
Never	4—Quite	Always
2—Seldom	Often	

*Noble, L., and Cox, R.H.: Development of a form to survey student reactions on instructional effectiveness of lifetime sports classes. Research Quarterly for Exercise and Sport, 54:3, 247–253, 1983. Used by permission of the authors and AAHPERD.

The Instructor:
1. Put material across in an interesting way.
2. Seemed enthusiastic about the subject matter.
3. Effectively demonstrated the skills needed.
4. Planned activities so that the whole class could participate maximally.
5. Explained course material clearly, and explanations were to the point.
6. Provided individual instruction when needed.
7. Made presentations which were dry and dull.*
8. Seemed to enjoy teaching.
9. Had knowledge that went beyond the textbook or readings.
10. Clearly stated the objectives of the course.
11. Introduced and explained the skills effectively.
12. Encouraged students to express themselves freely and openly.
13. Spoke with expressiveness and variety in tone of voice.
14. Made it seem like what he/she was teaching was worthwhile.
15. Answered students' questions in a way that demonstrated his/her expertise.
16. Made it clear how each topic fit into the course.
17. Gave me feedback on performance that was clear and meaningful.
18. Used different kinds of explanations or demonstrations if students were having trouble understanding.

Part II. The next eight questions ask you to describe yourself. Use the following code:

1 = Definitely false	3 = In between	5 = Definitely true
2 = More false than true	4 = More true than false	

19. I now possess the skills necessary to participate successfully in this activity on my own.
20. I understand the fundamentals sufficiently so that I will be able to improve my skills with further practice.
21. I believe I could teach the fundamentals of this activity to others.
22. During this term, I participated in this activity more than was required by the course.
23. I intend to participate in this activity after I leave college.
24. The skills I acquired in this course have made me more self-confident.
25. If the opportunity arose, I would welcome a chance to take another course from this instructor.
26. Overall, I gained more from this course than from the average course I have taken at this institution.

Scoring. Responses should be analyzed both by computing class averages for each item and by computing averages for each of the six dimensions of instructional effectiveness. The six dimensions and the items that comprise each dimension are:

Stimulation of Interest	Items 1, 7, 13
Enthusiasm for Subject Matter	Items 2, 8, 14
Knowledge of Subject Matter	Items 3, 9, 15
Preparation and Organization of the Course	Items 4, 10, 16
Clarity of Communication	Items 5, 11, 17
Sensitivity to Class Progress	Items 6, 12, 18

*The authors now recommend changing Item 7 to read, "The instructor gave interesting and stimulating presentations."

Comments. The authors emphasize that the instrument is still in development and encourage users to collaborate with them regarding possible improvements, additions, and/or psychometric analyses.

MEASURES FOR INTRAMURAL PROGRAMS

A Self-Appraisal Checklist for Intramurals in Ohio's Elementary and Secondary Schools*[9]

Purpose. To evaluate status and progress in the process of intramurals, and thereby to assist school personnel in their endeavors to improve the intramural program.

Development. The checklist has been validated by means of logical validity.

Level. The checklist is to be used to evaluate intramural programs in both elementary and secondary schools.

Uses. Self-evaluation of the intramural program.

Administration. The checklist is organized into major categories that represent essential aspects of the intramural program. Although the organization of the program, extent of facilities, activities available, staffing patterns, and other components of the program may vary widely among schools, the categories are represented to some degree in each school's program. The checklist, therefore, can be useful to school personnel in surveying and assessing its existing program and, in turn, comparing it to a quality program exemplified by the checklist items.

Ratings can be made by the members of the school administrative staff, by a team of evaluators, or by the intramural staff itself. All ratings must be made in as objective a manner as possible.

Scoring. A *possible score* is given for each category and for the total program, based upon a 4-point rating for each statement. The *actual score* is the total of the ratings given by the evaluator; the actual score should be compared to the possible score to determine the status of each category and of the total program.

When the checklist has been completed, needed program improvements should be identified on the basis of discrepancies between actual scores and possible scores. These needed improvements should be listed by categories. The list may then give direction to continuing efforts toward improving the quality of the intramural program.

Comments. The Summary of Scores and Score Comparison Chart should be used to facilitate interpretations.

---

*State of Ohio: A Self-Appraisal Checklist for Intramurals in Ohio's Elementary and Secondary Schools. Columbus, Division of Elementary and Secondary Education, Ohio Department of Education, 1978. Used by permission of the Ohio State Department of Education.

The Checklist

A Self-Appraisal Checklist for Intramurals in Ohio's Elementary and Secondary Schools*

I. Philosophy and Principles

Possible Score—28 points
Actual Score—___ points

Circle appropriate response

4 = Strongly agree
3 = Agree
2 = Undecided
1 = Disagree
0 = Strongly disagree

1. The intramural program is considered, by school personnel, as an expansion of the instructional program of physical education; and a means by which students may fulfill growth, development, and recreational needs.   4 3 2 1 0

2. The philosophy, principles, and objectives for the school intramural program are in writing and available to administrators, staff, students, parents, and other members of the community.   4 3 2 1 0

3. The stated philosophy and principles regard the school's intramural program as an integral part of the students' total educational experience.   4 3 2 1 0

4. Program objectives focus on activities which foster the physical, mental, emotional, and social development of the individual participant.   4 3 2 1 0

5. The intramural program provides a wide range of opportunities throughout the school year.   4 3 2 1 0

6. Participation in the intramural program is open and available to every student within the school.   4 3 2 1 0

7. An annual survey is conducted and the results are used to meet the needs and interests of the students.   4 3 2 1 0

II. Organization and Administration

Possible Score—48 points
Actual Score—___ points

Circle appropriate response

4 = Strongly agree
3 = Agree
2 = Undecided
1 = Disagree
0 = Strongly disagree

1. The administration of the intramural program is delegated to certificated teachers whose responsibilities include planning, scheduling, organizing, supervising, and evaluating the total intramural program.   4 3 2 1 0

2. Program directors are selected from the physical education instructional staff or other faculty members, with knowledge, interest, and enthusiasm for quality program management, development, and expansion.   4 3 2 1 0

*From State of Ohio: A Self-Appraisal Checklist for Intramurals in Ohio's Elementary and Secondary Schools. Columbus, Division of Elementary and Secondary Education, Ohio Department of Education, 1978. Used by permission of the Ohio State Department of Education.

3. In matters of policy, budget, use of facilities, equipment, scheduling, and extent of participation, equal opportunity is given to the development of programs for both sexes as well as coeducational intramural activities.   4 3 2 1 0

4. Adequate office space, clerical help, and supplies are available for use by the intramural staff.   4 3 2 1 0

5. A job description outlining duties and responsibilities of the staff is available for the total intramural program.   4 3 2 1 0

6. The intramural program provides leadership experiences for students and auxiliary personnel through their involvement in such phases of the program as planning, organizing, officiating, directing, and evaluating.   4 3 2 1 0

7. Responsibilities assigned to student personnel are commensurate with their age level, ability, and experience.   4 3 2 1 0

8. Selection of student assistants (managers, officials) is based upon personal qualities, skills, interest in giving service to the program, and ability to work with and for others.   4 3 2 1 0

9. Policies, rules, and regulations governing the intramural program are developed through a cooperative effort of the staff and students involved in intramurals and are endorsed by the administrative head of the school.   4 3 2 1 0

10. A staffing pattern or chart is developed which specifies relationships among staff in the intramural organization.   4 3 2 1 0

11. All personnel involved in intramurals follow the procedures and the organizational pattern as outlined.   4 3 2 1 0

12. Some form of systematic evaluation is used to maintain the effectiveness of the total program.   4 3 2 1 0

III. Finances, Facilities, and Equipment

Possible Score—36 points
Actual Score—___ points

Circle appropriate response

4 = Strongly agree
3 = Agree
2 = Undecided
1 = Disagree
0 = Strongly disagree

1. Finances to support and maintain the intramural progam are authorized and approved by the administrative head of the school.   4 3 2 1 0

2. Written policies and accounting procedures are established and adhered to in the management of funds and equipment.   4 3 2 1 0

3. Planning and scheduling of facilities are done cooperatively with other school departments and programs to insure maximum use of available facilities.   4 3 2 1 0

4. The facilities utilized by the intramural program are adequate, safe, and sufficient to provide activity for all who wish to participate.   4 3 2 1 0

5. The schedule of activities is flexible and organized at various times within the school day so that the maximum number of participants may take part.   4 3 2 1 0

6. Equipment and supplies are available in sufficient quantity.   4 3 2 1 0

7. Definite policies are established and in effect concerning proper care and maintenance of equipment used in the intramural program.   4 3 2 1 0

8. Community facilities and resources are used to augment and expand intramural opportunities.   4 3 2 1 0

9. Costs to the individual participant are kept at a minimum.   4 3 2 1 0

IV. Rules and Regulations

Possible Score—36 points

Actual Score—___ points

1. Procedures are clearly established which govern the intramural program in the following matters:
   a. Who is eligible to participate   4 3 2 1 0
   b. How individual and team activities are organized   4 3 2 1 0
   c. Appropriate means of communication to the participants   4 3 2 1 0
   d. Publicizing the entire program   4 3 2 1 0
   e. Types of tournaments to be scheduled   4 3 2 1 0
   f. Rules of play governing each sport and activity   4 3 2 1 0
   g. Selection and assignment of officials   4 3 2 1 0
   h. Criteria for awards and recognition of participants   4 3 2 1 0
   i. Protests, postponements, and forfeits   4 3 2 1 0

V. Management of Events

Possible Score—76 points

Actual Score—___ points

1. The extent of the activities to be offered during the yearly program of the intramurals is based upon the following:
   a. Number, age, and developmental level of students   4 3 2 1 0
   b. Physical education instructional program   4 3 2 1 0
   c. Student interests   4 3 2 1 0
   d. Available school facilities   4 3 2 1 0
   e. Available community resources and facilities   4 3 2 1 0
   f. Available staff   4 3 2 1 0
   g. Available financing   4 3 2 1 0

2. In scheduling intramural activities every effort is made to equalize levels of competition and experience of participants in both team and individual activities.   4 3 2 1 0

3. In comparative activities, every effort is made to maintain the interest of all participants throughout the schedule.   4 3 2 1 0

4. Activities are scheduled to accommodate the majority of student participants.   4 3 2 1 0

5. An effort is made to provide flexibility by scheduling activities prior to the school day, during the regular school day, after school, on weekends, and in the early evening.   4 3 2 1 0

6. Boys and girls have equal opportunity to participate in intramurals and have equal access to quality equipment, programming, and facilities.   4 3 2 1 0

7. Announcements, posting of schedules, team standings, and other forms of communication related to the intramural program are posted near the intramural office.

4 3 2 1 0

8. Records and data concerning the intramural program include the following:
   a. Individual and team rosters

   4 3 2 1 0

   b. Extent of total team and individual participation

   4 3 2 1 0

   c. Tournament standings

   4 3 2 1 0

   d. Organization pattern for conducting each intramural activity

   4 3 2 1 0

9. Records from each intramural activity are used in total program evaluation.

   4 3 2 1 0

VI. Scope of the Intramural Program

Possible Score—60 points
Actual Score—___ points

Circle appropriate response

4 = Strongly agree
3 = Agree
2 = Undecided
1 = Disagree
0 = Strongly disagree

1. The yearly program of intramurals encompasses a wide range of competitive activities in the following areas:
   a. Team sports

   4 3 2 1 0

   b. Individual sports

   4 3 2 1 0

   c. Rhythmics

   4 3 2 1 0

   d. Aquatics

   4 3 2 1 0

   e. Special interest areas

   4 3 2 1 0

2. The yearly program is planned to allow the student several options for each season—fall, winter, spring.

   4 3 2 1 0

3. The age and maturation of the students are considered in the selection of activities.

   4 3 2 1 0

4. Activities are offered for boys, girls, and corecreational groups.

   4 3 2 1 0

5. The range of activities in the intramural program includes the following:
   a. Activities which promote the development of physical, mental, emotional, and social skills

   4 3 2 1 0

   b. Highly structured activities

   4 3 2 1 0

   c. Informally organized activities

   4 3 2 1 0

   d. Vigorous activities

   4 3 2 1 0

   e. Passive activities

   4 3 2 1 0

   f. Activities engaged in for pure enjoyment

   4 3 2 1 0

6. Handicapped or atypical students are provided the opportunity to participate in the intramural program.

   4 3 2 1 0

VII. Program Promotion and Student Recognition

Possible Score—28 points
Actual Score—___ points

Circle appropriate
response
4 = Strongly agree
3 = Agree
2 = Undecided
1 = Disagree
0 = Strongly
disagree

1. Efforts are made to make every student in the school aware of the opportunities for participation in the intramural program.   4 3 2 1 0
2. Publications, brochures, announcements, and other means of communication are used to inform students of the existence of the intramural program and the number of activities available.   4 3 2 1 0
3. An ongoing program of public relations is used to communicate consistently the objectives, values, and activities of the intramural program to staff, students, parents, and members of the school community.   4 3 2 1 0
4. Opinions from participants, school personnel, and community members involved in the intramural program are sought in an effort to improve the total program.   4 3 2 1 0
5. There is a system of recognition for students who participate in the intramural program.   4 3 2 1 0
6. Recognition is given for service to the intramural program.   4 3 2 1 0
7. The monetary value of any award is kept to a minimum.   4 3 2 1 0

VIII. Intramural Program Safety

Possible Score—52 points
Actual Score—___ points

Circle appropriate
response
4 = Strongly agree
3 = Agree
2 = Undecided
1 = Disagree
0 = Strongly
disagree

1. Lines of communication are established between the intramural director and the school health service department so that the intramural staff can be aware of students' medical problems.   4 3 2 1 0
2. Less strenuous activities are provided for students with physical handicaps.   4 3 2 1 0
3. Parent's or physician's permission is required for participation in strenuous activities following illness, injury, or history of medical problems.   4 3 2 1 0
4. Provision is made for proper supervision by faculty during all aspects of the intramural program.   4 3 2 1 0
5. Officials are well-trained and safety conscious.   4 3 2 1 0
6. Equipment and facilities are inspected regularly to help insure the safety of all participants.   4 3 2 1 0
7. Safety equipment is provided as needed for various activities.   4 3 2 1 0
8. Safety awareness is emphasized to participants.   4 3 2 1 0
9. First aid equipment is readily available.   4 3 2 1 0
10. The intramural staff is aware of procedures to be followed in accidents, injuries, and other emergency situations.   4 3 2 1 0

11. All accidents, injuries, and incidents of an emergency nature are immediately reported in writing to the school administration.   4 3 2 1 0

12. Approved forms of transportation are authorized and provided when intramural activities are conducted after normal school hours or away from the school premises.   4 3 2 1 0

13. Parental permission forms are required of all students who participate in intramural activities away from school premises.   4 3 2 1 0

Summary of Scores

	Areas	*Possible Score*	*Actual Score*
Part I.	Philosophy and Principles	28	_____
Part II.	Organization & Administration	48	_____
Part III.	Finances, Facilities and Equipment	36	_____
Part IV.	Rules and Regulations	36	_____
Part V.	Management of Events	76	_____
Part VI.	Scope of the Intramural Program	60	_____
Part VII.	Program Promotion and Student Recognition	28	_____
Part VIII.	Intramural Program Safeguards	52	_____
	Total Score	364	_____

A Summary of Needed Improvements

    I. Philosophy and Principles
    II. Organization and Administration
    III. Finances, Facilities, and Equipment
    IV. Rules and Regulations
    V. Management of Events
    VI. Scope of the Intramural Program
    VII. Program Promotion and Student Recognition
    VIII. Intramural Program Safeguards

Score Comparison Chart

The asterisks on the diagram below indicate the highest score possible in each category. Chart the actual score based on your evaluation to determine strong and weak areas of your school's intramural program.

Points	Philosophy and Principles — I	Organization and Administration — II	Finances, Facilities, and Equipment — III	Rules and Regulations — IV	Management of Events — V	Scope of Intramural Program — VI	Program Promotion and Student Recognition — VII	Intramural Program Safeguards — VIII
80								
75					***			
70								
65								
60						***		
55								
50								***
45		***						
40								
35			***	***				
30								
25	***						***	
20								
15								
10								
5								
0								

Forward for review as applicable to the following staff:

_____   _____
Physical Education Teacher   Intramural Director

_____   _____
Department Chairman   Principal

_____   _____
Supervisor   Superintendent

Stobart Intramural Attitude Scale*[10,11]

Purpose. To assess positive and negative attitudes of individuals toward organized college intramural sports programs.

Development. A 20-member panel judged each of 106 attitudinal statements as positive, negative, or unclear. From their judgments, a list of 74 attitudinal statements was compiled and given to a test group of college students. The discriminatory factors and item reliability were determined for each of the original 74 statements. The 30 positive statements and 30 negative statements with the highest discriminatory factors were then divided equally into Forms A and B. A Spearman's rho of .84 was computed when scores from Form A were correlated to scores on Form B for 300 randomly selected college students. Forms A and B are designed to be parallel instruments.

Forms C and D, each consisting of 20 statements, were subsequently developed. Form C is a combined scale of the 20 statements from Forms A and B that had the highest discriminatory factors. Form D is a modification of Form C; certain items were re-worded so the final scale would have 10 positive and 10 negative statements.[11]

Level and Gender. For use with college level students of both genders.

Uses. This instrument may be used as part of the formal evaluation of the intramural sports program offered at colleges or universities.

The Instrument

Intramural Attitude Scale Form D†

SA = Strongly Agree   D = Disagree
A = Agree   SA = Strongly Disagree
U = Undecided

	SA	A	U	D	SD
1. A person would be better off emotionally if he/she did not participate in intramural sports.	( )	( )	( )	( )	( )
2. I would advise anyone who is physically able to actively participate in intramural sports.	( )	( )	( )	( )	( )
3. Intramural sports are not an important phase of education.	( )	( )	( )	( )	( )
4. If an extracurricular activity had to be dropped from the college program, intramural sports should not be the activity dropped.	( )	( )	( )	( )	( )
5. Intramural sports lessen opportunities for sociability by encouraging people to compete against each other in many of the activities.	( )	( )	( )	( )	( )
6. Intramural sports are not mainly for the physically gifted.	( )	( )	( )	( )	( )
7. Intramural sports develop desirable standards of conduct.	( )	( )	( )	( )	( )
8. The skills that one learns through intramural participation are of little value in everyday life.	( )	( )	( )	( )	( )

*Stobart, W.L.: A scale to measure attitudes toward organized college intramural sports programs. Dissertation. University of Arkansas, Fayetteville, 1984. Used with permission of the author.

†From Stobart, W.L.: Intramural Attitude Scale, Form D. Unpublished scale, 1988. Used with permission of the author.

9. Intramural sports are an important part of a school's activity program.	SA ( )	A ( )	U ( )	D ( )	SD ( )
10. Intramural sports have little to offer for the unskilled individual.	SA ( )	A ( )	U ( )	D ( )	SD ( )
11. No definite beneficial results come from participation in intramural sports.	SA ( )	A ( )	U ( )	D ( )	SD ( )
12. Participation in intramural sports makes for a more wholesome outlook on life.	SA ( )	A ( )	U ( )	D ( )	SD ( )
13. Intramural sports have no place in modern education.	SA ( )	A ( )	U ( )	D ( )	SD ( )
14. Time spent engaging in intramural sports could be more profitably spent in other ways.	SA ( )	A ( )	U ( )	D ( )	SD ( )
15. Intramural sports are a waste of time in college.	SA ( )	A ( )	U ( )	D ( )	SD ( )
16. Intramural sports participation contributes to the physical development of the participant.	SA ( )	A ( )	U ( )	D ( )	SD ( )
17. Intramural sports participation teaches the individual sportsmanship.	SA ( )	A ( )	U ( )	D ( )	SD ( )
18. Intramural sports participation increases the individual's ability to make decisions.	SA ( )	A ( )	U ( )	D ( )	SD ( )
19. Intramural sports participation does not teach the individual the importance of dedication to a cause.	SA ( )	A ( )	U ( )	D ( )	SD ( )
20. Intramural sports aid in the development of a well-rounded personality.	SA ( )	A ( )	U ( )	D ( )	SD ( )

Scoring. Each of the 20 items is scored from 1 to 5, with a *low score representing a positive attitude.* Total point values will range from 20 to 100. Positively stated items are 2, 4, 6, 7, 9, 12, 16, 17, 18, and 20. These items are to be scored: Strongly Agree = 1, Agree = 2, Undecided = 3, Disagree = 4, and Strongly Disagree = 5. Negatively stated items, to be scored in reverse, are 1, 3, 5, 8, 10, 11, 13, 14, 15, and 19.

Comments. Though designed for college level intramurals, this instrument may be modified for use with high school intramurals and non-school recreation programs.[11] The only item that would need modification is 15.

Forms A and B may be used as a pretest and posttest to assess the effects of formal or informal experimentation with the intramural program.[10]

MEASURES FOR ATHLETIC PROGRAMS

NASPE Player Performance Relative to Others*[8]

Purpose. To provide a second-party, end-of-season evaluation of a youth sport team or individual player, especially to reveal areas that need improvement.

Development. No explanation of development was given; however, the instrument appears to have logical validity.

Level. For use with youth sport programs.

Uses. This instrument may be used to assess changes through the season, relative to others in the league. It may be used for a team or an individual player.

Administration. To obtain the most useful second party information, the

*Seefeldt, V. (Ed.): Handbook for Youth Sport Coaches. Reprinted by permission of the American Alliance for Health, Physical Education, Recreation and Dance, 1900 Association Drive, Reston, Virginia 22091.

evaluator should be someone who is familiar with the coaching actions and the progress of the players. The evaluator should also be someone whose judgment is respected by the coach. Possible evaluators include players, parents, an assistant coach, an official, a supervisor, or a local youth sport expert.

The Instrument

Player Performance Relative to Others*

Evaluator: _____   Player/team _____   Date _____

EVALUATION QUESTION:	In comparison with other players in this league, how does the player (or team) listed above perform in the areas listed below?						
	PLAYER OR TEAM PERFORMANCE LEVELS						
	SEASON START			SEASON END			
PERFORMANCE AREAS	TOP 25%	MID 50%	BOTTOM 25%	TOP 25%	MID 50%	BOTTOM 25%	COMMENTS
SKILL — OFFENSIVE							
SKILL — DEFENSIVE							
KNOWLEDGE — RULES							
KNOWLEDGE — STRATEGIES							
KNOWLEDGE — OTHER							
FITNESS — STRENGTH							
FITNESS — ENDURANCE							
ATTITUDE — PERSONAL							
ATTITUDE — SOCIAL							

INDIVIDUAL EVALUATION:
   For each performance area indicate, by placing a check in the top, mid or bottom column, the beginning and ending performance level of the player.
TEAM EVALUATION:
   For each performance area estimate the number of players (% or actual numbers) in the top, mid or bottom performance levels at the beginning and at the end of the season.

*Seefeldt, V. (Ed.): Handbook for Youth Sport Coaches. Reprinted by permission of the American Alliance for Health, Physical Education, Recreation and Dance, 1900 Association Drive, Reston, VA 22091.

Scoring. For team evaluations, the evaluator should estimate the number of players (or percentage) in the top, mid, and bottom performance levels at the beginning and at the end of the season. For evaluations of individual players,

*From Seefeldt, V. (Ed.): Handbook for Youth Sport Coaches. Reprinted by permission of the American Alliance for Health, Physical Education, Recreation and Dance, 1900 Association Drive, Reston, Virginia 22091.

place a check in the top, mid, or bottom performance column for the beginning and end of the season.

The evaluation should be followed by a debriefing session between the coach and the evaluator. The purpose of the debriefing session should be to determine reasons for any low ratings, and to discuss what can be done to improve them.

Nebraska Youth Sports Inventory (NYSI)*[12,13]

Purpose. To determine the participants' attitudes, values, and perceptions toward a variety of variables pertinent to youth sport participation.[13]

Development. Item statements were: (a) modified from items used by the Joint Legislative Study on Youth Sports in the State of Michigan, (b) adapted from 1978 reseach by Thomas, or (c) designed by the authors to reflect the specific aims of the Spirit of 76 basketball league in Lincoln, Nebraska. Neither reliability nor validity evidence has been collected.

Level and Gender. The questionnaire was developed for 12- to 14-year-old males participating in a community youth basketball league.

Uses. To evaluate the effectiveness of the youth sport league in attaining its specific aims of maximum participation, having fun, improving fundamental skills, and maintaining players' level of interest in basketball. It was also used by the authors to evaluate the effectiveness of its "coaching endorsement" program by which coaches were provided through the University of Nebraska-Lincoln.

The authors employed the questionnaire in a pretest-posttest format, administering the questionnaire to players during the first week of practice and again at the end of the competitive season.

The Inventory

Nebraska Youth Sports Questionnaire

1. Team
2. Birth date
3. Did you participate in the league last year?   Yes   No
4. How would you rate your present skills in basketball in comparison to other players of the same age?

> Excellent
> Above Average
> Average
> Below Average
> Poor

*This information is reprinted with permission from the *Journal of Physical Education, Recreation & Dance,* October, 1985, 21–23. The *Journal* is a publication of the American Alliance for Health, Physical Education, Recreation and Dance, 1900 Association Drive, Reston, VA 22091.

Please circle the number that best describes how you feel about each of the following statements:

1. strongly agree
2. agree
3. no opinion
4. disagree
5. strongly disagree

5. I would rather do something else than play basketball in my free time. 1 2 3 4 5
6. I would rather play on a losing team than sit on the bench for a winning team. 1 2 3 4 5
7. Having fun and enjoying what I am doing is more important than winning. 1 2 3 4 5
8. I will continue to play the sport of basketball no matter how little I play in the future. 1 2 3 4 5
9. Players should be permitted to argue with referees. 1 2 3 4 5
10. Parents as spectators create many problems in basketball. 1 2 3 4 5
11. It is OK to argue with a teammate. 1 2 3 4 5
12. It is OK to break the rules in a game as long as I don't get caught. 1 2 3 4 5
13. Learning to play the game is more important than winning. 1 2 3 4 5
14. It is OK to argue with a player from another team. 1 2 3 4 5
15. If a referee makes a mistake in favor of my team, I should report it to him. 1 2 3 4 5
16. It is more important for the team to win than for everyone to get a chance to play. 1 2 3 4 5
17. It is OK to break the rules a little in order to win. 1 2 3 4 5
18. If I don't play very much in a game I have a good reason to be upset. 1 2 3 4 5
19. I have a good reason to be upset if a teammate doesn't play well. 1 2 3 4 5
20. I have a good reason to be upset when I don't play well. 1 2 3 4 5
21. I have a good reason to be upset when my team loses. 1 2 3 4 5
22. I think I am good enough to be a starter on my team. 1 2 3 4 5

Scoring. Items are scored on a 5-point scale that represents different levels of agreement with the statements. Because the order of response desirability is reversed for many of the items, scores for individual items should be recorded and evaluated according to the item content.

Comments. Although this instrument assesses qualities in the affective domain, it is recommended as a youth sport program evaluation tool because many programs have specific aims that legitimately fall within the affective domain. The instrument may be modified slightly to make it appropriate for use with sport programs other than basketball.

Eckman Evaluation Instrument (EEI)*[2]

Purpose. To evaluate the effectiveness of intercollegiate athletic coaches.

Development. A panel of experts on coaching, including Phyllis Bailey, Della Durant, Vonnie Gros, "Susie" Knierim, Matthew Maetozo, Gene Wettstone, and John Wooden, refined an original list of 95 competencies compiled by Eckman. Two rounds of Delphi questionnaires were then used to identify competency items for assessing coaching performance based on the consensus of the

---

*Eckman, C.A.: Development of an instrument to evaluate intercollegiate athletic coaches: A modified Delphi study. Dissertation. West Virginia University, Morgantown, 1983.

judges. The panel of judges for the Delphi process included 64 men's and women's athletic directors and 81 coaches of men's and women's teams from selected institutions in all nine of the AIAW regions. The judges were all from one of 62 state universities or colleges that offered a minimum of six sports at the AIAW Division II or III level, and from which at least one team had placed among the top teams in an AIAW championship between 1979 and 1981.

In the first Delphi round, judges rated the impact and desirability of each of 70 proposed competency items. In the second round, the participants reassessed previous ratings based on statistical feedback and provided an explanation for extreme ratings. The final instrument, a 5-point Likert rating scale, consists of the 42 items with the highest total mean scores and/or the highest modal scores for both impact and desirability.

Level and Gender. The EEI was designed for evaluation of coaches of intercollegiate athletic teams competing at the Division II or III level of AIAW.

Uses. The EEI could be used as part of the formal yearly evaluation of intercollegiate coaches by their athletic directors or as part of a self-evaluation. The instrument has the potential to identify strengths and weaknesses in the six major areas of personal qualities, administrative procedural abilities, knowledge and practice of medical-legal aspects, theory and techniques of coaching, personnel management, and public relations skills.

The Instrument

Eckman Evaluation (EEI) For Rating The Effectiveness of an Intercollegiate Athletic Coach©*

Name of Coach _____ Team _____ Date _____

Rate the coach using the following scale of 1 to 5:

   (1) Hardly Ever, (2) Occasionally, (3) Generally,
      (4) Frequently, (5) Almost Always

Circle the Appropriate Number

I. PERSONAL AND PROFESSIONAL ATTRIBUTES
   A. Personal Qualities
      1. Demonstrates self-confidence.   1 2 3 4 5
      2. Is enthusiastic.   1 2 3 4 5
      3. Presents a positive role model for the athlete, i.e.,   1 2 3 4 5
         appearance, language, and sportsmanship.
   B. Personal Conduct
      4. Exhibits ethical behavior.   1 2 3 4 5
      5. Maintains emotional control under stress.   1 2 3 4 5
      6. Places the welfare of the athlete above winning and   1 2 3 4 5
         would not sacrifice values/principles to win.
II. ADMINISTRATIVE PROCEDURAL ABILITIES
   A. Practice Organization
      7. Conducts well-planned practice sessions.   1 2 3 4 5
      8. Utilizes the coaching staff competently.   1 2 3 4 5
   B. Financial Resources   1 2 3 4 5
      9. Adheres to budget policies and procedures.

*From Eckman, C.A.: Development of an instrument to evaluate intercollegiate athletic coaches: A modified Delphi study. Dissertation. West Virginia University, Morgantown, 1983.

     10. Uses any supplemental funds in an accountable man-   1 2 3 4 5
         ner.

     11. Works within the constraints of the budget   1 2 3 4 5

III. KNOWLEDGE AND PRACTICE OF MEDICAL-LEGAL
    ASPECTS

     12. Exhibits reasonable and prudent conduct in prevent- 1 2 3 4 5
         ing and handling accidents and injuries.

     13. Follows the advice of the physician/trainer regarding 1 2 3 4 5
         the participation of injured athletes.

     14. Provides safe playing conditions and protective   1 2 3 4 5
         equipment.

IV. THEORY AND TECHNIQUES OF COACHING

  A. Coaching Methods

     15. Applies knowledge of the skills, techniques, and rules 1 2 3 4 5
         of the sport.

     16. Assists athletes in reaching their fullest potential.   1 2 3 4 5

     17. Demonstrates the ability to analyze and correct errors. 1 2 3 4 5

     18. Demonstrates the ability to teach fundamentals.   1 2 3 4 5

     19. Develops good team spirit and morale.   1 2 3 4 5

     20. Develops self-confidence and determination in ath-   1 2 3 4 5
         letes.

     21. Employs sound methods to teach skills and tech-   1 2 3 4 5
         niques.

     22. Maintains discipline in a firm and friendly manner. 1 2 3 4 5

     23. Provides an environment that makes participation en- 1 2 3 4 5
         joyable for the athletes.

  B. Strategy

     24. Demonstrates the ability to evaluate the performance 1 2 3 4 5
         of athletes/teams.

     25. Is knowledgeable of a variety of tactics and strategies. 1 2 3 4 5

     26. Selects appropriate strategies and tactics.   1 2 3 4 5

  C. Rules and Regulations

     27. Abides by the rules and regulations of the sport and 1 2 3 4 5
         appropriate governing bodies and complies with the
         academic policies of the institution.

     28. Demonstrates a knowledge of the rules and officiating 1 2 3 4 5
         techniques of the sport.

     29. Enforces team rules in an equitable and consistent   1 2 3 4 5
         manner.

V. PERSONNEL MANAGEMENT

  A. Recruiting

     30. Adheres to the policies and procedures of the appro- 1 2 3 4 5
         priate governing body.

     31. Demonstrates effective utilization of scholarship   1 2 3 4 5
         funds.

     32. Demonstrates the ability to identify potential ability 1 2 3 4 5
         in athletes.

     33. Effectively uses the monies budgeted for recruiting. 1 2 3 4 5

     34. Utilizes a consistent and fair criteria in judging ath- 1 2 3 4 5
         letes' abilities.

  B. Player-Coach Relationships

     35. Demonstrates the ability to communicate effectively 1 2 3 4 5
         with all athletes.

36. Develops and maintains a positive attitude among athletes.	1	2	3	4	5
37. Is able to motivate athletes.	1	2	3	4	5
38. Is concerned about the academic achievement of athletes.	1	2	3	4	5
39. Respects the rights and individual differences of athletes as long as it is not a detriment to the rest of the team.	1	2	3	4	5
40. Shows concern for the welfare of athletes.	1	2	3	4	5

VI. PUBLIC RELATIONS SKILLS

41. Communicates effectively with assistant coaches.	1	2	3	4	5
42. Cooperates with the athletic director in establishing and conducting a quality athletic program.	1	2	3	4	5

Possible Score—210   Total Score _____

Scoring. Each of the 42 items is scored with 1 to 5 points, indicating the frequency with which the coach demonstrates the behavior in question. Total scores will range from 42 to 210.

Comments. Though designed for AIAW Division II or III coaches, the EEI is appropriate for evaluation of coaches of men's or women's intercollegiate athletic teams competing in Division II or III of the NCAA or NAIA. Item 31 should, however, be eliminated when using the EEI for coaches of NCAA Division III teams for whom the granting of athletic scholarships is prohibited. Elimination of Items 31 and 33 would likely make the EEI appropriate for the evaluation of high school interscholastic coaches.

Although Eckman provided for a total score across all 42 competencies, it may be more useful to record subtotals for each of the six major areas. Individual competencies scored at the 1 or 2 level should be identified so that an improvement plan can be developed.

The Scale of Athletic Priorities (SAP)*[1]

Purpose. To assess the goal orientations of the constituencies served by intercollegiate sport programs. Also to facilitate organizational analysis and research.

Development. The development of the SAP occurred in three identifiable stages.

The first stage required identification of objectives of intercollegiate athletic programs as indicated by textbooks, annual reports and charters of universities, and newspaper items. The authors then generated criterion statements to reflect each of the objectives. These criterion statements and the objectives were evaluated by a panel of 13 experts. Subsequent to their recommendations, 74 items to reflect 11 objectives were selected and randomized on the initial version of the scale.

The second stage in the development of the SAP was concerned with the collecting of initial psychometric evidence. A total of 939 students from two Canadian universities responded to the scale. Their responses were used to determine item-total correlations, the range of scores on each item, internal consistency estimates, and the subjective evaluation of an item's conceptual

*Chelladurai, P., Inglis, S.E., and Danylchuk, K.E.: Priorities in intercollegiate athletics: Development of a scale. Research Quarterly for Exercise and Sport, 55(1):74–79, 1984. Used by permission of the authors and AAHPERD.

relationship to its associated objective. The results of the item-total correlations and the confirmatory factor analyses of the subscale structure indicated stability and generalizability of the scale across different samples. The scale was then modified to include four items to measure each of nine different objectives.

In the third stage, the revised version of the scale was administered to 90 administrators of intercollegiate athletic programs and to a new sample of 141 students. Fifty-five of these students responded to the scale a second time after an interval of four weeks to estimate test-retest reliability. Cronbach's alpha, an index of internal consistency, was calculated for each subscale; the coefficients ranged from .75 to .80 for administrators and from .66 to .80 for students. Test-retest reliability coefficients ranged from .62 for the Public Relations subscale to .83 for the Athlete's Personal Growth subscale.

Level and Gender. The scale is appropriate for use with college and university intercollegiate programs with sport offerings for either or both genders.

Uses. The authors of the SAP suggest that it "could be used to identify the specific objectives sought by key decision makers prior to evaluating the various programs. It could also be used to identify the differences in goal orientations of various publics of one institution as well as the differences between institutions."[1]

Administration. The evaluator is to read each of the 36 criterion statements and then indicate the degree of importance he/she would place on each criterion for decisions regarding *financial support for various sport teams.* Each statement is to be rated by circling a number on the 7-point scale ranging from "not important" to "very important." The evaluator is to assume that adequate coaching and facilities are available for all sports.

The evaluator is also to be told that there are no right or wrong answers, so he/she is to answer in his/her own way.

The Scale

Scale of Athletic Priorities*

A criterion to be considered in determining the degree of financial support for an intercollegiate athletic team is that:

	Not Important					Very Important
1. the sport attracts spectators from on campus	1 2	3	4	5	6	7
2. the student athletes are often selected to the national teams	1 2	3	4	5	6	7
3. the sport makes money through sale of admission and season tickets	1 2	3	4	5	6	7
4. the sport has a long tradition in the community	1 2	3	4	5	6	7
5. participation in the sport will develop the skills required in many jobs	1 2	3	4	5	6	7
6. the sport enhances the quality of university-community relations	1 2	3	4	5	6	7
7. the sport promotes fitness	1 2	3	4	5	6	7
8. the sport contributes to the status of the university	1 2	3	4	5	6	7

*From Chelladurai, P., Inglis, S.E., and Danylchuk, K.E.: Priorities in intercollegiate athletics: Development of a scale. Research Quarterly for Exercise and Sport, 55(1):74–79, 1984. Used by permission of the authors and AAHPERD.

9. the team (or individual athletes) is (are) often ranked high among the universities in the nation	1	2	3	4	5	6	7
10. the action in the sport is stimulating and exciting to watch	1	2	3	4	5	6	7
11. international competitions are available in the sport	1	2	3	4	5	6	7
12. the sport encourages businesses to make financial contributions to the university	1	2	3	4	5	6	7
13. the sport is felt to be part of the national culture	1	2	3	4	5	6	7
14. participation in the sport develops leadership qualities required in many jobs	1	2	3	4	5	6	7
15. the sport encourages alumni involvement in university affairs	1	2	3	4	5	6	7
16. the sport develops the spirit of healthy competition	1	2	3	4	5	6	7
17. the sport brings attention to the university	1	2	3	4	5	6	7
18. the student athletes perform at, or near national standards	1	2	3	4	5	6	7
19. the sport attracts spectators from outside the university community	1	2	3	4	5	6	7
20. the support of the sport will contribute to the national sport development	1	2	3	4	5	6	7
21. the sport earns money through corporate advertising	1	2	3	4	5	6	7
22. the sport is popular in our society	1	2	3	4	5	6	7
23. participation in the sport promotes the athlete's lifelong respect for authority and responsibility	1	2	3	4	5	6	7
24. the sport provides a rallying point for the students, alumni, faculty/staff, and community	1	2	3	4	5	6	7
25. the sport enhances the psychological well-being of the athletes	1	2	3	4	5	6	7
26. the sport enhances the prestige of the university	1	2	3	4	5	6	7
27. the student athletes exhibit a high level of excellence	1	2	3	4	5	6	7
28. the sport has spectator interest and appeal	1	2	3	4	5	6	7
29. there are university national championships in the sport	1	2	3	4	5	6	7
30. the sport promotes alumni and community donations to the university	1	2	3	4	5	6	7
31. the sport has an established tradition within the university	1	2	3	4	5	6	7
32. participation in the sport enhances the athlete's career opportunities after graduation	1	2	3	4	5	6	7
33. the sport fosters school spirit and is a unifying force	1	2	3	4	5	6	7
34. the athletes enjoy the competitive experience	1	2	3	4	5	6	7
35. the sport increases student enrollment in the university	1	2	3	4	5	6	7
36. the team has a favorable win-loss record in recent years	1	2	3	4	5	6	7

Scoring. Responses should be analyzed according to the nine objectives. A score for each objective may be calculated by summing the values for the four items that contribute to each subscale. The sum of scores on the items for one objective can be divided by 4 to derive the objective scale for a subject.

Entertainment (Items 1, 10, 19, 28): to provide entertainment to the student body, faculty/staff, and community.

National Sport Development (Items 2, 11, 20, 29): to contribute to the national sport development.

Financial (Items 3, 12, 21, 30): to generate revenue for the university.

Transmission of Culture (Items 4, 13, 22, 31): to transmit the culture and tradition of the university and society.

Career Opportunities (Items 5, 14, 23, 32): to provide those athletic experiences that will increase career opportunities for the athletes.

Public Relations (Items 6, 15, 24, 33): to enhance the university-community relations.

Athlete's Personal Growth (Items 7, 16, 25, 34): to promote the athlete's personal growth and health (physical, mental, and emotional).

Prestige (Items 8, 17, 26, 35): to enhance the prestige of the university.

Achieved Excellence (Items 9, 18, 27, 36): to support those athletes performing at a high level of excellence.

Comments. Fewer problems should arise if there is agreement about goals among the constituencies served by the intercollegiate athletic program. Athletic directors could use the SAP to identify differences and then take actions to reshape the goal orientation of any groups that are especially diverse.

REFERENCES

1. Chelladurai, P., Inglis, S.E., and Danylchuk, K.E.: Priorities in intercollegiate athletics: Development of a scale. Research Quarterly for Exercise and Sport, 55(1):74–79, 1984.
2. Eckman, C.A.: Development of an instrument to evaluate intercollegiate athletic coaches: A modified Delphi study. Dissertation. West Virginia University, Morgantown, 1983.
3. Illinois Association for Health, Physical Education and Recreation: 1980 Criteria for evaluating elementary physical education in Illinois schools. Illinois Journal, Fall 1984, 39–43.
4. Illinois Association for Health, Physical Education and Recreation: Criteria for evaluating physical education programs in Illinois schools (Form: 7–12), April, 1984. Illinois Journal, Fall 1984, 34–38.
5. McGee, R.: Program evaluation. In M.J. Safrit and Terry M. Wood, Measurement Concepts in Physical Education and Exercise Science. Champaign, IL, Human Kinetics. 1989.
6. Noble, L., and Cox, R.H.: Development of a form to survey student reactions on instructional effectiveness of lifetime sports classes. Research Quarterly for Exercise and Sport, 54(3):247–254, 1983.
7. Noble, L.: Personal correspondence, dated February 27, 1987.
8. Seefeldt, V. (Ed.): Handbook for Youth Sport Coaches. Reston, VA, American Alliance for Health, Physical Education, Recreation, and Dance, 1987.
9. State of Ohio: A Self-Appraisal Checklist for Intramurals in Ohio's Elementary and Secondary Schools. Columbus, Division of Elementary and Secondary Education. Ohio Department of Education, 1978.
10. Stobart, W.L.: A scale to measure attitudes toward organized college intramural sports programs. Dissertation. University of Arkansas, Fayetteville, 1984.
11. Stobart, W.L.: Personal correspondence, dated April 20, 1988.
12. Wandzilak, T., Potter, G., and Ansorge, C.: Reevaluating a youth sports basketball program. Journal of Physical Education, Recreation and Dance, 56(3):21–23.
13. Wandzilak, T.: Personal correspondence, dated March 4, 1987.

Glossary

Ability	—The present level of abilities or characteristics that describe the individual or group mentally, physically, socially, or emotionally.
Ability grouping	—Classifying pupils into homogeneous sections with reference to intelligence, mental or physical achievement, or any known or predicted ability.[15]
Ability test	—A test designed to measure the level of present status or present ability to function.[15]
Accountability	—(related to teachers) To demonstrate professional competence by producing measurable gains in student progress toward specified education objectives.[1]
Accreditation	—A professional, regional, state, or national recognition of an educational institution or program for meeting certain standards or evaluative criteria.[15]
Accuracy	—The ability of the individual to control voluntary movements toward an object.
Achievement	—The accomplishment of the individual beyond a defined starting point.
	—The change in ability as shown by the difference between two measurements.
Achievement standards	—Specific levels of attainment to be mastered for a particular purpose; specific requirements for marks or defined levels of attainment.[15]
Achievement test	—A test that measures the extent to which a person has acquired certain information or mastered certain skills, usually as a result of specific instruction.[20]
Activity	—Any learning situation involving change or motion; any mental or motor process in which students participate to derive satisfaction or to attain some desirable goal; in physical education, one of the organized games, sports, or elements in which students demonstrate skill and initiative, and which is selected and conducted for specific outcome.[15]
Adaptability	—Social—the ability of an individual to adjust his actions or mode of behavior to changes in social situations or general environment; Muscular—the ability of the neuromuscular system to activate appropriate motor units in adjusting muscular efforts to the load requirement.[15]
Adjustment	—The process of changing one's activities or environment to satisfy needs; the changes which an individual undergoes in order to fit environmental conditions; social adjustment usually refers to changes in habits or behavior which must be made by individuals with some deviation or conflict in association with others.[15]
Administrative evaluation	—Refers to the entire process of appraising or judging all of the procedures employed to accomplish the objectives of the program; includes the organization, policies, staff personnel, student achievement, methods and techniques, and facilities and their use.[6]

Aerobic	—Requiring the presence of oxygen.
Affective	—Concerned with sociopsychologic feelings and behavior such as attitudes, values, and adjustment.
Age-height-weight tables	—Tables showing the average height and the average weight of boys or girls of each chronological age.[15]
Age norms	—A score or value which represents the average performance for pupils of the given age in the trait or characteristic measured.[15]
Age scale	—A scale in which the units of measurement are the differences between successive age equivalents; each difference is considered as though equal to all others.[22]
Agility	—The ability of the body or parts of the body to change directions rapidly and accurately.
Alternative choice	—Type of selection test item including true-false, right-wrong, yes-no, cluster, and correction varieties.[23]
Anaerobic	—Occurring in the absence of oxygen, hence nonoxidation.[15]
Analysis of variance (ANOVA)	—Statistical technique, and a concept, used to determine whether there is a difference between groups and to isolate the origins of these differences, to break down the various sources which explain why groups differ, and to analyze the differences between any number of groups simultaneously.[24]
Anecdotal record	—A written objective record of an incident in the life of a student as observed by a teacher or leader.
Answer sheet	—A form used to make replies to written questions.
Anthropometry	—The measurement of the human body.
Apparatus	—Gymnastic horses, bucks, bars, ropes, booms, and other devices used as objects on which to exercise in a gymnasium; measurement—any instrument, device, or related group of devices designed or used to help control or measure skills, abilities, or conditions.[15]
Appraisal	—The process of determining the status, quality, quantity, or condition of anything; a process involving measurement and interpretation; used to determine the extent to which objectives are being achieved.[15]
Appreciation	—The ability to realize the value or worth of something which probably had as its beginning an attitude.
Aptitude	—A combination of abilities and other characteristics, whether native or acquired, known or believed to be indicative of an individual's ability to learn in some particular area.[20]
Aptitude test	—A test which measures the likelihood of an individual's succeeding in given subject area or line of work.[15]
Arithmetic mean	—The sum of a set of scores divided by the number of scores, commonly called average.[20]
Assessment	—A process involving both measurement and evaluation.[23]
Associated learning	—That which is learned incidentally or by implication or connection.[15]
Athletic ability	—Motor skills and abilities involved in the performance of athletic sports, measured in terms of achievement; present power to perform in athletic events.[15]
Athletic aptitude	—The inherent and acquired characteristics or traits which indicate an individual's ability to acquire proficiency in athletic skills; the ability of the individual to make future athletic achievement.[15]
Athletic index	—A score or value derived from several prognostic measurements relating to ability in sports and games; useful for classification or homogeneous grouping of pupils.[15]
Athletic type	—A type of body build characterized by broad shoulders, a well-developed chest, thick neck, flat abdomen, and large muscles; refers to mesomorphs.[15]

Attitude	—The beginning of feelings or ways of thinking about something which result in emotionalized tendencies to respond in certain ways.
Attitude scale	—An attitude measuring instrument with experimentally determined and equated units; gives a quantitative evaluation of an attitude.[15]
Attribute	—A characteristic or a quality.
Average	—A general term applied to measures of central tendency. The three most widely used averages are the arithmetic mean, the median, and the mode.[20]
Balance	—The ability of the individual to maintain his neuromuscular system in a static condition for an efficient response or to control it in a specific efficient posture while it is moving.
Basic skill	—(fundamental skill) A motor skill that is basic or essential to the mastery of an activity, such as running, jumping, throwing, kicking, or striking; a coordinated combination of basic movements.[15]
Battery	—A group of several tests standardized on the same population so that results on the several tests are comparable; sometimes loosely applied to any group of tests administered together, even though not standardized on the same subjects.[20]
Biomechanics	—The study of the motion of living organisms.[15]
Biserial correlation	—A technique used when one variable is interval data and one is dichotomous.
Body build	—See "Somatotypes."
Body image	—The way the body and its parts are perceived.
Body types	—See "Somatotypes."
Caliper	—An instrument used to measure the thickness or diameter of something.
Capacity	—The ultimate level of development in the ability or characteristic measured.
Cardiorespiratory	—An endurance item measured by activities requiring only moderate amounts of strength but a higher rate of energy expenditure so that the work load is sufficiently high to produce marked changes in the respiratory and heart rates.[9]
Cardiovascular	—Pertaining to the heart and circulatory functions.
Cardiovascular test	—A test which measures the response of the heart to regulated amounts of exercise.[15]
Ceiling	—The upper limit of ability measured by a test.[20]
Centile	—Any one of the 100 groups or divisions separated by percentile scores; *i.e.,* the first centile includes all scores below the first centile point; the 42nd centile includes all scores between the 41st and 42nd percentile points; the 100th centile includes all scores above the 99th percentile point.[15]
Central tendency	—A single score which is used to represent all the scores in a distribution.
Character	—The phase of personality comprising the more structural or enduring traits or characteristics which give continuity to personality over time, and which are of ethical and social significance; personality viewed in relation to some system of morality, and by which individuals may be compared.[15]
Character test	—A test designed to assess such ethical, volitional, or valuational aspects of a personality as honesty, persistence, loyalty, and values and ideals.[15]
Chart	—A sheet giving information in the form of diagrams, tables, and illustrations.
Checklist	—A list of things to look for as observations are being made.
Chronological age	—Age in years and months.

Classification	—The placement of individuals into groups for a particular purpose.
Classification test	—Any test used to group students according to abilities, age, weight, or any common factors for the purposes of instruction or competition.[15]
Coefficient of contingency	—Indication of whether resultant frequencies are distributed as might be expected from mere chance or whether there is a tendency for certain characteristics in the one distribution to be associated with the characteristics in the other.[5]
Coefficient of correlation	—(r) A measure of the degree of relationship, or "going-togetherness," between two sets of measures for the same group of individuals.[20]
Coefficient of determination (r²)	—The portion of variance in one variable that can be accounted for by the other variable.[16]
Coefficient of equivalence	—The type of reliability coefficient obtained from the administration of parallel or equivalent forms of a test to the same individuals.[15]
Coefficient of internal consistency	—The type of reliability coefficient obtained when using either the split-halves or Kuder-Richardson formulas for computations.[15]
Coefficient of stability	—The type of reliability coefficient obtained by retesting; or the administration of the same test twice to the same persons.[15]
Cognitive	—Concerned with intellectual abilities and skill such as knowledges and comprehension.
Comparable scores	—Scores having characteristics in common.
Completion item	—A test question calling for the filling in of a phrase or sentence, from which one or more parts have been omitted.[20]
Composite score	—A score which combines several scores, usually by addition; often different weights are applied to the contributing scores to increase or decrease their importance in the composite.[20]
Computer	—An electronic device for peforming high-speed arithmetic and logical operations . . . data are received, transmitted, stored, processed, and output with a minimum of human intervention.[8]
Computer (program)	—A logically arranged set of programming statements defining the operations to be performed by a computer to achieve the desired results.[8]
	—A set of instructions itemizing the kinds of data that will be entered, the functions to perform on them, and the form of the output.[14]
Concomitant learning	—Learning in a casual manner, without the intent to learn; learning which occurs while the intent or attention is focused on some other problems.[15]
Concurrent validity	—Validity based upon correlation with a criterion variable that is measured at about the same time as the test is administered.[15]
Construct validity	—That quality of a test having inferred value because of its demonstrated agreement with a theory; that involved whenever a test is to be interpreted as a measure of a quality or attribute that is not defined operationally.[15]
Content validity	—Validity of a test which can be demonstrated by a careful examination of the content of test items.[15]
Continuous data	—Data with any number of subdivisions like distance or time.
Continuum	—A line along which a trait, or set of scores, is conceived as being continuously distributed; a variable such that, no matter how close together any two values may be, it is always possible to have a third value between them; a continuous variable.[22]
Contract grading	—A student commitment to meet preset standards of mastery.

Coordination	—The ability of the performer to integrate types of movements into specific patterns.
Correction for guessing	—Subtracting a fraction of the number of wrong answers from the number of right answers.
Correlation	—The relation of two or more sets of paired data; pefect positive correlation is expressed as 1.00; perfect negative correlation as −1.00; and the absence of correlation as 0.00.[15]
Criterion	—A standard by which a test may be judged or evaluated; a set of scores or ratings that a test is designed to predict or to correlate with.[20]
	—A quality used as a basis for judging the value of something.
Criterion-referenced	—Interpretation of a person's score in relation to a previously identified standard.
Cumulative frequency	—A column in a frequency distribution table that shows, for any given interval, how many scores in the distribution lie below the upper limit of that interval.[15]
Cumulative percentage	—The percentage of cases falling at or below any given point is a frequency distribution; determined by adding all cases below the given point and determining the precentage of the total cases which this sum constitutes.[15] Its curve permits a quick determination of percentile ranks.[15]
Curricular validity	—Validity of a test shown by the extent of agreement between the test content and objectives with curricular content and objectives; demonstrated subjectively when test items cover the curricular content and objectives, are carefully constructed according to accepted rules or criteria, and are proportioned in number according to the percent of emphasis placed upon each objective.[15]
Curriculum	—A progressive series of courses and/or experiences in a particular educational level or in a specific field of learning for a definite social purpose; the sum or range of experiences, in or outside of school, whether consciously controlled and guided or undirected, that favorably influences the discovery, unfolding, and development of the personality, abilities, and traits of the individual in accordance with accepted education aims.[15]
Curve	—The line which results when scores are plotted against frequency.[27]
Data	—Facts or figures from which conclusions can be drawn.
Decile	—Any one of the 9 percentile points in a distribution that divides the distribution into 10 equal parts.[20]
Decision validity	—Evidence that the measurement instrument can accurately classify individuals as masters and nonmasters.
Development	—An increase in power to function; qualitative organization of behavior patterns as a result of heredity and activity supported by normal growth; an unfolding of abilities within the limits of inherent capacity.[15]
Deviation	—The amount by which the score differs from some reference value, such as the mean, the norm, or the score on some other test.[20]
Diagnosis	—The result of a procedure by which the nature of a problem is determined by a study of its history, signs, and symptoms; the conclusions drawn from facts derived from a process of discovering the nature of problems, or the interests, attitudes, motives, and aptitudes of an individual through tests, interviews, or case studies.[15]
Diagnostic test	—A test used to locate specific areas of weakness or strength, and to determine the nature of weaknesses or deficiencies; it

yields measures of the components or subparts of some larger body of information or skill.[20]

Dichotomous data —Data with a two-fold division like pass-or-fail.[20]

Difficulty rating —The proportion of the students who get an item correct. The higher the difficulty rating, the easier the item.

Discriminative index —The extent to which the observation or measures obtained from a group differ from one another or scatter about some measure of central tendency.[15]

Dispersion —The range or variability of a distribution.

Distractors —Any of the incorrect choices in a multiple-choice or matching item.[20]

Distribution —(frequency distribution) A tabulation of scores from high to low, or low to high, showing the number of individuals who obtain each score or fall in each score interval.[20]

Domain-Referenced validity —Evidence that the items sampled by the test adequately represent the criterion behavior. The domain needs to be thoroughly defined.

Dynamometer —An apparatus for measuring power, especially muscular effort of men or animals. It commonly embodies a spring to be compressed or a weight to be sustained by a force applied combined with an index, or automatic recorder, to show the work performed.

Educability —The ease and thoroughness with which one learns new motor skills.

Education —A change, a modification, or an adjustment on the part of an individual as a result of experience.

Empirical —A method that relies on practical experience and observations alone.[28]

Empirical measures —Measures assigned or obtained from observations or derived from tests constructed on the basis of experience rather than on some well-defined theory.[15]

Empirical validity —The worth or value of a test for a given purpose which has been proven through experience.[15]

Endurance —The result of a physiologic capacity of the individual to sustain movement over a period of time.

Equivalent form —Any one of several forms of a test that is similiar in content and item difficulty, and that yields very similar average scores, variability measures, and reliability estimates when administered to the same group.[15]

Ergograph —An instrument for recording the work done by a muscle or muscle group, used in studying fatigue.

Ergometer —An instrument used for measuring the amount of energy used or work done.[15]

Essay test —A form of test in which only the questions are supplied while the respondents compose the answers.

Ethical character —An individual's personality traits and behavior evaluated in terms of some moral code or set of ethical principles; usually connotes positive factors.[15]

ETS —Educational Testing Service.

Evaluation —The art of judgment scientifically applied according to some predetermined standards.

—A process of education that makes use of measurement techniques which, when applied to either the product or process of education, result in both qualitative and quantitative data expressed in both subjective and objective manner and used for comparisons with preconceived criteria.

Evaluative criteria —The bases of standards against which the worth or status of something may be checked or compared; factors used by an accrediting agency to determine if a school or department shall be accredited.[15]

Extrapolation —The process estimating values of a variable beyond the range of available data.[15]

Eye-hand coordination—Ability to use the eyes and hands together in such acts as fixating, grasping, and manipulating objects; important in all activities requiring fine accuracy, such as shooting a basketball or hitting a baseball.[15]

Face validity —Refers to the acceptability of a test and test situation by the tester in terms of apparent use to be made of a test. The test has face validity when it seemingly measures the variable in question.[19]

Factor —Any trait or variable considered in an investigation; any trait or characteristic, common to one or several variables, which causes or accounts for the correlations among a set of variables.[15]

Fitness —That state which characterizes the degree to which the person is able to function.

Flanagan method —A method of determining the index of discrimination of test items.

Flexibility —The range of movement in a joint.

Flexometer —An instrument used to measure flexibility of joints.[15]

Foil —An incorrect answer, a distractor.

Forced-choice item —Any test item when the examinee is required to select one or more of the given alternatives.[15]

Formative —Evaluation of learning during the instructional unit.[23]

Free-response test —A test on which the items require the subject to respond at his own volition, in his own words, without selecting from provided alternatives.[15]

Frequency —The number of actual individual occurrences in a specific class.

Frequency distribution—A tabulation of scores from high to low, or low to high, showing the number of individuals who obtain each score.[15]

Frequency polygon —A graphic representation of a frequency distribution, constructed by plotting each frequency as an ordinate above the midpoint of its class interval and connecting these plotted points by straight lines.[15]

Functioning of responses —Extent to which various responses are chosen in multiple-choice, multiple-response, and matching items.[19]

General athletic ability —(GAA) The present ability to perform in a variety of athletic events or sports; determined by a combination of basic elements such as speed, coordination, power, endurance, flexibility, strength, and agility.[15]

General motor ability —(GMA) Developed capacity; the present ability of an individual to perform in a variety of sports activities; the ability to successfully perform in most big muscular activities requiring neuromuscular coordinations, such as walking, running, jumping, and playing games involving these and other fundamental skills.[15]

General motor capacity —(GMC) The potentiality of an individual to perform in many motor (neuromuscular, psychomotor) activities involving large ranges of movement.[15]

Goniometer —An instrument, consisting of a protractor, a stationary arm, and a movable arm, for measuring angles in determining joint flexibility.[15]

Grade —Symbols used to denote an estimate of student status, progress, and achievement.

Grade-point —Numerical evaluation of scholastic achievement based upon a formula of equivalents that grants credit varying with the grade attained, as, for example, 4 points for an A, 3 for a B, with zero or negative points for failure.[15]

Graph —A diagram representing the successive changes in the value of a variable quantity.

Graphic rating scale —A form of recording a rating (subjective estimates), according to the strength of some quality or trait, along with a straight line (continuum); descriptive phrases of the trait being written below the line; the two extremes represent the highest and lowest degrees of the trait.[22]

Group test —A test that may be administered to a number of individuals at the same time by 1 examiner.[20]

Grouped data —The condensation of scores into step intervals which comprise a frequency distribution.

Grouped frequency distribution —The number that fall into each interval.[15]

Growth curve —A graphic representation of the changes that occur in a trait or function as a result of maturation; may apply to either physical or mental growth.[15]

Habit —A fixed way of behavior which comes from responding to a social situation in the same way many times.

Hand dynamometer —(manometer) An instrument used to measure strength of hand-grip, in which resistance is usually provided by powerful springs which must be compressed, the number of pounds of pressure exerted being registered on a dial.[15]

Health-related fitness —Refers to the physical qualities that have been found to contribute to one's general health by reducing the risk of degenerative diseases, chronic back problems, and diabetes; it is comprised of cardiorespiratory endurance, muscular endurance, muscular strength, body composition, and flexibility.[4]

Height-weight tables —Tables showing the average weight of boys and girls having a given height.[15]

Hierarchy —A group of items arranged in order from simple to complex. The simpler content and behaviors are prerequisites for those at the higher level of the hierarchy. Taxonomies by Bloom, Krathwohl, and Goldberger and Moyer are examples.

Histogram —A vertical bar graph of a frequency distribution.[19]

Homogeneous grouping —Classification by similar or identical elements.

Hull scale —A standard scale which has a mean of 50 and 3.5 standard deviations on each side of the mean.

Human movement —The change in position of the individual in time-space resulting from force developed from the individual's expenditure of energy interacting with his environment; may be expressive, communicative, or developmental, or adaptive (coping with environment).[15]

Hypothesis —A guiding idea, temporary explanation, or statement of probability used to begin and guide an investigation for relevant data and to predict certain results or consequences; a tentative solution set up for testing as to its tenability.[15]

Ideal —An appreciation on the positive side with a standard which is near perfect or in the upper quartile.

Ideal self —A composite of the expectations of society and the aspirations of the self.

Index —The relation or proportion of one amount or dimension to another.

Index of discrimination —The ability of a test item to differentiate between persons possessing much of some trait and those possessing little.[20]

Index of reliability —The square root of the reliability; used in test construction as a statement of the highest coefficient of validity that can possibly be obtained for a test with a given reliability coefficient; the correlation between true and obtained scores on a test, or the probable correlation between one test and the average of an infinitely large number of parallel tests.[15]

Individual test —A test that can be administered to only one person at a time.[20]

Interclass —A type of correlational technique used to determine consistency of performance *between* groups.

Interest —A subjective-objective attitude, concern, or condition involving a precept or an idea in attention and a combination of intellectual and feeling consciousness; may be temporary or permanent; based on native curiosity and conditioned by experience.[15]

Interpolation —Any process of estimating intermediate values between 2 known points.[20]

Interpretation —An unbiased, detailed description and explanation of the findings of an investigation, including a statement of the observed facts and their meanings as they relate to the source or general population.[15]

Interval —A space between 2 things.
—The extent of difference between 2 qualities or conditions.

Interval data —Having two features of the real number series: order and distance. (See real number system.)[23]

Interval scale —Characterized by equal units of measurement.[23,27]

Interview —An oral questionnaire.

Intraclass —A type of correlational technique used to determine sources of variability *within* a group.

Inventory —Usually a list of qualities, traits, or characteristics.

Isometric —A type of muscular contraction in which the muscle fibers do not shorten. No movement or work is accomplished, and the tension developed is given off in the form of heat.[15]

Isotonic —A type of muscular contraction during which muscle fibers shorten against resistance and result in the performance of work.[15]

Item —A single question or exercise in a test.[20]

Item analysis —The process of evaluating single test items by any of several methods. It usually involves determining the difficulty value and the discriminating power of the item, and often its correlation with some criterion.[20]

Item validity —Discriminative value of an item; the correlation between an item and some criterion of performance; correlation between an item and the whole test of which it is a part.[15]

Judgment —The ability to evaluate the facts in a problematic situation and/or ability to relate two or more concepts.[2]

Kinesthetic sense —The sense which give the individual an awareness of position of the body or parts of the body as it moves through space.

Knowledge —Awareness or cognizance of information.

Knowledge test —Any test designed to measure what an individual knows about a particular subject; distinguished from aptitude, attitude, and physical performance tests.[15]

Kuder-Richardson formula(s) —Formulas for estimating the reliability of a test from information about the individual items in the test, or from the mean score, standard deviation, and number of items in the test.[20]

Law of averages —The statistical law that the stability of a statistic tends to increase as the number of observations on which it is based is increased.[15]

Leadership —The ability and readiness to inspire and guide others, individuals or groups, toward specific objectives.[15]

Learning curve —A graphic representation of certain aspects of progress in ability

	during successive periods of practice, in terms of equal time or of equal accomplishment units.[15]
Leptokurtic	—Refers to a frequency curve that is more highly peaked than the normal probability curve.[15]
Level of confidence	—A statistical term to indicate the degree of confidence that may be placed upon an interval estimate, generally shown by a probability percentage, such as being 95% certain.[19]
Level of significance	—A statistical term describing the percentage that defines the likelihood of concluding that a difference between two means, percentages, or other comparable measures exists when in reality it does not; for example, if the difference in mean scores of boys and girls is reportedly significant at the .01 level, this means that there is only a 1 in 100 chance that a sample difference as large as or larger than the one observed would occur by chance sampling error if there is in reality no difference between the mean of the population of boys and the mean of the population of girls.[19]
Linear relationship	—(rectilinear correlation) A relationship between 2 or more variables that can be represented by a straight line; as one variable increases or decreases, the other moves likewise or inversely.[15]
Local norms	—Norms that have been made by collecting data in a certain school system and using them, instead of national or regional norms, to evaluate student performance.[15]
Logical validity	—A form of content validity.[23]
	—A precise definition and measurement of the trait are required to claim logical validity.[23]
Manometer	—Hand dynamometer.
Mark	—Grade.
Mastery learning	—Skills basic to further learning, or the minimum essentials required in criterion-referenced evaluation.[12]
Matching item	—A test item calling for the correct association of each entry in one list with an entry in a second list.[20]
McCall score	—T-Score.
Mean	—The point on a distribution of scores usually referred to as the average. It is the point about which the sum of the plus deviations is equal to the sum of the minus deviations.[28]
	—Sum of all measures divided by their number.
Measurement	—A technique of evaluation which makes use of procedures that are generally precise and objective, which will generally result in quantitative data, and which characteristically can express its results in numerical form.
Median	—The middle score in a distribution; the point that divides the group into two equal parts.[20]
	—That point along the score continuum above which and below which half of the cases fall.
Metric	—Used in measurement based on the meter and the gram.
Microcomputer	—A small low-cost computer containing a microprocessor.[8]
	—A sophisticated calculator with serial, single digit keyboard entry and a single, multi-digit, lighted display output.[11]
Midpoint	—The point or value midway between the real upper and real lower limits of a class interval.[15]
Mode	—The score or value that occurs most frequently in a distribution.[20]
Morphology	—Science of form and structure.[15]
Motor ability	—The present acquired and innate ability to perform motor skills of a general or fundamental nature, exclusive of highly specialized sports or gymnastic techniques.
Motor ability test	—A test designed to determine, measure, and evaluate physical

abilities, useful as a means of placing game contests on a fair competitive basis and for the classification of pupils for instruction in physical education.[15]

Motor capacity —The innate or inborn ability to learn complex motor coordinations.[15]

Motor educability —The ease and thoroughness with which one learns new motor skills.

Motor fitness —A readiness or preparedness for performance with special regard for big muscle activity without undue fatigue. It concerns the capacity to move the body efficiently with force over a reasonable length of time.

Motor learning —Learning in which the learner achieves new facility in the performance of bodily movements as a result of specific practice; distinguished from improvement of function resulting from maturation.[15]

—The integration of movement into a pattern for a purpose as a result of training procedures and environmental conditions.[18]

Movement —A design that is created in space.

Movement image —The way the moving body is perceived.

Multiple-choice item —A test item in which the examinee's task is to choose the correct or best answer from several given answers, or options.[20]

Multiple correlation —The correlation between a dependent or criterion variable and the sum of a number of independent variables, which are weighted so as to give a maximum correlation.[19]

Multiple-response item —A special type of multiple-choice item in which two or more of the given choices may be correct.[20]

N, n —The symbol commonly used to represent the number of cases in a distribution.[20]

National norm —A norm based on adequate nationwide sampling.[15]

Negative relationship —An inverse relationship between paired variables; as one variable increases, the other decreases.[15]

Neuromuscular —Pertaining to the relation between nerve and muscle.[15]

Nominal data —Having none of the features of the real number system.[23]

Nominal scale —A set of mutually exclusive categories.[23]

—There is no quantitative differentiation between the categories, and one is assumed to be as valuable as another.[27]

Nomograph —(alignment chart) A chart in which 3 variables are plotted on straight lines so that if any 2 are known, the third can be found with the use of a straight edge.[15]

Nonparametric —Statistic applied when the assumption cannot be made that the scores were drawn from a normally distributed population.[23]

—Statistic used with nominal and ordinal data.[23]

Nonverbal test —A paper-and-pencil test, usually used with children in the primary grades, in which the test items are symbols, figures, and pictures rather than words; instructions are given orally.[22]

Normal curve —The bell-shaped curve of a theoretical distribution that depicts a massing of scores or data at the center with gradually diminishing numbers toward both extremes; the mean, median, and mode coincide.[15]

Normal distribution —A frequency distribution in which the scores or values are so distributed that a normal probability curve is the best fitting curve.[15]

Norm-referenced —Interpretation of a person's score in relation to the score of others on the same test.

Norms —Statistics that describe the test performance of specific groups, such as pupils of various ages or grades, in the standardization group for a test. Norms are often assumed to be representative of some larger population.[20]

	—An experimentally derived index which enables teachers to compare the achievement or status of their students with those of a similar group.
Objective	—A precise and definite statement of the steps in the process of realization of an aim.
Objective test	—A test in the scoring of which there is no possibility of difference of opinion among scorers as to whether responses are to be scored right or wrong.[20]
Objectivity	—The degree of uniformity with which various persons score the same tests. This is often expressed by a correlation coefficient.[28]
Observation	—The act of watching the behavior, actions, or status of students for a specific purpose by a trained observer.
Ogive	—The graph of a cumulative percentage frequency distribution.
Ordinal data	—Reflecting one feature of the real number series, that of order. (See real number system.)[23]
Ordinal scale	—Determined by ranking a set of objects with regard to some specific characteristic.[23]
	—There is no absolute difference between the positions on an ordinal scale.[27]
Organic efficiency test	—A test of functional efficiency of bodily organic systems, especially circulatory and respiratory; early name for a test of response of the heart to exercise.[15]
Outcome	—A specific quality or characteristic of one who has participated in selected activities under desirable conditions and with effective technique.
Parallel tests	—Equivalent forms of a test.[15]
Parameter	—A value that is characteristic of a population.[24]
Parametric	—Statistics applied to data when the distribution approximates the normal distribution.[23]
Partial correlation	—The correlation between two variables with the influence of one or more other variables being eliminated.[19]
Pearson product-moment coefficient of correlation	—The r method of correlation that seeks a straight-line relationship from the scatter or spread of two or more groups of scores.[28]
Percent	—Per hundred; for every hundred.
Percentage	—Proportion in every hundred.
Percentile	—(P) A point in a distribution below which falls the percent of cases indicated by the given percentile. Thus, the 15th percentile denotes the score or point below which 15 percent of the scores fall.[20]
Percentile graph	—Ogive curve.[15]
Percentile rank	—The percent of scores in a distribution equal to or lower than the score corresponding to the given rank.[20]
Percentile score	—The score representing the percentage of persons who fall below a given raw score.[15]
Perception	—The total pattern arising from many sensations and resulting in a meaning which is more than the sum of its parts.[7]
	—Consciousness or awareness through the medium of the senses.[13]
Perceptual motor skills	—The skills which enable the individual to perceive (e.g., seeing, hearing, understanding, sensing); all of the mental and sensory attributes which contribute to the state of readiness.[15]
Performance test	—A test requiring motor or manual response on the examinee's part.[20]
Personality	—The total psychological and social reactions of an individual; the synthesis of his subjective, emotional, and mental life; his behavior and his reactions to the environment.[15]
PFI	—Physical fitness index.

Physical abilities	—Essentials to efficient functioning in the psychomotor domain.[13]
Physical capacity test	—A test of physical fitness and skill, based on a series of subtests of strength, agility, and physical achievement, for which standards have been established. Results are often expressed in terms of a strength index.[15]
Physical education	—An education by physical means where many of education's objectives are achieved through movement experiences.
Physical fitness	—Work capacity; the total functional capacity to perform some specified task requiring muscular effort; considers the individual involved, task to be performed, quality and intensity of effort; one aspect of total fitness; involves sound organic development, motor skill, and the capacity to perform physical work with biological efficiency.[15]
Physical performance tests	—Those objective tests to measure learnings which include motor ability, motor fitness, sport skill, posture, and nutrition.
Polygon	—Graphic representation of a frequency distribution, a line graph of a particular frequency distribution.
Posture	—The position of the whole body and its segments.
Potential ability	—The capacity to perform by virtue of some yet undeveloped or unrealized physical or mental attribute.
Power	—Capacity of the individual to bring into play maximum muscle contraction at the fastest rate of speed.
Power tests	—Knowledge tests in which the student has a reasonable opportunity to read all the items and indicate his answers in the time alloted.
	—A test intended to measure levels of performance rather than speed of response; hence one in which there is either no time limit or a very generous one.[20]
Predictive index	—An index used to transform the coefficient of correlation (r) to a better than a chance figure; $(1 - \sqrt{1 - r^2})$, expressed as a percent.[28]
Process	—The total physical education curriculum including personnel, program and environment.
Product	—The student.
Product moment coefficient	—See correlation and coefficient of correlation.
Proficiency test	—A test designed to determine the extent to which a performer can execute some skill or skills with ease and precision; usually involves a single skill or skills involved in a particular activity.[15]
Profile	—A graphic representation of the results on several tests, for either an individual or a group, when the results have been expressed in some uniform or comparable terms.[20]
Prognosis (prognostic test)	—A test used to predict future success or failure in a specific subject or field.[20]
Progress chart	—A graphic representation of achievement in schoolwork, consisting of a series of test scores or other marks taken from time to time and plotted in graphic form.[15]
Progress grade	—A grade based solely on the amount of progress made over a period of time, without regard to the final ability as compared with others in the group.[15]
Projective technique	—A method of personality study which avoids as much as possible any structuring of the situation; the subject responds freely to a series of stimuli such as inkblots, pictures, and unfinished sentences, and projects into his responses manifestations of personality characteristics.[15]
Psychomotor	—Observable voluntary human movement.[13]
Qualitative data	—Data according to kind or quality.
Quantitative data	—Data according to amount or number.

Quartile	—One of 3 points that divide the cases in a distribution into four equal groups. The lower quartile, or 25th percentile, sets off the lowest fourth of the group; the middle quartile is the same as the 50th percentile, or median; and the third quartile, or 75th percentile, marks off the highest fourth.[20]
Quartile deviation (semi-interquartile range) (Q)	—Half of the range between Q_1 and Q_3.
Question	—An item in a written test.
Questionnaire	—A method of obtaining information directly from an individual about his present status and practices.
Quotient	—The number obtained when one quality is divided by another; a ratio.
Random sample	—A sample so drawn that every member of a population has an equal chance of being included; excludes bias or selection. Inferences or generalizations may be made on the findings from such a representative sample.[15]
Range	—The difference between the highest and lowest scores obtained on a test by some group.[20]
Rank difference	—A type of correlation procedure used with ordinal data.[27]
Rank order correlation	—(rho) A method of computing a correlation coefficient by assigning ranks to each pair of scores of individuals, and determining the relationship between them; ranks of the magnitudes are used instead of the magnitudes themselves; usually used with a small number of cases.[15]
Rank scores	—All scores are ordered from the highest to the lowest with the highest score, 1, and the lowest, N.
Ranking	—Arranging the constituents of a group in order in terms of some measure. Rank numbers disclose the relative position of the constituents.[19]
Rating scale	—A subjective estimate which brings order to the processes of observation and self-apprasial and which provides for degrees of the quality, trait, or factor being examined.
Ratio scale	—A scale in which all units are equidistant from each other. There is a absolute zero point and proportional comparisons are appropriate.[27]
Raw score	—The first quantitative result obtained in scoring a test.[20]
Reaction time	—Time from the stimulus to the beginning of movement.[10]
Real number system	—Distinguished by three features: order, distance, and origin.[23]
Recall item	—An item that requires the examinee to supply the correct answer from his own memory or recollection, as contrasted with a recognition item, in which he need only identify the correct answer.[20]
Recognition item	—An item requiring the examinee to recognize or select the correct answer from among two or more given answers.[20]
Regression equation	—A technique used to predict the most likely measurement in one variable from the known measurement in another.
Reliability	—The extent to which a test is consistent in measuring whatever it does measure.[20]
Reliability coefficient	—The coefficient of correlation obtained between two forms of a test (alternate-form or parallel-form reliability); between scores on repeated administrations of the same test (test-retest reliability); between halves of a test properly corrected (split-half reliability); or by using the Kuder-Richardson formulas.[22]
Representative sample	—A sample that corresponds to or matches the population of which it is a sample with respect to characteristics important for the purposes under investigation.[20]

Research	—Careful, systematic, patient study and investigation in some field of knowledge to establish facts or principles.
	—To increase knowledge.
Rho	—Rank order correlation.
Sample	—Scores selected at random from a large group of population so that they have the characteristics of the whole population.[28]
Sampling	—The act or process of selecting a limited number of observations, individuals, or cases to represent a particular universe.[15]
Sampling error	—Errors caused by chance factors in random sampling; usually estimated statistically by the standard error.[15]
Scale	—A qualitative or quantitative graduation of scores used to differentiate the individuals from the group.[17]
Scattergram	—Correlation chart.
	—A two-dimensional chart affording a basis for computing a correlation coefficient for two variables or scores. Pairs of values are tallied on the chart, giving a visual picture of the relationship between the variables.[19]
Score	—A quantitative or qualitative record of the individual in the traits or characteristics concerned.
Score interval	—(class interval, step interval, class size) The range of scores, or the number of score units, between the upper and lower limits of a section, or interval, of test scores in a frequency distribution.[15]
Screening test	—A test designed to select from a group those individuals in a specified category; most commonly used for identifying those with exceptional or subnormal mental capacities or physical deviations.[15]
Self-apprasial	—Self-evaluation; the process of defining one's own status or progress toward specific goals; appraisal may involve measurement and opinion and is based on the individual's interpretation of his performance and ability.[15]
Self-evaluation	—The process of measuring one's own status or progress toward specific goals.[15]
Self-image	—The way the self is perceived.
Sigma	—(σ) A Greek letter used to represent the standard deviation.[28]
Skewness	—The tendency of a distribution to depart from symmetry of balance around the mean.[20]
Skill	—An art, craft, or science involving the use of the hands or body.
Skill-related fitness	—Refers to those physical qualities that contribute to successful athletic performance, including agility, balance, coordination, speed, power, and reaction time.[4]
Social development	—Refers to one's adjustment to the group and to other individuals in terms of his and their rights, privileges, and duties.[15]
Socialization	—The process by which individual members of society learn the ways of the group, become functioning members, act according to its standards, accept its rules, and in turn become accepted by the group.[15]
Sociogram	—A chart or diagram that graphically illustrates interactions, usually those desired or not desired, among individuals in a defined group; portrays social relationships within groups in terms of responses to stimulus questions on a sociometric test.[15]
Sociometry	—A technique or method of measuring the amount of organization of a social group in order to show the patterns of relationships and interrelationships.
Somatotype	—A classification of an individual according to body structure.[15]
Somatotype rating	—A series of three numbers, between 1 and 7, indicating the amount of ectomorphy, mesomorphy, and endomorphy in an individual's type of body build.[15]

Spearman Rho —A method of correlation by rank-difference: designed for use with small numbers.

Spearman-Brown prophecy formula —A formula giving the relationship between the reliability of a test and its length. The formula permits estimation of the reliability of a test lengthened or shortened by an amount, from the known reliability of a test of specified length.[20]

Speed —The capacity of the individual to perform successive movements of the same pattern at a fast rate.

Spirometer —An instrument for measuring the vital capacity of the lungs, or the volume of air which can be expelled from the chest after the deepest possible inspiration.

Split-half coefficient —A coefficient of reliability obtained by correlating scores on one-half of a test with scores on the other half. Generally, but not necessarily, the two halves consist of the odd-numbered and even-numbered items.[20]

Sport skills —Those physical activities constituting each sport which are distinctive to that sport.

Sportsmanship —Desirable attitude and actions on the part of sports participants and spectators; qualities and behavior befitting a sportsman; includes such qualities as abiding by the standards of fair play, cooperation, respect for the game, and the regard for the rights of others.[15]

Stadiometer —An instrument for measuring height.

Standard —The degree of attainment in a criterion and expressed as a quality or quantity.

Standard deviation —(SD) A measure of the variability or dispersion of a set of scores. The more the scores cluster around the mean, the smaller the standard deviation.[20]
—The square root of the average of the squared deviations from the mean.

Standard score —A general term referring to any of a variety of "transformed" scores, in terms of which raw scores may be expressed for reasons of convenience, comparability, or ease of interpretation.[20]
—Scores based on the standard deviation.

Standardized test —A systematic sample of performance obtained under prescribed conditions, scored according to definite rules, and capable of evaluation by reference to normative information. Some writers restrict the term to tests having the above properties, whose items have been experimentally evaluated, and/or for which evidences of validity and reliability are provided.[20]

Stanine —One of the steps in a 9-point scale of normalized standard scores. The stanine (short for standard-nine) scale has values from 1 to 9, with a means of 5, and a standard deviation of 2.[20]

Statistical validity —Test validity expressed numerically, usually as a coefficient of correlation between scores on the test and another set of measures such as scores on another test, teachers' marks, or ratings by experts.[15]

Statistics —The science which deals with the collection, organization, analysis, and interpretation of masses of numerical facts.

Status —Present condition, position, level.[15]

Stencil key —A scoring key which, when positioned over an examinee's responses, either in a test booklet, or more commonly, on an answer sheet, permits rapid identification and counting of all right answers.[20]

Strength —The capacity of the individual to exert muscular force.

Strength test —A test designed to measure muscular strength; often designates a test composed of a series of test items which when combined would give a measure of general bodily strength rather than the strength of specific muscles.[15]

Strip key —A scoring key arranged so that the answers for items on any page or in any column of the test appear in a strip or column that may be placed alongside the examinee's responses for easy scoring.[20]

Subjective —Resulting from the feelings or temperament of the subject or person thinking, rather than the attributes of the object thought of.

—Based on judgment and opinion.

Subjective test —A test scored on the basis of the scorer's personal judgment of the worth of each answer, rather than by reference to a pre-arranged scoring key or answer sheet (e.g., essay test).[15]

Summative —Evaluation at the end of a unit of instruction to reflect achievement.[23]

Survey —A systematic collection analysis, interpretation, and report of facts concerning an enterprise.

Taxonomy —A set of classifications.

Technical learning —The immediate, specific, and obvious results of teaching; for example, technical learnings in football are how to run, throw, kick, block, and tackle. See "associated" and "concomitant" learning.[15]

Test —A set of questions, problems, or exercises for determining a person's knowledge, abilities, aptitude, or qualifications.

—An examination.

—A specific tool of measurement for the collection of data, implying a response from the person being measured.

Test battery —A group of several tests intended to be administered in succession to the same subject or subjects; the tests are usually designed to accomplish a closely related set of measurement objectives.[15]

Test bias —Unfairness that may result whenever a test is administered to a group of individuals who have experiential backgrounds that are noticeably different from those of the group for whom the test was developed and on whom the test was standardized.[26]

Testing program —Any organized plan for systematically carrying out evaluative procedures in a school or school system or among school systems; involves the selection, administering, scoring, and interpretation of tests.[15]

Tetrachoric —A correlation technique used when both variables are dichotomous.

Trial —An attempt, endeavor, effort.

Trials-to-criterion —The number of trials needed to achieve a pre-set criterion score.

True-false item —A test question or exercise in which the examinee's task is to indicate whether a given statement is true or false.[20]

True score —A hypothetical value that can never be obtained by testing and which always involves some measurement error.[20]

T-Score —A derived score based upon the equivalance of percentile values of standard scores, thus avoiding the effects of skewed distributions, and usually having a mean equated to 50 and a standard deviation equated to 10.[19]

Understanding —The ability to grasp the significance of knowledges, to realize more fully their relationships, and to apply discriminatory powers where they are concerned.

Ungrouped data —Ranked or raw scores.

Utility —The ability of a test or measure to be employed for several purposes, such as for classification, assaying achievement, and drill.[15]

Validity	—The extent to which a test does the job for which it is used. Validity is always specific to the purposes for which the test is used, and different kinds of evidence are appropriate for appraising the validity of various types of tests.[20]
Variables	—The traits or factors that change from one case or condition to another; the representatives of the traits, usually in quantitative form, such as a measurement or an enumeration.[15]
Variability	—The scatter or spread of scores around a measure of central tendency within a distribution of scores.
Variance	—A measure of variability; the square of the standard deviation; arithmetic mean of the squares of the deviations from the mean.[15]
Weighting	—The relative importance of a single item in a battery of related items.
z-Score	—A raw score expressed in standard deviation units.[27]

GLOSSARY REFERENCES

1. Baumgartner, T.A., and Jackson, A.S.: Measurement for Evaluation in Physical Education. Boston, Houghton Mifflin Co., 1975.
2. Bookwalter, K.W.: Syllabus in Curriculum in Physical Education. School of Health, Physical Education and Recreation, Indiana University, Bloomington, 1951.
3. Bookwalter, K.W.: The Tyranny of Words. Journal of Health and Physical Education, *18*:714–715, 754, December, 1947.
4. Casperson, C., Powell, K., and Christenson, G.: Physical activity, exercise, and physical fitness: Definitions and distinctions of health-related research. Public Health Reports, *100*:126–131, 1985.
5. Clarke, H.H.: Application of Measurement and Physical Education. 5th Ed. Englewood Cliffs, Prentice-Hall, Inc., 1976.
6. Cowell, C.C., and France, W.L.: Philosophy and Principles of Physical Education. Englewood Cliffs, Prentice-Hall, Inc., 1963.
7. Cratty, B.J.: Movement Behavior and Motor Learning. 3rd Ed. Philadelphia, Lea & Febiger, 1973.
8. Darcy, L., and Boston, L.: Webster's New World Dictionary of Computer Terms. New York, Simon & Schuster, 1983.
9. Eckert, H.M.: Practical Measurement of Physical Performance. Philadelphia, Lea & Febiger, 1974.
10. Franks, B.D., and Deutsch, H.: Evaluating Performance in Physical Education. New York, Academic Press, 1973.
11. Gorsline, G.W.: Computer Organization. Englewood Cliffs, NJ, Prentice-Hall, Inc., 1980.
12. Gronlund, N.E.: Preparing Criterion-Referenced Tests for Classroom Instruction. New York, Macmillan Co., 1973.
13. Harrow, A.J.: A Taxonomy of the Psychomotor Domain. New York, David McKay Co., 1972.
14. Horine, L.: Administration of Physical Education and Sport Programs. Philadelphia, W.B. Saunders, 1985.
15. Hunter, M.D.: A Dictionary for Physical Education. P.E.D., Indiana University, Bloomington, 1966. One hundred eighteen definitions used by permission of the author.
16. Johnson, B.L., and Nelson, J.K.: Practical Measurements for Evaluation in Physical Education. 2nd Ed. Minneapolis, Burgess Publishing Co., 1974.
17. Larson, L.A., and Yocom, R.D.: Measurement and Evaluation in Physical, Health, and Recreation Education. St. Louis, C.V. Mosby Co., 1951.
18. Lawther, J.D.: Directing motor skill learning. Quest, *6*:68–76, May, 1966.
19. Meyers, C.R., and Blesh, T.E.: Measurements in Physical Education. New York, The Ronald Press, 1962. Eight definitions used by permission of the publisher.
20. Mitchell, B.C. (Consultant): A Glossary of Measurement Terms. Test Service Notebook No. 13, Test Department, Harcourt Brace Jovanovich, Inc. A few of the definitions used here are abridged.
21. Phillips, M., and Bookwalter, K.W.: Three little words. The Physical Educator, *5*:21, March, 1948.

22. Remmers, H.H., Gage, N.L., and Rummel, J.F.: A Practical Introduction to Measurement and Evaluation. New York, Harper & Brothers, 1960.
23. Safrit, M.J.: Evaluation in Physical Education. Englewood Cliffs, NJ, Prentice-Hall, Inc., 1973. Fourteen definitions used by permission of the publisher and the author.
24. Sheehan, T.J.: An Introduction to the Evaluation of Measurement Data in Physical Education. Reading, Massachusetts, Addison-Wesley Publishing Co., 1971.
25. Smithells, P.A., and Cameron, P.E.: Principles of Evaluation in Physical Education. New York, Harper & Brothers, 1962.
26. Thorndike, R.L.: Applied Psychometrics. Boston, Houghton Mifflin, 1982.
27. Vincent, W.J.: Elementary Statistics in Physical Education. Springfield, IL, Charles C Thomas, 1976. Seven definitions used by permission of the publisher and the author.
28. Willgoose, C.E.: Evaluation in Health Education and Physical Education. New York, McGraw-Hill Book Co., 1961. Six definitions used by permission of the publisher.

Index

Page numbers in *italics* indicate figures; numbers followed by "t" indicate tables.